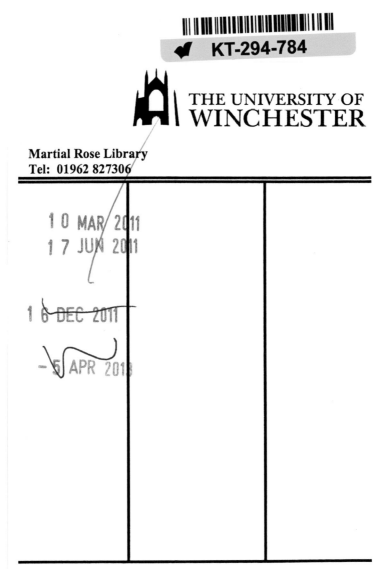

Interactions Between Short-Term and Long-Term Memory in the Verbal Domain

Interactions Between Short-Term and Long-Term Memory in the Verbal Domain

Edited by Annabel Thorn and Mike Page

Ψ Psychology Press
Taylor & Francis Group
HOVE AND NEW YORK

First published 2009 by Psychology Press
27 Church Road, Hove, East Sussex BN3 2FA

Simultaneously published in the USA and Canada
by Psychology Press
270 Madison Avenue, New York, NY 10016

*Psychology Press is an imprint of the Taylor & Francis Group, an
Informa business*

© 2009 Psychology Press

Typeset in Times by Garfield Morgan, Swansea, West Glamorgan
Printed and bound in Great Britain by MPG Books Ltd, Bodmin, Cornwall
Cover design by Design Deluxe

This publication has been produced with paper manufactured to strict
environmental standards and with pulp derived from sustainable
forests.

British Library Cataloguing in Publication Data
A catalogue record for this book is available from the British Library

Library of Congress Cataloging-in-Publication Data
Interactions between short-term and long-term memory in the verbal
domain / edited by Annabel Thorn and Mike Page.
    p. cm.
  ISBN 978-1-84169-639-3 (hardback)
  1. Memory. 2. Short-term memory. 3. Long-term memory. 4.
Verbal ability. 5. Verbal behavior. I. Thorn, Annabel, 1972– II. Page,
Mike, 1966–
  BF371.I56 2008
  153.1'3–dc22

                               2007048596

ISBN 978-1-84169-639-3 (hbk)

Contents

Figures

Tables

Contributors

Richard J. Allen, Department of Psychology, University of York, York, YO10 5DD, UK

Alan D. Baddeley, Department of Psychology, University of York, York, YO10 5DD, UK

Parveen Bhatarah, Department of Psychology, Keynes College, The University of Kent at Canterbury, Canterbury, Kent, CT2 7NP, UK

Zhijian Chen, Department of Psychological Sciences, University of Missouri, 207 McAlester Hall, Columbia, MO 65211, USA

Nelson Cowan, Department of Psychological Sciences, University of Missouri, 207 McAlester Hall, Columbia, MO 65211, USA

Clive R. Frankish, Department of Experimental Psychology, University of Bristol, 12a Priory Road, Bristol, BS8 1TU, UK

Susan E. Gathercole, Department of Psychology, University of York, York, YO10 5DD, UK

Prahlad Gupta, Department of Psychology, University of Iowa, Iowa City, IA 52242, USA

Charles Hulme, Department of Psychology, University of York, York, YO10 5DD, UK

Steve Majerus, Department of Cognitive Sciences, University of Liège, Boulevard du Rectorat, B33, B-4000 Liege, Belgium

Nadine Martin, Department of Communication Sciences, Temple University, 1701 N. 13th Street, Philadelphia, PA 19122, USA

Ian Neath, Department of Psychology, Memorial University of Newfoundland, St. John's, NL, A1B 3X9, Canada

Dennis Norris, MRC Cognition and Brain Sciences Unit, 15 Chaucer Road, Cambridge, CB2 2EF, UK

Mike P. A. Page, Psychology Department, University of Hertfordshire, College Lane, Hatfield, AL10 9AB, UK

Steven Roodenrys, Department of Psychology, University of Wollongong, Northfields Avenue, Wollongong, 2522, Australia

Elisabet Service, Centre de Recherche, Institut Universitaire de Gériatrie de

Montréal, 4565 chemin Queen Mary, Montréal, QC, H3W 1W5, Canada

George P. Stuart, Università Cattolica del Sacro Cuore, Faculty of Psychology, Largo A. Gemelli 1, Milano, 20123, Italy

Aimée M. Surprenant, Department of Psychology, Memorial University of Newfoundland, St. John's, NL, A1B 3X9, Canada

Lydia Tan, Department of Psychology, University of Essex, Wivenhoe Park, Colchester, CO4 3SQ, UK

Annabel S. C. Thorn, Department of Experimental Psychology, University of Bristol, 12a Priory Road, Bristol, BS8 1TU, UK

Geoff Ward, Department of Psychology, University of Essex, Wivenhoe Park, Colchester, CO4 3SQ, UK

1 Current issues in understanding interactions between short-term and long-term memory

Annabel S. C. Thorn and Mike P. A. Page

Introduction

Investigation of the association between memory systems dedicated to the retention of information over the short or long term has occupied the minds of psychologists for many years. The idea that human memory is not a single system that operates across all time frames, but rather comprises dissociable short- and long-term memory components, goes back to William James (1890). James distinguished between primary memory, which he viewed as our awareness of what has just happened, and secondary memory, proposed to be our knowledge of events that have left our consciousness and are therefore part of the "psychological past". More than fifty years later the notion of dissociable short- and long-term memory systems was supported by Hebb (1949), who suggested that the distinction between primary and secondary memory has a neurophysiological basis; the former, he proposed, reflects temporarily reverberating electrical activity in the brain, whereas the latter results from permanent synaptic changes.

The distinction between short- and long-term memory systems was captured in the highly influential "modal model" of memory proposed by Atkinson and Shiffrin (1968). According to this model, incoming information is first processed by parallel sensory buffers and then enters a limited capacity short-term store. To enter long-term memory, Atkinson and Shiffrin proposed that information must be "copied" from the short-term store, with transfer occurring via rehearsal processes. The proposal that information can only gain access to long-term memory via short-term storage has been one of the most widely debated features of this model. For example, a number of reports document neuropsychological patients with grossly impaired short-term memory span who show generally unimpaired long-term learning (Basso et al., 1982; Shallice & Warrington, 1970), a cognitive profile that is not consistent with the assumption that all information must pass through short-term memory in order to be stored in long-term memory. Having said that, such patients do show a specific deficit in their ability to learn long-term representations of sequences (e.g., novel word-forms), suggesting that a modified view may be viable, in which the representation of a *sequence* in short-term memory is a necessary precursor of the storage of that sequence in long-term memory.

Notwithstanding the problems with the modal model account, consideration of the extent to which short- and long-term memory systems are interrelated continues to drive memory research today. Understanding of the detailed mechanisms and processes underpinning the operation of short-term memory has considerably advanced since the modal model was first proposed, with the publication of a number of successful models, both conceptual and computational, that have proved capable of accounting for a wide range of experimental data. At the conceptual level, much work has been driven by the working memory (WM) model of Baddeley and Hitch (1974), and its influence has been seen in computational models of immediate serial recall, such as those of Burgess and Hitch (1992, 1999), Henson (1998) and Page and Norris (1998). Other modellers, notably Neath and Brown (2006), have constructed models that depart from the WM framework and that challenge some of its core assumptions, while alternative conceptual frameworks have been proposed by Jones and colleagues, among others (Jones, Macken, & Nicholls, 2004).

A key issue in the discussion that surrounds these alternative conceptions, is the relationship between short-term and long-term memory. Our aim in bringing this book together was to document where researchers are currently positioned, both empirically and theoretically, with respect to their understanding of the interrelationship between the two. Because understanding of verbal memory systems is relatively better advanced, the focus of this volume is on memory in the verbal domain. The chapters contributed to the book have been written by leading researchers in the field, and represent research perspectives and techniques from both sides of the Atlantic. These chapters draw on cognitive, developmental and neuropsychological research and reflect both conceptual and computational approaches to theorising. Each chapter makes an important contribution in its own right towards a fuller understanding of the interrelationship between short- and long-term memory in the verbal domain. As a collection, the chapters also raise a number of important questions that will undoubtedly inform and direct future research endeavours in this field.

Current perspectives

The book opens with two chapters from research groups for whom the notion of separable short- and long-term memory systems remains questionable. The chapter by Surprenant and Neath (Chapter 2) is a robust denial of the distinction between short- and long-term memory. The authors draw attention to problems with the evidence-base upon which the distinction has traditionally been built, discussing what they see as the nine "lives" of short-term memory. Surprenant and Neath present a powerful argument on a number of grounds. It would be disingenuous to pretend that we, as Editors, are neutral in this matter and we remain of the belief that the notion of a short-term verbal store, dedicated to the storage of ordered information, can be spared most, if not all, of the lives they claim it has lost. Life 1, for example, concerns the extent to which the proposed rapid rate of decay of information in short-term memory (which contrasts with long-lasting retention in long-term memory) is really demonstrated by the Brown–Peterson paradigm, yet the filled retention intervals associated with this paradigm are typically much longer than the assumed duration of the short-term store. Surprenant and Neath give only the briefest consideration to Baddeley and Scott's (1971) finding of a sharp drop in performance over the first five seconds of a single-trial Brown–Peterson style experiment, a finding that we believe merits further discussion, particularly given that Baddeley and Scott used only a single trial, thus ruling out an effect of proactive interference. Life 2 questions the dual-store logic with respect to the representational form of information in short- and long-term memory but the phonological-store hypothesis (and many of the computational models based on it) asserts that it is the order of list items that is stored in the short term, not, for example, their status as words, their meaning, etc. Long-term memory is undoubtedly consulted during presentation of a novel word-list (at the very least to recognise the words), but there can be no prior long-term memory representation of the word-order that can be so consulted. Life 3 concerns capacity estimates, proposed to be limited in short-term memory and unlimited in long-term memory. The argument here is again not as strong as it might be, first, because the task in which Nairne and Neath (2001) demonstrated comparable "capacity limits" in long-term memory did not require serial recall of memory items, and second because many recent computational, process models (as opposed to abstract, mathematical models like that of Schweickert, Guentert, & Hersberger, 1990) can simulate differences, for words and nonwords, in the function that relates span to speech rate, without abandoning the notion of a short-term store for serial order. Lives 4 and 5 are about free recall, and therefore are outside the (necessary) application of the phonological loop that is specialised for immediate serial recall (though see below, with reference to Ward et al., Chapter 3). Life 6 discusses the time-based word-length effect as evidence for time-based decay but here we would note that failures to replicate Baddeley, Thomson, and Buchanan's (1975) original word-length effect finding have rarely measured the *times* at which words were recalled, which seems likely to be relevant to a test of *time-based* decay. Life 7, regarding the extent to which the phonological similarity effect can be seen as a manifestation of proactive interference, provides some defence of the unitary view, but does not contradict the separate stores' view: there are several successful computational models of the phonological similarity effect that correspond to the type of short-term memory that Surprenant and Neath argue against. Life 8 concerns the merits or otherwise of decay, particularly in relation to a two-stimulus comparison task used by Cowan, Saults, and Nugent (2001). However, since this task is not one that demands memory for serial order, the results are not immediately relevant to the discussion of a component of short-term memory dedicated to maintenance of order information. Likewise, the discussion in regard to Life 9, the extent to which neuropsychological dissociations provide evidence for a separable short-term memory system, covers many interesting topics, including patients' performance on tasks other than those that require serial recall, but does not discuss a key finding in relation to the so-called short-term memory patients, that is, their almost complete inability to perform immediate serial recall, in the presence of almost completely preserved long-term memory.

By giving these very brief counter-arguments to some of Surprenant and Neath's points, it is far from our intention to attempt to close the issue down. Rather, in the absence of a chapter here dedicated to a response to Surprenant and Neath's analysis, we did not want to leave the general reader with the impression that the matter is decided either one way or the other. Undoubtedly though, on the issue of whether or not human memory comprises a separable short-term memory system, Surprenant and Neath's contribution constitutes perhaps the most powerful case for the prosecution yet committed to print.

Ward et al. raise similar issues in their chapter (Chapter 3). They examine the distinction between a short-term store (STS) and a long-term store (LTS). The distinction is suggested by classic results using the free recall and serial recall tasks, and they describe the results of experiments designed to examine its continued viability. With regard to free recall, and on the basis of several of their own recent experiments, they argue forcefully that both primacy and recency effects can be accounted for by a single recency-based mechanism. Their approach, in which participants' rehearsals are made explicit by requiring them to be overt, has also revealed ways in which other factors, like presentation frequency and list length, can be seen to operate via effects on rehearsal schedules, and thence item recency. The authors do acknowledge, though, that the apparent selectively disruptive effect of a short, filled retention interval on the recency effect remains somewhat difficult to explain under their pure recency account.

In a similar vein, they question the evidence for a mechanism involved in the immediate serial recall (ISR) task that is distinct from that employed in free recall. Their arguments are made with respect to a strict interpretation of Baddeley and Hitch's (1974) position. Baddeley and Hitch's original data suggested that the size of the recency effect in free recall was unaffected by a serial-recall load. Ward and colleagues describe more rigorous and, it turns out, successful attempts to replicate and extend this result, but express some unease about the seemingly clean division, between mechanisms underlying such ostensibly similar tasks, that the results imply. Proponents of the working memory model (like ourselves) might be less uneasy. The phonological loop component of working memory has always been characterised as a system specialised for keeping speech-based material in the correct serial order in the short term. From this perspective, it would not be considered a *necessary* component underlying performance in the free recall task. That is not to say, however, that it might not be used in some forms of the free recall task, such as the free recall of shortish lists without a retention interval. Any mechanism capable of serial recall of a list of a given length is also *sufficient* for free recall of that list. For example, if asked to free recall the list *2,8,4*, it would not be surprising if an experimental participant replied "2, 8, 4", thus maintaining serial order above and beyond the requirements of the task. In experiments with lists that are short by the standards of free recall experiments (eight words), Bhatarah, Ward, and Tan (2008) did indeed find that participants were flexible in the resources that they could bring to bear on the task. Whether this means that a short-term serial ordering mechanism is used *whenever* free recall is required, even for lists of twenty or thirty words or, over the long term, in memory for parking spots or last season's rugby fixtures, is less clear.

Their results have led Ward and colleagues to a preferred position in which STS and LTS, as manifested in ISR and free recall tasks, are considered to be aspects of a unitary "episodic" store that is sensitive to recency. This position will not be that adopted by all their readers, but their experimental work continues to challenge "classical" views of the relationship between short- and long-term memory. In their future work they identify the key issue of forward report-order in a recency-based episodic system. It is easy to forget that many of the classic models of short-term serial recall are themselves recency-based, because stored material is sensitive to either delay or interference. In models such as that of Burgess and Hitch (1999) or Page and Norris (1998), though, the recency is that of the forward-going representation of the list itself, rather than just that of the items within it. It will be interesting to see whether and how that notion is incorporated within a unitary episodic store.

For the remaining chapters in the book, the notion of separable systems for the retention of information over the short or long term is less controversial. These chapters look in detail at various facets of the ways in which short- and long-term memory are interrelated. Allen and Baddeley (Chapter 4) discuss data that bear on the recently proposed "episodic buffer" component of the working memory model, the function of which is to bind information from the short-term storage subsystems and from long-term memory into integrated representations or episodes. Allen and Baddeley explore the role of the episodic buffer in relation to experiments on recall of meaningful sentences. They propose, with reference to the results of two experiments, that within-sentence binding proceeds relatively automatically, that is, in the absence of significant executive resources. They are careful to make a distinction between the sort of binding that is a function of long-term memory (such as might be manifest in the recall of the sentence "To be or not to be"), and that which reflects the more temporary association of lexical items (as in their example, "Noisy flashes emit careful floods"). In relation to the work of Gupta, and Page and Norris (both this volume), we might want to make the distinction even clearer by referring to the former as chunking (cf. Miller, 1956) and the latter as genuine binding. We will return to this point below.

An important message of Allen and Baddeley's chapter is that binding is not simply coactivation in long-term memory. In the classic statement of the "binding problem", namely the correct association of shape with colour when presented with a red triangle and a green square, it is importantly the case that all the long-term lexical concepts "red", "green", "triangle" and "square" are activated at the same time. It is the ability to associate these concepts together temporarily and flexibly that is crucial to a discussion of binding. It seems from Allen and Baddeley's work that the process of building a bound representation from a sentence, or series of related sentences, is less resource demanding than might have been supposed. As the authors note, these data, together with those of Jefferies, Lambon Ralph, and Baddeley (2004), suggest some modification of the way in which the episodic buffer is presumed to interact with the phonological loop component of the WM model. Specifically, there appears to be some relatively automatic generation, in the buffer, of a thematically bound representation of sentence material, driven by the arrival of (in this case) verbal material over time, though not necessarily via its storage as a sequence (cf. Caplan & Waters, 1999). In this respect, the buffer truly lives up to its "episodic" tag, inasmuch as its contents comprise a relationally bound configuration, as opposed to simply an array of activated items.

Cowan and Chen's chapter (Chapter 5), although at first sight located in the same theoretical territory as Allen and Baddeley's, is, on closer inspection, more specifically concerned with chunking. Cowan and Chen begin by exploring the possibility that immediate memory performance results from the combining of information from two sources, namely from the immediate focus of attention and from an activated portion of long-term memory. Important to their conception is the idea that long-term memory can encompass a system that is capable of rapid learning of new associations. In this regard, their long-term memory is more redolent of an episodic memory system than, say, a semantic system, given that rapid (indeed, single-trial) learning is a defining characteristic of the former. Cowan and Chen suggest that chunk formation can proceed quickly enough to be of use in tasks such as free recall of supra-span lists of words or, in the case of the experiments they describe, lists of previously associated word-pairs; they also propose a role for a more traditional-style phonological short-term memory specialised in the retention of order information across list items, at least for lists short enough for such a mechanism to be effective. Importantly, the chunking to which Cowan and Chen refer seems likely to involve distinct mechanisms from those involved in the binding which Allen and Baddeley describe. The data described by Cowan and Chen show that prelearning pairs of words extends memory capacity for lists containing those pairs. These data seem to specifically demonstrate chunking insofar as it is the list of words that is overfamiliar rather than any of the bindings that it implies. For example, while the sentence "The cat sat on the mat" might inspire certain bindings (e.g., the cat as the agent of the sitting), its cliché status relies not on the familiarity of this, or any other, role binding, but rather on the fact that the word-sequence is familiar from being oft repeated in exactly this form. In Cowan and Chen's demonstration of the role of learned chunks in extending the effective capacity of short-term memory, it is likely, therefore, that we are seeing long-term sequence learning in action rather than the binding that Allen and Baddeley propose to be the province of the episodic buffer. Long-term sequence learning is exactly the topic of the chapters by Gupta and Page and Norris, to which we now turn.

Both Gupta and Page and Norris take very seriously the well-known association between ability in immediate serial recall (or nonword repetition) and the learning of phonological word-forms (e.g., Baddeley, Gathercole, & Papagno, 1998). This strongly suggests a common representation of serial order underlying both abilities. Gupta (Chapter 6) has developed and implemented a quantitative, connectionist model that seeks to make explicit the overlap between the short- and long-term memories for serial order. There are several ways in which this model might be regarded as a hybrid model. Firstly, it employs several different means of representing serial order: a slot-based mechanism to represent word-forms as concatenated syllables and, similarly, to represent syllables as concatenated phonemes; a simple recurrent network, to permit the unpacking of these word-forms/ syllable forms into sequences of their constituent syllables/phonemes; and an overarching serial ordering mechanism that effectively associates positional codes with the localist representations at each of the model's representational levels. Gupta's model is also hybrid with respect to its representational scheme: at each level, there are both distributed and localist representations of the items at that level. This is principally a consequence of the fact that serial order in the long term (e.g., of syllables in a word) is decoupled, over the course of learning, from the positional mechanism underlying serial order in the short term, although Gupta argues that retention in the short term is vital to allowing the long-term representation to develop, primarily by affording an additional learning episode each time a list is recalled. Gupta's model gives a quantitative account of the relationships between immediate serial recall, nonword repetition and, to a certain extent, word-form learning, and elucidates the specific way in which some of these processes fail in, for instance, short-term memory patients. One point that may merit further investigation concerns whether or not Gupta's implementation of a pure short-term memory deficit, namely the slashing of the learning rate for connections to the serial ordering module, is sufficient to account for the loss of long-term word-form learning that is characteristic of the corresponding patients. On the face of it, long-term word-form learning remains possible even in the lesioned model, via the distinct ordering system embodied in the simple recurrent nets. Nonetheless, in pulling together a variety of data under the umbrella of an explicit quantitative model, Gupta's chapter is, we believe, a landmark contribution to the field of enquiry addressed by this book.

The model outlined in Page and Norris's chapter (Chapter 7) is directed towards very much the same data-set as that which motivates Gupta. In addition, they set considerable store by observations of the so-called Hebb effect (Hebb, 1961), and use these to place further constraints on modelling. As they note, the Hebb effect is a paradigmatic example of transfer from short- to long-term memory, and one that seems to be robustly present under a number of different experimental manipulations. The authors consider the possibility that the Hebb effect can be viewed as a laboratory analogue of word-form learning, inasmuch as both paradigms involve the gradual learning of repeatedly presented sequences of categorically perceived items. A number of different experimental variations are described which somewhat bolster this working hypothesis, and the results are used to motivate the outline of a chunking model built around the ordering mechanism that lies at the heart of the primacy model of immediate serial recall. Unlike Gupta's model, this model has only a single flavour of serial-ordering mechanism that runs across the boundary between short- and long-term memory. It also uses localist representation throughout, with representations of list items (be they phonemes/syllables in words, or words/nonwords in lists), being chunked together via the formation of new localist representations of higher order. One of the principal reasons for adhering to this chunking principle relates to the observation that the Hebb effect appears to involve neither reinforcement of position–item associations, nor the item–item associations characteristic of so-called chaining models. It would be interesting to see whether an account of these Hebb effect data could be modelled within Gupta's framework, or whether they would be considered beyond its scope of application. Another factor that has motivated this ordinal chunking mechanism is its applicability to the learning of words from, and recognition of words within, continuous speech, within which "position" is not normally explicitly marked. It is certainly possible that this chunking mechanism is appropriate for application to Cowan and Chen's data described above.

The contributions of Stuart and Hulme, Roodenrys and Thorn et al. look at the association between short- and long-term memory from the opposite perspective, considering the impact that long-term knowledge has on our ability to temporarily remember verbal material. Stuart and Hulme (Chapter 8) and Roodenrys (Chapter 9) focus on a process widely viewed to underpin the effects of long-term knowledge on short-term memory, namely, redintegration, in which established phonological representations are used to reconstruct information in the temporary memory trace. Stuart and Hulme

(Chapter 8) look at this mechanism as an account of the effects of word frequency on the ability to immediately recall an auditorily (or visually) presented string of words. To accommodate findings showing that the effect of word frequency on immediate recall changes depending on the list context in which the item is presented, and specifically on the comparative frequency of other words presented in the list, Stuart and Hulme propose that the long-term memory representations called upon during redintegration are dynamic and context dependent rather than fixed. They propose an account in which there is spreading activation across pathways connecting all memory items encountered in a presented memory list, with the degree of activation-spread determined by the connection strength between the items, which in turn is determined by the degree to which the items have previously co-occurred. As the authors acknowledge, such a redintegration process, dependent on context-determined long-term memory representations, could be implemented in a number of current models of short-term memory. What is not clear is whether a spreading activation hypothesis can account for sublexical long-term knowledge effects, such as the influence of lexical neighbours and phonotactic frequency, on the ability to recall nonword memory items. Stuart and Hulme propose that the sawtooth pattern obtained for recall of alternating word and nonword lists can be accounted for by the spreading activation hypothesis if it is supposed that there are no established nodes for nonwords and hence pathways between word and nonword memory items cannot be established. However, the view that nonwords have no established nodes necessarily dictates that activation could not be spread between nonword items and consequently predicts no difference in recall for nonwords, irrespective of their sublexical status. As the contribution by Roodenrys shows, the impact of sublexical characteristics of memory items on immediate recall can be found in both word and nonword recall.

The chapter by Roodenrys (Chapter 9) looks at the redintegration mechanism as an account of the influence of lexical neighbours on the recall of verbal memory items in the immediate serial recall task. Roodenrys argues that a redintegration process of the type commonly incorporated in recent models of verbal short-term memory, which operates on the basis of comparisons of degraded traces against whole-item long-term memory representations, is not sufficient to accommodate findings that close lexical neighbours of a given memory item not only intrude on it in recall, but also support the correct recall of that item. Roodenrys proposes that both competitive and facilitative effects of lexical neighbourhoods can be explained as a result of a redintegration-type process in which a degraded memory trace is taken as the input to an interactive phonological network that has distinct representations of phonemes (giving rise to facilitative effects of lexical neighbours) and words (giving rise to inhibitory lexical neighbourhood effects). This account of the redintegration process and that proposed by Stuart and Hulme are not necessarily mutually exclusive. Indeed, Roodenrys' account might plausibly be assimilated with Stuart and

Hulme's proposal that the activation strength of long-term memory representations is influenced by context-dependent spreading activation between representations. However, it remains difficult to accommodate the sawtooth pattern obtained for recall of mixed lists of words and nonwords within such an account since the interpretation of this finding offered by Stuart and Hulme necessitates no links between nonwords (represented at the phoneme level in Roodenrys' model) and word memory items. Importantly though, both Roodenrys and Stuart and Hulme add significant detail to a hitherto relatively underspecified reconstruction process and, although we are clearly still some way from a full specification of the redintegration process, the contributions by Roodenrys and Stuart and Hulme take an important step towards achieving this.

One important implication of the view of redintegration proposed by Roodenrys is that the reconstruction process is an inherent part of the recall process for all items. Thorn, Frankish, and Gathercole (Chapter 10) argue against this view. A redintegration process that operates on all memory traces would predict that all types of recall attempt would be influenced by long-term knowledge, irrespective of the degree of target information produced in that attempt. Thorn et al. present data indicating that while this is true for a number of long-term knowledge variables, it is not always the case. In a detailed error analysis of serial recall protocols it is shown that lexicality influences the production of completely correct responses (more completely correct recalls for words than nonwords) and partially correct responses (fewer partially correct recalls for words than nonwords), but makes no impact on the rate at which completely incorrect responses are produced. This response profile is not consistent with an account of the effects of lexicality on short-term memory in terms of a redintegration process that operates on all memory items. Other evidence presented in the chapter demonstrates inconsistent effects of long-term knowledge variables on short-term memory tasks that reduce the demands on the overt retrieval of item information. On the basis of these converging lines of evidence, Thorn et al. argue that the effects of permanent knowledge structures on temporary memory processes cannot be attributed to a single mechanism operating at a single point in the memory system. They suggest instead a model in which long-term knowledge impacts on immediate memory at two stages, influencing the initial strength of the temporary memory trace and subsequently determining the success of a redintegration process which attempts to rebuild partially degraded memory items on the basis of remaining phonemes in the temporary trace. This dual-mechanism account might go some way towards reconciling the redintegration literature with a parallel literature which attributes long-term knowledge effects to storage rather than retrieval processes. This literature has developed largely from a literature that views short-term memory as being intimately related to systems involved in language processing, a topic that forms the focus of the final three chapters in this volume.

The contributions of Martin (Chapter 11) and of Majerus (Chapter 12) look directly at the association between short-term memory and the language system, drawing on insights from both behavioural experiments and neuropsychological work. Martin (Chapter 11) looks for convergent evidence on the association between language and short-term memory across a range of short-term memory tasks, focusing on both normal and impaired processing. On the basis of the specific patterns of performance observed in patients and normal controls, Martin argues that processes responsible for activating and maintaining activation of language representations in verbal tasks are involved in the temporary storage of language representations and their integration into long-term memory. The core evidence in support of this view comes from studies of people with aphasia. Martin suggests that word processing deficits in aphasia are essentially short-term memory impairments, insofar as they reflect an impairment of the ability to maintain activation of semantic and phonological representations of words, an impairment that impacts on any language processing task whether it involves processing single or multiple words. In the case of an activation maintenance deficit that affects the ability to maintain activation of semantic representations of words, Martin argues that learning of novel verbal information is also disrupted. Investigations of people with aphasia also suggests a possible answer to the principal limitation of such an account of immediate memory, which relates to the absence of a specific mechanism for maintaining order in short-term memory. Martin presents evidence suggesting that semantic and phonological deficits differentially impair items at the beginning and end of a sequence, which she interprets to indicate that "maintenance activation" might not only provide content, but also, in part, underpin the maintenance of serial order in verbal short-term memory. This provides a novel account of the retention of order in immediate memory, and one that is intriguingly different from that advanced in the principal models of short-term memory to date. The extent to which such a mechanism can account for the abundance of documented serial order phenomena will be interesting to see.

Majerus (Chapter 12) also argues that activation of language representations plays a crucial role in temporary memory processing, but in contrast to Martin, Majerus proposes that temporary activation of the language network is involved only in the retention of item information, and that verbal short-term memory tasks requiring the retention of order information require a separate distinct mechanism for maintaining the order of the items, this being a specific function of a dedicated short-term memory system. Majerus's chapter draws on behavioural, developmental, neuropsychological and neuro-imaging data suggesting that short-term memory for item information and for order information rely on distinct cognitive processes and are underpinned by distinct neuro-anatomical substrates: the temporary retention of item information, Majerus argues, shares many processes with language processing, reflects the organisation of the phonological, lexical and semantic networks that underlie language representations and involves the temporary activation of language representations in the temporal lobes, whereas the retention of order information does not show any such associations and neuro-anatomically is supported by a distinct network distributed over right fronto-parieto-cerebellar areas. To model this multiple-component system Majerus proposes a short-term memory framework that integrates language processing systems (responsible for the retention of item information) and serial order processing systems (dedicated to the retention of order), which is supported by an "attentional modulator", a common flexible pool of attentional resources. This modulator is capable of steering attentional resources towards either language representations (item processing), serial order processing, or both. The idea of separate systems for storing item information and serial order information in the short term fits well with some current computational models of temporary memory (e.g., Burgess & Hitch, 1999; Gupta, 2003; Page & Norris, 1998). What sets Majerus's framework apart from these models, and draws it together as a unified account of memory rather than two entirely independent systems, is the postulation of the attentional modulator in addition to the systems responsible for retaining item and order information. Majerus acknowledges that the principal empirical support for this component comes largely from neuro-imaging studies, although he likens the attentional modulator to Cowan's (1995) "focus of attention". The future success of Majerus's short-term memory framework seems likely to lie in the ability of this component to hold up under closer scrutiny. Nevertheless, Majerus's chapter provides a compelling case for the distinction between item and order information in short-term memory, which future revisions of models that do not currently attend to such a distinction would benefit from heeding.

The final chapter by Service (Chapter 13), like those of Gupta and Page and Norris, examines the relationship between phonological short-term memory and long-term learning. The focus of Service's chapter is on the nature of the representational systems that are involved in the temporary retention of verbal information and in the long-term learning of new word-forms and is driven very much by consideration of normal and impaired language processing. Service suggests that the well-documented link between short-term memory and new word learning is likely to lie in the quality of the phonological representations that subserve short- and long-term memory systems. This suggestion is based on three principal lines of evidence: (a) that ERP (event-related potential) MMN (mismatch negativity) amplitude, which is thought to reflect sensory processing, appears to be related to nonword repetition accuracy (and hence verbal short-term memory), suggesting that sensory memory and/or representations may subserve verbal short-term memory processing; (b) that developmental dyslexia may be caused by a core deficit in the processing of rapid stimulus changes, and that such a generalised temporal storage/processing deficit might result in phonological short-term memory problems and may also limit long-term storage/learning, specifically by compromising the specification of a trace at encoding; and (c) that data bearing on the neural substrate of phonological short-term memory indicate that brain areas that are involved in the encoding and maintenance of complex phonological stimuli in working memory, such as attention and rehearsal, appear to also play a role in the learning of new words. On the basis of these three distinct lines of evidence Service concludes that what links verbal short-term memory performance and processes involved in new word learning is the representational efficiency of the neural language networks that encode and maintain complex phonological stimuli. What distinguishes Service's contribution from that of Gupta and Page and Norris is that unlike Gupta and Page and Norris, Service does not explicitly consider the role of ordering mechanisms in the link between short-term memory and new word learning. Service nonetheless provides an interesting elucidation of the mechanistic nature of the well-established association between the systems involved in the temporary retention of verbal information and the long-term learning of new words, which complements the more detailed modelling approaches of the contributions of Gupta and Page and Norris.

Summary

All the chapters contributed to this book have in common the view that short- and long-term memory systems are intimately related. For some, like Surprenant and Neath and Ward et al., the debate as to whether or not these systems are one and the same thing rages on. For others, the most fruitful lines of enquiry lie in elucidating the precise nature of the links between temporary and permanent memory systems. Across these chapters a number of key theoretical issues are apparent: that understanding of binding/chunking mechanisms is central to understanding the integration of short- and long-term memory representations (Allen & Baddeley, Cowan & Chen), that sequencing mechanisms are of critical import (Gupta, Page, & Norris), that the link between short- and long-term memory is bi-directional and that long-term knowledge impacts on short-term retention in significant ways (Roodenrys, Stuart & Hulme, Thorn et al.) and that, in the case of temporary and permanent retention of verbal information, the role of the language system and its associated processes cannot be ignored (Martin, Majerus, Service). These chapters highlight the importance of the interrelations between short- and long-term memory to current memory research, both to modelling endeavours and to understanding normal and impaired processing. Together we hope the chapters in this volume will provide the reader with an advanced appreciation of current understanding of interactions between short- and long-term memory in the verbal domain, and of the most recent empirical work and critical theoretical issues that currently drive research in this field.

References

Atkinson, R. C., & Shiffrin, R. M. (1968). Human memory: A proposed system and control processes. In K. W. Spence & J. D. Spence (Eds.), *The psychology of learning and motivation* (Vol. 2, pp. 89–195). New York: Academic Press.

Baddeley, A. D., Gathercole, S. E., & Papagno, C. (1998). The phonological loop as a language learning device. *Psychological Review, 105*, 158–173.

Baddeley, A. D., & Hitch, G. (1974). Working memory. In G. A. Bower (Ed.), *Recent advances in learning and motivation* (Vol. 8, pp. 47–90). New York: Academic Press.

Baddeley, A. D., & Scott, D. (1971). Short-term forgetting in the absence of pro-active interference. *Quarterly Journal of Experimental Psychology, 23*, 275–283.

Baddeley, A. D., Thomson, N., & Buchanan, M. (1975). Word length and the structure of short-term memory. *Journal of Verbal Learning and Verbal Behaviour, 14*, 575–589.

Basso, A., Spinnler, H., Vallar, G., & Zanobio, M. E. (1982). Left hemisphere damage and selected impairment of auditory verbal short-term memory: A case study. *Neuropsychologia, 20*, 263–274.

Bhatarah, P., Ward, G., & Tan, L. (2008). Examining the relationship between free recall and immediate serial recall: The serial nature of recall and the effect of test expectancy. *Memory & Cognition, 36*, 20–34.

Burgess, N., & Hitch, G. (1992). Toward a network model of the articulatory loop. *Journal of Memory and Language, 31*, 429–460.

Burgess, N., & Hitch, G. J. (1999). Memory for serial order: A network model of the phonological loop and its timing. *Psychological Review, 106*, 551–581.

Caplan, D., & Waters, G. S. (1999). Verbal working memory and sentence comprehension. *Behavioral and Brain Sciences, 22*, 77–126.

Cowan, N. (1995). *Attention and memory: An integrated framework*. New York: Oxford University Press.

Cowan, N., Saults, S., & Nugent, L. (2001). The ravages of absolute and relative amounts of time on memory. In H. L. Roediger III, J. S. Nairne, I. Neath, & A. M. Surprenant (Eds.), *The nature of remembering: Essays in honor of Robert G. Crowder* (pp. 315–330). Washington, DC: APA.

Gupta, P. (2003). Examining the relationship between word learning, nonword repetition and immediate serial recall in adults. *Quarterly Journal of Experimental Psychology, 56A*, 1213–1236.

Hebb, D. O. (1949). *Organization of behavior*. New York: Wiley.

Hebb, D. O. (1961). Distinctive features of learning in the higher animal. In J. F. Delafresnaye (Ed.), *Brain mechanisms and learning* (pp. 37–46). Oxford: Blackwell.

Henson, R. N. A. (1998). Short-term memory for serial order: the start-end model. *Cognitive Psychology, 36, 73–137.*

James, W. (1890). *Principles of Psychology, Vol. 1*. New York: Holt.

Jefferies, E., Lambon Ralph, M., & Baddeley, A. D. (2004). Automatic and controlled processing in sentence recall: The role of long-term and working memory. *Journal of Memory and Language, 51*, 623–643.

Jones, D. M., Macken, W. J., & Nicholls, A. P. (2004). The phonological store of working memory: Is it phonological and is it a store? *Journal of Experimental Psychology: Learning, Memory, and Cognition, 30*, 656–674.

Miller, G. A. (1956). The magical number seven, plus or minus two: Some limits on our capacity for processing information. *Psychological Review*, *63*, 81–97.

Nairne, J. S., & Neath, I. (2001). Long-term memory span. *Behavioral and Brain Sciences*, *24*, 134–135.

Neath, I., & Brown, G. D. A. (2006). SIMPLE: Further applications of a local distinctiveness model of memory. In B. H. Ross (Ed.), *The psychology of learning and motivation* (pp. 201–243). San Diego, CA: Academic Press.

Page, M. P. A., & Norris, D. (1998). The primacy model: A new model of immediate serial recall. *Psychological Review*, *105*, 761–781.

Schweickert, R., Guentert, L., & Hersberger, L. (1990). Phonological similarity, pronunciation rate, and memory span. *Psychological Science*, *1*, 74–77.

Shallice, T., & Warrington, E. K. (1970). Independent functioning of verbal memory stores: A neuropsychological study. *Quarterly Journal of Experimental Psychology*, *22*, 261–273.

2 The nine lives of short-term memory

Aimée M. Surprenant and Ian Neath

Overview

In this chapter we review nine arguments that have been used, at one time or another, to support the idea that there is a fundamental difference between short- and long-term memory. For each point, we show why there is no support for the idea that there exists a separate short-term memory that follows fundamentally different laws than long-term memory. We thus wholeheartedly endorse Melton's (1963) claim that results from experiments on short-term memory are readily interpretable in terms of factors known to operate in long-term memory.

Introduction

In 1963, Arthur Melton wrote a paper entitled "Implications of short-term memory for a general theory of memory" in which he argued against the idea that short-term memory (STM) was distinct from long-term memory (LTM) and laid out the case that the results from experiments on STM are readily interpretable in terms of "factors known to operate in LTM" (p. 8). Almost 20 years later, one of his students, Bob Crowder, noted that Melton's paper "has been remembered with great respect, . . . but mainly as a last ditch argument in a losing cause" (Crowder, 1982, p. 293). The negative assessment of the impact of Melton's paper notwithstanding, Crowder's own review led him to a similar conclusion: The evidence pointed "grimly to the demise of short-term memory as a concept" (p. 320).

Nonetheless, there are still investigators declaring that "reports of the demise of short-term memory may have been much exaggerated" (Davelaar, Goshen-Gottstein, Ashkenazi, Haarmann, & Usher, 2005, p. 30; see also Healy & McNamara, 1996; Raaijmakers, 1993). In this chapter we review nine arguments that have been used, at one time or another, to support or refute the idea that there is a fundamental difference between short- and long-term memory. Some of the points were made previously by Melton, Crowder, and other critics of the dual-store notion (e.g., Nairne, 2002), and some reflect more recent evidence. For each point, we show why there is no support for the idea that there exists a separate short-term memory that follows fundamentally different laws than long-term memory. Given the response to Melton's and Crowder's papers, however, we hold out little hope that our arguments will settle the debate once and for all. Perhaps STM has even more lives than the proverbial cat.

Clarifications and caveats

What exactly is meant by the term *short-term memory*? At one point in time, researchers agreed to a distinction such that short-term memory and long-term memory referred to tasks whereas short-term store and long-term store referred to the underlying hypothetical memory store (Crowder, 1976). However, this distinction is not always followed and the task and the concept are now conflated. To further confuse the issue, there are the terms *primary* and *secondary memory*, as well as *working memory* and *immediate memory*.

Typically, primary memory still refers to the Jamesian idea (James, 1890, pp. 608–609) that an object in primary memory "never was lost; its date was never cut off in consciousness from that of the immediately present moment. In fact, it comes to us as belonging to the rearward portion of the present space of time, and not to the genuine past." In contrast, an object from secondary memory "is one which has been absent from consciousness altogether, and now revives anew". The critical distinction here is that if something has not been continuously in consciousness, then it has left primary memory and must be retrieved from secondary memory.

The most common use of short- and long-term memory are as replacements for short- and long-term stores in the modal model of the late 1960s. So termed by Murdock (1967), this conception of memory had information first pass through a sensory register before it was recoded into the short-term store. If the items in the short-term store were rehearsed appropriately, they were copied into the long-term store, otherwise they were lost to decay. Retrieval from the long-term store required that the information be copied back into the short-term store, from which it could then be output. The short-term store within the modal model reflects many features of the information-processing metaphor of memory: it was of limited capacity, short duration, and functioned as a buffer in which to temporarily store information. Information in the short-term store was forgotten if attention was withdrawn from it.

Usually, the term *working memory* is taken as referring to the Baddeley and Hitch (1974; Baddeley 2000) model, one of whose principal components is the phonological loop. The phonological loop component is similar to the short-term store in the modal model, except that capacity is defined in terms of the number of items that can be rehearsed within about 2 seconds rather than an absolute number of items. Information in the phonological loop is verbal in nature and is subject to time-based decay unless refreshed by rehearsal. A different usage of the term working memory refers to the activated portions of long-term memory, which has quite different implications (e.g., Cowan, 2001). Miyake and Shah (1999) include chapters that represent 10 different models of working memory (including the two mentioned here).

The term *immediate memory* has many different usages, sometimes being a synonym for James' (1890) primary memory, sometimes a synonym for the modal model's short-term store, and sometimes as a term designed specifically to be neutral with respect to the STM–LTM distinction.

In this chapter we will use the term *short-term memory* (STM) to refer to a concept that has the following properties: (1) there is a fundamental difference between the form of memory responsible for remembering over the short term and the form that is responsible for remembering over the long term; (2) forgetting over the short term is due to decay; and (3) decay can be offset by rehearsal. Some of the arguments will apply only to more specialized uses of the term (e.g., particular architectural assumptions), but most will apply to all of the various incarnations of the concept.

It should be noted that there do exist alternative conceptions of STM in which capacity limitations can arise from sources other than just decay (e.g., Barrouillet, Bernardin, & Camos, 2004; Cowan, 2001). However, such accounts typically retain time-based decay of at least some portion of the information within the system and, as such, are at least partially vulnerable to the points we make below. A model of STM that completely rejects the notion of decay and instead has the capacity of the system limited by some other factor could still be a form of memory that is qualitatively different from LTM. As this conception does not reflect the common usage of the term "STM" in the literature, we do not address the limitations of this type of model here.

Our major point is that regardless of the various theoretical manifestations of the concept, the data do not support the idea that STM is fundamentally different than LTM. Moreover, we gain no additional insight or explanatory power by requiring two memory stores to what we have when we do not make the distinction. As Edwin Starr might have put it, short-term memory: what is it good for? Absolutely nothing.

The nine lives

Life 1: Brown–Peterson

Within the modal model, one of the fundamental differences between short- and long-term memory is the rate at which information is forgotten. Information in long-term memory is long-lasting, and there is no compelling evidence that it is ever permanently lost (Capaldi & Neath, 1995).[1] In contrast, information in short-term memory decays quickly, unless the decay is offset by rehearsal. The rapid rate of information decay in short-term memory was demonstrated using what would later be named the

"Brown–Peterson task" (after Brown, 1958; Peterson & Peterson, 1959). In this task subjects are given three items, usually consonants, and are asked to recall them after a distraction-filled delay. The number of items (three) is meant to be well below the capacity of short-term memory and the distractor task is meant to be different enough from the to-be-remembered items to cause no interference while at the same time being difficult enough to prevent active rehearsal and recoding of the target items. The major variable is the duration of the distractor interval. Thus, this paradigm was supposed to give a relatively pure estimate of how long information remained in short-term memory after attention was withdrawn. The data showed that there was rapid forgetting of the consonants as the filled delay increased; after 18 seconds' delay, the consonants were recalled only 10% of the time. This loss of information was hypothesized to be due to the decay of information in the limited capacity short-term buffer.

The conclusion that forgetting in the Brown–Peterson task is due to rapid decay of information was proven wrong in a number of different ways. First, Keppel, and Underwood (1962) showed no differential forgetting on the first recall trial regardless of the retention interval. That is, recall was equivalent regardless of whether the item had to be retained for 3 seconds or 18 seconds; differential forgetting was observed only on subsequent trials. This finding strongly argues against a decay explanation of forgetting in short-term memory because such an account has to predict that forgetting will occur during any filled retention interval. Keppel and Underwood explained their results as being due to the build-up of interference from previous trials. This type of interference is known as proactive interference (PI).[2]

Wickens and colleagues (1970, 1972; Wickens, Born, & Allen, 1963) tested the build-up of PI explanation of performance on the Brown–Peterson task. Theoretically, PI increases over multiple retrieval attempts of similar information. Therefore, if there is a change in materials, there should be less PI and better recall. In contrast, if the information simply decays as a function of time, switching materials should have no effect on recall. Wickens et al. asked subjects to recall lists of three consonants for three trials. Replicating Keppel and Underwood (1962), performance dropped sharply over those three trials. However, in the fourth trial, the materials were changed from consonants to numbers. Performance in this switched condition was much better than that of an unswitched control group who continued to recall letters.[3] This release from proactive interference has since been demonstrated using a variety of materials ranging from vegetables and professions (Wickens, Dalezman, & Eggemeier, 1976) to news stories (Gunter, Berry, & Clifford, 1981) and standardized tests (Dempster, 1985).

If recall in the Brown–Peterson task is due to interference from previous trials, another way to reduce the interference is to separate the trials by having a very long inter-trial interval. Loess and Waugh (1967) found that with very long intervals between trials (such as 300 seconds), there was no difference in performance as a function of trial number, even when the subjects were counting backwards for 18 seconds.

A final nail in the coffin of the idea that forgetting in the Brown–Peterson paradigm is due to decay of information in the short-term store was provided by Turvey, Brick, and Osborn (1970). They had three groups[4] of subjects perform a standard Brown–Peterson task. However, one group counted backwards for 10 seconds, one counted backwards for 15 seconds, and one counted backwards for 20 seconds. Contrary to a decay explanation of forgetting in the Brown–Peterson task, on the fourth trial all groups were performing equivalently; doubling the duration of the distractor activity had no effect on the level of recall. On the fifth trial all subjects were given the same retention interval (15 seconds). For the subjects whose retention interval increased, performance was much worse. For the subjects whose retention interval was the same as in the other trials, performance did not change. However, for the subjects whose retention interval decreased, performance increased substantially. Thus, it is not the absolute amount of time spent doing the distractor task that is the determining factor in performance in the task (as predicted by a decay explanation) but the relative time compared to other trials (Baddeley, 1976; Neath & Surprenant, 2003).

For many researchers, these studies, along with a great many other ones, convincingly demonstrated that forgetting in the Brown–Peterson task is due to PI and cannot be accounted for by decay (for a recent summary, see Nairne, Whiteman, & Kelley, 1999). Instead of taking these results as evidence against the idea of a separate short-term memory, however, many proponents of the dual-store account recast the argument. For example, Healy and McNamara (1996) argue that these results are not problematic because "information can be encoded in secondary memory even with rapid stimulus presentation so that retention can derive from secondary memory as well as primary memory in the distractor task" (p. 147). Thus, according to Healy and McNamara, the Keppel and Underwood (1962) result of no differential forgetting on the first trial is due to a lack of PI build-up in secondary memory. Secondary memory supports first-trial retention but, because it is susceptible to PI, cannot support further recall attempts very well. The end result is that short-term memory is not needed as part of the explanation of the very phenomenon that was used to justify the concept of decay in the first place, and hence the existence of short-term memory.

Like Crowder (1982), we interpret the data as showing that forgetting within the Brown–Peterson task is explainable solely in terms of mechanisms thought to underlie long-term memory, consistent with Melton's (1963) thesis.

Life 2: Dual-store logic

Almost from the very beginning, researchers who tried to separate the contributions of STM from those of LTM ran into problems inherent in the architecture of the modal model. As discussed above, this account describes the flow of information through a multi-component information processing system. Stimuli are taken up through the senses, stored briefly in a sensory buffer, are recoded and transferred into STM, and then, if rehearsed for long enough, copied into LTM. Although the modal model sounds reasonable at first, problems begin to arise the more one thinks about how the stages must interact.

One problem concerns how the sensory information is converted into a form for deposit into short-term memory. Presumably, there must be direct contact between sensory memory and long-term memory in order to identify the item. If information can go directly from the sensory register to long-term store, why does it then go back to the sensory register before proceeding to long-term store via short-term store? Why not just stay in long-term store?

A second logical problem is that there will always be contamination of one presumed store with the other (Crowder, 1993a; Nairne, 1996). Information recalled from long-term memory has to pass through short-term memory on the way in and on the way out. Information in short-term memory has to be linked to information in long-term memory so that it can be identified and categorized in the first place. Any response from any task will reflect contributions from both stores, and, thus, will be contaminated. Many of the chapters in this very volume further illustrate this point.

A related issue concerns the nature of the representation. Traditionally, it was thought that the primary mode of representation in short-term memory was phonological or acoustic whereas information in long-term memory was primarily coded semantically (e.g., Kintsch & Buschke, 1969). This leads to a common inference that if a task shows acoustic (or phonological) errors, it is a sign that the task relies on short-term memory. Similarly, the absence of acoustic errors or presence of semantic errors is seen as indicative of a task that taps long-term memory. However, all acoustic knowledge necessarily needs to be stored in long-term memory, so it is unclear which system is responsible for producing the information. Combine this with evidence of acoustic interference (and thus acoustic coding) in tasks supposed to tap long-term memory (Dale & McGlaughlin, 1971) and semantic confusion errors (and thus semantic coding) in tasks thought to tap short-term memory (Shulman, 1970, 1972), and the reasoning that phonological processing signals STM involvement comes perilously close to specious.

At the risk of belabouring the point, it should be obvious that most conceptions of short-term memory absolutely require the ability of information in the store to take on *any* form of coding. Atkinson and Shiffrin (1968) recognized this need, and allowed for codes other than what they termed "auditory-verbal-linguistic", including a haptic code. The reason is that within the architecture of the model, information is recalled via short-term memory; if you recall something haptic, then either the information has to pass from long-term memory into short-term memory before being produced or the information is still in short-term memory. Short-term memory has to allow all possible codes, including those ascribed to long-term memory.

Life 3: Estimates of short-term memory capacity

Given that a researcher has proposed a distinction between a limited capacity short-term memory and a (potentially) unlimited long-term memory, the question arises, what is the nature of the limit? There have been many different ways proposed to measure the capacity of short-term memory; here, we focus on just three.

Memory span

One common measure of the capacity of short-term memory is based on the number of items that can be immediately recalled in order.[5] The logic behind this is as follows. Say you are trying to determine the capacity of a bucket. You place seven apples in and they all stay nicely in the bucket. However, when you place the eighth apple in, it falls out. Thus, we have determined that the capacity of the bucket is seven apples. Notice that we could have precariously perched the eighth apple on top of some of the other apples, in which case it would fall out only if the bucket were jostled. Alternatively, we could have used larger apples, in which case the estimates of the capacity of the bucket may be smaller than seven. However, over multiple trials, with many different apples, we converge to about the same estimate of the capacity of our bucket, about seven (plus or minus two) apples. Transferring that analogy to short-term memory, the way the capacity of short-term memory is determined is that we place information into the store until some of it "falls out" or is not recalled accurately. We then infer that this is the amount of information that can "fit" or be stored in short-term memory.

If this logic is correct, we should be able to use the same method to determine the capacity of long-term memory. Nairne and Neath (2001) did exactly this: they simply used delayed recall rather than immediate recall. Given that approximately 5 minutes elapsed between presentation and test, no proponent of the STM–LTM distinction could argue that the items were still in STM; recall therefore must be from LTM. Nairne and Neath determined that the capacity of long-term memory is about five items, well within the range of estimates of the capacity of short-term memory. Their point, of course, was not that you can retain only five pieces of information in long-term memory. Rather, they suggested that tasks used as measures of short-term memory might be measuring something else.[6] The fact that span is about the same for both short- and long-term memory suggests that the span technique is *not* measuring capacity of short-term memory.

Non-zero intercept

A second common measure of short-term memory is based not on items but on time. Specifically, the capacity limit is due to two opposing processes: items decay over time but this decay can be offset by subvocal rehearsal. This time-based capacity is often expressed as a simple equation. Given the assumption that overt reading rate is highly correlated with subvocal rehearsal rate, memory span, s, can be described as a linear function of the pronunciation rate, r, and the duration of the verbal trace, t:[7]

$$s = rt$$

Experimenters can measure both span, s in the equation, and also pronunciation rate, r. They can then solve for the third variable, the duration of the trace, t. If memory span, s, really is solely a function of pronunciation rate and the duration of the verbal trace, then when there is no rehearsal rate, span must be zero (Schweickert, Guentert, & Hersberger, 1990). When memory span is plotted as a function of speech rate and the best-fitting line is calculated, the key issue is whether this line intercepts the y-axis at 0.

When words are used, the intercept is greater than 0 (e.g., Brown & Hulme, 1992; Hulme, Maughan, & Brown, 1991; Hulme, Roodenrys, Brown, & Mercer, 1995; Multhaup, Balota, & Cowan, 1996). This has been interpreted as showing a long-term influence on short-term memory, and is further taken as showing that span is not a pure measure of short-term memory. This reinforces conclusions from earlier studies (e.g., Watkins, 1977).

However, a more critical test concerns non-words as stimuli: because these words are not known to the subject, they cannot be in long-term memory prior to beginning the experiment and thus there should be no way for long-term memory to contribute. The evidence from non-words is mixed: Multhaup et al. (1996) found a non-zero intercept for both younger and older adults, and Experiment 1 of Hulme et al. (1991) also resulted in a non-zero intercept. However, a second experiment reported by Hulme et al. did find a zero intercept for Italian words (and the subjects knew no Italian). When the subjects became more familiar with the Italian words, however, the intercept became non-zero. Brown and Hulme (1992) and Hulme et al. (1995) both found an approximately zero intercept for non-words. Again, when subjects became more familiar with the stimuli, the intercepts all increased. Stuart and Hulme (2000) even found that familiarizing subjects with low frequency words 24 hours prior to the memory span assessment improved subjects' performance. That is, being exposed to a set of stimuli on Tuesday increased your memory span for those items on Wednesday. Unless you are recalling items that you have never experienced before, your span is likely to be contaminated by long-term memory.

If one wants to give most weight to the studies showing a zero intercept for non-words and conclude that memory span is not affected by contributions from long-term memory, there is still a problem. This conclusion requires the prediction that immediate serial recall of short lists of non-words is also immune to the effects of long-term memory, because memory span is essentially an immediate serial recall task. The problem is that studies show that immediate serial recall of non-words in both four-item (Roodenrys & Hinton, 2002) and five-item lists (Thorn & Frankish, 2005) is so affected.

Inferential procedures

Crowder (1976, pp. 146–150) reviews many methods proposed to measure the capacity of short-term memory based on the idea that short- and long-term memory both contribute to recalling a list of items. Each method makes different assumptions and uses different equations, but most seem to produce an answer less than half of the typical memory span estimate. Glanzer and Razel (1974) report a mean of 2.2 words, with a standard deviation of 0.64, computed from examining some thirty-odd studies. Despite this convergence, the estimate changes considerably if one adopts a different unit of analysis: Using a chunk[8] rather than the word, then the estimate almost doubles to about four items (Cowan, 2001).

There is no consensus on the answer to the question, what is the capacity of short-term memory? Consensus does not even exist about the basic unit – time? item? chunk? – that should be used. The lack of consensus is due, we suggest, to the fact that the bucket, whose capacity we are trying to measure, does not exist.

Life 4: Recency effect in free recall

A common memory task is to ask people to recall a list of items in any order they like, so-called free recall. Memory performance is typically plotted as a function of the item's original position in the list, and the resulting graph is usually termed a serial position curve. Typically, recall of the first few items is very good (the primacy effect), recall of the final few items is excellent (the recency effect), and recall of the middle items is much worse (e.g., Murdock, 1962). According to the modal model (e.g., Atkinson & Shiffrin, 1968; Glanzer, 1972), the primacy effect is due to long-term memory whereas the recency effect is due to short-term memory. The first few items get additional rehearsal, which leads to a greater likelihood that the items are copied into long-term memory. When the first item is presented, subjects can devote 100% of their rehearsal to this item; when the second item is presented, subjects must now split rehearsal time between two items. At some point, there are more items than can be rehearsed.

When presentation of the list ends, the last few items are still in short-term memory and can be "dumped" before they decay.

If the recency effect is due to dumping items from short-term memory, then the recency effect should be eliminated if sufficient time passes that the items should have decayed and if rehearsal is prevented so that the items cannot be copied to long-term memory. Glanzer and Cunitz (1966; see also Postman & Phillips, 1965) report such an experiment. When the list was followed by 30 seconds of distractor activity (counting backwards), the recency effect was eliminated but the primacy effect was unaffected. This dissociation of primacy and recency effects has been taken as strong evidence supporting the distinction between STM and LTM.

Problems with this account of recency in free recall began to emerge with the introduction of the continual distractor paradigm.[9] Whereas Glanzer and Cunitz (1966) added just one period of distractor activity, Bjork and Whitten (1974) added distractor activity after *every* item in the list, including the final item. When subjects are continually distracted, the recency effect re-emerges. This long-term recency effect caused Bjork and Whitten (1974, p. 189) to conclude that "the customary two-process theoretical account of immediate free recall is certainly incomplete, if not wrong".

An attempt to save the modal model's account was proposed by Koppenaal and Glanzer (1990). They noted that in the typical continual distractor paradigm, subjects receive the same distractor task on each trial. Given practice, the subjects might be able to learn to time-share, alternating their processing between maintenance rehearsal to keep the last few items in short-term memory and performing the distractor task. This view predicts that if the distractor task changes, the time-sharing mechanism should be disrupted and the long-term recency effect should again be eliminated. In their changing condition, the subjects experienced one type of distractor task after every item until the final list item was presented. Then, a second type of distractor task was used. The recency effect was eliminated when the distractor task changed.

Neath (1993) suggested a different explanation. Processing of the to-be-remembered item does not instantly cease the second the distractor task begins. Rather, the two co-occur, and thus the type of distractor task can serve as a contextual retrieval cue. In the changing distractor recall task, the last list item is associated with a different context than the other list items and so is less likely to be recalled when the main distractor task is used as a contextual retrieval cue. If, however, subjects experienced a different distractor task after every list item, the final item should not be penalized: all items are associated with a different specific context (e.g., item 1 with distractor task A, item 2 with distractor task B, item 3 with distractor task C) and thus subjects should refrain from using just one distractor task as a contextual retrieval cue. This predicts that the recency effect should re-emerge if the distractor task changes after every item; an experiment confirmed this prediction (see Neath, 1993, Experiment 2).

Some researchers have tried to resurrect the modal model by arguing that the long-term recency effect is somehow different than the short-term recency effect. However, two types of experimental data question this assertion. First, if short- and long-term recency effects are qualitatively different, the ratio rule (Bjork & Whitten, 1974) should not link the two. The ratio rule describes the magnitude of the recency effect as a function of the temporal spacing of the to-be-remembered items. Essentially, when the ratio of the time between the presentation of each item (the inter-item presentation interval or IPI) to the retention interval (or RI) is held constant, the size of the recency effect is constant also. Thus, the standard immediate free recall case might be one in which there is an IPI of 1 s and an RI of 1 s. A continual distractor task in which the IPI is 10 s and the RI is 10 s should lead to the same level of recency. Numerous studies have generally supported the accuracy of this type of prediction (e.g., Glenberg, Bradley, Kraus, & Renzaglia, 1983; Nairne, Neath, Serra, & Byun, 1997). Second, if short- and long-term recency effects are qualitatively different, Greene (1986a) should not have found that many variables have similar effects in both immediate free recall and continual distractor recall.

Despite all the similarities, Davelaar et al. (2005) noted five dissociations between recency in immediate free recall and continual distractor recall, and these dissociations, they argue, strongly support the idea of a separate short-term memory. We mention two of the dissociations here, a third in the next section ("Life 5: Negative recency"), and a fourth in the final section ("Life 9: Neuropsychological dissociations"); Neath and Brown (2006) offer a systematic and more detailed account.

The first dissociation noted by Davelaar et al. (2005) is that recency is present in immediate free recall tasks when subjects are asked to begin recall with the last item but recency is absent when subjects are asked to begin recall with the first item (e.g., Dalezman, 1976). However, there are "no significant differences" in recall as a function of directed output order with continual distractor recall (Whitten, 1978, p. 689). The second dissociation concerns PI: a prior list interferes only with recall of pre-recency items; recency items are immune to PI in immediate free recall. However, a prior list interferes with recall of all items in continual distractor recall; recency items are not immune. Davelaar et al. take these differences as supporting the idea that STM and LTM are distinct.

Neither of these dissociations requires a distinction between STM and LTM. Neath and Brown (2006) offer an existence proof in which a model that assumes no difference between short- and long-term memory produces exactly these dissociations. The model, SIMPLE (Scale Invariant Memory and Perceptual Learning; Brown, Neath, & Chater, 2007), assumes that memory retrieval, regardless of the paradigm, is discrimination in terms of location along a dimension, whether that dimension is frequency, temporal position, ordinal position, etc., or some combination. Items with fewer close neighbours on the relevant dimension(s) will be better remembered than items with more close neighbours. The pattern of results seen with immediate free recall, delayed recall, continual distractor recall, and so on, are all due to how the distribution of items along a primarily temporal dimension change. This view also accounts for the ratio rule and the effects of rehearsal on free recall (Tan & Ward, 2000).

The recency effect in free recall, then, is readily explainable by accounts in which STM does not exist. The dissociations noted by Davelaar et al. (2005) and others are real, they simply do not require two stores to explain them. Ward, Tan, and Bhatarah (this volume) arrive at a similar conclusion, although from a slightly different perspective. Again, the basic processes and mechanisms of LTM do just fine accounting for data commonly attributable to STM.

Life 5: Negative recency

The demonstration of a negative recency effect in final free recall has often been cited as evidence supporting the distinction between short- and long-term memory. On each trial in an experiment, subjects see a list of items and are given an immediate free recall task. After the last trial, the subjects receive a surprise test that asks them to recall all of the items from all of the lists, a so-called final free recall test. On this surprise test, items from the recency portions of the individual lists are typically recalled worse than all other list items (Craik, 1970). This finding is consistent with the claim that the final few items in immediate free recall are held in STM from which they are dumped whereas earlier list items are recalled from LTM. On the final free recall test, only the items that were in LTM can be recalled, and thus, recall of the final few items from each list is impaired. This result is also consistent with the claim that long-term recency is somehow different from short-term recency because negative recency effects are typically not seen on final free recall tests that follow continual distractor (or delayed) initial tests (e.g., Bjork & Whitten, 1974).

However, as Greene (1986b) has noted, this pattern of results is also consistent with views that deny the distinction between short- and long-term memory; all that is required is a view that attributes the results, at least in part, to differential processing. There is a lot of evidence that negative recency is due to a strategy that subjects adopt in which they rehearse the final few items in each list less than other items (e.g., Maskarinec & Brown, 1974; Tan & Ward, 2000; Watkins & Watkins, 1974). If you know you are going to dial a number immediately, you typically just say it over and over to yourself. This method is "good enough" for the short term. If you know you will need the number in an hour's time, then you will probably use a different method.

Negative recency itself, then, does not require a distinction between STM and LTM. Moreover, some aspects of these negative recency effects pose a problem for the dual store account. Assume that items from the recency portion of each list were originally in STM and were not in LTM. This is the claim to explain the basic negative recency effect. What if, however, right before the final free recall test, the subjects were asked to try to recall the last few items from each list first before trying to recall the items from the other parts of each list? When subjects are given these instructions, the negative recency effect turns into a positive recency effect (Dalezman, 1976; Wixted, 1991). If one wants to attribute negative recency to the idea that the final few items from each list were not copied to long-term memory, how can they be well recalled when the output order on the final free recall test is changed? Even if some aspects of the negative recency effect are what a dual-store account would predict, the pattern of results does not require such a distinction and there are aspects of the data that cannot be accounted for by a dual-store account.

Life 6: The word-length effect

A currently popular conception of short-term memory assumes that "memory traces decay over a period of a few seconds, unless revived by articulatory rehearsal" (Baddeley, 2000, p. 419). Recall of items from short-term memory, then, is a joint function of the decay rate and the time needed to rehearse them sufficiently to offset decay. Assuming a positive correlation between the rate of subvocal rehearsal and overt pronunciation time, this view predicts worse recall of items that take longer to pronounce than otherwise comparable items that take less time to pronounce. The word-length effect is the name given to this finding: lists of shorter words are recalled better than otherwise comparable lists of longer words.

There are really two versions of the effect: The time-based word-length effect is when the short and long items differ only in pronunciation time; everything else (e.g., number of phonemes, number of syllables, frequency, familiarity, etc.) is equated. The segment-based word-length effect still requires that the two sets of items are equated on as many dimensions as possible, but allows them to differ in the number of "segments" (e.g., syllables, phonemes, etc).

The time-based word-length effect

For whatever reason, most experiments on the time-based word-length effect use the stimulus set created by Baddeley, Thomson, and Buchanan (1975) in the first detailed examination of the basic effect. The short words are BISHOP, DECOR, EMBER, HACKLE, PECTIN, PEWTER, PHALLIC, TIPPLE, WICKET, WIGGLE. The long words are COERCE, CYCLONE, FRIDAY, HARPOON, HUMANE, MORPHINE, NITRATE, TYCOON, VOODOO, ZYGOTE. In a typical study, the pronunciation time for the short set is shorter than for the long set and, when tested by immediate serial recall, memory is also better for the short set (e.g., Cowan, Day, Saults,

Keller, Johnson, & Flores, 1992; Longoni, Richardson, & Aiello, 1993; Lovatt, Avons, & Masterson, 2000; Nairne, Neath, & Serra, 1997; Neath, Bireta, & Surprenant, 2003).[10]

The problem is that although the stimuli listed above readily result in a word-length effect, "four [different] sets of English stimuli and one set each of Finnish and Chinese stimuli yield no difference or a reverse effect" (Neath et al., 2003, p. 432). The stimuli created by Caplan, Rochon, and Waters (1992) yield a reverse word-length effect (i.e., better recall of the temporally longer items), as does one set created by Lovatt et al. (2000). Another set used by Lovatt et al. produced no advantage for the temporally shorter items, the same results found with the stimulus set created by Neath et al. Given that currently only one out of seven sets of stimuli produce a pure time-based word-length effect, it seems reasonable to conclude that the time-based word-length effect is due to some artefact.[11] Even if six other sets of stimuli were created that resulted in a time-based word-length effect, you would still obtain the effect with only 50% of the stimulus sets predicted to show it.

The segment-based word-length effect

The case is quite different for the segment-based word-length effect, which has been demonstrated with many different sets of stimuli. If one wishes to use the segment-based effect as reflecting the trade-off between rehearsal and decay evidence in a short-term memory system, there are still two problems. First, why is there so little evidence of a pure time-based effect? Second, why does the syllable-based word-length effect disappear when short and long items appear in the same list?

Hulme, Surprenant, Bireta, Stuart, and Neath (2004) report two experiments in which subjects heard or saw lists of six items and were asked to recall the items in order. One list type had only short items (one or two syllables) and another list type had only long items (three, four, or five syllables). Recall of the pure short lists was substantially higher than recall of the pure long lists, the standard finding. However, Hulme et al. also include two types of mixed lists. In the alternating lists, short and long items alternated. In the random lists, short and long items again were mixed together, but this time in random order. Recall of the mixed lists was equivalent to recall of the pure short lists. In particular, recall of the long items in the mixed lists was just as good as recall of the short items in the pure lists and substantially better than recall of the long items in the pure lists (see also Bireta, Neath, & Surprenant, 2006).

Hulme et al. (2004; see also Hulme, Neath, Stuart, Shostak, Surprenant, & Brown, 2006) argued that this refutes all existing accounts of the word-length effect, including the standard decay offset by rehearsal view.[12] Accounts that focus on the temporal duration of the entire list must predict that recall of the items from mixed lists will be in-between that of the pure lists. In contrast, accounts that focus on item-specific causes predict no difference between items from pure and mixed lists.

The major point is that a decay offset by rehearsal view has problems explaining the lack of temporal effects with the time-based word-length effect, and the excellent recall of temporally long items in the mixed list paradigm. Space precludes a discussion of SIMPLE's explanation; rest assured that it uses factors known to operate in LTM as the primary reason for the word-length effect (for details, see Neath & Brown, 2006, pp. 222–224).

Life 7: Proactive interference

Proactive interference occurs when an earlier item interferes with memory for a newer item. Everyone agrees that PI occurs in long-term memory; the controversial claim is that certain types of short-term memory are immune to PI (e.g., Cowan, 2001[13]; Healy & McNamara, 1996). One peculiar aspect of this claim is that the demonstration of an absence of PI in tasks thought to rely only on short-term memory is taken as evidence that PI cannot be obtained in tasks thought to rely only on short-term memory. We term this "peculiar" because it is trivially easy to construct a long-term memory task in which PI is absent, yet no one would claim that long-term memory is immune to the effects of proactive interference. Surprenant and Neath (forthcoming) review in detail the evidence that shows that PI is readily observable in short-term memory tasks as long as the experimenter takes great care to ensure that the interfering material is processed appropriately by the subjects. Here, we mention just two examples.

First, both proactive and retroactive interference are readily observable in short-term memory experiments that examine the acoustic confusion effect (Conrad, 1964), the finding that lists of similar sounding items are harder to recall than lists of dissimilar sounding items. The decrement affects items at all positions, including the final item. This point is important because the reduction in recall of the final item cannot be due to retroactive interference; it must be due to proactive interference. Baddeley, Lewis, and Vallar (1984, Experiment 3) had subjects listen to lists of 2, 3, 4, 5, 6, or 7 letters that either were dissimilar-sounding or were similar-sounding. Although there was no effect for the two-item list, there were more errors for three-item lists of similar-sounding letters than dissimilar-sound letters in the slow condition (one item every 1.5 s) and for four-item lists in all conditions. Baddeley et al. (1984, p. 241) argue that their results are "not attributable to mishearing".

As a second example, consider a task in which subjects are presented with a list of items followed immediately by a test probe. The subject is asked to respond as quickly as possible whether the test item was in the list just seen. One way to induce PI in this situation is to have two (or more) lists in a row that contain items from the same semantic or rhyming category. The proponents of the idea that short-term memory is immune to PI point to several studies like this in which PI was induced for list lengths greater than four but was absent for list lengths of four or less (e.g., Cowan, Johnson, & Saults, 2005; Halford, Maybery, & Bain, 1988; Tehan & Humphreys, 1995). However, there exist other studies in which PI was observed with lists of four or fewer items (e.g., Atkinson, Herrmann, & Wescourt, 1974; Monsell, 1978; McElree & Dosher, 1989).

A third example, in a neuropsychological setting (Hamilton & Martin, in press), is reviewed below.

Again, we do not claim that PI must be observed in every short-term memory task, just as we do not claim that PI must be observed in every long-term memory task. Rather, the general claim is that PI is observable in tasks often ascribed to short-term memory under appropriate conditions. There are sufficient demonstrations of PI in tasks thought to tap short-term memory that it renders the statement "short-term memory is immune to PI" false.

Life 8: Decay

As outlined at the beginning of this chapter, one characteristic all conceptions of short-term memory have is that loss of information is due to a fundamentally different cause than in long-term memory: decay. No one doubts that interference is a basic cause of forgetting, at least as far as tasks thought to tap long-term memory are concerned. Our approach to this debate is to assume that decay does not exist. Then, we search for one positive instance of forgetting that can unequivocally be attributed to decay. To anticipate, we cannot find any such data.[14]

Three paradigms stand out, either historically or currently, as candidates for providing evidence in favour of decay. Two paradigms have already been discussed. Forgetting in the Brown–Peterson task used to be attributed to decay (as noted above) but is now attributed to proactive interference. Second, the word-length effect has been taken as evidence (as noted above); however, the critical results – differential forgetting when the only difference between the two sets of items is time – can be found for only one set of stimuli out of seven (Neath et al., 2003). Given that the finding does not replicate to other sets of stimuli, this is not convincing evidence.

Evidence for decay can be claimed only when one can show a decrease in memory performance as a function solely of the passage of time. All other possible factors (e.g., interference effects, distinctiveness effects, etc.) must be controlled for. The final area we consider is notable for trying to take into account these possible alternative explanations.

Cowan, Saults, and Nugent (1997) asked subjects to judge whether two pure tones were the same or different in frequency. They varied both the time between the two tones as well as the time between tone pairs. They suggested that the absolute amount of time that has passed before a memory test takes place does have an effect on subsequent performance.

However, Cowan, Saults, and Nugent (2001) performed further analyses to take into account an explanation based on differential distinctiveness. The details of the analyses are too complex to be presented here; suffice it to quote Cowan et al.'s own conclusions: "The present data provide no clear evidence for the importance of the absolute amount of time in recall, that is, for decay. All of the forgetting that we see could have to do with the loss of distinctiveness. This is true also of the vast two-stimulus comparison literature, which basically has ignored distinctiveness issues . . . We have failed to find clear evidence of decay in a situation that has often been viewed as one of the simplest paradigm cases for decay, namely in two-tone comparisons" (p. 326).

Life 9: Neuropsychological dissociations

One of the key findings taken to support the distinction between short- and long-term memory is the pattern of memory loss observed in amnesia. People with amnesic syndrome typically have relatively normal performance on tasks thought to tap short-term memory, such as digit span, but are unable to form lasting new episodic memories. That is, amnesia is characterized by impairment of long-term memory but preservation of short-term memory. It has often been argued that this pattern of lost and spared functioning cannot be explained except with reference to an anatomically and functionally distinct short-term memory system. For example, Tulving (2002) stated that, "it is difficult to imagine how, for instance, brain pathology could occur in which the patient loses all episodic memory functions while retaining those that rely on other systems unless there exists the potentiality for such a division in the healthy brain" (p. 12).

Despite this prevailing view, there are a number of alternative explanations of the amnesic syndrome that do not presuppose separate short- and long-term storage systems. One suggestion is that amnesics are deficient in their ability to make use of contextual information and lack the ability to bind the memory of an event to its context (Chun & Phelps, 1999; Ryan & Cohen, 2003). This hypothesis predicts that amnesics will be impaired when contextual binding is required, even when the task is implicit and does not require conscious awareness of learning. To test this hypothesis, Chun and Phelps asked normal and amnesic subjects to find a rotated *T* among a background of variously oriented and arranged *L*s. Unbeknownst to the subjects, some of the exact configurations of the background were repeated across trials. Control subjects showed an improvement in accuracy and response time on the repeated trials even though they were at chance when asked to discriminate old from new displays. Amnesic subjects, on the other hand, showed no improvement of performance on repeated, as compared to new, displays. Importantly, both groups improved in performance overall, showing normal perceptual learning. The crucial difference was in the use of the context to aid in the search process. According to this analysis, the reason that there appears to be a difference between conscious memory for new information that is retained over a short compared to a long period of time is that in the short term the context is relatively unchanging between study and test whereas over longer time scales the context changes substantially. Individuals who cannot use the context change as a cue will be disadvantaged compared to those who can use the context. This explanation is similar to the associative deficit hypothesis that has been successfully used to explain the pattern of loss and spared functioning in older adults (e.g., Naveh-Benjamin, 2000).

Another compatible explanation of the amnesic syndrome is that amnesics suffer from massive interference from other material. Cowan, Beschin, and Della Sala (2004) examined the role of interference in patients diagnosed with anterograde amnesia. They presented the patients with lists of words or stories and tested verbatim recall both immediately after the material was presented and after 10 minutes or an hour's delay. During the regular interference conditions the subjects were asked to complete a variety of interpolated tasks. In the minimal interference condition subjects were asked to lie down in a darkened, quiet room in order to minimize interference. Although the amnesic subjects showed worse performance than healthy controls in both delay conditions, most (but not all) showed substantial improvement under conditions of minimal interference. Cowan et al. argued that the amnesic subjects could not have maintained the story in short-term or working memory as some of the patients who benefited quite substantially from the minimal interference condition were observed to snore during the unfilled delays. These results are not due to the particular sample of patients tested: Della Sala, Cowan, Beschin, and Perini (2005) replicated this study using a more homogeneous group of patients diagnosed with mild cognitive impairment who showed the symptoms of anterograde amnesia without overt dementia. Cowan and his colleagues argued that anterograde amnesia is characterized by an increased susceptibility to retroactive interference. If this is the case, we would predict that amnesic individuals will have impaired short-term memory if they are given distracting information before being asked to recall, thus adding potentially interfering material. This is exactly what occurs (Chao & Knight, 1995; Scoville & Milner, 1957).

A third way in which amnesic data can be accommodated without recourse to separate memory stores was offered by Zaki, Nosofsky, Jessup, and Unverzagt (2003; see also Nosofsky & Zaki, 1998; Zaki & Nosofsky, 2001). It has been shown that amnesic individuals perform normally on tasks in which they learn to assign category labels to objects but are severely impaired when asked to recognize or recall previously presented exemplars. Zaki et al. argued that the type of specificity of detail needed to accomplish a recognition or recall task is much greater than that of most implicit tasks, particularly categorization. In the generalized context model (Nosofsky, 1986), both categorization and recognition are accomplished using a single representational system. For the present purposes the crucial parameter in the model is the memory sensitivity parameter that determines the discriminability among different exemplars in each category. Nosofsky and Zaki (1998) successfully simulated the dissociation between categorization and recognition in amnesiacs solely by reducing the memory sensitivity parameter.

Zaki et al. (2003) tested a prediction drawn from this hypothesis that suggests that amnesics will show impaired performance on tasks in which the categorization task is more demanding and relies on memory sensitivity. They tested normal and amnesic subjects in easy and difficult categorization tasks. Along with the single-category tasks they also presented a two-category task in which the subjects had to learn to assign one of two category labels to unique objects. The amnesic subjects showed the usual dissociation with the single-category task (good categorization performance but poor recognition) but showed uniformly poor performance in the two-category task. Zaki et al. further supported their results by simulating the entire pattern of results using the generalized context model and changing just the memory sensitivity parameter.

In addition to syndromes in which short-term memory is spared and long-term memory is damaged, the opposite pattern can also emerge: semantic and phonological short-term memory deficits accompanying relatively spared long-term memory. Again this was initially used as an argument for a separate short-term store that could be selectively damaged. Initially it was thought that such individuals suffered from a very fast decay rate of information in short-term memory. However, later research has indicated that the deficit is more likely to be due to massive proactive interference due to abnormal persistence of previously presented material (Hamilton & Martin, 2005, 2007). Hamilton and Martin (2007) investigated proactive interference in patient ML who has a semantic short-term memory deficit. ML's memory span is less than three items although his one-word repetition is nearly normal. Hamilton and Martin (in press) used a probe recognition task in which a list of items is followed by a probe. The subject is asked to determine whether the probe had appeared on the list that was just presented. On some trials the probe was a letter that had appeared in the list prior to the current target list, the "recent negative" probe. These trials are compared to a condition in which the letter had appeared more than three lists before, the "nonrecent negative" condition. Control subjects showed a significant interference effect of the recent compared to nonrecent negatives. However, patient ML showed a greatly exaggerated effect with many intrusions and extremely slow response times on the recent compared to the nonrecent probes. Experiment 2 replicated the finding with words that were either phonologically or semantically related to the probe item. Patient ML showed abnormal amounts of interference from both the semantic and the phonologically related lures. Importantly, if ML's deficit was due to rapid decay of representations in a short-term memory store he should actually show *less* interference from previous trials.

A final account of how a single system can explain dissociations observed in free recall between amnesic and control subjects has been offered by Brown and Lamberts (2003; see also Brown, Della Sala, Foster, & Vousden, 2007).

Thus, although the pattern of loss and spared functioning in amnesia has always been pointed to as a fundamental flaw in single-system explanations of memory, there is quite a bit of evidence showing that single-system explanations are a viable alternative to multiple-system views of memory.

Discussion and conclusions

What evidence requires that we distinguish between STM and LTM that cannot be readily explained by accounts that do not require such a distinction? We have outlined nine areas above that require no such distinction. What additional understanding do we gain by positing such a distinction? We have suggested previously (Neath & Surprenant, 2003) that the notion of distinct stores adds nothing to our understanding. According to a dual-store theorist, STM is the explanatory concept for why you can remember only a limited number of items coded in a phonological format for a short period of time whereas LTM is the explanatory concept for why you can remember a large (infinite?) number of items coded in a semantic format for a long period of time (forever?). If we deleted reference to the two stores, we could still explain the same findings: if you process items phonologically, you can remember only a few items for a short period of time but if you process items semantically, you can remember a far larger number for far longer. The processing is the key, not the store (cf. Craik & Lockhart, 1972). We thus wholeheartedly endorse Melton's (1963) claim that results from experiments on STM are readily interpretable in terms of factors known to operate in LTM.

There is one topic that we have not yet covered but which we suspect is at the root of the continued existence of STM: the phenomenological experience (see also Crowder, 1993b). It certainly does feel as if we have a limited capacity STM in which items fade away once we stop thinking about them. As compelling as this type of experience is, it is still introspection. We do not deny conscious awareness; we do, however, question whether it is sufficient grounds for constructing a fundamentally different type of memory. The feeling might arise out of our processing, but this does not make it an accurate description of the nature of the processing.

In an unpublished paper, Bob Crowder (1990) considered this type of conscious awareness and drew an analogy with kidney functioning. He argued that intuitions based on experience are of equal value for both mental processes, such as memory, and other bodily processes, such as kidney functioning.[15] As much as we might want evidence to confirm our introspection, it might be worth remembering that introspection has had a "dismal record of failure" in psychology (Bower & Clapper, 1989, p. 245).

Our analysis of the evidence for a distinct short-term memory that obeys fundamentally different principles from long-term memory suggests that this might be yet another area in which our introspections and intuitions have led us astray. As Crowder (1993b, p. 145) put it, "Our intuitive observations about how our memories work must resemble people's intuitive observations, in earlier times, of how astronomy worked. Those intuitions are the same ones that led to a firm belief in a geocentric universe and a flat earth."

Author notes

Portions of this chapter were developed while the authors were Visiting Professors at the Department of Psychology, City University, London, and much of the chapter was written while the authors were at Purdue University, West Lafayette, IN, USA.

Notes

1 Excluding situations in which there is brain trauma.
2 A similar study used longer intervals (up to 36 s) and more items per list (3, 5, and 7 digits) and did report differential forgetting (Baddeley & Scott, 1971). However, these data are readily explainable in terms of intra-sequence interference and thus do not require decay or invocation of a separate short-term memory (Neath, 2006).
3 This type of experiment usually includes the other switch, in this case from numbers to consonants, and the release from PI is typically equivalent.
4 We ignore another two groups for ease of exposition.
5 There are numerous minor variations, such as whether span is the length of the longest list recalled at all, or the length of the longest list recalled 50% of the time, and so on.
6 The issue of what span tasks are measuring is beyond the remit of the current paper. However, a preliminary answer might be that for these types of tasks, subjects use a form of representation that is subject to cue overload.
7 This equation is sometimes given as $s = rt + c$.
8 Note that there is no precise definition of a chunk.
9 This is often referred to as the "continuous" distractor paradigm despite the fact that no one, to our knowledge, has ever used continuous distraction.
10 Note that the time-based word-length effect can be seen as a less restrictive prediction of the zero-intercept problem noted above.
11 Ellis and Hennelly (1980) tested bilingual speakers of Welsh and English and showed that lists of Welsh digits take longer to pronounce than lists of English digits and also result in lower span scores. However, Murray and Jones (2002) showed that it is the complex between-item articulatory gestures that cause the Welsh decrement. In fact, Welsh digits spoken in isolation are spoken more quickly than English digits.
12 Annoyingly, the Hulme et al. (2004, 2006) papers also rule out two accounts proposed by a subset of the authors of the Hulme et al. papers, i.e., the feature model (Neath & Nairne, 1995) and the Brown and Hulme (1995) model.
13 Cowan (2001) states that only items in the focus of attention, part of his view of short-term memory, are immune to PI.
14 The only other area of memory research that invokes decay is sensory memory. A review of sensory memory is beyond the scope of this chapter. However, two

recent reviews argue against the concept of sensory memory as a separate memory system on the grounds that the bit that's sensory isn't memory, and the bit that's memory isn't sensory (Nairne, 2003; Surprenant & Neath, forthcoming).

15 Note that Crowder (1990) characterized these intuitions as being of "equal" value rather than of "no value at all: We all carry with us a naive theory of kidney function based on observed input-output relationships. I call this the 'asparagus and beer' process."

References

Atkinson, R. C., Herrmann, D. J., & Wescourt, K. T. (1974). Search processes in recognition memory. In R. L. Solso (Ed.), *Theories in cognitive psychology: The Loyola Symposium* (pp. 101–146). Potomac, MD: Lawrence Erlbaum Associates, Inc.

Atkinson, R. C., & Shiffrin, R. M. (1968). Human memory: A proposed system and its control processes. In K. W. Spence & J. T. Spence (Eds.), *The psychology of learning and motivation: Advances in research and theory, Vol. 2* (pp. 89–195). New York: Academic Press.

Baddeley, A. D. (1976). *The psychology of memory*. New York: Basic Books.

Baddeley, A. D. (2000). The episodic buffer: A new component of working memory? *Trends in Cognitive Sciences, 4*, 417–423.

Baddeley, A. D., & Hitch, G. (1974). Working memory. In G. H. Bower (Ed.), *The psychology of learning and motivation: Advances in research and theory* (Vol. 8, pp. 47–89). New York: Academic Press.

Baddeley, A. D., Lewis, V., & Vallar, G. (1984). Exploring the articulatory loop. *Quarterly Journal of Experimental Psychology, 36A*, 233–252.

Baddeley, A. D., & Scott, D. (1971). Short-term forgetting in the absence of pro-active interference. *Quarterly Journal of Experimental Psychology, 23*, 275–283.

Baddeley, A. D., Thomson, N., & Buchanan, M. (1975). Word length and the structure of short-term memory. *Journal of Verbal Learning and Verbal Behavior, 14*, 575–589.

Barrouillet, P., Bernardin, S., & Camos, V. (2004). Time constraints and resource sharing in adults' working memory spans. *Journal of Experimental Psychology: General, 133*, 83–100.

Bireta, T. J., Neath, I., & Surprenant, A. M. (2006). The syllable-based word length effect and stimulus set specificity. *Psychonomic Bulletin & Review, 13*, 434–438.

Bjork, R. A., & Whitten, W. B. (1974). Recency-sensitive retrieval processes in long-term free recall. *Cognitive Psychology, 6*, 173–189.

Bower, G. H., & Clapper, J. P. (1989). Experimental methods in cognitive science. In M. I. Posner (Ed.), *Foundations of Cognitive Science* (pp. 245–300). Cambridge, MA: MIT.

Brown, G. D. A., Della Sala, S., Foster, J. K., & Vousden, J. I. (2007). Amnesia, rehearsal, and temporal distinctiveness models of recall. *Psychonomic Bulletin & Review, 14*, 256–260.

Brown, G. D. A., & Hulme, C. (1992). Cognitive psychology and second language processing: The role of short-term memory. In R. J. Harris (Ed.), *Cognitive approaches to bilingualism* (pp. 105–121). Amsterdam: Elsevier.

Brown, G. D. A., & Hulme, C. (1995). Modeling item length effects in memory span: No rehearsal needed? *Journal of Memory and Language, 4*, 594–621.

Brown, G. D. A., & Lamberts, K. (2003). Double dissociations, models, and serial position curves. *Cortex, 39*, 148–152.

Brown, G. D. A., Neath, I., & Chater, N. (2007). A temporal ratio model memory. *Psychological Review, 114*, 539–576.

Brown, J. (1958). Some tests of the decay theory of immediate memory. *Quarterly Journal of Experimental Psychology, 10*, 12–21.

Capaldi, E. J., & Neath, I. (1995). Remembering and forgetting as context discrimination. *Learning & Memory, 2*, 107–132.

Caplan, D., Rochon, E., & Waters, G. S. (1992). Articulatory and phonological determinants of word length effects in span tasks. *Quarterly Journal of Experimental Psychology, 45A*, 177–192.

Chao, L. L., & Knight, R. T. (1995). Human prefrontal lesions increase distractibility to irrelevant sensory inputs. *Neuroreport, 6*, 1605–1610.

Chun, M. M., & Phelps, E. A. (1999). Memory deficits for implicit contextual information in amnesic patients with hippocampal damage. *Nature Neuroscience, 2*, 844–847.

Conrad, R. (1964). Acoustic confusions in immediate memory. *British Journal of Psychology, 55*, 75–84.

Cowan, N. (2001). The magical number 4 in short-term memory: A reconsideration of mental storage capacity. *Behavioral and Brain Sciences, 24*, 87–114.

Cowan, N., Beschin, N., & Della Sala, S. (2004). Verbal recall in amnesiacs under conditions of diminished retroactive interference. *Brain, 27*, 825–834.

Cowan, N., Day, L., Saults, J. S., Keller, T. A., Johnson, T., & Flores, L. (1992). The role of verbal output time in the effects of word-length on immediate memory. *Journal of Memory and Language, 31*, 1–17.

Cowan, N., Johnson, T. D., & Saults, J. S. (2005). Capacity limits in list item recognition: evidence from proactive interference. *Memory, 13*, 293–299.

Cowan, N., Saults, J. S., & Nugent, L. D. (1997). The role of absolute and relative amounts of time in forgetting within immediate memory: The case of tone pitch comparisons. *Psychonomic Bulletin & Review, 4*, 393–397.

Cowan, N., Saults, S., & Nugent, L. (2001). The ravages of absolute and relative amounts of time on memory. In H. L. Roediger III, J. S. Nairne, I. Neath, & A. M. Surprenant (Eds.), *The nature of remembering: Essays in honor of Robert G. Crowder* (pp. 315–330). Washington, DC: APA.

Craik, F. I. M. (1970). The fate of primary memory items in free recall. *Journal of Verbal Learning and Verbal Behavior, 9*, 143–148.

Craik, F., & Lockhart, R. (1972). Levels of processing: A framework for memory research. *Journal of Verbal Learning and Verbal Behavior, 11*, 671–684.

Crowder, R. G. (1976). *Principles of learning and memory*. Hillsdale, NJ: Lawrence Erlbaum Associates, Inc.

Crowder, R. G. (1982). The demise of short-term memory. *Acta Psychologica, 50*, 291–323.

Crowder, R. G. (1990). *The brain, the kidney, and consciousness*. Unpublished manuscript.

Crowder, R. G. (1993a). Systems and principles in memory theory: Another critique of pure memory. In A. F. Collins, S. E. Gathercole, M. A. Conway, & P. E.

Morris (Eds.), *Theories of memory* (pp. 139–161). Hove, UK: Lawrence Erlbaum Associates Ltd.

Crowder, R. G. (1993b). Short-term memory: Where do we stand? *Memory & Cognition, 21*, 142–145.

Dale, H. C. A., & McGlaughlin, A. (1971). Evidence of acoustic coding in long-term memory. *Quarterly Journal of Experimental Psychology, 23*, 1–7.

Dalezman, J. J. (1976). Effects of output order on immediate, delayed, and final recall performance. *Journal of Experimental Psychology: Human Learning and Memory, 2*, 597–608.

Davelaar, E. J., Goshen-Gottstein, Y., Ashkenazi, A., Haarmann, H. J., & Usher, M. (2005). The demise of short-term memory revisited: Empirical and computational investigations of recency effects. *Psychological Review, 112*, 3–42.

Della Sala, S., Cowan, N., Beschin, N., & Perini, M. (2005). Just lying there, remembering: Improving recall of prose in amnesic patients with mild cognitive impairment by minimizing interference. *Memory, 13*, 435–440.

Dempster, F. N. (1985). Proactive interference in sentence recall: Topic-similarity effects and individual differences. *Memory & Cognition, 13*, 81–89.

Ellis, N. C., & Hennelly, R. A. (1980). A bilingual word-length effect: Implications for intelligence testing and the relative ease of mental calculation in Welsh and English. *British Journal of Psychology, 71*, 43–51.

Glanzer, M. (1972). Storage mechanisms in recall. In G. H. Bower & J. T. Spence (Eds.), *The psychology of learning and motivation, Vol. 5* (pp. 129–153). New York: Academic Press.

Glanzer, M., & Cunitz, A. R. (1966). Two storage mechanisms in free recall. *Journal of Verbal Learning and Verbal Behavior, 5*, 351–360.

Glanzer, M., & Razel, M. (1974). The size of the unit in short-term storage. *Journal of Verbal Learning and Verbal Behavior, 13*, 114–131.

Glenberg, A. M., Bradley, M. M., Kraus, T. A., & Renzaglia, G. J. (1983). Studies of the long-term recency effect: Support for the contextually guided retrieval hypothesis. *Journal of Experimental Psychology: Learning, Memory and Cognition, 9*, 231–255.

Greene, R. L. (1986a). A common basis for recency effects in immediate and delayed recall. *Journal of Experimental Psychology: Learning, Memory and Cognition, 12*, 413–418.

Greene, R. L. (1986b). Sources of recency effects in free recall. *Psychological Bulletin, 99*, 221–228.

Gunter, B., Berry, C., & Clifford, B. R. (1981). Proactive interference effects with television news items: Further evidence. *Journal of Experimental Psychology: Learning, Memory, and Cognition, 7*, 480–487.

Halford, G. S., Maybery, M. T., & Bain, J. D. (1988) Set-size effects in primary memory: An age-related capacity limitation? *Memory & Cognition, 16*, 480–487.

Hamilton, A. C., & Martin, R. C. (2005). Dissociations among tasks involving inhibition: A single-case study. *Cognitive, Affective and Behavioral Neuroscience, 5*, 1–13.

Hamilton, A. C., & Martin, R. C. (2007). Proactive interference in a semantic short-term memory deficit: Role of semantic and phonological relatedness. *Cortex, 43*, 112–123.

Healy, A. F., & McNamara, D. S. (1996). Verbal learning and memory: Does the modal model still work? *Annual Review of Psychology, 47*, 143–172.

Hulme, C., Maughan, S, & Brown, G. D. A. (1991). Memory for familiar and unfamiliar words: Evidence for a long-term memory contribution to short-term memory span. *Journal of Memory and Language, 6,* 685–701.

Hulme, C., Neath, I., Stuart, G., Shostak, L., Surprenant, A. M., & Brown, G. D. A. (2006). The distinctiveness of the word-length effect. *Journal of Experimental Psychology: Learning, Memory, and Cognition, 32,* 586–594.

Hulme, C., Roodenrys, S., Brown, G. D. A., & Mercer, R. (1995). The role of long-term memory mechanisms in memory span. *British Journal of Psychology, 86,* 527–536.

Hulme, C., Surprenant, A. M., Bireta, T. J., Stuart, G., & Neath, I. (2004). Abolishing the word-length effect. *Journal of Experimental Psychology: Learning, Memory, and Cognition, 30,* 98–106.

James, W. (1890). *Principles of psychology.* New York: Henry Holt.

Keppel, G., & Underwood, B. J. (1962). Proactive inhibition in short-term retention of single items. *Journal of Verbal Learning and Verbal Behavior, 1,* 153–161.

Kintsch, W., & Buschke, H. (1969). Homophones and synonyms in short-term memory. *Journal of Experimental Psychology, 80,* 403–407.

Koppenaal, L., & Glanzer, M. (1990). An examination of the continuous distractor task and the long-term recency effect. *Memory & Cognition, 18,* 183–195.

Loess, H., & Waugh, N. C. (1967). Short-term memory and inter-trial interval. *Journal of Verbal Learning and Verbal Behavior, 6,* 455–460.

Longoni, A. M., Richardson, J. T., & Aiello, A. (1993). Articulatory rehearsal and phonological storage in working memory. *Memory & Cognition, 21,* 11–22.

Lovatt, P., Avons, S. E., & Masterson, J. (2000). The word-length effect and disyllabic words. *Quarterly Journal of Experimental Psychology, 53A,* 1–22.

Maskarinec, A. S., & Brown, S. C. (1974), Positive and negative recency effects in free recall learning. *Journal of Verbal Learning and Verbal Behavior, 13,* 328–334.

McElree, B., & Dosher, B. A. (1989). Serial position and set size in short-term memory: The time course of recognition. *Journal of Experimental Psychology: General, 118,* 346–373.

Melton, A. W. (1963). Implications of short-term memory for a general theory of memory. *Journal of Verbal Learning and Verbal Behavior, 2,* 1–21.

Miyake, A., & Shah, P. (Eds.) (1999). *Models of working memory: Mechanisms of active maintenance and executive control.* New York: Cambridge University Press.

Monsell, S. (1978). Recency, immediate recognition memory, and reaction time. *Cognitive Psychology, 10,* 465–501.

Multhaup, K. S., Balota, D. A., & Cowan, N. (1996). Implications of aging, lexicality, and item length for the mechanisms underlying memory span. *Psychonomic Bulletin & Review, 3,* 112–120.

Murdock, B. B. Jr (1962). The serial position effect of free recall. *Journal of Experimental Psychology, 64,* 482–488.

Murdock, B. B. Jr (1967). Recent developments in STM. *British Journal of Psychology, 58,* 421–433.

Murray, A., & Jones, D. M. (2002). Articulatory complexity at item boundaries in serial recall: The case of Welsh and English digit span. *Journal of Experimental Psychology: Learning, Memory, and Cognition, 28,* 594–598.

Nairne, J. S. (1996). Short-term/working memory. In E. L. Bjork & R. A. Bjork (Eds.), *Memory* (pp. 101–126). New York: Academic Press.

Nairne, J. S. (2002). Remembering over the short-term: The case against the standard model. *Annual Review of Psychology, 53*, 53–81.

Nairne, J. S. (2003). Sensory and working memory. In A. H. Healy & R. W. Proctor (Eds.), *Comprehensive handbook of psychology: Volume 4. Experimental Psychology* (pp. 423–446). New York: Wiley.

Nairne, J. S., & Neath, I. (2001). Long-term memory span. *Behavioral and Brain Sciences, 24*, 134–135.

Nairne, J. S., Neath, I., & Serra, M. (1997). Proactive interference plays a role in the word-length effect. *Psychonomic Bulletin & Review, 4*, 541–545.

Nairne, J. S., Neath, I., Serra, M., & Byun, E. (1997). Positional distinctiveness and the ratio rule in free recall. *Journal of Memory and Language, 37*, 155–166.

Nairne, J. S., Whiteman, H. L., & Kelley, M. R. (1999). Short-term forgetting of order under conditions of reduced interference. *Quarterly Journal of Experimental Psychology, 52A*, 241–251.

Naveh-Benjamin, M. (2000). Adult age differences in memory performance: Tests of an associative deficit hypothesis. *Journal of Experimental Psychology: Learning, Memory, and Cognition, 26*, 1170–1187.

Neath, I. (1993). Contextual and distinctive processes and the serial position function. *Journal of Memory and Language, 32*, 820–840.

Neath, I. (2006). A SIMPLE account of Baddeley & Scott (1971). Memory Lab Technical Report 2006-01, Memorial University of Newfoundland. Retrieved February 7, 2008 from http://memory.psych.mun.ca/pubs/t06.shtml

Neath, I., Bireta, T. J., & Surprenant, A. M. (2003). The time-based word length effect and stimulus set specificity. *Psychonomic Bulletin & Review, 10*, 430–434.

Neath, I., & Brown, G. D. A. (2006). SIMPLE: Further applications of a local distinctiveness model of memory (pp. 201–243). In B. H. Ross (Ed.), *The Psychology of Learning and Motivation*. San Diego: Academic Press.

Neath, I., & Nairne, J. S. (1995). Word-length effects in immediate memory: Overwriting trace decay theory. *Psychonomic Bulletin & Review, 2*, 429–441.

Neath, I., & Surprenant, A. M. (2003). *Human memory: An introduction to research, data, and theory* (2nd ed.). Belmont, CA: Wadsworth.

Nosofsky, R. M. (1986). Attention, similarity, and the identification-categorization relationship. *Journal of Experimental Psychology: General, 115*, 39–57.

Nosofsky, R. M., & Zaki, S. R. (1998). Dissociations between categorization and recognition in amnesic and normal individuals: An exemplar-based interpretation. *Psychological Science, 9*, 247–255.

Peterson, L. R., & Peterson, M. J. (1959). Short-term retention of individual items. *Journal of Experimental Psychology, 61*, 12–21.

Postman, L., & Phillips, L. W. (1965). Short-term temporal changes in free recall. *Quarterly Journal of Experimental Psychology, 17*, 132–138.

Raaijmakers, J. G. W. (1993). The story of the two-store model of memory: Past criticisms, current status, and future directions. In D. E. Meyer & S. Kornblum (Eds.), *Attention and performance XIV: Synergies in experimental psychology, artificial intelligence, and cognitive neuroscience* (pp. 467–488). Cambridge, MA: MIT Press.

Roodenrys, S., & Hinton, M. (2002). Sublexical or lexical effects on serial recall of nonwords? *Journal of Experimental Psychology: Learning, Memory, and Cognition, 28*, 29–33.

Ryan, J. D., & Cohen, N. J. (2003). Evaluating the neuropsychological dissociation evidence for multiple memory systems. *Cognitive, Affective, & Behavioral Neuroscience, 3,* 168–185.

Schweickert, R., Guentert, L., & Hersberger, L. (1990). Phonological similarity, pronunciation rate, and memory span. *Psychological Science, 1,* 74–77.

Scoville, W. B., & Milner, B. (1957). Loss of recent memory after bilateral hippocampal lesions. *Journal of Neurological and Neurosurgical Psychiatry, 20,* 11–21.

Shulman, H. G. (1970). Encoding and retention of semantic and phonemic information in short-term memory. *Journal of Verbal Learning and Verbal Behavior, 9,* 499–508.

Shulman, H. G. (1972). Semantic confusion errors in short-term memory. *Journal of Verbal Learning and Verbal Behavior, 11,* 221–227.

Stuart, G., & Hulme, C. (2000). The effects of word co-occurrence on short-term memory: Associative links in long-term memory affect short-term memory performance. *Journal of Experimental Psychology: Learning, Memory, and Cognition, 26,* 796–802.

Surprenant, A. M., & Neath, I. (forthcoming). *Principles of memory.* New York: Psychology Press.

Tan, L., & Ward, G. (2000). A recency-based account of the primacy effect in free recall. *Journal of Experimental Psychology: Learning, Memory, and Cognition, 26,* 1589–1625.

Tehan, G., & Humphreys, M. S. (1995). Transient phonemic codes and immunity to proactive interference. *Memory & Cognition, 23,* 181–191.

Thorn, A. S. C., & Frankish, C. R. (2005). Long-term knowledge effects of serial recall of nonwords are not exclusively lexical. *Journal of Experimental Psychology: Learning, Memory, and Cognition, 31,* 729–735.

Tulving, E. (2002). Episodic memory: From mind to brain. *Annual Review of Psychology, 53,* 1–25.

Turvey, M. T., Brick, P., & Osborn, J. (1970). Proactive interference in short-term memory as a function of prior-item retention interval. *Quarterly Journal of Experimental Psychology, 22,* 142–147.

Watkins, M. J. (1977). The intricacy of memory span. *Memory & Cognition, 5,* 529–534.

Watkins, M. J., & Watkins, O. C. (1974). Processing of recency items for free recall. *Journal of Experimental Psychology, 102,* 488–493.

Whitten, W. B. (1978). Output interference and long-term serial position effects. *Journal of Experimental Psychology: Human Learning and Memory, 4,* 685–692.

Wickens, D. D. (1970). Encoding categories of words: An empirical approach to meaning. *Psychological Review, 77,* 1–15.

Wickens, D. D. (1972). Characteristics of word encoding. In A. W. Melton & E. Martin (Eds.), *Coding processes in human memory.* Washington, DC: Winston.

Wickens, D. D., Born, D. G., & Allen, C. K. (1963). Proactive inhibition and item similarity in short-term memory. *Journal of Verbal Learning and Verbal Behavior, 2,* 440–445.

Wickens, D. D., Dalezman, R. E., & Eggemeier, F. T. (1976). Multiple encoding of word attributes in memory. *Memory & Cognition, 4,* 307–310.

Wixted, J. T. (1991). Conditions and consequences of maintenance rehearsal. *Journal of Experimental Psychology: Learning, Memory, and Cognition, 17,* 963–973.

Zaki, S. R., & Nosofsky, R. M. (2001). A single-system interpretation of dissociations between recognition and categorization in a task involving object-like stimuli. *Cognitive, Affective, and Behavioral Neuroscience, 1,* 344–359.

Zaki, S. R., Nosofsky, R. M., Jessup, N. M., & Unverzagt, F. W. (2003). Categorization and recognition performance of a memory-impaired group: Evidence for single-system models. *Journal of the International Neuropsychological Society, 9,* 394 406.

3 The roles of short-term and long-term verbal memory in free and serial recall: Towards a recency-based perspective

Geoff Ward, Lydia Tan and Parveen Bhatarah

Overview

In this chapter, we reinterpret classic empirical evidence that has been argued previously to support a theoretical distinction between short-term and long-term memory stores (STS and LTS, respectively) within a recency-based framework of episodic memory. Our discussion centres on the free recall and immediate serial recall tasks, from which, historically, measures of the recency effect and memory span respectively have provided some of the most important lines of empirical evidence in establishing the dichotomy.

Free recall

In the free recall task, participants are presented with a sequence of unrelated items for study, one at a time, and immediately after the presentation of the last item, they must try to remember as many of the list items as possible, freely recalling the items in any order that they wish. Typically, free recall gives rise to U-shaped or J-shaped serial position curves, which show that the early items and the later items in the list tend to be recalled more often than the middle list items, and these advantages are known as the primacy effect and the recency effect, respectively (e.g., Murdock, 1962).

The classic interpretation of the serial position curve is that performance on the early and middle list items is due to retrieval from LTS, whereas performance on the later list items is due to retrieval from STS and LTS. Within this account, the primacy effect is assumed to reflect the increased associative strength of the early items in LTS that results from additional rehearsals afforded to these list items (Atkinson & Shiffrin, 1968, 1971; Rundus, 1971), whereas the recency effect is assumed to be the result of the direct output of items residing in STS at the time of test (e.g., Atkinson & Shiffrin, 1971; Glanzer, 1972).

An LTS–STS interpretation of free recall is strengthened by the findings that different variables selectively affect different portions of the serial position curve. For example, the recency effect is selectively eliminated by a filled 30 s period of distracting activity immediately prior to recall (Glanzer

& Cunitz, 1966; Postman & Phillips, 1965), whereas the earlier list items are selectively influenced by variables assumed to affect long-term learning (LTS-variables), such as presentation rate, word frequency, list length, and the age of participants, that have little effect on recall in the recency region (for a review, see Glanzer, 1972).

However, there are two potential problems for such dual-store accounts. First, a number of subsequent studies have shown that the probability of recalling a word from LTS is not always an increasing function of the number of rehearsals that an item receives (e.g., Craik & Watkins, 1973). Second, recency effects have been found in a number of methods and over a range of timescales for which an STS explanation is untenable (e.g., Baddeley & Hitch, 1974, 1977; Bjork & Whitten, 1974).

Over recent years we have attempted to reinterpret the classic data used to support the STS–LTS dichotomy in free recall. We have assumed that the accessibility of items from episodic memory varies along a continuum of episodic experience, with the most recently experienced items or events being those that were the most accessible and the least recently experienced items or events being those that were least accessible (see e.g., Tan & Ward, 2000; Ward, 2001).

We have been heavily influenced in our thinking by unitary accounts of memory (e.g., Brown, Neath, & Chater, 2007; Crowder, 1982, 1993; Crowder & Neath, 1991; Glenberg, 1984, 1987; Glenberg et al., 1980) and empirical evidence for the *ratio rule* (e.g., Baddeley & Hitch, 1977; Bjork & Whitten, 1974; Crowder, 1976; Glenberg, Bradley, Kraus, & Renzaglia, 1983; Greene, 1986; Nairne, Neath, Serra, & Byun, 1997; Neath & Brown, 2006). The ratio rule predicts that the magnitude of the recency effect in free recall will be proportional to the fraction $\Delta t/T$, where Δt refers to the inter-presentation interval and T refers to the retention interval. The ratio rule has been applied successfully across a wide range of timescales and conditions.

When taken at face value, it might seem that the ratio rule is not well suited for explaining primacy effects – the earliest list items are least recent and therefore should be the least well recalled. However, it is widely accepted that the primacy effect is associated with rehearsal, and Tan and Ward (2000) proposed that participants' rehearsal of early list items might result in additional copies of these items in the mnemonic record, such that copies of the early items appeared more often, appeared more recently, and were distributed more widely throughout the continuum of episodic memory than those items that were less well rehearsed.

Tan and Ward (2000) combined the free recall task with the overt rehearsal procedure (Rundus & Atkinson, 1970), in which participants are asked to say out loud what they are currently thinking during the study period. When we plotted the free recall data by the position in the experimenter's list, we obtained the classic J- or U-shaped serial position curves. However, when the same recall data were re-plotted by when the words were last rehearsed or experienced, we obtained extended recency effects, with little or no primacy, consistent with a recency-based account of the primacy effect in free recall (for similar findings, see also Brodie, 1975; Brodie & Murdock, 1977; Brodie & Prytulak, 1975).

Subsequently, we have shown that many of the effects of LTS-variables can also be reinterpreted within a recency-based framework. The effects of presentation rates (Tan & Ward, 2000), word frequency (Tan & Ward, 2000; Ward, Woodward, Stevens, & Stinson, 2003), list length (Ward, 2002) and participants' age (Ward & Maylor, 2005) on free recall can all be accommodated within a recency-based account of free recall.

Figure 3.1 shows one of the most elegant demonstrations of using overt rehearsals to reinterpret free recall data. It summarises the main findings from Ward (2002) in which participants performed the free recall task on lists of 10, 20 and 30 words. In this experiment, participants saw a total of 15 lists of words, five from each of the three list lengths, and on each trial participants were asked to try to say out loud what they were currently thinking during the study period. As Figure 3.1A shows, when the data are plotted by the experimenter's list order (the nominal serial position) there are classic U-shaped serial position curves, which could be interpreted as evidence for the STS–LTS dichotomy. However, as Figure 3.1B shows, when the data are re-plotted by when the words were last experienced or last rehearsed, the list length effects can be readily reinterpreted in terms of the subjective retention interval of the items.

A recency-based continuum has a number of advantages over the STS–LTS dichotomy. First, the recency-based nature of the continuum provides a clear reason why increased rehearsal sometimes does (e.g., Rundus, 1971) and sometimes does not (e.g., Craik & Watkins, 1973) improve recall: increased rehearsal is more likely to improve recall if participants' rehearsals are distributed and recent (as in Rundus, 1971; Tan & Ward, 2000), and less likely if participants' rehearsals are massed and less recent (e.g., Craik & Watkins, 1973). Second, a recency-based perspective can be readily applied to recency effects over the full range of timescales and a full range of experimental methodologies. Third, there is an attraction in the simplicity of a recency-based continuum, since there is no need to detail how information is transferred from one memory store to another (nor in attempting to detail the patterns of interaction between these different components).

We have used the term "recency-based" to describe our account of free recall (e.g., Tan & Ward, 2000; Ward, 2002) and episodic memory (Ward, 2001) in order to highlight the prevalence of recency throughout the entire serial position curve in free recall (and episodic memory more generally), and to contrast our position with those theories that have postulated that recency is limited to STS, and indeed absent from LTS (e.g., see Shiffrin, 1970a, 1970b, below).

However, we should make it clear that the term "recency-based" is an incomplete description of our account. First, not all LTS-factors are

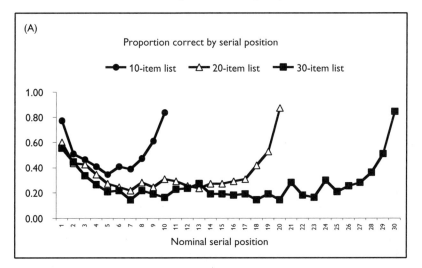

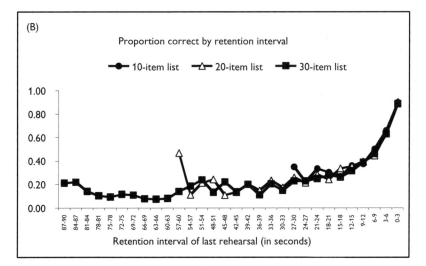

Figure 3.1 The effect of list length on free recall. Participants saw lists of 10, 20 or 30 words for free recall under overt rehearsal instructions. Panel A shows the data when plotted by the position on the experimenter's list. Panel B shows the same data re-plotted by when the words were last experienced/rehearsed. Adapted with permission from Ward G. (2002). A recency-based account of the list length effect in free recall. *Memory & Cognition, 30*(6), 885–892.

entirely explainable in terms of differences in the rehearsal schedules: analyses of word frequency effects demonstrate the importance of inter-item associations as well (see Howard & Kahana, 1999, 2002a, 2002b; Ward, Woodward, Stevens, & Stinson, 2003; and for effects of inter-item association on ISR, see also Stuart & Hulme, 2000, this volume). Second, a strict interpretation of the term "recency-based" might presume that the words in free recall must be output in reversed order (most recent first), but this is rarely the case. Items tend, if anything, to be recalled more often in the same order as that in which they were presented. The forwards ordering of recall may arise under some circumstances through the cumulative forwards-order nature of rehearsal (Ward ct al., 2003). However, this is unlikely to be the full story, as forwards-order recall is observed throughout the list even when rehearsal is prevented (Howard & Kahana, 1999, 2002a, 2002b).

The most apparent weakness with our position is its inability to provide a satisfactory account of the selective effect of a filled delay on the recency component of free recall (e.g., Glanzer & Cunitz, 1966; Postman & Phillips, 1965). This classic finding is problematic for our recency-based account because we predict that a filled delay should reduce the recency of *all* the list items along the continuum of episodic memory, and we therefore incorrectly predict reduced recall performance throughout the list following a filled delay (although we do correctly predict that the greatest disruption will be for the words presented at the end of the list which do not receive large numbers of distributed rehearsals).

Despite this weakness, our recency-based account has been able to reinterpret the even more drastic finding of Shiffrin (1970a; Atkinson & Shiffrin, 1971), who appeared to show that recall from LTS was not only unaffected by a delay filled by a period of distractor activity, but was also unaffected by whether an intervening list was 5 or 20 items in length. In Shiffrin's (1970a) three experiments, participants were presented with lists of 5 or 20 words and immediately after the end of a list they had to recall the words from the *penultimate* list. The ordering of the lists was so arranged that Shiffrin could examine separately the effects on free recall of the to-be-remembered (TBR) list lengths (5 and 20) and the effects of the intervening list lengths (also 5 and 20). Shiffrin showed that there was a large effect of TBR list length but absolutely no effect of intervening list length, a finding that is clearly contrary to the predictions of recency-based accounts of episodic memory (and indeed all accounts of temporal discrimination, retroactive interference, or trace decay). Instead, Shiffrin argued that retrieval from LTS involved using a readily available probe to cue the search through long-term memory images of the items in the TBR list and, within this framework, the probability of recall was affected by the size of the TBR search set (the TBR list length, see also Shiffrin, 1970b) but not by the length of the retention interval nor the number of intervening items.

However, Ward and Tan (2004) showed that the original Shiffrin (1970a) findings may be confounded by covert rehearsal. We noted that performance was low in the original Shiffrin data (participants were only recalling around 2–3 words from lists of 5 or 20 words) and we argued that such a pattern of recall could arise through the covert rehearsal of a few TBR items through the intervening lists. When we replicated and extended the method using the overt rehearsal method we indeed found evidence of rehearsal throughout the list, and also found evidence of extended recency effects within the lists.

In a third experiment, we presented participants with either one or two lists, each of either 5 or 20 words, and then cued participants to recall either the only list, the first list of two, or the second list of two. In this experiment, participants did not know in advance of each trial whether there would be one or two lists, or which list would be cued. Under these conditions, we also found evidence of extended recency effects within the lists. Critically, we also found that the recall of the first list of a pair of lists was affected by the length of the intervening list. This latter finding is not only consistent with recency-based accounts of free recall, it is also consistent with the large effect of a filled delay found throughout the serial position curve in the final free recall task (Craik, 1971), in which participants are given an unexpected free recall test at the end of a testing session and are asked to remember as many words as they can from all the lists used in the preceding free recall trials.

In summary, the recency-based account of free recall can account for the shape of the serial position curve in free recall, the effects of various "LTS-factors", and the effect of moderate to large filled delays. However, it cannot as yet account for the effect of a modest filled delay that abolishes selectively the very last items. Nevertheless, we believe that recency-based accounts of episodic memory may provide a useful framework within which to understand free recall, and arguably provide a more elegant and simple account than those that promote the STS–LTS distinction.

Immediate serial recall

The second classic line of evidence supporting a distinction between STS and LTS comes from the immediate serial recall (ISR) task. In this task, participants are presented with a sequence of items for study, one at a time, and then immediately after the presentation of the last item, they must recall as many of the list items as possible in exactly the same order as that in which they were presented.

In ISR, the serial position curves show more extended primacy and an only one- or perhaps two-item recency (e.g., Conrad & Hull, 1964; Drewnowski & Murdock, 1980). An STS interpretation of ISR is strengthened by the findings that there is a limit to the number of items that can be regularly recalled in exactly the same order as that presented (the memory span, Miller, 1956), and that ISR is greatly affected by the phonological characteristics of speech, such as the phonological confusability of list items (Baddeley, 1966a), and the word length or the word duration (Baddeley, Lewis, & Vallar, 1984; Baddeley, Thomson, & Buchanan, 1975), whereas long-term learning is more affected by the meaning of the words (Baddeley, 1966b).

One might think that if an STS explanation of the recency effect in free recall was correct then that same STS might play an important role in ISR. However, it appears that this may not be the case. In a series of experiments, Baddeley and Hitch (1974, 1977) compared the free recall of lists of 16 words with and without a concurrent 6-digit ISR memory load. They found that the concurrent ISR load had a small but significant effect throughout the free recall serial position curve but the magnitude of the recency advantage was unaffected by the load, a finding that they argued was inconsistent with the recency effect being within the remit of a general limited-capacity working memory.

We believed that this finding was important enough to warrant a replication and we felt that we could make two key improvements. First, in the original Baddeley and Hitch method, the free recall with concurrent 6-digit load condition was compared to a control condition, in which participants wrote down the digits as they were presented. We argued that listening to and writing down digits might itself constitute an STS load, and so we decided to use a free recall alone condition as our control condition. Second, the timing of the digits and the words was suboptimal in the original concurrent 6-digit load condition: sometimes words were presented on their own, sometimes words were presented whilst digits were also being presented, and sometimes words were presented whilst digits were being recalled. We argued that in the concurrent 6-digit load condition, each word should first be presented and then followed by a different sequence of 6 digits for ISR.

Thus, in our recent replication and extension, Bhatarah, Ward, and Tan (2006) showed participants lists of 16 words for free recall and, in the 6-digit ISR load condition, participants were required to hear and then repeat back a different 6-digit sequence after each and every word (including the last). This condition was compared with a free recall alone condition, in which participants experienced the words at the same presentation rate but with no digits. Over three experiments, we compared the effects of concurrent load on free recall under visual silent and visual reading aloud conditions, under overt rehearsal conditions, and under fixed rehearsal conditions (in which participants rehearsed only the currently presented word, e.g., Fischler, Rundus, & Atkinson, 1970). In all experiments, we replicated the critical Baddeley and Hitch (1974, 1977) finding: the magnitude of the recency effect was unaffected by the concurrent digit load, a result that confirmed that the recency effect in free recall and ISR performance cannot both be underpinned by a unitary STS. Our subsequent analyses of the secondary task further confirmed that our participants were indeed following instructions and maintaining satisfactory and relatively consistent ISR performance in the concurrent load conditions.

Having replicated Baddeley and Hitch's (1974, 1977) findings, we then reconsidered their interpretation. They concluded that the phonological loop mechanism of working memory (WM) was responsible for underpinning ISR, but the recency effect in free recall was outside the remit of the

WM model. They later claimed that the recency effect (Baddeley & Hitch, 1993) was the result of an explicit retrieval mechanism operating on implicit priming in LTS. Although consistent with their data, their conclusion necessitated that free recall and ISR were encoded rather differently. Since early and middle list items in free recall were presumed not to be underpinned by WM, the exclusion of the recency effect from WM meant that, at the time of test, no words in a list of words for free recall were recalled from WM, a conclusion that contrasted with the phonological loop's role in underpinning ISR. Ward (2001) has previously commented on the uneasy tension that he experiences when considering this conclusion: it seems unreasonable that two similar immediate memory tasks should be underpinned by completely different memory mechanisms.

In a second series of experiments, Bhatarah, Ward, and Tan (2008) aimed to address this unease in a further examination of the relationship between free recall and ISR. Rather than asking participants to perform the two tasks concurrently, we asked participants to perform just one of the two tasks on each trial, but we varied whether or not participants knew in advance which task they were to perform. We were interested in the possibility that participants strategically encoded the words differently when they knew in advance which task they were to perform: perhaps the phonological loop would be used for the ISR task, whereas some other more LTS-based memory mechanism might be used for free recall.

In two experiments, participants were presented with lists of eight different words for immediate recall. In the pre-cued conditions, the participants always knew in advance that they would be tested by free recall or ISR (the pre-cued free recall and pre-cued ISR conditions, respectively). In the post-cued conditions, the participants did not know the task in advance of the list. Rather, the participants saw lists of words as before, but were cued to perform free recall or ISR only after the last item in the list had been presented (the post-cued free recall and post-cued ISR conditions, respectively). The results of Experiment 1 are shown in Figure 3.2, which shows that the manipulation of test expectancy had little effect on either the serial position curves for free recall or the serial position curves for ISR. Both the pre-cued and post-cued ISR curves showed extended primacy with little or no recency, whereas both the pre-cued and post-cued free recall curves showed U-shaped serial position curves with both primacy and recency.

In addition, these findings were observed when test expectancy was manipulated between subjects, suggesting that our results were not due to carryover effects between the conditions. Furthermore, in a third experiment an analysis of the overt rehearsals showed that the patterns of rehearsals were also very similar for the two tasks. Our results therefore suggest that our participants used similar or at least compatible strategies when encoding words for free recall, and as such provide little evidence that different memory mechanisms were used for the two tasks.

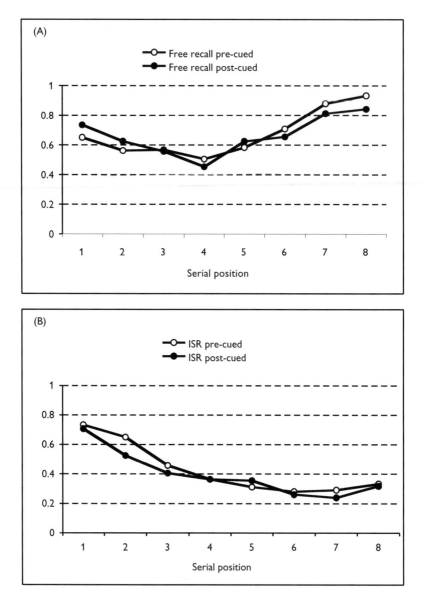

Figure 3.2 The effect of test expectancy on free recall and immediate serial recall. Participants received four blocks of trials. On each trial participants saw eight words one at a time for a test of immediate memory. In different blocks participants either knew in advance (pre-cued) or did not know until after the list was presented (post-cued) whether they would be required to recall using free recall (Panel A) or immediate serial recall (Panel B). Adapted from Experiment 1 of Bhatarah, P., Ward, G., & Tan, L. (2008). Examining the relationship between free recall and immediate serial recall: The serial nature of recall and the effect of test expectancy. *Memory & Cognition, 36,* 20–34.

What is the relationship between free recall and ISR?

Our results made us reassess the relationship between ISR and free recall. Were these tasks underpinned by similar or different memory mechanisms, and could one or both of these tasks be underpinned by STS (or WM)? We consider in turn three hypothetical memory architectures.

Hypothetical Architecture 1 refers to an architecture in which the same unitary limited-capacity STS is responsible for both the recency effects in free recall and ISR. One exemplar is the architecture sometimes referred to as the modal model (Murdock, 1967) in some texts. The advantages of this architecture are that it elegantly explains the limitations in the capacity of recency effects and memory spans, and it helps explain why relatively small amounts of recently presented items are forgotten in delayed free recall (e.g., Glanzer, 1972; Glanzer & Cunitz, 1966), or in delayed serial recall (e.g., Brown, 1958; Peterson & Peterson, 1959) when rehearsal is prevented. Unfortunately for Hypothetical Architecture 1, the data from Bhatarah et al. (2006) show that the recency effect in free recall is unaffected by a concurrent 6-digit ISR task, and this finding is inconsistent with both the capacity and the duration aspects of an STS explanation of recency.

An alternative is Hypothetical Architecture 2. In this architecture, STS is responsible for ISR but not recency, which is assumed to be underpinned by a separate, non-STS mechanism. A candidate architecture is the WM model of Baddeley and Hitch (1974; Baddeley, 1986). In this account, ISR is underpinned by the phonological loop (an STS or WM mechanism), whilst recency is due to explicit retrieval of implicit priming in LTS (Baddeley & Hitch, 1993). This account can explain the preserved size of the recency effects observed in Bhatarah et al. (2006) because the magnitude of the recency effect and the limitations in ISR do not stem from the same shared limited-capacity mechanism. However, for Architecture 2 to be able to account for the findings of Bhatarah et al. (2008) one must assume that the encoding in ISR and free recall are similar (or at least compatible) and that the words are processed and maintained *in parallel* in both the phonological loop (to be potentially used for later ISR) and into LTS (to be potentially used for later free recall). Note that each memory mechanism must be selectively used for just one task in order to explain why there is no trade-off between the two tasks in Bhatarah et al. (2006).

A third possibility is Hypothetical Architecture 3 in which there is no separate STS or LTS distinction; rather, the most recent and earlier list items are represented along a continuum of episodic memory. One candidate exemplar is the framework proposed by Ward (2001), which assumes that retrieval from episodic memory is recency-based, and sensitive to the ratio of the inter-stimulus interval to the retention interval of the list items. This account assumes that the same representations in episodic memory support recall in both the ISR and free recall tasks. Recency is predicted to be unaffected by the concurrent ISR task in Bhatarah et al. (2006), because the fraction ($\Delta t/T$) of the recency items is unaffected by whether the recency items are embedded in rehearsals of primacy items or concurrent digits. In addition, all episodic memory tasks may share a common forwards-order rehearsal mechanism, and this may be used for rehearsal and output in ISR and for rehearsal and output in free recall.

The main difference between Hypothetical Architectures 2 and 3 is that in Hypothetical Architecture 2, ISR and free recall are underpinned by separate mechanisms, whereas in Hypothetical Architecture 3, ISR and free recall are underpinned by the same mechanisms: a recency-based episodic memory and a forwards-order rehearsal and recall mechanism. We argued that one line of evidence that would help discriminate between these candidates was to examine whether different variables would have similar or different effects on recall in the two tasks: similar effects might be most elegantly explained by Hypothetical Architecture 3, whereas different effects might be better explained by Hypothetical Architecture 2.

Bhatarah and Ward (in preparation; Bhatarah, 2004) examined the effects of articulatory suppression, word length and presentation rate in free recall and ISR. Participants were presented with blocks of trials for free recall or ISR. On each trial, participants saw a sequence of eight words one at a time. The words were taken from an open pool such that no participant saw the same word twice within the experiment. In one experiment, the effects of word length and presentation rate were manipulated. The words in the sequences were short, medium or long words (1, 3 or 5 syllables, respectively) and the presentation rate was fast or slow (1 or 2.5 seconds per word). In a second experiment, the effects of word length and articulatory suppression were manipulated. The words in the sequences were short or long words (1 or 5 syllables, respectively) and the words were presented in silence or under conditions of articulatory suppression. Bhatarah (2004) found that performance on the free recall task tended to result in U-shaped curves and performance on the ISR tended to result in more extended primacy and less recency. Critically, there were broadly similar effects of presentation rate, word length and articulatory suppression for free recall and ISR: recall decreased with faster rates, longer words, and under conditions of articulatory suppression – findings that suggest similarities rather than differences between the tasks.

In the final three experiments reported here, Tan and Ward (2007, in press) explored whether the extended primacy effects typically observed in ISR could be explained within a recency-based view. In so doing we examined the patterns of rehearsals and effects of output orders in ISR.

In one experiment (Tan & Ward, in press), we examined the effect of presentation rate on ISR of a 6-item list using the overt rehearsal method. Many researchers assume that at slow rates any decrease in ISR due to increased retention interval is compensated for by increases in rehearsal. Despite such assumptions, there are few, if any, studies on adults examining the rehearsal schedules that occur during ISR at different presentation rates. We tested two groups of participants, one under visual silent conditions and one under overt rehearsal instructions. All participants received a total of 48 lists of 6 words for ISR, presented in three blocks of 16 trials at different presentation rates (fast, 1 s/word; medium, 2.5 s/word; and slow, 5 s/word). We found that the patterns of recall were broadly similar in the overt rehearsal and the visual silent conditions: there were extended primacy effects with little or no recency, and in both conditions, recall in ISR increased with slower rates.

In order to look at which words were rehearsed at different points during encoding of a list, we borrowed the term "rehearsal set" (RS) from the overt rehearsal method in free recall (e.g., Rundus, 1971) to refer to the set of words that was rehearsed immediately after the presentation of a particular word in the list. Thus, RS 1 refers to the set of rehearsals that immediately followed the presentation of the first word, RS 2 refers to the set of rehearsals that immediately followed the presentation of the second word, and so on, such that RS 6 refers to the set of rehearsals that immediately followed the last word in the list. For each presentation rate and RS, we calculated the proportion of rehearsals in which the first one (1), the first two (1, 2), the first three (1, 2, 3), the first four (1, 2, 3, 4), the first five (1, 2, 3, 4, 5) or all six (1, 2, 3, 4, 5, 6) words in the list were rehearsed in their correct serial order. We found that participants typically choose to rehearse in a cumulative forwards order throughout the list for the first four items, after which they experience items 5 and 6 before recalling the items in order. Indeed, for RSs 2–4, if the first word was rehearsed at all, it tended to be rehearsed along with all the other words up to that point in the list in the correct order. It was only at RS 5 and RS 6 that some participants produce incomplete or inaccurate sequences of rehearsals. This pattern of rehearsals is in line with that assumed by Page and Norris (1998). It is consistent with a recency-based account of ISR, in that it shows the importance of participants' rehearsals in reducing the retention interval of the entire list when the presentation rate is slow, However, these data do not help us understand, from a recency-based view, why ISR gives rise to such extended primacy effects with little or no recency; to explain this, we examined output orders.

A second series of experiments by Tan and Ward (2007) helps to explain the standard primacy-based serial position curve in ISR within a recency-based account of episodic memory. In two experiments, participants were presented with lists of 8 words (Experiment 1) or 6 words (Experiment 2) and were always required to recall the words in their correct serial positions by writing the words in the correct row of a lined response grid. Participants were asked either to recall in strict forwards order, or were free to respond in any order (whilst maintaining the requirement to write the words in the correct serial positions in the response grid). In addition, in each experiment participants were either pre-cued as to the method of responding or post-cued. Tan and Ward (2007) found that participants who were required to recall in a strict forwards order recalled the first items far better than later items – the classic ISR serial position curve. However, participants who were free to recall in any order (although still maintaining the correct serial position in the lined response grid) recalled the later items more often than the earlier items. This was true whether participants knew the method of testing in advance (pre-cued) or did not (post-cued), and for both 6- and 8-item lists. Additional analyses showed that participants often started their recall from the last half of the list when they were free to do so, and these results suggest that the recency items are more accessible at the time of test than the poor performance on strict forwards-ordered ISR would suggest. Finally, when the data were re-plotted by output order there were strikingly similar curves for all conditions in each experiment (for related data, see also Cowan, Saults, & Brown, 2004; Cowan, Saults, Elliott, & Moreno, 2002; Oberauer, 2003).

Our examinations of ISR and free recall suggest that there are more similarities than differences between the two tasks. Performance on both tasks is affected in similar ways by variables such as word length, presentation rate, and articulatory suppression. The use of the overt rehearsal method in ISR confirms that rehearsal is used to effectively reduce the functional retention interval of list items at slow rates, but the examination of the effect of output order suggests that it is output order that has the greatest bearing on the shapes of the serial position curves between the tasks. We therefore propose that Hypothetical Architecture 1, in which a common STS explains both performance in the ISR task and the recency effect in free recall, cannot account for the findings of Bhatarah et al. (2006), and that the third unified store account (Hypothetical Architecture 3) provides a more elegant and parsimonious account than the second independent, parallel store account (Hypothetical Architecture 2) in explaining the data presented here.

Future directions and speculations

Our work is driven by the desire to integrate performance on different episodic memory tasks within a unified theoretical framework. A central theme of our research programme has been to demonstrate that, even though there may appear to be little difference in recall performance across large ranges of serial positions (e.g., the asymptote in free recall, Murdock, 1962; Shiffrin, 1970a), performance across the entire list is nonetheless highly sensitive to recency (e.g., Tan & Ward, 2000; Ward, 2002; Ward & Tan, 2004). In line with this theme, we are currently applying the overt rehearsal procedure to free recall and cued recall of categorised and uncategorised lists of different lengths and compositions, and have found considerable and extended recency effects within lists and within categories. In addition, recent evidence by Talmi and Goshen-Gottstein (2006) suggests that recognition memory may also be sensitive to recency.

One crucial future area requiring examination is the relationship between rehearsal and recall in free recall and rehearsal and recall in ISR. Some accounts of ISR suggest that there is a direct relationship between rehearsal and recall in ISR – indeed, Burgess and Hitch (1999) assume that rehearsal and ISR are underpinned by the same cognitive mechanisms. Similarly, recent accounts of free recall also seek increasing similarity between the mechanisms underpinning rehearsal and recall (e.g., Laming, 2006; Tan & Ward, 2000). Our research into ISR and free recall can be considered to be an attempt to integrate the mechanisms of rehearsal and recall across the free recall and ISR tasks. Not only do there appear similarities between rehearsal and recall across these tasks in our studies, a common rehearsal account of ISR and free recall may also help interpret the high correlations between memory span measures of ISR and secondary memory components of free recall (see, e.g., Crowder, 1976, pp. 149–150; Craik, 1971).

At first, suggestions seeking similarities between rehearsal and recall in free recall and rehearsal and recall in ISR may seem far-fetched. The forwards-ordered nature of ISR seems to set ISR apart from free recall. However, there is abundant evidence for the forwards-ordered nature of recall in free recall (Beaman & Morton, 2000; Kahana, 1996; Howard & Kahana, 1999, 2002b; Laming, 2006; Ward et al., 2003) over a range of different serial positions, whether rehearsal is encouraged or discouraged, such that it is tempting to argue that both recency and the forwards-ordered nature of rehearsal and recall are general properties of episodic memory across a wide range of tasks and timescales.

We hope to concentrate more closely on the forwards-ordered nature of recall in future work. A wide range of different mechanisms for forwards order have been proposed, and it remains to be determined which, if any, can account for data on rehearsal and recall of both free recall and ISR.

Summary and conclusions

There are five main conclusions. First, we believe that it is unnecessary to explain the pattern of data from free recall by proposing the STS–LTS dichotomy. Rather, we assume that all episodic memory is sensitive to recency, and factors that have been previously thought to selectively influence LTS (such as presentation rate, word frequency and list length) affect recall because they affect the subjective ordering and schedule of the items along a recency-based continuum of episodic memory. We note that a recency-based account of free recall has difficulty in explaining why a brief filled delay only affects the recency portion of the curve, but does correctly predict the effect throughout the list (and particularly on the recency items) of longer filled delays such as are found in the Shiffrin (1970a) method and the final free recall task (Craik, 1971).

Second, we believe that an STS explanation of recency in free recall would be more convincing if there was additional evidence for a unitary STS that was used in a wide range of immediate memory tasks. However, we have confirmed that the recency effect in free recall can withstand a concurrent 6-digit ISR task, which itself is believed to be a signature of STS. Our preferred explanation of this finding is that neither task is supported by a limited-capacity STS, but we do accept that it is logically possible that only one of the two effects (recency or span) is underpinned by STS.

Third, we believe that the hypothesis that ISR alone is underpinned by STS does not provide a very parsimonious account of our data. The data from our manipulation of test expectancy suggests that the method of encoding for ISR is highly similar to that used in the free recall task. Furthermore, the two tasks are affected similarly by word length, articulatory suppression, and presentation rate. It seems more parsimonious to assume that the two tasks are underpinned by the same memory mechanisms than to assume that there exist two separate memory mechanisms which are affected similarly by a range of different variables.

Fourth, we propose that the serial position curves of both tasks can be explained if one takes into account both rehearsal and output interference. We have shown that rehearsal largely helps explain why (despite the recency-based nature of episodic memory) there might be a slight improvement in ISR at slower presentation rates. We have also shown that it is the recency items (and not the earlier items) that are most accessible at the time of test in tests of immediate serial memory. However, this preference for recalling the most accessible later items first is only manifested when participants are allowed to output in any order. This finding suggests that the typical primacy-based ISR serial position curves arises at least in part from the increased output interference that builds up as successive list items are output.

Finally, we acknowledge the importance of a forwards-order mechanism in episodic memory, which is perhaps most clearly seen in ISR tasks, but which is influential in all episodic tasks, including free recall. Future research is required to determine which of the many proposed forwards-ordering mechanisms is best suited to explaining the extant data across these tasks.

Acknowledgements

The first and second authors were supported by an ESRC research grant R000239674, and the third author was supported by an ESRC research studentship number R42200134058.

References

Atkinson, R. C., & Shiffrin, R. M. (1968). Human memory: A proposed system and its control processes. In K. W. Spence & J. T. Spence (Eds.), *The psychology of learning and motivation* (Vol. 2, pp. 89–195). New York: Academic Press.

Atkinson, R. C., & Shiffrin, R. M. (1971). The control of short-term memory. *Scientific American, 225,* 82–90.

Baddeley, A. D. (1966a). Short-term memory for word sequences as a function of acoustic, semantic, and formal similarity. *Quarterly Journal of Experimental Psychology, 18,* 362–366.

Baddeley, A. D. (1966b). The influence of acoustic and semantic similarity on long-term memory for word sequences. *Quarterly Journal of Experimental Psychology, 18,* 302–309.

Baddeley, A. D. (1986). *Working memory.* Oxford: Clarendon Press.

Baddeley, A. D., & Hitch, G. J. (1974). Working memory. In G. Bower (Ed.), *Recent advances in learning and motivation* (Vol. 8, pp. 47–90). London: Academic Press.

Baddeley, A. D., & Hitch, G. J. (1977). Recency re-examined. In S. Dornic (Ed.), *Attention and performance VI* (pp. 647–667). Hillsdale, NJ: Lawrence Erlbaum Associates, Inc.

Baddeley, A. D., & Hitch, G. J. (1993). The recency effect: Implicit learning with explicit retrieval? *Memory & Cognition, 21,* 146–155.

Baddeley, A. D., Lewis, V. J., & Vallar, G. (1984). Exploring the articulatory loop. *Quarterly Journal of Experimental Psychology, 36,* 233–252.

Baddeley, A. D., Thomson, N., & Buchanan, M. (1975). Word length and the structure of short-term memory. *Journal of Verbal Learning and Verbal Behavior, 14,* 575–589.

Beaman, C. P., & Morton, J. (2000). The separate but related origins of the recency and the modality effect in free recall. *Cognition, 77,* B59–B65.

Bhatarah, P., (2004). *An experimental investigation of the similarities between free recall and immediate serial recall.* PhD Thesis, University of Essex.

Bhatarah, P., & Ward, G. (in preparation). *Free recall and immediate serial recall share common rehearsal mechanisms.*

Bhatarah, P., Ward, G., & Tan, L. (2006). Examining the relationship between immediate serial recall and free recall: The effect of concurrent task performance. *Journal of Experimental Psychology: Learning, Memory, and Cognition, 32,* 215–229.

Bhatarah, P., Ward, G., & Tan, L. (2008). Examining the relationship between free recall and immediate serial recall: The serial nature of recall and the effect of test expectancy. *Memory & Cognition, 36,* 20–34.

Bjork, R. A., & Whitten, W. B. (1974). Recency-sensitive retrieval processes in long-term free recall. *Cognitive Psychology, 6,* 173–189.

Brodie, D. A. (1975). Free recall measures of short-term store: Are rehearsal and order of recall data necessary? *Memory & Cognition, 3,* 653–662.

Brodie, D. A., & Murdock, B. B. (1977). Effect of presentation time on nominal and functional serial-position curves of free recall. *Journal of Verbal Learning and Verbal Behavior, 16,* 185–200.

Brodie, D. A., & Prytulak, L. S. (1975). Free recall curves: Nothing but rehearsing some items more or recalling them sooner? *Journal of Verbal Learning and Verbal Behavior, 14,* 549–563.

Brown, G. D. A., Neath, I., & Chater, N. (2007). A temporal ratio model of memory. *Psychological Review, 114,* 539–576.

Brown, J. (1958). Some tests of the decay theory of immediate memory. *Quarterly Journal of Experimental Psychology, 10,* 12–21.

Burgess, N., & Hitch, G. (1999). Memory for serial order: A network model of the phonological loop and its timing. *Psychological Review, 106,* 551–581.

Conrad, J., & Hull, A. J. (1964). Information, acoustic confusion and memory span. *British Journal of Psychology, 55,* 75–84.

Cowan, N., Saults, J. S., & Brown, G. D. A. (2004). On the auditory modality superiority effect in serial recall: Separating input and output factors. *Journal of Experimental Psychology: Learning, Memory and Cognition, 30,* 639–644.

Cowan, N., Saults, J. S., Elliott, E. M., & Moreno, M. (2002). Deconfounding serial recall. *Journal of Memory and Language, 46,* 153–177.

Craik, F. I. M. (1971). Primary memory. *British Medical Bulletin, 27,* 232–236.

Craik, F. I. M., & Watkins, M. J. (1973). The role of rehearsal in short term memory. *Journal of Verbal Learning and Verbal Behavior, 12,* 599–607.

Crowder, R. G. (1976). *Principles of learning and memory.* Hillsdale, NJ: Lawrence Erlbaum Associates Inc.

Crowder, R. G. (1982). The demise of short-term memory. *Acta Psychologica, 50,* 291–323.

Crowder, R. G. (1993). Short-term memory: Where do we stand? *Memory & Cognition, 21,* 142–145.

Crowder, R. G., & Neath, I. (1991). The microscope metaphor in human memory. In W. E. Hockley & S. Lewandowsky (Eds.), *Relating theory and data: Essays in human memory in honour of Bennet B. Murdock.* Hillsdale, NJ: Lawrence Erlbaum Associates, Inc.

Drewnowski, A., & Murdock. B. B., Jr (1980). The role of auditory features in memory span for words. *Journal of Experimental Psychology: Learning, Memory, and Cognition, 6,* 319–332.

Fischler, I., Rundus, D., & Atkinson, R. C. (1970). Effects of overt rehearsal procedures on free recall. *Psychonomic Science, 19,* 249–250.

Glanzer, M. (1972). Storage mechanisms in recall. In G. H. Bower (Ed.), *The psychology of learning and motivation: Advances in research and theory Vol. V* (pp. 129–193). New York: Academic Press.

Glanzer, M., & Cunitz, A. R. (1966). Two storage mechanisms in free recall. *Journal of Verbal Learning and Verbal Behavior, 5,* 351–360.

Glenberg, A. M. (1984). A retrieval account of the long-term modality effect. *Journal of Experimental Psychology: Learning, Memory, and Cognition, 10,* 16–31.

Glenberg, A. M. (1987). Temporal context and recency. In D. S. Gorfein & Robert R. Hoffman (Eds.), *Memory and learning: The Ebbinghaus Centennial Conference.* Hillsdale, NJ: Lawrence Erlbaum Associates, Inc.

Glenberg, A. M., Bradley, M. M, Kraus, T. A., & Renzaglia, G. J. (1983). Studies of the long-term recency effect: Support for a contextually guided retrieval hypothesis. *Journal of Experimental Psychology: Learning, Memory, and Cognition, 9,* 231–255.

Glenberg, A. M., Bradley, M. M., Stevenson, J. A., Kraus, T. A. Tkachuk, M. J., Gretz, A. L., et al. (1980). A two-process account of long-term serial position effects. *Journal of Experimental Psychology: Human Learning and Memory, 6,* 355–369.

Greene, R. L. (1986). Sources of recency effects in free recall. *Psychological Bulletin, 99,* 221–228.

Howard, M. W., & Kahana, M. J. (1999). Contextual variability and serial position effects in free recall. *Journal of Experimental Psychology: Learning, Memory, and Cognition, 25*, 1–19.

Howard, M. W., & Kahana, M. J. (2002a). When does semantic similarity help episodic retrieval? *Journal of Memory and Language, 46*, 85–98.

Howard, M. W., & Kahana, M. J. (2002b). A distributed representation of temporal context. *Journal of Mathematical Psychology, 46*, 269–299.

Kahana, M. J. (1996). Associative retrieval processes in free recall. *Memory & Cognition, 24*, 193–109.

Laming, D. (2006). Predicting free recalls. *Journal of Experimental Psychology: Learning, Memory, and Cognition, 32*, 1146–1163.

Miller, G. A. (1956). The magic number seven plus or minus two: Some limits on our capacity to process information. *Psychological Review, 63*, 81–97.

Murdock, B. B. (1962). The serial position curve of free recall. *Journal of Experimental Psychology, 64*, 482–488.

Murdock, B. B., Jr (1967). Recent developments in short-term memory. *British Journal of Psychology, 58*, 421–433.

Nairne, J. S., Neath, I., Serra, M., & Byun, E. (1997). Positional distinctiveness and the ratio rule in free recall. *Journal of Memory and Language, 37*, 155–166.

Neath, I., & Brown, G. D. A. (2006). SIMPLE: Further applications of a local distinctiveness model of memory. In B. H. Ross (Ed.), *The psychology of learning and motivation*, pp. 201–243. San Diego, CA: Academic Press.

Oberauer, K. (2003). Understanding serial position curves in short-term recognition and recall. *Journal of Memory and Language, 49*, 469–483.

Page, M. P. A., & Norris, D. (1998). The primacy model: A new model of immediate serial recall. *Psychological Review, 105*, 761–781.

Peterson, L. R., & Peterson, M. J. (1959). Short-term retention of individual items. *Journal of Experimental Psychology, 61*, 12–21.

Postman, L., & Phillips, L. W. (1965). Short-term temporal changes in free recall. *Quarterly Journal of Experimental Psychology, 17*, 132–138.

Rundus, D. (1971). Analysis of rehearsal processes in free recall. *Journal of Experimental Psychology, 89*, 63–77.

Rundus, D., & Atkinson, R. C. (1970). Rehearsal processes in free recall: A procedure for direct observation. *Journal of Verbal Learning and Verbal Behavior, 9*, 99–105.

Shiffrin, R. M. (1970a). Forgetting, trace erosion or retrieval failure? *Science, 168*, 1601–1603.

Shiffrin, R. M. (1970b). Memory search. In D. A. Norman (Ed.), *Models of memory* (pp. 375–447). New York: Academic Press.

Stuart, G., & Hulme, C. (2000). The effects of word co-occurrence on short-term memory: Associative links in long-term memory affect short-term memory performance. *Journal of Experimental Psychology: Learning, Memory, and Cognition, 26*, 796–802.

Talmi, D., & Goshen-Gottstein, Y. (2006). The long-term recency effect in recognition memory. *Memory, 14*, 424–436.

Tan, L., & Ward, G. (2000). A recency-based account of primacy effects in free recall. *Journal of Experimental Psychology: Learning, Memory, and Cognition, 26*, 1589–1625.

Tan, L., & Ward, G. (2007). Output order effects and immediate serial recall. *Memory & Cognition, 35*, 1093–1106.

Tan, L., & Ward, G. (in press). Rehearsal in immediate serial recall. *Psychonomic Bulleting & Review*.

Ward, G. (2001). A critique of the working memory model. In J. Andrade, (Ed.), *Working Memory in Perspective* (pp. 219–239). Hove, UK: Psychology Press.

Ward, G. (2002). A recency-based account of the list length effect in free recall. *Memory & Cognition, 30*, 885–892.

Ward, G., & Maylor, E. A. (2005). Age-related deficits in free recall: The role of rehearsal. *Quarterly Journal of Experimental Psychology, 58A*, 98–119.

Ward, G., & Tan, L. (2004). The effect of the length of to-be-remembered lists and intervening lists on free recall: A re-examination using overt rehearsal. *Journal of Experimental Psychology: Learning, Memory, and Cognition, 30*, 1196–1210.

Ward, G., Woodward, G., Stevens, A., & Stinson, C. (2003). Using overt rehearsals to explain word frequency effects in free recall. *Journal of Experimental Psychology: Learning, Memory, and Cognition, 29*, 186–210.

4 Working memory and sentence recall

Richard J. Allen and Alan D. Baddeley

Overview

Meaningful sequences of words, such as sentences and passages of prose, are easier to remember than sequences that lack syntactic and semantic structure. In this chapter we explore the interactions between short-term memory and stored language knowledge in long-term memory that give rise to this effect. Previous research on sentence processing in the areas of working memory and language comprehension is discussed. We then report two experiments demonstrating a sentence effect in serial recall, indicating that stored language knowledge is applied to the temporary retention of single sentences in a relatively automatic manner, without requiring additional working memory resources. This "within-sentence binding" is contrasted with memory for complex, multi-sentence sequences. The work is interpreted within the context of working memory models, with particular reference to the multi-component framework proposed by Baddeley (2000).

Introduction

The notion that the capacity of short-term memory can be increased through the binding of information into larger chunks has remained popular since initially proposed by Miller (1956). In this seminal work, Miller suggested capacity to be chunk- rather than item-dependent, and that the more efficiently larger chunks of information are created, the better subsequent memory performance will be. Processes of chunking have been shown to utilize features of the to-be-remembered stimuli, such as rhythm and timing (Ryan, 1969), as well as word meaning. One important variant of information binding, which presumably involves interaction between temporary processing and stored knowledge, concerns memory for redundant material such as text.

Memory for words placed within a sentential context has been consistently shown to be superior to memory for word strings that do not resemble language sequences (e.g., Brener, 1940), with level of recall strongly linked to approximation of word sequences to natural text (Marks & Jack, 1952; Miller & Selfridge, 1950). Extending the evidence for a chunking advantage in memory for sentences, Tulving and Patkau (1962) found that, while order of approximation to language was not linked to the number of chunks of information participants recalled, it was connected to the size of these recalled chunks. Thus, the sequential redundancy inherent in prose increases the amount of information that can be bound into a chunk, rather than increasing the overall number of chunks that can be held, which appears to have an approximate limit of around four items (e.g., Broadbent, 1975; Cowan, 2001).

Following on from this early work, researchers have attempted to more clearly establish the factors involved in sentence processing. Much of this work has focused on the role of syntactic structure. For example, Epstein (1961) demonstrated that the addition of grammatically correct morphemes to nonsense word strings (e.g., *the yigs were vumly rixing* vs. *yig vum rix*) improved recall, though sequential rather than simultaneous presentation removed this effect (Epstein, 1962), and O'Connell, Turner, and Onushka (1968) only observed it with auditory presentation when appropriate intonation was introduced, thus suggesting an effect of prosody rather than syntax. However, Marks and Miller (1964) identified both semantic and syntactic factors as being important. They compared memory for normal sentences and for grammatically correct but semantically anomalous sentences (e.g., *noisy flashes emit careful floods*), with memory for scrambled word strings. While recall was superior for normal sentences, thus illustrating the role of semantic processing, it was also better for the anomalous sentences than for scrambled word strings, indicating a separable effect of syntactic structure on memory.

Regardless of the relative roles of syntax, semantics, and other factors in language processing, the sentence advantage has been consistently observed both in normal participant samples and in a variety of patients with memory deficits. Baddeley, Vallar, and Wilson (1987) reported that, while recall was generally depressed in a group of patients with specific phonological STM impairments, these individuals still recalled around four or five words when presented in a sentential context (relative to one or two words from an unrelated sequence). Furthermore, a group of patients with preserved STM but grossly impaired LTM have shown both normal span for word strings and a typically increased span for words in sentences (up to 16 items) and prose passages (Baddeley & Wilson, 1988, 2002). However, effective prose memory in these patients was strictly limited to temporary storage, as the interpolation of a pre-test delay resulted in total loss of the prose information. These findings indicate important interactions between short-term and long-term memory in the binding of information into chunks within sentences, and the subsequent boost to memory capacity for such information. The observation that amnesic patients were less capable of immediate prose recall when their memory problems were concomitant with an executive processing deficit (Baddeley & Wilson, 2002) also indicates a role for attentional processes.

How are models of memory able to account for the sentence and prose advantage? One interpretation is that the semantic and syntactic structure of such information enables temporary storage within LTM. For example, Ericsson and Kintsch (1995) proposed a form of long-term working memory, with temporary retention of information achieved through integration with activated LTM-based knowledge structures. In this approach, LTM serves as an extension of working memory, with short-term memory only required to hold cues to retrieval structures, rather than provide the entire basis for temporary storage. Meaningful material is more easily and rapidly integrated with the meaning-based knowledge structures of LTM. In contrast, word lists lack any sequential redundancy or meaningful structure, so the scope for storage within long-term knowledge structures is extremely limited. However, while this model is effective in accounting for skilled memory performance (e.g., chess players' memory for board positions, or sports fans' memory for game commentaries), it is not clear how the creation and manipulation of new structures is achieved (with immediate benefits for memory performance) in a system that only involves the simple activation of existing structures in LTM.

A similar conception has been proposed by Cowan (1995, 1999) in his "embedded processes" model. According to this account, information is temporarily retained as an activated portion of LTM, though only a subset of this activation is held within the focus of attention at any one time. Sentence processing receives both active and automatic support in this model, thereby serving to improve recall relative to word lists. Active binding processes occur through the application of attentional focus to the creation of new links between different levels of linguistic knowledge in LTM. In addition, connections can also be established and subsequently strengthened between activated representations that are outside the focus of attention, thus providing a more automatic binding process.

These models describe how pre-existing linguistic knowledge may contribute to verbal memory performance and the sentence/prose advantage through storage within LTM itself. However, it remains unclear how novel information may be initially integrated. For example, while being anomalous on the basis of prior knowledge, the sentence *noisy flashes emit careful floods* (Marks & Miller, 1964) can be held and manipulated in working memory, and an understanding can develop of what a "careful flood" might involve, and how it might interact with a "noisy flash". This ability to integrate novel information would instead appear to indicate an active and flexible temporary working memory capacity.

Multi-component working memory and the episodic buffer

A distinction between temporary and long-term storage capacities is a key component of the working memory model proposed by Baddeley and Hitch (1974). This model comprises an attentional control system, termed the central executive, and two independent sub-systems, the phonological loop and the visuo-spatial sketchpad. The sketchpad is associated with the retention of visual, spatial and possibly kinaesthetic information, and is principally located within the right hemisphere (Smith & Jonides, 1995). The phonological loop is assumed to hold auditory-verbal information over a few seconds, and consists of a temporary store and an articulatory rehearsal system, based within Brodmann areas 6, 40 and 44 (e.g., Paulesu, Frith, & Frackowiak, 1993). Auditory input can directly and automatically enter the phonological store, while visually presented information requires conversion via subvocal articulation for a phonological memory trace to be created. This sub-system directly interacts with stored language knowledge in LTM, and is assumed to play an important role in the acquisition of vocabulary in children and foreign language learners, through the temporary storage of novel phonological word forms (e.g., Baddeley, Gathercole, & Papagno, 1998; Gathercole & Baddeley, 1989, 1990).

While this simple model accounts for a wide range of data, it has become clear that the model in its original state has trouble addressing a number of questions, principal among them being memory for sentences and prose passages. If the phonological loop has a limited capacity of just a few seconds as assumed, how is the working memory system able to hold information that grossly exceeds this capacity, and where does this boost to memory performance come from? Although it presumably must involve interaction between temporary memory and stored language knowledge in LTM, it is unclear where this integration of information occurs, and where the resulting chunks are retained, particularly considering the patient data discussed earlier (Baddeley et al., 1987; Baddeley & Wilson, 1988, 2002). In response to these and other shortcomings of the working memory model, Baddeley (2000) proposed a fractionation of the central executive into its original attentional control system and a further store, the "episodic buffer" (Figure 4.1). This buffer is assumed to be a limited-capacity, modality-independent store capable of binding information from the sub-systems and from LTM into integrated representations or episodes. It is described as providing the interface between memory and conscious awareness, serving to integrate information from disparate sources and form the basis for the creation of mental models. The multi-dimensional code retained within the episodic buffer is controlled by the central executive, and is accessible for the purposes of recall through conscious awareness. This proposed component increases the compatibility with alternative approaches such as that of Cowan (1995), which also emphasizes the integrative and executive capacities of working memory.

Thus, while the original working memory model isolates the separable sub-components of the system, the episodic buffer emphasizes the way in which these sub-components interact, and in doing so provides an account of how interaction between STM and LTM may benefit memory. For sentences and passages of prose presented aurally, information is initially processed by the

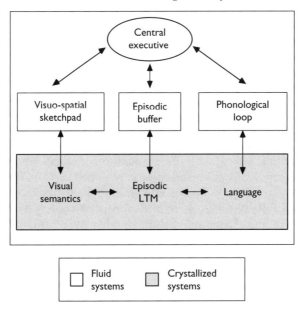

Figure 4.1 The multi-component working memory model (Baddeley, 2000).
Reprinted from *Trends in Cognitive Sciences*, *4*(11), Baddeley, A. D., The episodic
buffer: A new component of working memory? p. 421, Copyright (2000), with
permission from Elsevier.

phonological loop. As the auditory sequence unfolds and sequential
redundancy develops, knowledge structures in LTM concerning syntactic
and semantic processing are applied. This binding of initial phonological
representations into chunks, using long-term language knowledge to
capitalize on the sequential redundancy, proceeds within the episodic
buffer. In contrast, interactive support from LTM for random word strings is
generally limited to effects at the individual word level (e.g., Hulme,
Maughan, & Brown, 1991; Hulme, Roodenrys, Schweickert, Brown, Martin,
& Stuart, 1997; Walker & Hulme, 1999). The lack of any internal semantic or
syntactic structure, and in turn, the absence of sequential redundancy, makes
the binding of words into larger chunks more difficult. Thus, short-term
memory for redundant material such as sentences benefits from episodic
buffer-based binding and storage, resulting in improved recall relative to
word lists, which are generally limited to phonological loop storage. Patients
with pure phonological STM deficits therefore show generally depressed
performance, as the phonological loop is still critical to performance
(through the interaction with LTM). However, subsequent storage within
the episodic buffer still provides a small boost to sentence recall (Baddeley
et al., 1987).

It is important to note from Figure 4.1 that, while the phonological loop
and visuo-spatial sketchpad have direct access to language knowledge and

visual semantics respectively (in LTM), they are not assumed to automatically access the episodic buffer. Active central executive processing is required for information to be effectively bound into chunks and retained in the buffer, indicating these processes to be particularly resource demanding. In addition, "rehearsal" within the episodic buffer would take the form of continued attention to a representation. Therefore, while memory for sentences and prose passages is greater than for random word strings, this advantage comes at a greater cost to central executive resources. Some amnesic patients demonstrate normal sentence recall as binding and retention occurs within a separate buffer, though this depends on whether these patients have intact executive capacities available to perform the demanding process of binding these sentences into chunks (Baddeley & Wilson, 2002).

It does not follow, however, that all forms of binding are particularly resource demanding. There may well be different types of binding, with the system having evolved to integrate certain stimuli automatically, without requiring anything extra in terms of attention or back-up storage. Allen, Baddeley, and Hitch (2006) suggested a distinction between automatic, passive binding processes that proceed using low-level perceptual mechanisms and/or the sub-systems, and active, demanding binding processes. While any binding directly achieved within the episodic buffer is assumed to be of the latter type, this store may also be capable of holding information that has already been automatically bound elsewhere. Indeed, Allen et al. observed that visual features such as shape and colour could be bound together without requiring additional resources. These representations may be automatically created elsewhere in the perceptual or working memory system and then retained in the episodic buffer.

Within-sentence binding

If a broad distinction can be made between different forms of information binding, where does sentence and prose memory fit into this framework? It is possible that different processes contribute to binding within sentences, in which syntactic and semantic structure is utilized to chunk the constituent words into meaningful representations, and binding across sentences, in which the content of larger prose passages is integrated together. It therefore seems instructive to consider these cases separately, before attempting to draw the findings together under a larger banner. We will begin by looking more closely at within-sentence binding.

It has already been suggested that the binding of words in sentences into larger chunks involves not only interaction between the phonological loop and LTM, but also the episodic buffer, and that these processes are particularly dependent on attentional resources. There is considerable evidence to support the assumption that syntactic processing and the extraction of meaning from sentences requires the allocation of processing resources. Sentences with complex syntactic structures are more difficult and time-consuming to understand (see MacDonald, 1997). For example, assigning the thematic roles (who did what to whom), a process we would assume to be crucial in binding a sentence into meaningful chunks, is more demanding for object-relativized sentences (e.g., *The boy that the girl pushed kissed the baby*) than for subject-relativized sentences (e.g., *The girl that pushed the boy kissed the baby*). "Garden path" sentences, that is, sentences that are ambiguous before being resolved as the less preferred interpretation (e.g., *The experienced soldiers warned about the dangers conducted the midnight raid*), are also thought to have heavy processing demands. Problems in assigning thematic roles arising from the complexity and lack of redundancy in these sentences would make binding into accurate integrated representations in memory much more difficult. In line with this, detailed on-line measurements such as eye-fixation durations and self-paced listening and reading times have been shown to increase at the most complex points of a sentence (e.g., Caplan, Hildebrandt, & Waters, 1994; Ferreira, Henderson, Anes, Weeks, & McFarlane, 1996; Frazier & Rayner, 1982; King & Just, 1991).

Just and Carpenter (1992) proposed that a single set of verbal processing resources is applied to the performance of any verbal task, and that the processing of syntactic and semantic structure is demanding of these resources. They suggested that individuals with low working memory capacity, or individuals performing a demanding concurrent task, have fewer resources available for sentence processing, and are therefore less able to perform such tasks, particularly when the sentences have greater syntactic complexity. King and Just (1991) reported that the largest differences between high and low working memory span participants in self-paced reading times (a task in which a sentence is presented, one word at a time) occurred at the syntactically complex points of sentences. Similarly, Baddeley and Hitch (1974) observed that performance on a syntactic reasoning task was more disrupted by a six-digit concurrent load when using passive sentences (e.g., *A is followed by B: AB*) than when sentences were active (e.g., *B follows A: AB*).

The single resource theory therefore assumes that the interaction between the phonological loop and LTM in the initial processing of semantic and syntactic structure (for the purposes of both sentence comprehension and memory formation) can be resource demanding, at least when sentences are complex. However, Waters and Caplan have proposed an alternative approach in a series of papers (e.g., Caplan & Waters, 1999; Rochon, Waters, & Caplan, 2000; Waters & Caplan, 2004; Waters, Caplan, & Rochon, 1995). They have drawn a distinction between the processes involved in extracting meaning from a linguistic signal, what they term "interpretive processing", and the use of this meaning to perform further tasks, termed "post-interpretive processing". Waters and Caplan argue that interpretive processing is served by a separate resource specialized for the first-pass processing of auditory-verbal information, which is capable of assigning syntactic structure and determining sentence meaning automatically. Under this approach, interaction between the phonological loop and stored language knowledge, and the resultant creation of temporary representations of sentence meaning, is achieved at no extra cost to general working memory capacity or central executive processes. It is only when individuals are required to use the determined syntactic and semantic structure in the performance of further tasks, such as action planning, reasoning, or sentence recall (Caplan & Waters, 1999), that is, aspects of post-interpretive processing, that additional demands are placed on working memory resources and conscious, controlled processing is required.

Waters and Caplan (2004; see also Caplan & Waters, 1995) reported that, in a series of studies using the "auditory moving window" technique in which participants heard segments of a sentence at their own pace, they failed to replicate previous findings (e.g., King & Just, 1991) of an increased complexity effect for individuals with low working memory span. In addition, while the overall effects of syntactic complexity remained consistent, these effects were not influenced by concurrent memory load, and were no larger in elderly participants or in patients with dementia of the Alzheimer's type (DAT), across a wide variety of techniques such as self-paced listening and sentence–picture matching (e.g., Feier & Gerstman, 1980; Rochon et al., 2000; Waters, Caplan, & Yampolsky 2003; Waters et al., 1995). As the participants in these studies were expected to have reduced central executive resources (either artificially, through the performance of concurrent tasks, or neurologically, in the case of DAT patients), they should have struggled with syntactically complex sentences, if syntactic processing and the subsequent derivation of meaning were resource demanding. Instead, the findings indicate that initial interactions between the phonological loop and LTM for the purposes of sentence comprehension and chunking occur relatively automatically.

While syntactic complexity does not appear to interact with availability of executive resources, the number of propositions (i.e., the number of thematic roles) in a sentence does, with memory and comprehension worse for sentences containing more propositions (see Caplan & Waters, 1999, for a review). For example, Rochon et al. (2000) manipulated syntactic complexity and number of propositions in sentence–picture and sentence–video matching tasks with a group of DAT patients, and found that the individuals with Alzheimer's disease showed a much larger proposition effect, relative to a normal complexity effect. Similarly, Waters et al. (1995) demonstrated that the addition of a concurrent load increased the proposition effect in DAT patients, while it had no effect on syntactic complexity. Caplan and Waters argued that, while syntactic complexity effects reflect the separable and relatively automatic interpretive stage of processing (in which STM and LTM interact and meaningful representations of sentences develop), proposition effects reflect conscious, controlled processing within the post-interpretive phase. The propositions contained in a sentence are encoded by the interpretive stage, but they place resource demands primarily on post-interpretive processing, during which the thematic roles of a sentence are held in memory and utilized in the performance of further tasks (e.g., matching the sentence to a picture or video, re-enacting the sentence, or making acceptability judgements).

Applying this framework to the concept of the episodic buffer (Baddeley, 2000) implies that the derivation of structure and meaning (and therefore redundancy) through STM–LTM interaction and the resultant within-sentence chunking occurs automatically, and that the memory advantage for sentences over word lists will arise at no extra cost to attention. These bound representations of sentence content may then be retained in the episodic buffer, and it is only when further manipulation or action is required that executive resources are required.

Within-sentence binding: Is it resource demanding?

Experiment 1

We decided to investigate directly whether memory for sentences places particular demands on executive resources. In a first experiment, we assessed the effect of performing a concurrent visual reaction time task on memory for aurally presented natural sentences, constrained sentences, and for each participant's digit span. The natural, or "open" sentences were drawn from national newspapers, with length set at 16 content words in an attempt to avoid ceiling effects. Brener (1940) found that span for normal sentences was at least twice that for random sequences, and our own exploratory studies revealed that open sentence recall varied greatly between individuals and between different types of sentence. In order to study sentence memory while minimizing the possibility of LTM storage, and to also enable comparisons of concurrent task effects with non-sentence information (digit span) without the confound of large variations in item length and recall capability, we used a constrained sentence methodology. Each constrained sentence comprised 8 words (not including function words such as "the" and "and") drawn from a limited pool, all of which were constantly reused in other sentences in the experiment and so were highly primed.

Open: CAR HEADLIGHTS THAT CAN HELP MOTORISTS SEE ROUND CORNERS WILL FINALLY BE INTRODUCED SOMETIME in the NEXT YEAR

Constrained: LUCY the OLD PILOT RAPIDLY BORROWED the SMALL RED BOOK

Digits: 2 7 9 3 8 6 1 5

It was hoped that, in order to take advantage of the structure and redundancy within the constrained sentences, participants would have to form new bindings between words on each trial while discarding those previously created. This would emphasize the role of working memory and the limits that linguistic processing places on order and redundancy within the sentence, while minimizing any contribution from long-term storage. Initial interactions between the phonological loop and LTM would still be crucial in enabling the processing of syntactic structure and meaning, but the bindings between words would have to be created anew on each trial. If this binding and chunking required by sentences is particularly reliant on executive resources, constrained sentence recall should show a relatively larger disruptive effect of concurrent task than digit span.

The role of executive resources in sentence memory was assessed through the addition of a visual-motor concurrent task previously shown by Craik, Govoni, Naveh-Benjamin, and Anderson (1996) to disrupt LTM performance. In this continuous response task, one of four on-screen locations was occupied by a dot to which participants made a corresponding key-press response. As soon as this response was made, the dot shifted to a new location, thus requiring continuous monitoring and responding. This visual-motor task was performed throughout both auditory presentation and subsequent immediate recall of the sentence or digit string. Twenty-four undergraduate and postgraduate students from the University of Bristol performed each of the open and constrained sentence and digit recall conditions on their own and under concurrent task conditions, in a counterbalanced order, as well as baseline blocks of the visual task both before and after the main experimental phase. There were 8 open and 8 constrained sentences used in each of the baseline and concurrent task conditions. Digit span was assessed using 4 sequences at each length, continuing until participants failed to correctly recall 2 of the 4 sequences at that length. The sentence and digit sequences were presented aurally through headphones, with verbal serial recall immediately following the end of each sequence.

A word was scored as being correctly recalled in the open and constrained sentence conditions if it was recalled in the correct position relative to an adjacent word, with the exception of the first and last words in a sequence, which were also scored in terms of serial position. This relative order scoring method emphasized sequential redundancy and the binding of words to their immediate context, rather than using a strict serial position approach. The mean performance levels are displayed in Table 4.1. It is clear that the visual concurrent task did not have a disruptive effect on any

Table 4.1 Mean number of words correctly recalled in each condition (with standard deviations) in Experiment 1

	Open sentences	Constrained sentences	Digit span
Baseline	8.91 (2.32)	6.58 (0.87)	7.54 (1.18)
Visual CRT	9.41 (2.49)	6.75 (0.73)	7.56 (1.33)

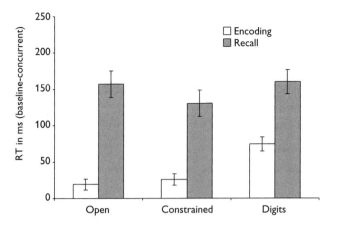

Figure 4.2 Mean differences between reaction times in baseline visual performance and performance as a concurrent task in Experiment 1 (with standard error).

of the conditions, and indeed there was a trend towards a beneficial effect on performance. Estimates of the concurrent task effect size (Cohen's *d*) revealed small and beneficial task effects of 0.17 on open sentences, 0.36 on constrained sentences, and 0.02 on digit span. This would indicate that the processing of sentences and digit sequences in an immediate recall task requires little in the way of executive resources. However, examination of reaction times in the visual concurrent task revealed the presence of trade-off effects. Performing the immediate verbal recall task resulted in slower reaction times on the concurrent visual task, relative to baseline. Figure 4.2 illustrates the pattern of trade-offs as a difference score (mean reaction time in the visual CRT when performed as a concurrent task minus mean reaction time in the baseline visual CRT measure) for each verbal item condition. The trade-off effects are further divided into whether they may have occurred during presentation and encoding of the verbal item, or during the recall phase.

A 3 × 2 repeated measures ANOVA on the reaction time trade-offs revealed significant effects of verbal memory condition, F (2,46) = 5.98, *MSE* = 3309.41, *p* < .01, task stage, F (1,23) = 82.20, *MSE* = 5237.97, *p* < .001, and the interaction, F (2,46) = 6.26, *MSE* = 1345.27, *p* < .01. Visual task reaction times were much slower during the response phase than during auditory-verbal presentation and encoding. This is in line with previous findings that indicate a larger disruption of secondary task performance by retrieval than by the encoding stage across a variety of tasks, while retrieval itself is not influenced by the secondary task (e.g., Naveh-Benjamin, Craik, Gavrilescu, & Anderson, 2000). Reaction times were only marginally slower during verbal encoding than during the visual baseline blocks, and were no slower for open or constrained sentences than for the non-sentence condition. Indeed, visual task responses were actually slower during digit sequence encoding than open sentences, t (23) = 5.39, p < .001, or constrained sentences, t (23) = 4.77, p < .001, while the sentence conditions did not differ during encoding, t (23) = 1.32, p = .201, *ns*. Effect sizes (Cohen's d) relative to baseline visual performance were 1.60 for visual performance during digit encoding, 0.51 during open sentence encoding, and 0.66 during constrained encoding. There were no significant differences during verbal output between digits and open sentences, t (23) = 0.17, *ns*, digits and constrained, t (23) = 1.43, p = .165, *ns*, and open and constrained conditions, t (23) = 1.95, p = .063, *ns*. Effect sizes were 1.96 during digit recall, 1.76 during open recall, and 1.47 during constrained. It is unclear why concurrent task performance should slow more during encoding of digit sequences than during encoding of sentences. Perhaps the absence of meaningful internal structure within digit sequences forced participants to turn to a strategy of temporal chunking within the phonological loop, thus disrupting the timing of their key press responses in the visual task.

Nevertheless, the absence of a disruptive concurrent task effect on memory for open or constrained sentences, and the minimal concurrent task trade-off effect during auditory-verbal encoding, indicates that sentential structure is processed at no extra cost to working memory resources. As the unfolding sentence is processed and entered into the phonological loop, stored knowledge about syntactic and semantic structure in LTM is accessed automatically, enabling sequential redundancy and chunking to develop within the sentences. These automatically bound representations may then be retained in the episodic buffer until recall is required. Thus, within-sentence binding in working memory appears to be located primarily at the level of automatic interactions between phonological processing and LTM.

There were a number of limitations to this initial study, however. While recall of open sentences was superior to non-sentence memory (digit span), our constrained sentence measure, with which we attempted to emphasize working memory capacities, was not. It is obviously crucial that we are able to demonstrate that participants are able to utilize to their advantage the structure and sequential redundancy within constrained sentences. Secondly, digit span was not a direct non-sentence control for the constrained condition, as both the content (digits) and span procedure (increasing item length) differed. A more appropriate non-sentence control would be to use a fixed list length and draw items from the same word pool as the one used for constrained sentences, presenting these words in a random, non-structured order without any sequential redundancy. These issues were addressed in a second experiment.

Experiment 2

In this experiment, we examined the effects of the concurrent visual task on memory for 16-word open sentences and 8-word constrained sentences. We

Table 4.2 Mean number of words correctly recalled in each condition (with standard deviations) in Experiment 2

	Open sentences	Constrained sentences	Constrained lists
Baseline	10.57 (1.95)	7.21 (0.46)	5.20 (0.59)
Visual CRT	10.15 (1.94)	7.05 (0.49)	5.07 (0.61)

also added a test of memory for the words used in the constrained sentences, without their sentential context. Thus, participants were presented with lists of words drawn from the same constrained word pool, in random order (e.g., *car borrowed Lucy red old rapidly*). As these lists involved the same words as the constrained sentences, but lacked any kind of internal structure or redundancy, we predicted that immediate recall would be less accurate. For this reason, list length was set at 6 words, in an attempt to match overall difficulty level with the constrained sentences, and therefore allow a direct comparison of concurrent task effects. Although proportionally less accurate on the open sentences in Experiment 1, participants nevertheless recalled a greater number of words from open sentences, and performance on these items was so variable that we decided to once again set length at 16 words. The stimulus presentation and concurrent task procedure were the same as in Experiment 1. Twenty-four participants from the University of Bristol performed each of the memory conditions with 10 sentences or lists in each condition, plus pre- and post-test baseline measures of visual task performance.

The relative order scoring method from Experiment 1 was used again here, with numbers of words recalled in the correct order in each condition provided in Table 4.2. A 3 × 2 ANOVA revealed a significant effect of item set, $F (2,46) = 195.96$, $MSE = 1.70$, $p < .001$, a marginally non-significant effect of visual task, $F (1,23) = 4.07$, $MSE = 0.49$, $p = .056$, *ns*, and no interaction between item set and visual task, $F (2,46) = 0.67$, $MSE = 0.50$, *ns*. Immediate recall of open sentences was superior to constrained sentence recall, which in turn was better than recall of the same words in random order. Therefore we observed evidence of the effects of sentential structure on immediate word recall, using our constrained sentence methodology. However, there was only a small and marginally non-significant effect of performing the concurrent visual task on recall performance, and this was consistent across conditions. Effect size (Cohen's *d*) estimates for the concurrent task were 0.26 for open sentences, 0.48 for constrained sentences, and 0.34 for word lists. While there was a small disruptive effect of concurrent task on recall in this experiment, we found no evidence that the use of sentential structure to bind words into chunks is any more resource demanding, relative to memory for random word sequences.

While there was a numerical recall advantage for constrained sentences over lists of words, this comparison is undermined to an extent by the use of

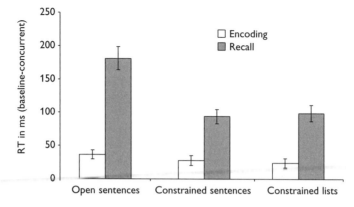

Figure 4.3 Mean differences between reaction times in baseline visual performance and performance as a concurrent task in Experiment 2 (with standard error).

differing sequence lengths. It is important to establish that sentential binding did occur for the constrained sentences in a way that produced a meaningful boost to memory performance, relative to unstructured lists. If there was no actual recall advantage for sentences over lists of words, proportional recall rates should be higher for lists than sentences, as the former sequence type were two words shorter than the latter, and therefore should have been easier to recall. In fact, mean proportion correct rates of .90 (SD = 0.06) in constrained sentence (baseline) and .88 (SD = 0.06) in constrained sentence (visual CRT) conditions were obtained, relative to rates of .87 (SD = 0.10) in list (baseline) and .85 (SD = 0.10) in list (visual CRT) conditions. A 2 × 2 ANOVA revealed significant effects of item set F $(1,23)$ = 11.15, MSE = 2.76^{-03}, p < .01, and concurrent task $F (1,23)$ = 9.86, MSE = 9.92^{-04}, p < .01, but not the item set by task interaction, $F (1,23)$ = 0.01, MSE = 1.76^{-03}, *ns*. Therefore, we actually observed an advantage for sentences versus lists in proportion correct despite the differences in sequence length, indicating that sentential structure did indeed impact on constrained recall performance.[1]

Turning to performance on the concurrent visual task, we again observed evidence of trade-offs between the verbal and visual measures. Response latencies are reported in Figure 4.3 as the difference between mean baseline performance and reaction times during either presentation or recall of the sentence or list. A 3 × 2 repeated measures ANOVA revealed significant effects of item set, $F (2,46)$ = 19.65, MSE = 1843.40, p < .001, test stage, F $(1,23)$ = 108.63, MSE = 2992.44, p < .001, and the interaction, $F (2,46)$ = 26.03, MSE = 855.62, p < .001. As in the first experiment, visual task performance was disrupted to a far greater extent by sentence/list recall than by encoding. The auditory-verbal presentation phase did have a disruptive influence on visual task performance, with effect size estimates

(Cohen's *d*) relative to baseline reaction time of 1.13 for open sentences, 0.76 for constrained sentences, and 0.70 for word lists. There were no differences in visual task performance between the open and constrained sentences' conditions, *t* (23) = 1.35, *p* = .189, *ns*, between open and constrained lists, *t* (23) = 1.85, *p* = .077, *ns*, or between the two constrained item conditions, *t* (23) = 0.75, *ns*. Effect sizes were somewhat larger during the recall phase relative to visual task baseline, with *d* = 2.14 for open sentences, 1.79 for constrained sentences, and 1.64 for word lists. There were significant differences in reaction times during recall between open and constrained sentences, *t* (23) = 6.20, *p* < .001, between open sentences and word lists, *t* (23) = 5.13, *p* < .001, but not between the constrained sentences and word lists, *t* (23) = 0.47, *ns*. To summarize, we observed a relatively small disruption of visual task performance during the encoding phase, to a similar extent across all three item set conditions. A much larger degree of concurrent task disruption emerged during the recall phase, particularly during recall of the open sentences. As these items were at least twice as long as the constrained sets, processes of output may have been more demanding, producing a particular slow-down in concurrent task performance during the recall phase.

Nevertheless, the immediate recall and concurrent visual task findings across two experiments indicate that sentential structure does benefit verbal memory performance, and that this emerges relatively automatically, at no extra cost to executive resources. What are the implications for STM–LTM interaction and the episodic buffer? We would suggest that the unfolding auditory-verbal signal is temporarily retained in phonological short-term memory, during which time stored language knowledge in LTM is applied in the analysis of syntactic structure and the derivation of meaning. These processes occur automatically, enabling the binding of words within a sentence into larger chunks, the development of sequential redundancy, and the formation of meaningful representations. These may be temporarily retained in the episodic buffer, either in parallel as the sentence is unfolding through interactions between STM and LTM (with the buffer receiving the chunked sentence in stages), or after it has been completed and a full representation is available. It is therefore reasonably clear from our data, and work by Waters, Caplan, and colleagues, that the initial processes of syntactic and semantic analysis through interaction between temporary representations of the auditory-verbal signal and stored language knowledge and the subsequent chunking for the purposes of retention proceed at no extra cost to central executive resources. This would indicate that the working memory model as set out by Baddeley (2000) requires modification, with direct links between the phonological loop, stored language knowledge in LTM, and the episodic buffer, rather than access to the buffer being dependent on executive resources.

It is plausible that the working memory system has evolved to accomplish essential within-modality binding such as the chunking of structured sequences of words into meaningful representations without requiring additional active processing. We would argue that the episodic buffer is involved in retention, as phonological short-term memory would not possess the capacity to store long sequences, nor the capability for semantic or syntactic coding. Furthermore, it is not clear how long-term memory could repeatedly create and retain new associations on the basis of single exposures to stimuli. However, the role of the episodic buffer would be limited in these circumstances to that of a passive recipient for chunking achieved elsewhere in the system, rather than an active creator of bound representations.

Across-sentence binding

Where then might the episodic buffer and executive resources become involved in the active formation of bindings in working memory? One possibility is that, in contrast to the within-modality binding described above, the binding of information across modalities is particularly demanding, requiring integration from different sub-systems of working memory and storage in a multi-dimensional code provided by the episodic buffer. Another possibility is that the processes of binding vary with level of scale and the precise form of information integration that is required. Thus, while words can be bound into sentences relatively automatically using stored language knowledge, the binding of multiple sentences on a larger scale into meaningful representations of prose passages could plausibly be a more demanding process.

Hambrick and Engle (2002) examined the effects of working memory capacity, domain knowledge, and age on memory for prose passages, by presenting artificial baseball commentaries to individuals who varied in their degree of baseball expertise. They found that while all three factors were related to memory for passage content, domain knowledge was by far the strongest predictor, particularly for the recall of baseball-relevant information (e.g., state of play). In addition, there was a "rich-get-richer" interaction between knowledge and working memory capacity for baseball-relevant recall, with younger participants and those with higher working memory spans making better use of their baseball knowledge. This was not the case for baseball-irrelevant information (e.g., the weather). These findings would suggest both LTM and working memory to be involved in prose passage binding, and that working memory resources can influence how effectively long-term knowledge is applied. For new information to be integrated with existing knowledge structures, it must be maintained in an activated state during ongoing processing. Thus, access to domain knowledge is automatic, but it can only be more effectively applied when sufficient working memory resources are available to keep new information active. Hambrick and Engle suggest that this information is integrated directly into knowledge structures in LTM, as proposed by Ericsson and Kintsch (1995). Alternatively, pre-existing domain knowledge held in LTM might be applied to the binding of prose passages within a temporary store such as the episodic buffer, before assimilation into LTM can occur. Under this account, the continued activation of new information during ongoing processing and its binding into larger chunks using long-term knowledge will be resource demanding. However, it is important to note that, though significant, working memory capacity predicted only a small amount of variance in passage memory, relative to domain knowledge.

Baddeley, Emslie, and Anderson (unpublished) administered passages of prose that varied in readability from simple fairy stories up to passages about philosophy, with the role of executive resources examined using a wide range of demanding concurrent tasks. Prose memory was measured using questions about the presented passages. While performance varied with prose passage difficulty and was impaired by concurrent tasks, the degree of concurrent task impairment was consistent across easy, moderate, and difficult passages. Similarly, level of prose passage difficulty had little effect on concurrent task performance. It appears that the binding of prose passages into larger coherent chunks in memory was influenced by passage difficulty, and that this was independent of the amount of executive resources that could be applied. These resources are clearly involved in prose passage binding, as concurrent tasks did influence performance, but they seem to be applied in a manner that is separable from whatever the difficulty level variable is tapping.

The role of working memory resources and their interaction with LTM in the encoding and binding of prose passages in memory therefore remains somewhat unclear. Though Hambrick and Engle (2002) found evidence for a contribution from executive resources when individuals possessed high levels of domain knowledge, this contribution was relatively small. Furthermore, the measures of retention in such studies of prose memory have tended to be somewhat inexact. For example, both Baddeley et al. (unpublished) and Hambrick and Engle (2002) used a question format as a measure of passage memory, which may emphasize prior knowledge over other aspects of performance.

Jefferies, Lambon Ralph, and Baddeley (2005) avoided this problem by assessing memory performance with verbatim recall. They compared recall of a series of unrelated sentences with recall of the same words placed in non-sentential context, using auditory presentation. Each sentence and word sequence was tested three times, to assess the rate of learning. The role of attention resources in the sentence and word list conditions was examined with a concurrent task, specifically using the visual-motor continuous response task described earlier and used in our constrained sentence studies. Jefferies et al. observed that, on the first trial, this concurrent task had a significant disruptive effect on recall of unrelated sentence strings but not for lists of words. By the third trial, however, word list recall was significantly impaired by concurrent task, while the effect remained constant across learning trials for sentences. Similarly, visual-motor task reaction times were initially higher during sentence than list processing, but significantly increased during subsequent presentations of the same word lists. Attentional resources therefore appear to play an important role in the binding of novel information into chunks when placed within sentential structure. For novel, unstructured lists of words, the absence of frameworks of association between these words in LTM will result in a reliance on less demanding phonological coding, though increased familiarity through repeated presentation can improve the applicability of chunking processes (at a greater cost to attentional resources).

In a key final experiment, Jefferies et al. compared word list and unrelated sentence sequence recall with recall of sentence sequences that formed a meaningful and coherent story. They found that memory for the latter type of information was not significantly impaired by the concurrent task, though unrelated sentence recall was again disrupted. These findings support our earlier assertion and other work (e.g., Caplan & Waters, 1999; Rochon et al., 2000; Waters et al., 1995) suggesting that within-sentence binding arises relatively automatically through interactions between working memory and pre-existing linguistic knowledge in LTM. In addition, the creation of mental models on the basis of meaningful prose passages does not appear to require additional executive resources. Instead, it is the binding together and retention of arbitrary combinations of sentences that is resource demanding. In line with this, we have already noted that processing demands increase when sentences contain multiple propositions that require maintenance and binding (see Caplan & Waters, 1999). Similarly, Radvansky and Copeland (2004) observed that working memory span correlated with the ability to remember information that was poorly integrated within a wider prose passage (though there was no relation with the processing of prose meaning generally). It appears that the chunking together of multiple unrelated propositions, often across sentence boundaries, requires additional active processing resources that are not involved in simple within-sentence binding or the processing of coherent and meaningful prose passages.

Implications for models of working memory

It is important to consider the range of findings discussed as a whole, and their implications for concepts of working memory and interaction with stored language knowledge. We have established that recall of words is superior when they are presented in a sentential context, with accompanying syntactic and semantic structure and improved sequential redundancy, with linguistic structure enabling the binding of words into larger chunks. Furthermore, it appears that this within-sentence binding emerges relatively automatically through interaction between initial phonological processing and pre-existing language knowledge stored in LTM (which itself seems to be important to all forms of verbal binding). Relatively automatic binding, through the application of LTM knowledge, is also applied to the chunking of multiple sentences, provided they unite to form a coherent and meaningful story. Additional central executive resources only become important when binding is required between multiple unrelated propositions and/or sentences (e.g., Jefferies et al., 2005). In contrast, memory for novel sequences of words presented without any sentential structure is limited to relatively automatic phonological coding, though increased familiarity with a word sequence appears to enable the application of more effective but demanding chunking processes.

In order to account for this pattern of findings, models of verbal memory must outline how LTM-based language knowledge is applied to the processing of sentential structure, while also describing how this interacts with attentional resources. The Ericsson and Kintsch (1995) model describes a system in which information can be temporarily retained within stored knowledge structures in LTM, with STM simply required to retain active retrieval cues. Under this approach, coherent stories and simple sentences are easily integrated into LTM, as the knowledge structures already exist for the processing of such information. However, effective pre-existing structures are not available for the integration of unrelated sentences. These items instead require the creation of novel connections between knowledge structures, or the retention of numerous retrieval cues in short-term memory. Novel unstructured lists of words also lack corresponding support in LTM, and so performance is based primarily on temporary phonological coding.

The Cowan (1995, 1999) embedded processes model is also able to account for many aspects of the findings, with the binding and retention of sentences across coherent prose passages and within sentences themselves proceeding through activation of LTM representations. As syntactic and semantic knowledge is already being held in LTM, the integration of such information would not necessarily require the focusing of attention. In contrast, this focus of attention is required for the binding of and creation of links between unrelated sequences of sentences.

These models are able to describe many aspects of verbal memory processing in terms of storage within long-term knowledge structures, without the need for any kind of temporary integrative storage capacity. However, it is not clear how they account for the memory advantage for constrained sentences over word lists. The repeated presentation of the same words in different configurations of meaningful sentential structures would presumably require the creation and subsequent suppression of so many activated representations as to make LTM-based storage unreliable, ineffective, and highly demanding. It may instead be more plausible to postulate a separable integrative store such as the episodic buffer (Baddeley, 2000).

In line with the work by Caplan and Waters (e.g., Caplan & Waters, 1999, Waters & Caplan, 2004), we would argue that the syntactically and semantically guided chunking and the development of sequential redundancy involved in within-sentence binding arises automatically, at no extra cost to attentional resources. This may emerge through the interaction between phonological STM and stored language knowledge in LTM, with subsequent storage of the chunked representations in the episodic buffer. Similarly, binding across sentences into integrated representations of coherent prose passages would also emerge relatively automatically through the application of pre-existing semantic knowledge. For the processing of unrelated sentence sequences, within-sentence binding would proceed automatically, but active and resource-demanding integrative processes would be required to bind each sentence together within the episodic buffer itself. Memory for novel and unstructured lists of words would initially rely primarily on automatic phonological coding, though the development of a degree of familiarity over time could enable the use of more effective, active chunking processes, again illustrating the integrative benefits of the episodic buffer. Constrained sentence memory could also be accounted for, as the temporary and flexible nature of the buffer would enable the discarding of old bindings and the development of new chunks on every trial. Thus, the episodic buffer perspective provides a broad description of how temporary storage and processing resources interact with LTM in the encoding of structured verbal information, provided that the model proposed by Baddeley (2000) is adapted so that direct links run between the buffer and the sub-systems. This would enable information automatically bound elsewhere in the system to access the episodic buffer, as opposed to the previously described indirect route via the central executive.

Further exploration is certainly required to outline more clearly how temporary storage and processing capacities and LTM may interact under a range of conditions, and to establish with greater precision how within- and across-sentence binding is achieved. Nevertheless, it is apparent that language knowledge held within LTM can make a large and often crucial contribution to temporary verbal memory functioning, with within- and between-sentence processing a particular example of this. For intra-sentence binding and many types of inter-sentence binding, the application of language knowledge structures is achieved automatically. The language processing system has developed to process sentential structure and bind within- and between-sentences. It appears to do so without placing additional demands on executive resources, therefore allowing such resources to be applied to the matter in hand, rather than to the demands of language processing. This is only possible, however, when the passage forms a coherent whole. Individual sentences or phrases that appear to be unrelated require the application of attentional resources if they are to be chunked together in memory.

Note

1 We also have data from further experimental work (Allen, Baddeley, & Hitch, in preparation) using constrained sentences and lists of matched length, in which a consistent and robust sentence advantage emerges.

References

Allen, R. J., Baddeley, A. D., & Hitch, G. J. (2006). Is the binding of visual features in working memory resource-demanding? *Journal of Experimental Psychology, General, 135*(2), 298–313.

Allen, R. J., Baddeley, A. D., & Hitch, G. J. (in preparation). *Linguistic structure, binding, and working memory: Evidence from immediate serial recall and recognition.*

Baddeley, A. D. (2000). The episodic buffer: A new component of working memory? *Trends in Cognitive Sciences, 4*, 417–423.

Baddeley, A. D., Gathercole, S., & Papagno, C. (1998). The phonological loop as a language learning device. *Psychological Review, 105*(1), 158–173.

Baddeley, A. D., & Hitch, G. J. (1974). Working memory. In G. H. Bower (Ed.), *The psychology of learning and motivation: Advances in research and theory* (Vol. 8, pp. 47–90). New York: Academic Press.

Baddeley, A. D., Vallar, G., & Wilson, B. A. (1987). Sentence comprehension and phonological memory: Some neuropsychological evidence. In M. Coltheart (Ed.), *Attention and performance XII: The psychology of reading* (pp. 509–529). Hillsdale, NJ: Lawrence Erlbaum Associates, Inc.

Baddeley, A. D., & Wilson, B. A. (1988). Frontal amnesia and the dysexecutive syndrome. *Brain and Cognition, 7*(2), 212–230.

Baddeley, A. D., & Wilson, B. A. (2002). Prose recall and amnesia: Implications for the structure of working memory. *Neuropsychologia, 40*(10), 1737–1743.

Brener, R. (1940). An experimental investigation of memory span. *Journal of Experimental Psychology, 27*, 467–482.

Broadbent, D. E. (1975). The magic number seven after fifteen years. In A. Kennedy & A. Wilkes (Eds.), *Studies in Long-Term Memory* (pp. 3–18). London: John Wiley & Sons.

Caplan, D., Hildebrandt, N., & Waters, G. S. (1994). Interaction of verb selectional restrictions, noun animacy and syntactic form in sentence processing. *Language and Cognitive Processes, 9*, 549–585.

Caplan, D., & Waters, G. S. (1995). Aphasic disturbances of syntactic comprehension and working memory capacity. *Cognitive Neuropsychology, 12*, 637–649.

Caplan, D., & Waters. G. S. (1999). Verbal working memory and sentence comprehension. *Behavioral and Brain Sciences, 22*, 77–126.

Cowan, N. (1995). *Attention and memory: An integrated framework.* New York: Oxford University Press.

Cowan, N. (1999). An embedded-processes model of working memory. In A. Miyake & P. Shah (Eds.), *Models of working memory: Mechanisms of active maintenance and executive control* (pp. 62–99). Cambridge: Cambridge University Press.

Cowan, N. (2001). The magical number 4 in short-term memory: A reconsideration of mental storage capacity. *Behavioral and Brain Sciences, 24*, 87–114.

Craik, F., Govoni, R., Naveh-Benjamin, M., & Anderson, N. (1996). The effects of divided attention on encoding and retrieval processes in human memory. *Journal of Experimental Psychology: General, 125*, 159–180.

Epstein, W. (1961). The influence of syntactical structure on learning. *American Journal of Psychology, 74*, 80–85.

Epstein, W. (1962). A further study of the influence of syntactical structure on learning. *American Journal of Psychology*, *75*, 121–126.

Ericsson, K., & Kintsch, W. (1995). Long-term working memory. *Psychological Review*, *102*, 211–245.

Feier, C. D., & Gerstman, L. J. (1980). Sentence comprehension abilities throughout the adult life span. *Journal of Gerontology*, *35*, 722–728.

Ferreira, F., Henderson, J. M., Anes, M. D., Weeks, P. A., Jr, & McFarlane, D. K. (1996). Effects of lexical frequency and syntactic complexity in spoken language comprehension: Evidence from the auditory moving window technique. *Journal of Experimental Psychology: Learning, Memory, and Cognition*, *22*, 324–335.

Frazier, L., & Rayner, K. (1982). Making and correcting errors during sentence comprehension: Eye movements in the analysis of structurally ambiguous sentences. *Cognitive Psychology*, *143*, 178–210.

Gathercole, S. E., & Baddeley, A. D. (1989). Evaluation of the role of phonological memory in the development of vocabulary in children: A longitudinal study. *Journal of Memory and Language*, *28*, 200–213.

Gathercole, S. E., & Baddeley, A. D. (1990). The role of phonological memory in vocabulary acquisition: A study of young children learning new names. *British Journal of Psychology*, *81*, 439–454.

Hambrick, D. Z., & Engle, R. W. (2002). Effects of domain knowledge, working memory capacity, and age on cognitive performance: An investigation of the knowledge-is-power hypothesis. *Cognitive Psychology*, *44*, 339–387.

Hulme, C., Maughan, S., & Brown, G. D. A. (1991). Memory for familiar and unfamiliar words: Evidence for a long-term memory contribution to short-term memory span. *Journal of Memory and Language*, *30*, 685–701.

Hulme, C., Roodenrys, S., Schweickert, R., Brown, G. D. A., Martin, S., & Stuart, G. (1997). Word frequency effects on short-term memory tasks: Evidence for a redintegration process in immediate serial recall. *Journal of Experimental Psychology: Learning, Memory, and Cognition*, *23*, 1217–1232.

Jefferies, E., Lambon Ralph, M., & Baddeley, A. D. (2005). Automatic and controlled processing in sentence recall: The role of long-term and working memory. *Journal of Memory and Language*, *51*, 623–643.

Just, M. A., & Carpenter, P. A. (1992). A capacity theory of comprehension: Individual differences in working memory. *Psychological Review*, *99*(1), 122–149.

King, J., & Just, M. A. (1991). Individual differences in syntactic processing: The role of working memory. *Journal of Memory and Language*, *30*, 580–602.

MacDonald, M. C. (1997). Lexical representations and sentence processing: An introduction. *Language and Cognitive Processes*, *12*(2–3), 121–136.

Marks, M. R., & Jack, O. (1952). Verbal context and memory span for meaningful material. *American Journal of Psychology*, *65*(2), 298–300.

Marks, L. E., & Miller, G. A. (1964). The role of semantic and syntactic constraints in the memorization of English sentences. *Journal of Verbal Learning and Verbal Behavior*, *3*, 1–5.

Miller, G. A. (1956) The magical number seven, plus or minus two. *Psychological Review*, *63*, 81–97.

Miller, G. A., & Selfridge, J. A. (1950). Verbal context and the recall of meaningful material. *American Journal of Psychology*, *63*(2), 176–185.

Naveh-Benjamin, M., Craik, F. I., Gavrilescu, D., & Anderson, N. D. (2000).

Asymmetry between encoding and retrieval processes: Evidence from divided attention and a calibration analysis. *Memory & Cognition, 28*(6), 965–976.

O'Connell, D. C., Turner, E. A., & Onushka, L. A. (1968). Intonation, grammatical structure, and contextual association in free recall. *Journal of Verbal Learning and Verbal Behaviour, 7,* 110–116.

Paulesu, E., Frith, C. D., & Frackowiak, R. S.J. (1993). The neural correlates of the verbal component of working memory. *Nature, 362,* 342–344.

Radvansky, G. A., & Copeland, D. E. (2004). Working memory span and situation model processing. *American Journal of Psychology, 117,* 191–213.

Rochon, E., Waters, G. S., & Caplan, D. (2000). The relationship between measures of working memory and sentence comprehension in patients with Alzheimer's disease. *Journal of Speech, Language, and Hearing Research, 43,* 395–413.

Ryan, J. (1969). Grouping and short-term memory: Different means and patterns of grouping. *Quarterly Journal of Experimental Psychology, 21,* 137–147.

Smith, E. E., & Jonides, J. (1995). Working memory in humans: Neuropsychological evidence. In M. S. Gazzaniga (Ed.), *The cognitive neurosciences* (pp. 1009–1020). Cambridge, MA: MIT Press.

Tulving, E., & Patkau, J. E. (1962). Concurrent effects of contextual constraint and word frequency on immediate recall and learning of verbal material. *Canadian Journal of Psychology, 16,* 83–95.

Walker, I., & Hulme, C. (1999). Concrete words are easier to recall than abstract words: Evidence for a semantic contribution to short-term serial recall. *Journal of Experimental Psychology: Learning, Memory, and Cognition, 25,* 1256–1271.

Waters, G. S., & Caplan, D. (2004). Verbal working memory and on-line syntactic processing: Evidence from self-paced listening. *Quarterly Journal of Experimental Psychology, 57A*(1), 129–163.

Waters, G. S., Caplan, D., & Rochon, E. (1995). Processing capacity and sentence comprehension in patients with Alzheimer's disease. *Cognitive Neuropsychology, 12,* 1–30.

Waters, G. S., Caplan, D., & Yampolsky, S. (2003). On-line syntactic processing under concurrent memory load. *Psychonomic Bulletin and Review, 10*(1), 89–95.

5 How chunks form in long-term memory and affect short-term memory limits

Nelson Cowan and Zhijian Chen

Overview

We address the question of whether information in short-term memory can be conceived of as the activated portion of long-term memory. The main problem for this conception is that short-term memory must include new associations between items that are not already present in long-term memory (or sometimes between items and serial positions). Relevant evidence is obtained from a task in which new word pairings are taught and then embedded within a short-term serial-recall task. We conclude that rapid long-term learning occurs in short-term memory procedures, and that this rapid learning can explain the retention of new associations. We propose that new associations are formed between elements concurrently held in the focus of attention, and that these new associations quickly become part of long-term memory. An understanding of rapid learning appears to be necessary to understand capacity limits in short-term memory.

Introduction

This chapter is about how long-term memory information is activated and used when one carries out short-term memory tasks, and how new long-term memory information is formed during short-term memory tasks. The topic is related to Miller's (1956) famous article. He not only pointed out capacity limits in short-term memory (seven plus or minus two units in serial recall, and about the same number of categories along a dimension in perceptual tasks); he also indicated how long-term knowledge can greatly increase short-term memory. It can do so through a process Miller termed *chunking*, the combination of multiple items to form a larger, meaningful item. To offer a simple example, it is much easier to recall the letter sequence *i-b-m-c-b-s-r-c-a* if one recognizes within it acronyms for three American corporations in succession: IBM, CBS, and RCA. This reduces the number of chunks in the list from nine to three.

The issues of capacity and chunking that Miller (1956) raised become entangled with one another when it is considered that people might form new chunks during a short-term memory task, as a mnemonic strategy. For example, given the telephone number *662-5892*, one might memorize three chunks: 662, 58, and 92. In this way, what was a rather taxing list of seven single-digit numbers becomes a less taxing list of three multi-digit numbers. Indeed, the reason that telephone numbers are listed with a break in the middle is probably to facilitate this type of memorization. If one allows this "on-line" basis of chunk formation, though, the true limit in capacity is in question. Can people recall about seven chunks of information or, when seven items are recalled in a memory task such as serial recall, do these items actually make up a smaller number of multi-item chunks that the participants have formed? This chapter will examine the basic capacity limit of short-term memory and the role of long-term learning in the use of this limit. First, though, a brief history of research on this topic lends perspective.

Brief history of research on interactions between short- and long-term memory

Some researchers believe that a single set of rules applies across all memory procedures (e.g., Crowder, 1993; McGeoch, 1932; Melton, 1963; Nairne, 2002; Surprenant & Neath, this volume). Other researchers believe that a distinction must be made between at least two types of memory, which James (1890) called primary and secondary memory. Primary memory is the limited amount of information that one is actively thinking about, whereas secondary memory is the vast amount of information about the past that one can call up at various times. These types of memory have been known by various names with different theoretical origins (for a review see Cowan, 2005a) but they are commonly called short-term memory and long-term memory (e.g., Atkinson & Shiffrin, 1968).

The basis for the distinction between these two types of memory includes patients with dense amnesia, who respond normally on immediate-recall tasks and yet perform poorly on delayed-recall tasks, in which a distracting task comes between the presentation of a list of items and the recall period (e.g., Baddeley & Warrington, 1970; Squire, 1987; Warrington & Weiskrantz, 1970). In rare cases, the converse occurs; certain patients perform poorly on immediate-recall tasks but perform normally on delayed-recall tasks (Shallice & Warrington, 1970).

In normal participants, the evidence for separate functions of short- and long-term memory has been controversial. Nevertheless, one can find important dissociations between patterns of performance on immediate-versus delayed-recall tasks (for reviews, see Cowan, 1995; Davelaar, Goshen-Gottstein, Ashkenazi, Haarmann, & Usher, 2005). For example, some relevant results involve immediate free recall tasks, in which items can be recalled in any order. Those items near the end of the list (recency items) typically are recalled first, and are recalled at a level that is very high, at least relative to items in the middle of the list. Similarly, items at the beginning of the list (primacy items) are recalled well. However, the results are different when recall is delayed by several seconds filled with distraction. Then, recency items lose their advantage over items in the middle of the list, even though primacy items are still recalled well (Glanzer & Cunitz, 1966; Postman & Phillips, 1965).

The original interpretation of this pattern of results regarding primacy and recency advantages was that the early list items are remembered well because they can be rehearsed with undivided attention at first, allowing a strong long-term memory code to form; whereas later list items are remembered well only if they have not yet been displaced from short-term memory by the time of recall. Later research questioned the interpretation of the recency effect on the basis of experiments in which there were distracting periods between items as well as in the retention interval at the end of the list (e.g., Bjork & Whitten, 1974; Tzeng, 1973). An alternative interpretation was that the important factor was the ratio between the inter-item intervals and the retention interval (the *ratio rule*). However, there are important differences between recency effects in immediate versus delayed recall. For example, differences show up in a final free recall task, in which the participant has to try to recall all of the words from all of the lists that had been used in immediate recall. When ordinary immediate recall was followed by a final free recall test, there was a *negative recency effect* in which items that had been presented in the recency portions of lists in immediate recall were now, in final free recall, remembered less well than items that had been recalled in intermediate list positions (even though the primacy effect remained positive, not negative). Because the recency items had been recalled from short-term memory, they presumably were not deeply encoded in long-term memory, and therefore were not recalled well in final free recall. In contrast, when list items were separated by distracting tasks, a recency effect was obtained but it did not lead to a negative recency effect in final free recall (for a review see Davelaar et al., 2005). So there appear to be multiple sources of recency advantages: one based on retrieval from short-term memory, and another based on distinctiveness of the last few items in a way that aids retrieval from long-term memory.

More generally, the most fundamental reason why investigators have questioned the existence of separate short- and long-term stores is that there are strong similarities between performance patterns in immediate and delayed memory tasks, and there is the possibility of accounting for these similarities in terms of general rules of memory such as cue-driven perform-ance and temporal distinctiveness (e.g., Bjork & Whitten, 1974; Keppel & Underwood, 1962; Nairne, 2002). In order to understand both the similari-ties and the differences between immediate and delayed memory tasks, though, one must carefully consider the relation between short- and long-term memory.

Theorists who believe in a single set of principles for all memory tasks have pointed to interference between items as an important principle. In responding to this type of theorist, Broadbent (1971) stated the following:

There remain to be considered two points urged by interference theory: the existence of effects on short-term memory from previous long-term experiences, and the continuity which seems to exist between memory at long and short periods of time. The first of these must be admitted straight away, and is perfectly consistent with a view of short-term memory as due to recirculation into and out of a decaying buffer storage . . . In general one must beware of concluding that the appearance in short-term memory of an effect known from longer-term studies is evidence for identity of the two situations . . . Only the success or failure of attempts to show differences between the two situations is of interest in distinguishing the theories.

(Broadbent, 1971, pp. 342–343)

He suggested that immediate and delayed memory tasks involve similar mechanisms, but that the contribution of the recirculation of information in and out of a buffer store will be greater in immediate-recall procedures, with a greater influence of retrieval cues and interference in delayed-recall procedures.

Activation and attention: Two components of short-term memory storage?

The possible relation between short- and long-term memory becomes clearer if one distinguishes between different potential components of short-term storage. In the model of Alan Baddeley and colleagues (Baddeley & Hitch, 1974; Baddeley, 1986; Baddeley & Logie, 1999), short-term storage was said to take place in dedicated, code-specific buffers (the phonological loop and the visuospatial sketchpad). In contrast, in the conception of Cowan (1988), similar to some previous papers (e.g., Massaro, 1975; Shiffrin, 1975, 1976), there were said to be two separate types of storage component that cut across domains. One component is the set of currently activated items and features from long-term memory, and a second component is the information currently in the focus of attention. The latter information is a subset of the activated portion of long-term memory, and it may be in a more deeply-analyzed form than information that is activated without the involvement of the focus of attention. For example, suppose that a person is listening to someone on a telephone and, concurrently, ignoring a conversation going on in the room. Both sources of speech will activate features from long-term memory. However, the ignored speech may activate primarily physical features related to the voice quality and the identity of some of the speech phonemes, whereas the attended speech is more likely to activate long-term memory features related to the lexical identity and meaning of the speech, in addition to physical features. The information in the focus of attention is presumably categorical information and that is not true of all of the information in the activated portion of long-term memory, although items that were attended a few seconds ago may remain temporarily active in the more categorical form.

One source of evidence in favor of the type of processing that we have suggested comes from experiments on selective listening, in which two different messages are presented to the two ears through headphones and the message presented to one ear is to be attended (monitored or repeated). Cherry (1953) found that people do not notice and cannot recall much of the information presented to the ignored message, although changes in physical features, such as the speaker's voice, are usually noticed. Moray (1959) then found that, in an exception to this pattern, people do sometimes notice their own name presented in the channel to be ignored. However, Conway, Cowan, and Bunting (2001) found that it is most often individuals with low working memory span who notice their names in the ignored channel. Given a great deal of other evidence relating low working memory span to the relatively poor control of attention (e.g., Kane, Bleckley, Conway, & Engle, 2001; Kane & Engle, 2003), Conway et al. suggested that noticing one's own name may occur only in individuals who do not have very good control of attention, which may sometimes wander to the channel that is supposed to be ignored.

The overall concept, then, is that the focus of attention is the core of primary memory and that the activated portion of long-term memory is its fringe. One difference between these two components would be that the focus of attention would be limited to just a few chunks of information at a time (normally 3 to 5 chunks in adults; see Cowan, 2001), whereas the activated portion of long-term memory would be limited only by interference from other stimuli with similar features, and possibly by decay over time.

The processing of new links between items in short-term memory

One problem with the conception of short-term memory as comprising the activated portion of long-term memory is that, taken literally, it cannot account for everything that must be held in short-term memory. Often, it is the serial order of items or the particular new associations between items that must be remembered, and such new information does not exist within the previously learned knowledge stored in long-term memory. For example, one might need to store the association between each item in a list and its serial position, between adjacent items in a list, or between each object in a spatial array and its location. One might have to save associations between features that are coded quite differently, such as associations between names and faces in a group of people. This problem was noted by Cowan (1995, 1999) and also by Baddeley (2000).

Cowan (1999, 2001, 2005a, 2005b) suggested that new associations or links between elements are stored as a specific function of the focus of attention, a point that will be explained further a bit later on, in conjunction with Figure 5.2. Baddeley (2000) saw these new links as one of the main justifications for a new component in his model of working memory, the episodic buffer. It could hold associations between elements that could not be held in the other two buffers (cf. Allen & Baddeley, this volume). One important question is how similar or different these two theoretical views really are.

One might suggest that the episodic buffer is entirely a function of the focus of attention, in which case the two theoretical approaches would not differ. Another possibility is that what is taken as the result of an episodic buffer is actually a composite of information in the focus of attention and the preservation of associations in newly-formed long-term memory traces.

Recent information from amnesic individuals suggests that there may be something more to the episodic buffer, outside of either the focus of attention or long-term memory. In particular, Cowan, Beschin, and Della Sala (2004a) found that some densely amnesic individuals could remember considerable information for up to an hour in the absence of any interference (in a quiet, dark room), even on trials in which they slept during this retention interval. This suggests that they must have used some sort of storage mechanism outside of the focus of attention that does not depend on long-term memory, at least not as we normally think of it. This theoretically could be the same as an episodic buffer. Although we will not pursue that question further, we provide evidence and ideas suggesting that, in normal individuals, immediate memory performance can be accounted for by a combination of information in the focus of attention and activated elements of long-term memory, if the latter includes the results of rapid long-term learning of new associations.

Evidence on long-term memory contributions to capacity limits

Evidence, Part 1: Basic capacity limits

Given that long-term memorization can be used to increase the size of chunks to be recalled in an immediate-memory task, there is no practical limit on how much can be recalled. This point was dramatically demonstrated by Ericsson, Chase, and Faloon (1980). They studied an individual who could remember only about seven digits at a time, like most people; but, in the course of a year of practice, his immediate-memory span for digits increased to about 80. This appeared to happen through a process in which he learned to group several digits together on the basis of past knowledge of athletic times, supplemented by other knowledge (e.g., 89.5 could be remembered as the age of a very old man). That process allowed him to retain lists of up to about 20 digits. Then he mastered a process of grouping the multi-digit groups together into higher-order super-groups, bringing the span up to about 80.

Because of this sort of finding, researchers sometimes have maintained that there is no basic capacity limit. However, that conclusion does not follow from the data. One could recall any number of items based on a higher-order grouping, and there still could be a basic limit to how many groups can be retained at once. Cowan (2001) examined a wide variety of experimental situations in which it seemed reasonable to assume that items could not be grouped, for one reason or another (e.g., because they could not be fully attended and rehearsed at the time of their presentation). This can occur when the items are presented quickly in a list of unpredictable length, when they are presented in a multiple-item simultaneous array, or when they are presented along with a secondary task that suppresses rehearsal or causes distraction. In such circumstances, each item recalled should represent a separate, 1-item chunk in memory. It appeared that, across many different situations of this general type, a common limit of 3 to 5 items applies in young adults. Thus, the hypothesis emerging from this review was that the basic capacity limit is in the range of 3 to 5 chunks.

Evidence, Part 2: Chunk limits and length limits in verbal memory

The limitation in the evidence described by Cowan (2001) is that the capacity limit was observed entirely with 1-item chunks. It remained possible that the capacity limit would depend on the size of the chunks. To rule out this possibility and establish a more general capacity limit, Cowan, Chen, and Rouder (2004b) and Chen and Cowan (2005) took a different approach. Instead of preventing new chunks from being formed, the process of chunking was carefully monitored.

It had already been shown that associations between items can assist in short-term recall (Stuart & Hulme, 2000) and that the increased availability of prior knowledge about the associations between items tends to increase the size of chunks rather than the number of chunks recalled (Tulving & Patkau, 1962). For a controlled investigation, Cowan et al. (2004b) used a training session in which words were presented a variable number of times, singly or in consistent pairs, to assess the effects of pairing. Memory was then tested in serial recall of 8-item lists that included pairs that had been used in a particular amount of associative training, and in cued recall. In that study, which will be presented in greater detail later, the basic findings were (1) that both serial and cued recall improved as a function of the number of prior training exposures to the consistent word pairings, and (2) that the increase in serial recall could be attributed entirely to an increase in the proportion of recalled chunks comprising two words rather than one.

The number of chunks recalled (2-item pairs plus singletons) did not appear to increase with training. This conclusion of Cowan et al. (2004b) was dependent on a model that was used to estimate how often the recall of two items in a pair could be interpreted as recall of a single, 2-item chunk as opposed to the separate recall of the two items comprising the pair as two 1-item chunks. The model suggested that the recall of two items in a pair that was familiar from the training session almost always could be interpreted as the recall of a single 2-item chunk. The number of chunks recalled averaged about 3.5 across training conditions, closely in line with the expectations of Cowan (2001) based on a review of very different procedures.

Chen and Cowan (2005) addressed the issue of boundary conditions for capacity limits in serial and free recall. In serial recall at least, there is a large body of work suggesting that the limit in recall is not so much in the number of chunks to be recalled, but rather in the phonological length of the list to be recalled. Baddeley, Thomson, and Buchanan (1975) found that memory for lists of multisyllabic words was poorer than memory for lists of an equivalent number of monosyllabic words; memory was equivalent to the number of words that could be recalled in about 2 s. The theoretical explanation given in that paper was that a phonological form of memory lasts about 2 s and that an individual can recall as much as he or she can rehearse in a repeating loop before it decays. Although the existence of time-based decay is controversial (e.g., Lewandowsky, Duncan, & Brown, 2004; Lovatt, Avons, & Masterson, 2002; Mueller, Seymour, Kieras, & Meyer, 2003), the finding of the word length effect based on how much phono-logical material is in each word in the list is highly replicable, being found even by those who question the existence of a time-based effect (Service, 1998; Tolan & Tehan, 2005). A word length effect has been obtained also in free recall (Turner & Engle, 1989). The issue becomes, then, when a chunk capacity limit applies and when a length limit applies instead.

Chen and Cowan (2005) addressed the issue by manipulating the length of lists composed of singletons or well-learned pairs. In the training con-dition, the entire set of singletons and pairs was re-presented over and over until the participant performed 100% successfully on the set. On each training trial, a word was presented that was either a singleton or the first word in a pair that had already been presented. The correct response was to recall the associated word, if any, and otherwise to indicate that the word was a singleton. Responses were typed into the computer; the words were easy enough that remembering the spelling was not an important issue. Then feedback was received. For pairs, the complete pair was presented as feedback.

The training session was followed by serial or free recall. Each list was composed entirely of singletons or of learned pairs. Given the high criterion of training, it was possible to assume that, when a pair within a list was recalled, it was recalled as a single, two-word chunk. Therefore, it was possible to compare performance on lists of short chunks (singletons) and lists of long chunks (learned pairs) to assess an analogue to the word length effect.

One comparison was for lists of 6 learned pairs. If a chunk limit governs performance, the proportion of words correct on such lists should be equivalent to that for lists of 6 singletons. If, in contrast, a length limit governs performance, the proportion of words correct on lists of 6 learned pairs should be equivalent to that for 12 singletons (a much lower level than for 6 singletons). Similarly, lists of 4 learned pairs were examined and, according to a chunk limit, the proportion of words correct on such lists should be equivalent to that for lists of 4 singletons. If a length limit governs performance, the proportions should be similar for 4 learned pairs and 8 singletons (much lower than for 4 singletons).

For free recall of the longer lists, a chunk capacity limit worked very well. Lists of 6 learned pairs were recalled at about the same proportion of words correct as lists of 6 singletons. The same was true for serial recall when it was scored in a free manner, not deducting points for words recalled in the incorrect serial positions. However, for serial recall of shorter lists strictly scored, a length limit applied instead. With that scoring of serial recall, lists of 4 learned pairs were recalled only at about the same proportion of words correct as lists of 8 singletons. Other conditions produced results that were intermediate, not conforming closely to either prediction. These intermediate results were obtained for free recall (or free scoring of serial recall) of the shorter lists, and for serial recall (strictly scored) of the longer lists.

Figure 5.1 shows one way in which these results might be explained. A mechanism could exist that holds a limited number of chunks at once; it could be the focus of attention that holds the information (Cowan, 1988, 1995, 2001). A phonologically based storage and rehearsal mechanism, such as the phonological loop mechanism of Baddeley (1986), may come into play primarily when items have to be recalled in the correct serial order, although it theoretically also might be of some use in retaining a limited amount of item information. Information from both sources would be considered in recall, and the weight given to each mechanism would depend on its suitability to the task. The phonological mechanism is best suited when one needs to repeat a sequence lasting about 2 s in order, and the chunk mechanism is better suited when order is not needed and/or the sequence is too long for the phonological mechanism. Also, the availability of within-list structure (e.g., lists of mixed short and long words: Cowan, Baddeley, Elliott, & Norris, 2003; Hulme, Surprenant, Bireta, Stuart, & Neath, 2004) may encourage the use of the chunk-based mechanism because the structure can be used to form groups, whereas phonological memory may be more useful when the list is homogeneous.

In the view of Cowan (1999, 2001, 2005a, 2005b), the focus of attention is used to remember information, and the process by which this occurs involves new long-term memory formation, as illustrated in Figure 5.2. Each panel of the figure shows one state of the memory system, which always includes two components of short-term memory: the activated portion of long-term memory, and the focus of attention as a subset of that activated portion. As shown in Panel 1, new inputs result in the activation of elements in long-term memory. These elements may represent only some of the features by which the stimuli can be encoded (e.g., physical but not semantic features, as is often the case for unattended stimuli). Associations

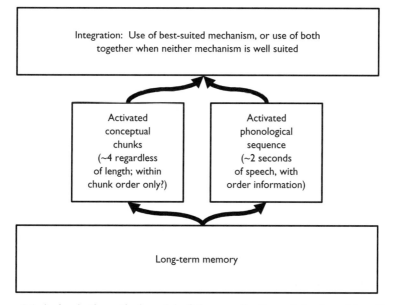

Figure 5.1 A simple theoretical model of the coordination of chunk and length limits in immediate recall.

to the stimuli also may be activated (the basis of priming), or features may be activated through internal thoughts alone. As shown in Panel 2, some of the activated features may enter the focus of attention. Panel 3 shows that concurrently attended features are linked together to form a new structure. Finally, as shown in Panel 4, the new structure is available for memory responses, in either short- or long-term memory tasks. This structure may be sufficient for retaining serial order information for the items within a newly formed chunk, but it would be deficient in between-chunk serial order information.

The phonological storage mechanism may be another instance of the use of the focus of attention to assemble a new structure in long-term memory. It is clear that a phonological storage mechanism is involved in learning new vocabulary (Baddeley, Gathercole, & Papagno, 1998). Perhaps the mechanism contributing to immediate recall is one that uses the temporal aspect of language to avoid the capacity limit. Suppose a list of six words, A-B-C-D-E-F, is presented. It might be that A-B-C can be in the focus of attention at one time, forming a structure that, when followed by D, can be knitted into A-B-C-D; and so on until the entire list is rapidly assembled into a new, united long-term memory representation even though six separate elements would not fit into the focus of attention. The limit on formation of that sort of associative structure might depend on the assembly taking place fast enough so that the earlier segments remain available throughout the process; hence the mechanism is limited to the

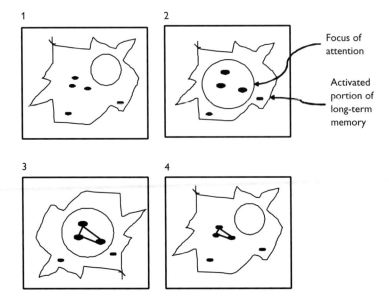

Figure 5.2 A depiction of how new associations between items may be remembered. (1) Elements are activated in long-term memory. (2) Concurrent with this activation or slightly afterward, these particular activated elements happen to be represented in the focus of attention concurrently. (3) New associations are formed between elements in the focus of attention, resulting in a new structure. (4) The new structure quickly becomes a new entry into long-term memory and is available for responses in short- or long-term memory tasks.

amount that can be recited in about 2 s. Any such newly-formed long-term memory representation will be very susceptible to subsequent interference, given that it shares many properties with other lists in the experiment. However, it may allow immediate recall because there has not yet been interference with a structure that is now held as a single chunk.

The chunk-storage mechanism would hold items to be recalled, some of which are multi-word chunks. The phonological mechanism would provide additional cues to a time-limited number of items in the list along with strong cues to their order. For items held in the chunk-storage mechanism (such as the focus of attention), order information could be forgotten without the loss of item information, but that event is less likely for infor-mation held in the phonological storage mechanism because the structure is explicitly serial.

This model helps to explain why a chunk limit governs recall for long lists in free recall (because the phonological ordering mechanism was not critical), whereas a length limit governs recall for shorter lists in serial recall (because the ordering mechanism is both critical and useful) (Chen & Cowan, 2005). Lists of more than about 8 syllables would exceed the limits of the phonological mechanism and would especially hurt order information. Intermediate results would occur when both the chunk-limited mechanism and the phonological storage mechanism are used and contribute to recall. Both meaningful chunks and phonological representations may be used for both item and order information, but to different degrees, with more extensive item information based on chunks and more coherent order information based on phonology. We are engaged in further research to determine how the mechanisms interact.

Evidence, Part 3: On-line chunk formation and storage in long-term memory

The data of Cowan et al. (2004b) can be used to explore further the interaction between short- and long-term memory stores. A reanalysis of the results of Cowan et al. (2004b) supports this theoretical account. The procedure of that study needs further explanation before the results are presented. A training phase was followed by a serial-recall phase (recall of 8-word lists) and a cued-recall phase (recall of the second word in each pair, given the first). In Experiment 1, list recall came before cued recall whereas, in Experiment 2, it was the reverse. In the training phase that began the experiment, the total number of presentations of a word was four. Some words were presented four times as singletons. Others were presented three times as singletons and once in a pair; twice as singletons and twice in consistent pairs; or four times in consistent pairs. These comprised the 0-, 1-, 2-, and 4-pairing conditions, respectively. They differ in the number of presentations of each word pairing, but not in the number of presentations of each word itself. There also were words in a control condition that were not included in the training phase at all.

In cued recall, the task was to recall the second word in a learned pair, given the first. Participants in Experiment 2 had no prior exposure to the pairings in the unstudied-word control or the 0-pairing condition (given that the cued-recall test came before list recall), whereas participants in Experiment 1 had seen the words in these two conditions paired together previously one time, namely within the list presentations.

In serial recall, the 8 items in a list were presented in pairs. The words in each of the four pairs within a list were presented concurrently for 2 s, with the words on both sides of the center of the screen, and with each successive pair replacing the previous one. All of the pairs in a list were drawn from pairs used in one particular training phase although, in the 0-paired and unstudied-control conditions, the particular pairings themselves had not been seen in the training phase. In the unstudied-control condition, the words had not been seen in training, either.

The training manipulation was highly effective. In both experiments, cued recall increased steadily with the number of training exposures to the pairs (0 through 4; the no-study control condition produced results slightly lower than the 0-paired condition). Cowan et al. (2004b) plotted the results

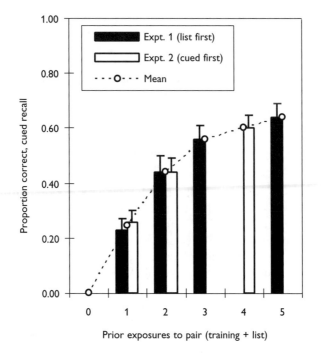

Figure 5.3. The cued-recall results of Cowan et al. (2004b), redrawn to show the proportion correct as a function of the total number of prior presentations of each pair, including presentations received either in training itself (in both experiments) or in a serial-recall task when it came before cued recall (in Experiment 1 only). The number of presentations that preceded cued recall was 0, 1, 2, or 4 in Experiment 2 (white bars) because of training presentations of the pair, whereas it was 1, 2, 3, or 5 in Experiment 1 (black bars) because of the additional contribution of a list presentation before cued recall. Notice the smooth learning function. Error bars are standard errors.

as a function of the number of paired presentations in training. However, a more accurate impression of how the pairs were learned (as measured in cued recall) could be obtained by taking into account the further presentation of word pairs within list recall, which preceded cued recall in Experiment 1. The cued-recall data of Cowan et al. (2004b) are re-plotted in Figure 5.3 with list presentations taken into account. This adds one presentation to every condition in Experiment 1, but not Experiment 2. (In the 0-paired condition in Experiment 2, there was no basis for cued recall, unlike Experiment 1 in which the pairing had been seen once, in list recall.) One can see from the figure that the effect of pair presentation within a list in serial recall caused about the same amount of learning as in the training phase. The overall learning function is smooth and decelerating. This experimental example approximates the practical example given earlier, of people rapidly learning grouping information for telephone numbers.

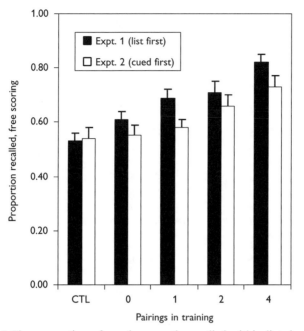

Figure 5.4 The proportion of words correctly recalled within lists in Cowan et al. (2004b) in each training condition, with credit given for each recalled word regardless of the serial position in which it was recalled (free scoring). CTL = unstudied-control condition. The list-recall task was presented either before cued recall (Experiment 1, black bars) or after cued recall (Experiment 2, white bars). Error bars are standard errors.

Figure 5.4 shows the proportion of words correctly recalled from lists in each training condition used by Cowan et al. (2004b), based on free scoring of serial recall (i.e., full credit for words recalled even in the wrong serial position). It is clear from this figure that learned associations between words did contribute to list recall when the lists included learned pairs.

One finding that warrants further discussion is that the proportion of words recalled was slightly higher in Experiment 1, in which the list-recall procedure came before cued recall, than in Experiment 2, in which the list-recall procedure came only after cued recall (Figure 5.4). Apparently, then, a cued-recall test did not help list recall. In this experiment, there was no feedback within cued recall (or within list recall, for that matter). Therefore, it appears that retrieving what was already known, in cued recall, did not reinforce knowledge of the pair; at least, not in a way that was of discernible use in list recall. This is in contrast to the finding that *presentation* of a pair in list recall did aid cued recall (see Figure 5.3).

Further supporting this conclusion are data on the rates of success with individual pairs of words in list and cued recall in both experiments, shown in Table 5.1. First, successes on both the first and second item in a pair in

Table 5.1 Frequency of cases in which each item within a list pair was recalled along with successful or unsuccessful cued recall for the second item in that pair

	Cued recall		Fisher's Exact Test p
List recall	Successful	Unsuccessful	Lax (strict)
	Experiment 1 (list recall, then cued)		
First item			
recalled	305 (261)	170 (150)	.001 (.07 marginal)
not recalled	47 (91)	54 (74)	
Second item			
recalled	324 (291)	177 (145)	.000 (.000)
not recalled	28 (61)	47 (79)	
	Experiment 2 (cued recall, then list)		
First item			
recalled	204 (164)	237 (197)	.01 (n.s.)
not recalled	45 (85)	90 (130)	
Second item			
recalled	200 (176)	272 (235)	n.s. (n.s.)
not recalled	49 (73)	55 (92)	

Note: Primary data, lax scoring of item recall; in parentheses, strict serial order scoring. The data are collapsed across the 1-, 2-, and 4-pairing conditions. Significance in Fisher's Exact Test here indicates that rates of success in list and cued recall tasks were associated.

list recall were scored free, without regard to serial order. When list recall preceded cued recall (Experiment 1), recall of the first and second items in a pair were both associated with success for the same word pair in cued recall. In contrast, when cued recall preceded list recall (Experiment 2), success on the first, but not on the second, item in a pair in list recall was associated with prior success in cued recall. A strict serial order scoring of list recall produced a statistical pattern that differed only in that the associations with the first item in a pair were no longer significant.

The associations in Table 5.1 need not indicate learning effects, inasmuch as certain words may just be more memorable than others in either list-recall or cued-recall procedures. However, the finding that the associations with the second word in a pair in list recall were significant only when the list procedure was presented first (i.e., in Experiment 1, but not Experiment 2) seems to reinforce the notion that presentation of the item caused learning, not its recall. Thus, in cued recall, only the first item in a pair is presented, and successful cued recall did not cause the second item to be remembered better in list recall.

This pattern of results seems to go against an often-observed effect in which items are recalled better when generated by the participant than when actually presented (e.g., Hendry & Tehan, 2005). However, it could indicate that, in Experiment 2, the frequent mistakes committed during

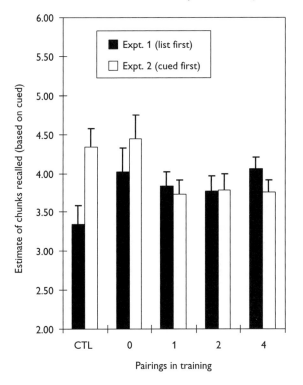

Figure 5.5 Number of chunks per list recalled in each training condition by participants in Cowan et al. (2004b). CTL = unstudied-control condition. The list-recall task was presented either before cued recall (Experiment 1, black bars) or after cued recall (Experiment 2, white bars). The chunks were estimated here under the assumption that the proportion correct in cued recall in a particular training condition mirrors the proportion of pairs forming 2-item chunks in lists. Error bars are standard errors. There are reasons to believe that the most valid capacity estimate occurs in Experiment 1 for the 0- through 4-pairing conditions (see text).

cued recall and the absence of feedback discouraged participants from using the cued-recall episode as a source of information for the subsequent list-recall task.

Finally, Figure 5.5 is an examination of the number of chunks recalled. (It uses free scoring of item recall whereas, if strict serial order scoring is used, the estimates are similar but lower, ranging from 2.2 to 3.2.) In the article of Cowan et al. (2004b), a multinomial model was used to estimate what proportion of the recalled word pairs actually were two-word chunks, as opposed to being two words separately recalled. Here, instead of that multinomial-model-based approach, cued recall was used to validate the estimate of chunking. In particular, the mean number of chunks recalled in each adjacent pair of odd–even serial positions i and $i+1$ was judged according to Equation 1:

$$chunks_{[i, (i+1)]} = [pc_i + pc_{(i+1)}] / (1 + cued_{[i, (i+1)]}) \tag{1}$$

where pc_i and $pc_{(i+1)}$ are the proportions correct in list recall at Serial Position i and $i+1$ according to a free scoring, and $cued_{[i, (i+1)]}$ is the proportion correct in cued recall for this word pair. If list recall at these serial positions is perfect, for example, then the number of chunks recalled in those two positions could be as high as 2 (if $cued_{[i, (i+1)]} = 0$) or as low as 1 (if $cued_{[i, (i+1)]} = 1$). In the latter case, the two words in the pair are consistently considered to contribute to a single 2-word chunk. The formula works essentially by dividing *items recalled* by *items per chunk* to arrive at an estimate of *chunks*. The better cued recall is, presumably the more items per chunk there are, the allowed range being from 1 to 2.

Figure 5.5 shows that the number of chunks recalled stayed roughly constant across training conditions and across experiments, except for the unstudied-control and 0-pairing conditions. There are several factors underlying discrepancies in these conditions. First, the assumption embodied in Equation 1, that cued recall reflects the amount of long-term learning available at the time of list recall, should produce an underestimate in Experiment 2 because its cued-recall test cannot take into account any learning of pairings that occurred during the list-recall presentation itself, as it followed cued recall. The effect of neglecting learning of pairings during the list presentation itself is most important in the unstudied-control and 0-pairing conditions because, in those conditions, the list presentation provided the only possible exposure to the pairing in the experimental session.

In Experiment 1, which presumably yields the best estimates of capacity because of the considerations just mentioned, the capacity estimate was fairly constant across the 0- through 4-pairing conditions. The fact that it was lower in the unstudied-control condition than in the 0-studied condition suggests that there was a benefit from the training exposure to isolated words but that it did not benefit list recall as much as it benefited subsequent cued recall. In Experiment 2, in which there was no basis at all to retrieve the paired word in cued recall in the unstudied-control or 0-pairing conditions, the estimates of chunks recalled from the list were probably inflated by this method of estimation, inasmuch as the estimate of words per chunk was in principle limited to 1.0, probably unrealistically.

To summarize, we have discussed a theoretical framework to examine capacity limits in a serial-recall task using long-term learning information from a cued-recall task (Cowan et al., 2004b). This framework suggests certain boundary conditions for an accurate estimate. The boundary conditions were best met for 0-, 1-, 2-, and 4-pairing conditions in Experiment 1 because the words were made equally familiar across these conditions and the cued-recall data could take into account on-line memorization of word pairings during the list presentation itself. The capacity limits across these conditions ranged narrowly between about 3.75 and 4 chunks, convergent with results from a previous literature review on memory for sets of 1-item chunks (Cowan, 2001).

Summary and conclusions

This chapter addresses a basic question about the nature of short-term or working memory. Cowan (1988) suggested that it consists of the activated portion of long-term memory along with a capacity-limited subset of that activated memory, the focus of attention. The two components supposedly serve complementary roles, with deeper perceptual analyses taking place in the focus of attention. A problem with this view (noted by Cowan, 1995, 1999) is how to understand the formation of new links between elements in a short-term memory task when those elements have not previously been linked in long-term memory.

Baddeley (2000) suggested that there is a mechanism that can hold new links of diverse types, the episodic buffer. A way to accomplish what the episodic buffer does, but without adding a new component to the model of Cowan (1988), is to add the assumption that new long-term memories can form on line during a short-term or working memory task, contributing to performance (Cowan, 2005a, 2005b). We have demonstrated that this is possible in a reanalysis of results from the serial-recall and cued-recall tasks of Cowan et al. (2004b). Learning of word pairings from a training phase summated with learning from list presentations to produce a smooth learning curve (Figure 5.3), and this long-term learning proved to be a good basis upon which to estimate the use of multi-word chunks in recall. Using that basis, evidence of a constant capacity limit of about 4 chunks was obtained. Learning changed the frequency of recalling longer (2-word) as opposed to shorter (1-word) chunks, but did not appear to influence the basic capacity of short-term memory expressed in chunks. One of the functions of the focus of attention may be to allow items that are represented concurrently to be bound into new structures (i.e., multi-item chunks).

Other evidence of the use of long-term memory to bind items together in short-term or working memory tasks also exists in the literature (e.g., Stuart & Hulme, 2000, and in this volume). One source of evidence, very different from what we have been discussing, comes from the examination by Cowan et al. (2003b) of response timing in working memory tasks. In the tasks examined, each processing episode terminates in a verbal item to be retained for subsequent recall after several processing episodes. This type of task shows a high relation to cognitive aptitudes so it is important to learn what processes operate in such tasks. When the items to be recalled could be remembered on the basis of recall cues from the processing (because they were the final words of sentences to be comprehended), Cowan et al. found that the response times were much longer than when the processing episodes served as poor cues to recall (screens with objects to be counted, all looking much like one another) or when there were no processing episodes (in digit span). These response times suggest that recall cues from long-term memory can be used in working memory tasks. Specifically, sentences may be retrieved to provide cues for retrieval of the sentence-final words in reading and listening span tasks.

One complication for the model of Cowan (1988) is that amnesic individuals presumably form new links between items in short-term memory, but nevertheless do not save the information in a way that allows it to be remembered later. Somehow, this needs to be accounted for in terms of neural mechanisms. A large amount of research has suggested that memory representations are formed in diverse cortical regions, whereas the conscious retrieval of those memories at first depends on temporal lobe regions surrounding and including the hippocampus (e.g., Cowan, 1995, 2005a; Schacter, 1989; Squire, 1987). However, the focus of attention itself involves frontal and parietal areas (as reviewed in these same articles). If the focus of attention is intact in amnesic individuals, then it would be expected that new links between items could be formed as usual without becoming available for later long-term recall.

We thus propose that although the mechanisms of short-term memory are separate from those of long-term memory, they are closely related. Everything in memory has to be returned to short-term memory in order to be recalled. As an analogy, cooked food typically should be warm at the time it is served, either from its initial cooking (analogous to short-term retrieval) or from re-heating (analogous to long-term retrieval). Similarly, the rules of short-term memory should influence even long-term recall (and, for evidence suggesting that they do, see Nairne & Neath, 2001).

One purpose of the focus of attention may be to hold information in a form that is relatively immune to the types of interference that otherwise can occur in both short- and long-term retrieval (Cowan, Johnson, & Saults, 2005; Halford, Maybery, & Bain, 1988). Overall, the most fundamental distinction within the memory system may not be the short- versus long-term memory distinction, but rather the distinction between the retrieval of information from the current focus of attention and other types of memory retrieval (Cowan, 1995, 2005a).

Acknowledgments

Preparation of this chapter was supported by NIH Grant R01 HD-21338.

References

Atkinson, R. C., & Shiffrin, R. M. (1968). Human memory: A proposed system and its control processes. In K. W. Spence & J. T. Spence (Eds.), *The psychology of learning and motivation: Advances in research and theory* (Vol. 2, pp. 89–195). New York: Academic Press.

Baddeley, A. D. (1986). *Working memory*. Oxford Psychology Series #11. Oxford: Clarendon Press.

Baddeley, A. (2000). The episodic buffer: A new component of working memory? *Trends in Cognitive Sciences, 4*, 417–423.

Baddeley, A., Gathercole, S., & Papagno, C. (1998). The phonological loop as a language learning device. *Psychological Review, 105*, 158–173.

Baddeley, A., & Hitch, G. J. (1974). Working memory. In G. Bower (Ed.), *Recent advances in learning and motivation* (Vol. VIII, pp. 47–89). New York: Academic Press.

Baddeley, A. D., & Logie, R. H. (1999). Working memory: The multiple-component model. In A. Miyake & P. Shah (Eds.), *Models of working memory: Mechanisms of active maintenance and executive control* (pp. 28–61). Cambridge, UK: Cambridge University Press.

Baddeley, A. D., Thomson, N., & Buchanan, M. (1975). Word length and the structure of short-term memory. *Journal of Verbal Learning and Verbal Behavior, 14*, 575–589.

Baddeley, A. D., & Warrington, E. K. (1970). Amnesia and the distinction between long- and short-term memory. *Journal of Verbal Learning and Verbal Behavior, 9*, 176–189.

Bjork, R. A., & Whitten, W. B. (1974). Recency-sensitive retrieval processes in long-term free recall. *Cognitive Psychology, 6*, 173–189.

Broadbent, D. E. (1971). *Decision and stress*. London: Academic Press.

Chen, Z., & Cowan, N. (2005). Chunk limits and length limits in immediate recall: A reconciliation. *Journal of Experimental Psychology: Learning, Memory, and Cognition, 31*, 1235–1249.

Cherry, E. C. (1953). Some experiments on the recognition of speech, with one and with two ears. *Journal of the Acoustical Society of America, 25*(5), 975–979.

Conway, A. R. A., Cowan, N., & Bunting, M. F. (2001). The cocktail party phenomenon revisited: The importance of working memory capacity. *Psychonomic Bulletin & Review, 8*, 331–335.

Cowan, N. (1988). Evolving conceptions of memory storage, selective attention, and their mutual constraints within the human information processing system. *Psychological Bulletin, 104*, 163–191.

Cowan, N. (1995). *Attention and memory: An integrated framework*. Oxford Psychology Series, No. 26. New York: Oxford University Press.

Cowan, N. (1999). An embedded-processes model of working memory. In A. Miyake & P. Shah (Eds.), *Models of working memory: Mechanisms of active maintenance and executive control* (pp. 62–101). Cambridge, UK: Cambridge University Press.

Cowan, N. (2001). The magical number 4 in short-term memory: A reconsideration of mental storage capacity. *Behavioral and Brain Sciences, 24*, 87–114.

Cowan, N. (2005a). *Working memory capacity*. New York: Psychology Press.

Cowan, N. (2005b). Working-memory capacity limits in a theoretical context. In C. Izawa & N. Ohta (Eds.), *Human learning and memory: Advances in theory and applications* (pp. 155–175). The 4th Tsukuba international conference on memory. Mahwah, NJ: Lawrence Erlbaum Associates, Inc.

Cowan, N., Baddeley, A. D., Elliott, E. M., & Norris, J. (2003). List composition and the word length effect in immediate recall: A comparison of localist and globalist assumptions. *Psychonomic Bulletin & Review, 10*, 74–79.

Cowan, N., Beschin, N., & Della Sala, S. (2004a). Verbal recall in amnesiacs under conditions of diminished retroactive interference. *Brain*, *127*, 825–834.

Cowan, N., Chen, Z., & Rouder, J. N. (2004b). Constant capacity in an immediate serial-recall task: A logical sequel to Miller (1956). *Psychological Science*, *15*, 634–640.

Cowan, N., Johnson, T. D., & Saults, J. S. (2005). Capacity limits in list item recognition: Evidence from proactive interference. *Memory*, *13*, 293–299.

Cowan, N., Towse, J. N., Hamilton, Z., Saults, J. S., Elliott, E. M., Lacey, J. F., et al. (2003). Children's working-memory processes: A response-timing analysis. *Journal of Experimental Psychology: General*, *132*, 113–132.

Crowder, R. G. (1993). Short-term memory: Where do we stand? *Memory & Cognition*, *21*, 142–145.

Davelaar, E. J., Goshen-Gottstein, Y., Ashkenazi, A., Haarmann, H. J., & Usher, M. (2005). The demise of short-term memory revisited: Empirical and computational investigations of recency effects. *Psychological Review*, *112*, 3–42.

Ericsson, K. A., Chase, W. G., & Faloon, S. (1980). Acquisition of a memory skill. *Science*, *208*, 1181–1182.

Glanzer, M., & Cunitz, A. R. (1966). Two storage mechanisms in free recall. *Journal of Verbal Learning and Verbal Behavior*, *5*, 351–360.

Halford, G. S., Maybery, M. T., & Bain, J. D. (1988). Set-size effects in primary memory: An age-related capacity limitation? *Memory & Cognition*, *16*, 480–487.

Hendry, L., & Tehan, G. (2005). An item/order trade-off explanation of word length and generation effects. *Memory*, *13*, 364–371.

Hulme, C., Surprenant, A., Bireta, T. J., Stuart, G., & Neath, I. (2004). Abolishing the word-length effect. *Journal of Experimental Psychology: Learning, Memory, and Cognition*, *30*, 98–106.

James, W. (1890). *The principles of psychology*. New York: Henry Holt.

Kane, M. J., Bleckley, M. K., Conway, A. R. A., & Engle, R. W. (2001). A controlled-attention view of working-memory capacity. *Journal of Experimental Psychology: General*, *130*, 169–183.

Kane, M. J., & Engle, R. W. (2003). Working-memory capacity and the control of attention: The contributions of goal neglect, response competition, and task set to Stroop interference. *Journal of Experimental Psychology: General*, *132*, 47–70.

Keppel, G., & Underwood, B. J. (1962). Proactive inhibition in short-term retention of single items. *Journal of Verbal Learning and Verbal Behavior*, *1*, 153–161.

Lewandowsky, S., Duncan, M., & Brown, G. D. A. (2004). Time does not cause forgetting in short-term serial recall. *Psychonomic Bulletin & Review*, *11*, 771–790.

Lovatt, P., Avons, S. E., & Masterson, J. (2002). Output decay in immediate serial recall: Speech time revisited. *Journal of Memory and Language*, *46*, 227–243.

Massaro, D. W. (1975). *Experimental psychology and information processing*. Chicago: Rand McNally.

McGeoch, J. A. (1932). Forgetting and the law of disuse. *Psychological Review*, *39*, 352–370.

Melton, A. W. (1963). Implications of short-term memory for a general theory of memory. *Journal of Verbal Learning and Verbal Behavior*, *2*, 1–21.

Miller, G. A. (1956). The magical number seven, plus or minus two: Some limits on our capacity for processing information. *Psychological Review*, *63*, 81–97.

Moray, N. (1959). Attention in dichotic listening: Affective cues and the influence of instructions. *Quarterly Journal of Experimental Psychology*, *11*, 56–60.

Mueller, S. T., Seymour, T. L., Kieras, D. E., & Meyer, D. E. (2003). Theoretical implications of articulatory duration, phonological similarity, and phonological complexity in verbal working memory. *Journal of Experimental Psychology: Learning, Memory, and Cognition, 6*, 1353–1380.

Nairne, J. S. (2002). Remembering over the short-term: The case against the standard model. *Annual Review of Psychology, 53*, 53–81.

Nairne, J. S., & Neath, I. (2001). Long-term memory span. *Behavioral and Brain Sciences, 24*, 134–135.

Postman, L., & Phillips, L. W. (1965). Short-term temporal changes in free recall. *Quarterly Journal of Experimental Psychology, 17*, 132–138.

Schacter, D. L. (1989). On the relation between memory and consciousness: Dissociable interactions and conscious experience. In H. L. Roediger & F. I. M. Craik (Eds.), *Varieties of memory and consciousness: Essays in honor of Endel Tulving.* Hillsdale, NJ: Lawrence Erlbaum Associates, Inc.

Service, E. (1998). The effect of word length on immediate serial recall depends on phonological complexity, not articulatory duration. *Quarterly Journal of Experimental Psychology, 51A*, 283–304.

Shallice, T., & Warrington, E. K. (1970). Independent functioning of verbal memory stores: A neuropsychological study. *Quarterly Journal of Experimental Psychology, 22*, 261–273.

Shiffrin, R. M. (1975). The locus and role of attention in memory systems. In. P. M. A. Rabbitt & S. Dornic (Eds.), *Attention and performance V* (pp. 168–193). New York: Academic Press.

Shiffrin, R. M. (1976). Capacity limitations in information processing, attention, and memory. In W. K. Estes (Ed.), *Handbook of learning and cognitive processes* (pp. 177–236). Hillsdale, NJ: Lawrence Erlbaum Associates, Inc.

Squire, L. R. (1987). *Memory and brain.* New York: Oxford University Press.

Stuart, G., & Hulme, C. (2000). The effects of word co-occurrence on short-term memory: Associative links in long-term memory affect short-term memory performance. *Journal of Experimental Psychology: Learning, Memory, and Cognition, 26*, 796–802.

Tolan, G. A., & Tehan, G. (2005). Is spoken duration a sufficient explanation of the word length effect? *Memory, 13*, 372–379.

Tulving, E., & Patkau, J. E. (1962). Concurrent effects of contextual constraint and word frequency on immediate recall and learning of verbal material. *Canadian Journal of Psychology, 16*, 83–95.

Turner, M. L., & Engle, R. W. (1989). Is working memory capacity task dependent? *Journal of Memory and Language, 28*, 127–154.

Tzeng, O. J. L. (1973). Positive recency effect in a delayed free recall. *Journal of Verbal Learning and Verbal Behavior, 12*, 436–439.

Warrington, E. K., & Weiskrantz, L. (1970). Amnesic syndrome: Consolidation or retrieval? *Nature, 228*, 629–630.

6 A computational model of nonword repetition, immediate serial recall, and nonword learning

Prahlad Gupta

Overview

A computational model is presented that tackles the issue of serial ordering both across word forms (as in list recall) and within word forms (as in nonword repetition). The model was set up to simulate performance in these two tasks. A number of patterns of relationship between performance in these tasks then fell out of the model, including the well-documented correlation between performance in the two tasks, and the typical profile of impairment in the "pure STM" neuropsychological syndrome. The model thus provides a concretely instantiated means of thinking about relationships between list recall and nonword repetition, and has the potential to play a useful role in investigation of these relationships.

Introduction

There is now abundant evidence to suggest that immediate list recall ability, nonword repetition ability, and the learning of new words are related in some way. There is also a measure of agreement that immediate serial recall (ISR) and nonword repetition are both tasks that draw on the mechanisms of phonological short-term memory fairly directly, and that the learning of new words is also in some way supported by phonological short-term memory (e.g., Baddeley, Gathercole, & Papagno, 1998; Brown & Hulme, 1996; Gathercole, Service, Hitch, Adams, & Martin, 1999; Gupta, 2003; Gupta & MacWhinney, 1997). Insofar as this is the case, these abilities constitute a fascinating domain of interaction between short-term and long-term learning and memory systems, and, moreover, one that is fundamental to some of the most centrally human cognitive abilities. However, there is no current widely-accepted mechanistic account of the observed patterns of relationship.

From the point of view of an individual learner, every new word is in effect a nonword when first encountered, and every known word was once a nonword to that learner. Greater facility in processing nonwords would therefore be expected to lead to greater facility in eventually learning them, thus providing intuition for why there might be a relationship between nonword repetition and word learning. But why are immediate list recall and nonword repetition related? – in what sense might immediate repetition of a nonword be a phonological short-term memory task? In thinking about this, it is useful to consider that an auditorily presented nonword is a novel sequence of sounds, in much the same way that the typical list in an ISR task is a novel sequence of words or digits. This raises the possibility that a nonword may literally be processed like a list (i.e., like a novel sequence of speech units) when it is first encountered (Cumming, Page, & Norris, 2003; Gupta, 1996, 2002, 2005; Gupta & MacWhinney, 1997; Gupta, Lipinski, Abbs, & Lin, 2005; Hartley & Houghton, 1996). If this were the case, it would provide a simple explanation of the relationships observed between immediate serial recall and nonword repetition. Moreover, if mechanisms similar to those underlying immediate serial recall are operative in the repetition of nonwords, we would expect to observe serial position effects in repetition of the sequence of sounds comprising nonwords. Following this reasoning, Gupta (2002, 2005; Gupta et al., 2005) examined immediate repetition of individual auditorily presented polysyllabic nonwords, to determine whether repetition accuracy broken down by syllables within the nonwords would manifest primacy and recency; that is, whether the first and last syllables within the nonwords would be repeated more accurately than middle syllables. In a series of experiments, such primacy and recency effects were indeed obtained in repetition of individual nonwords of lengths four through seven syllables. These results are consistent with the idea that similar serial ordering mechanisms are operative in immediate serial recall of lists and in repetition of nonwords, especially when taken together with the considerable body of evidence indicating an association between nonword repetition and list recall.

These results serve, among other things, to emphasize the fact that some sequencing mechanism is needed to encode, maintain, and retrieve the serial order of these components of a nonword. The question then arises of exactly how this mechanism might be related to the mechanism underlying immediate serial recall of lists. Are these mechanisms identical? If so, how? If not, how do they differ? The present chapter describes a computational model that simulates performance in list recall and nonword repetition tasks, and uses these simulations to offer an account of the empirically observed relationships between performance in these tasks.

Functional requirements for a model

What would a model need to address, in order to provide an account of performance in immediate serial recall as well as nonword repetition? To simulate nonword repetition, a model clearly would need to address the serial ordering of sublexical constituents such as syllables/phonemes *within* word forms. That is, it would need, first, to *represent* such sublexical constituents, and second, to provide a means for the encoding and retrieval of their *serial order*. Without this, it could not offer an account of how the novel sequence of sounds comprising a nonword such as *zitricaymus* can be immediately repeated, in sequence. To simulate immediate serial recall of lists of verbal items, a model would clearly need to address the serial ordering of the words constituting the list elements. That is, it would need, first, to *represent* these lexical elements, and second, to provide a means for the encoding and retrieval of their *serial order*. Without this, it could not offer an account of how the novel sequence of words comprising a list such as *cat dog ball chair* can be immediately repeated, in sequence.

To simulate performance in both tasks, therefore, a model would need to incorporate both lexical and sublexical representations, and to provide for serial ordering at both these levels of representation. However, these requirements have not so far been addressed by current models. Although there are now several important and insightful computational models of immediate serial recall (e.g., Botvinick & Plaut, 2006; Brown, Preece, & Hulme, 2000; Burgess & Hitch, 1992, 1999; Hartley & Houghton, 1996; Houghton, 1990; Page & Norris, 1998; Vousden, Brown, & Harley, 2000), and indeed, the present work draws importantly on some of these models, most have been concerned primarily with addressing the numerous phenomena of immediate serial recall per se, rather than with the relationship between immediate serial recall and novel word processing. An exception to this is the work of Burgess and Hitch (1999) which did indeed seek to address this relationship (along with an impressive range of phenomena from ISR per se), but, like other models, it did not address the issue of serial ordering at multiple levels of representation. Addressing this issue is, however, a central motivation of the present work (see also Gupta, 1995, 1996; Gupta & MacWhinney, 1997), which is less concerned with achieving wide coverage of the phenomena of immediate serial recall. The aims of the present work can thus be seen as complementary to those of much existing computational modelling work in the domain of phonological short-term memory. Indeed, the central focus of the present work can be seen as lying precisely at the nexus of short-term memory and long-term memory and serial ordering in the verbal domain.

The current model: Overview

The core conceptualization underlying the present model essentially mirrors the preceding discussion of functional requirements: it incorporates lexical and sublexical levels of representation, and a serial ordering mechanism that provides for the encoding, maintenance and retrieval of sequences that are activated at these levels. Thus, as shown in Figure 6.1, the model incorporates word form and semantic levels of lexical representation, and syllabic and phonemic levels of sublexical representation. It may be worth noting that the incorporation of such levels of representation is completely

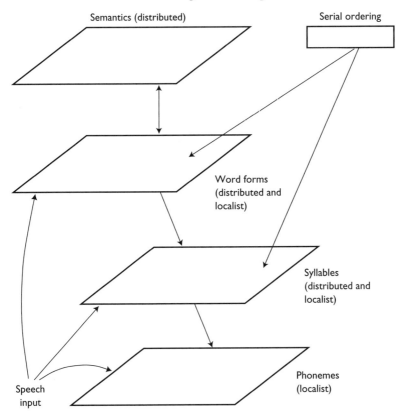

Figure 6.1 Overview of model.

consistent with the assumptions commonly made in models of lexical processing (e.g., Dell, 1986; Levelt, Roelofs, & Meyer, 1999).

Presentation of a word form to the model (depicted by the "speech input" arrows in Figure 6.1) results in sequences of representations being activated at the various levels of representation. For instance, presentation of the word form *zitricaymus* is manifested in the model as activation of the relevant sequence of phoneme representations at the phoneme level, activation of the relevant sequence of syllable representations at the syllable level, and activation of the relevant word form representation at the word form level. New representations are created on the fly as necessary at each of these levels, using mechanisms of the kind proposed by Grossberg (1987). Presentation of either a known word form or a novel word form thus gives rise to sequences of activations at the phoneme and syllable levels, and of a single activation at the word form level. A "list" is simply a sequence of these sequences. For instance, presentation of the list *cat dog ball chair* leads to activation of the sequences of phonemes and syllables constituting each word in the list, and, additionally, gives rise to a sequence of activations at the word form level (the representations of the word forms cat, dog, ball, and chair). Thus in a real sense, a word form is just a list of length one. For both a list or a single word form, the activated representation(s) at the word form level will lead to activations at the semantic level of representation. For known word forms, these will be the specific semantic representation that is associated with that word form, whereas for nonwords the evoked semantic representation will tend to be an indeterminate semantic representation that is a blend of those corresponding to known word forms that are similar to the nonword. Figure 6.1 also shows a "serial ordering mechanism" (to be discussed in greater detail below). This mechanism encodes (and maintains and retrieves) the serial order of a sequence of activations, at any level of representation it is connected to. As shown in the figure, the serial ordering mechanism has connections to both the word form and syllable levels of representation. Thus, the model provides for serial ordering at both lexical and sublexical levels of representation, thus completing the functional requirements outlined in the previous discussion.

The current model: Details

More details of the model's architecture are shown in Figure 6.2. The word form and syllable levels of representation are actually each composed of two sets of representations. One set of representations is *localist*, i.e., there is an individual unit representing the entire entity (a word form, at the word form level, or a syllable, at the syllable level). In the second set of representations at each level, the entity (word form or syllable) is represented as a pattern of activation that is *distributed* across a pool of units, with each unit in the pool representing a feature that comprises the entity; there is no individual unit that represents the whole entity, and this constitutes the critical difference between what are termed localist and distributed representations. The word form and syllable levels thus incorporate *both* localist and distributed representations (see Page, 2000, for a discussion of the merits of each type of representation).

As is typical in such artificial neural network or parallel distributed processing or connectionist models, the "units" are to be thought of as highly abstract neuron-like elements ("artificial neurons"). Such a unit has connections to and from other units. The outgoing connections from a unit are thought of loosely as axonal projections from a neuron. These projections make contact with other units, with such contacts being thought of loosely as synapses. The strength of any given "synapse" from unit a to unit b in such a model is instantiated as a *weight* on the connection from a to b. Thus a unit in such a model receives input from other units via the weighted incoming connections, summates its input, and, if the summed input crosses some threshold, transmits an output on its outgoing connections, thus providing input to other units to which it is connected. The input received by unit *b* from unit *a* is the product of the output emitted by *a* and the weight on the connection from *a* to *b*. The connection weights in such a model at any given point are thought of as encoding the model's *long-term knowledge* at that point. They start at some initial random value, and are adjusted following each stimulus processing event. The gradual adjustment of connection weights in this way modifies the long-term knowledge, and is therefore thought of as *learning*. A variety of weight-adjustment or learning procedures exist for such models.

In the present model, the localist and distributed representations at each level (word form and syllable) are bidirectionally connected, with every unit in the localist pool having a connection to every unit in the distributed pool, and vice versa. The weights on all these connections are adjusted during training of the model, using a Hebbian learning algorithm, in which the adjustment of connection weights is a simple function of the activation of the sending and receiving units (and does not make use of the notion of divergence from some target activation for the receiving unit, which is termed *error*, and would additionally be used in an *error-driven* learning procedure; see McLeod, Plunkett, & Rolls, 1998, for an accessible treatment of such learning procedures). Therefore, after learning, at the word form level, activation of the localist unit representing a word form leads to activation of the corresponding distributed representation, and vice versa; and analogously at the syllable level.

As shown in Figure 6.2, the semantic level of representation is connected to the word form level (specifically, to the distributed representations at the word form level) via an intermediate set of "hidden units". All these connection weights are also learned during training of the model, using a Hebbian learning algorithm. Again, these constitute long-term memory in the model.

The distributed representations at the word form level are the phonologically structured representations of an entire word form. Specifically, the word form is represented as a string of syllables. The representation of a syllable is in terms of a CCVCC (i.e., Consonant-Consonant-Vowel-Consonant-Consonant) template. That is, the representation scheme for a syllable consists of a pool of units divided into five slots. Activation of units in the first slot denotes the first C (if any) of the syllable, activation of units in the second slot denotes the second C (if any) of the syllable, activation of units in the third slot denotes the V of the syllable, and so on. The entire word form is represented as a string of such syllable templates, stringing together as many syllables as needed to represent the whole word form. Thus the word form is represented in a CCVCC-CCVCC-CCVCC . . . format (note that the hyphens are shown here to clarify the fact that there are multiple syllables, but have no counterpart in what is presented to the model).

The long-term connections from the word form level to the syllable level are in fact from the distributed word form representations to the localist

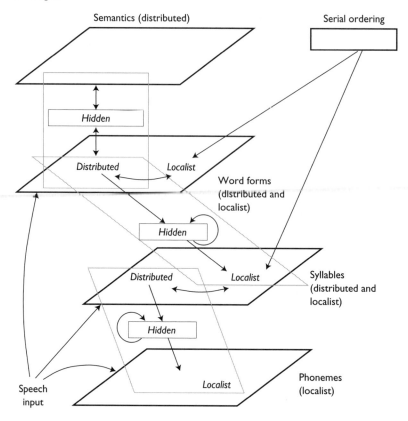

Figure 6.2 Detailed architecture of model.

syllable representations. The distributed representation at the word form level constitutes the input layer of a type of simple recurrent network (SRN; Elman, 1990a; Jordan, 1986) which is shown in the middle parallelogram in Figure 6.2. For present purposes, the crucial feature of such a network is that it can take as its input an unchanging (and hence *non-sequential*) representation of an entire sequence (the "plan" for the entire sequence), and combine this non-sequential input with information about its own sequence of internal states over time, so as to produce *sequential* output that "spells out" the constituent elements of the sequence represented by the plan, in serially ordered fashion, across successive time steps (for further detail on such networks, see Elman, 1990a; Gupta & Cohen, 2002; Jordan, 1986). In the present model, this SRN translates its input representation (the "plan" for the entire word form) into a sequence of localist outputs representing the sequence of syllables constituting that word form. This aspect of the model also constitutes long-term memory or knowledge. The SRN acquires its knowledge through adjustment of connection weights during training of the model, which employs the back-propagation learning algorithm (an *error-driven* learning procedure; Rumelhart, Hinton, & Williams, 1986), as is typical for an SRN (e.g., Elman, 1990a, 1990b; Jordan, 1986).

The long-term connections from the syllable level to the phoneme level are in fact from the distributed syllable representations to the (localist) phoneme representations. The distributed representations at the syllable level are the phonologically structured representations of an entire syllable, arranged in a CCVCC format. (The representation scheme is identical to that used at the word form level for *each* of the syllables constituting the entire word form.) These constitute the input to a second SRN which is shown in the bottom parallelogram in Figure 6.2. This SRN translates its input representation, the "plan" for the entire syllable, into a sequence of localist outputs representing the sequence of phonemes constituting that syllable. This SRN is also trained via back-propagation, and it also constitutes long-term memory/knowledge in the system.

The serial ordering mechanism is a variant of the *avalanche* (Grossberg, 1978), and is a time-varying context signal of the general kind that has been employed in a number of computational models of verbal short-term memory (e.g., Brown et al., 2000; Burgess & Hitch, 1992, 1999; Hartley & Houghton, 1996; Houghton, 1990; Vousden et al., 2000). It encodes the serial order of linguistic representations as they are activated at the word form and syllable levels. The mechanism is an endogenous generator of a waveform. It automatically sweeps through the same waveform whenever it is reset. A useful metaphor (Brown et al., 2000; Vousden et al., 2000) is that the mechanism is like a "clock", which recreates the same waveform whenever it is reset to the 12:00 position. As the clock proceeds through its waveform, it takes "snapshots" of the activation of linguistic representations as they occur in sequence at the word form and syllable levels of representation as a result of presentation of speech inputs, and can later re-display these snapshots in sequence, thus recalling the previously presented list. The "snapshots" are implemented by decaying (and hence *short-term*) weights on connections to the localist representations at both the word form and syllable levels. Hebbian learning occurs in these short-term connections, when representations are activated in sequence by input at the word form and syllable levels. The mechanism can subsequently cause those sequences of activations to be replayed and thus recalled, as long as the connection weights have not decayed too much. The replaying consists literally of a recreation of the original sequence of activations in the linguistic system (for further detail, see Gupta, 1996; Gupta & MacWhinney, 1997).

The serial ordering device thus constitutes the model's short-term sequence memory. It is important to note, however, that no "copies" of the to-be-remembered item(s) are made or "stored". Rather, the short-term sequence memory is a serial ordering device that sets up associations to a sequence of activations in the linguistic system (which consists of long-term representations). A consequence of this is that the short-term and long-term aspects of the model are inextricably linked in performance in a task such as immediate list recall or word form repetition. Performance depends critically on *both* the short-term and long-term memory systems in the model.

Development of the model

Development of the model to the present point has proceeded in three phases. The first step has been to construct a computational model (incorporating the architecture discussed in the previous section) that exhibits the basic ability to perform the two tasks of nonword repetition and immediate serial recall. The second step has been to calibrate the model so that its performance on the nonword repetition and immediate serial recall tasks is qualitatively similar to human behavioral performance. The third step has been to employ the model, as thus developed, to examine the relationship between immediate serial recall and nonword repetition.

As a precursor to simulations of nonword repetition and immediate serial recall, the model was "pretrained" to establish pre-existing linguistic knowledge and a known vocabulary. A set of approximately 3000 real words of English one through seven syllables in length was presented to the model. Each of the three components of the model representing long-term linguistic knowledge was trained on this set. The task for the system consisting of the semantic and distributed word form representations (see Figure 6.2) was to produce the correct semantic vector in response to a particular distributed word form representation and vice versa, for each of the 3000 words. Connection weights in this component were adjusted via a Hebbian learning algorithm, to and from the hidden layer localist units.[1] The task for the SRN system shown in the upper parallelogram in Figure 6.2 (consisting of the distributed word form representations and localist syllable representations) was to produce the correct sequence of localist syllable outputs in response to the distributed word form representation for each of the 3000 words. The task for the SRN system shown in the lower parallelogram in Figure 6.2 (consisting of the distributed syllable representations and localist phoneme representations) was to produce the correct sequence of phoneme representations in response to each distributed syllable representation contained in the 3000 words. Connection weights in these two SRNs were adjusted via back-propagation of error in each of their respective tasks. New units were created as necessary at the localist word form and localist syllable levels of representation, and connection weights between the localist and distributed representations at each level were also established during pretraining on the 3000 words. After each epoch of training, the model's performance on each word was tested by presenting the semantic representation for that word to the model's semantic level, allowing the activations to propagate from the semantic level to the word form, syllable, and phoneme levels, and examining the sequence of phonemes that was produced as a result. The word was considered to have

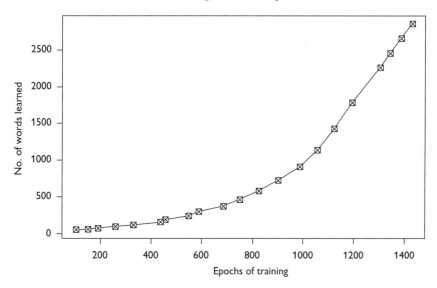

Figure 6.3 Growth of the model's vocabulary during pretraining.

been "learned" if all its phonemes were correctly produced, in correct order. Figure 6.3 shows the progress of vocabulary learning during pretraining. It is worth noting, however, that no claims are made about the psychological plausibility of the pretraining procedure as just described, nor about its correspondence with human vocabulary learning or development. The aim of pretraining was simply to establish a corpus of words that were known to the system (i.e., for which appropriate connection weights existed throughout the long-term components of the model). Achieving this aim provided the model with a vocabulary of known words that could be drawn on for simulated immediate serial recall, and provided a distinction in the model between known words and nonwords, for which there would be no appropriate pre-existing connection weights.

Simulation of nonword repetition and immediate serial recall

The goal of the simulations of nonword repetition (NWR) and immediate serial recall (ISR) was to achieve performance qualitatively similar to human empirical data. Moreover, the aim was to achieve this with a single set of parameters, so that the identical model would be performing each task and exhibiting humanlike behavior in both tasks (rather than have separate versions of the model for each task). The phenomenon chosen as the target for modeling of nonword repetition was the serial position functions that have recently been reported in human nonword repetition (Gupta, 2005; Gupta et al., 2005). For simulation of immediate serial recall, the phenomena chosen as modeling targets were the classic serial position effects in list recall, list length effects, and the movement error gradients that have been documented for ISR (e.g., Henson, Norris, Page, & Baddeley, 1996). In each case, the aim was simply to achieve qualitatively similar behavior in the model (rather than precise quantitative fits).

Simulations of NWR were conducted by presenting nonwords of lengths one through seven syllables (25 of each length) to the model. The nonwords were drawn from the same corpus used in behavioral investigation of serial position effects in nonword repetition (Gupta et al., 2005). Each nonword was presented individually, and the model's repetition response recorded after each presentation. Each presentation consisted of activation of the appropriate sequence of representations at the syllable and phoneme levels in the model, and of a single representation at the word form level. The word form level representation consisted of a new localist node and the distributed representation of the entire word form. During this presentation, learning occurred in the connections from the word form level to the syllable level, the connections from the syllable level to the phoneme level, and bidirectionally between localist and distributed representations at each of the word form and syllable levels. All of these constituted learning in the long-term components of the model, and embodied the notion that learning occurs constantly in the system. Learning did not occur, however, between the semantic level and the word form level because for nonword representation, there is assumed to be no specific semantic representation that is activated. In addition to learning in these long-term components, learning occurred in the short-term connection weights from the serial ordering mechanism to the word form level (to the new word form that had been created and activated) and to the syllable level (to the sequence of syllable level representations that had been activated). Following this presentation, nonword repetition was simulated by resetting the serial ordering mechanism to its original state, followed by regeneration of its waveform. The recreated waveform, together with the connection weights created during presentation, led to reactivation of the previously presented patterns of activation at the word form and syllable levels.[2] The accuracy of this recall depends on a variety of factors including the extent to which adjacent portions of the waveform overlap in the "snapshots" they take of the word form and syllable levels, the rate of decay of the short-term connection weights, and the level of noise in the activations of word form level and syllable level units. Thus, accuracy of recall is not guaranteed to be perfect, and tends to yield serial position functions for recall at the target level. The model's performance in simulated NWR is shown in Figure 6.4. As can be seen, simulated NWR performance exhibits clear serial position effects, which are qualitatively similar to those observed behaviorally (Gupta et al., 2005).

Simulations of ISR were conducted by presenting lists of 1 to 12 known words (25 lists of each length) to the model, employing exactly the same model and parameters as in simulation of NWR. The lists were composed of one-syllable words drawn from the model's vocabulary. Each list was

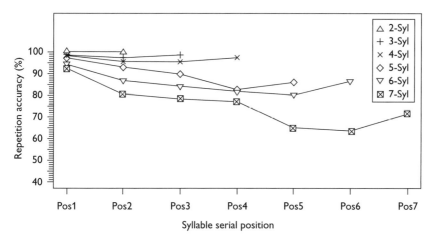

Figure 6.4 Serial position functions from simulated repetition of nonwords of 2 through 7 syllables in length.

presented one word at a time, and the model's recall of the list was recorded at the end of list presentation. Presentation of each word consisted of activation in the model of the appropriate sequence of representations at the phoneme level, and of a single representation at each of the word form and syllable levels. At every time step of this presentation, learning occurred in the short-term connection weights from the serial ordering mechanism to the word form level (to the currently activated word form representation) and to the syllable level (to the currently activated syllable representation).[3]

As with nonword repetition, recall of the list was simulated by resetting the serial ordering mechanism to its original state. Endogenous regeneration of the waveform, together with the connection weights created during presentation, led to reactivation of the previously presented patterns of activation at the word form and syllable levels, with accuracy of recall being dependent on the same factors as discussed above for nonword repetition. Figure 6.5 shows serial position functions for simulated ISR of lists of various lengths. As can be seen, the functions exhibit bowing and primacy and recency effects qualitatively similar to those characteristic of human list recall.

The errors observed in human immediate serial recall also follow characteristic patterns. In particular, when a list item that was presented in a particular serial position N is recalled in an incorrect position, the incorrect position is most likely to be very close to N, and relatively unlikely to be far from N. Thus the probability of an item presented in position N being recalled in an incorrect position M ($M = N \pm e$, $e > 0$) decreases with the distance of M from N, i.e., decreases as a function of e (e.g., Henson et al., 1996). Figure 6.6 shows that the model's ISR performance exhibits this property. The figure depicts movement error gradients for the model's ISR

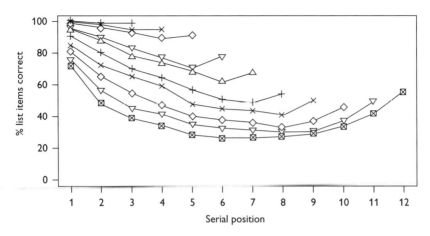

Figure 6.5 Serial position functions from simulated immediate serial recall of lists of 1 through 12 words.

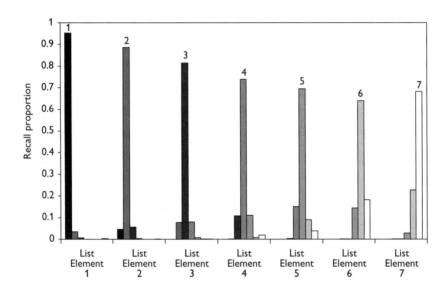

Figure 6.6 Movement error gradients for 7-item lists. Each set of bars arrayed along the x-axis corresponds to the item from a particular serial position in the stimulus list. From left to right within each set, the specific bars indicate the proportion of trials on which that stimulus item was recalled in each of the seven recall positions. (Some bars are not visible because some proportions are negligible.) Numerals at the top of each set of bars indicate, for that stimulus item, the output serial position at which it was most frequently recalled.

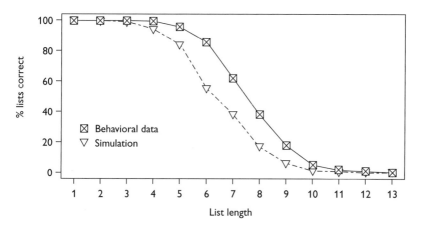

Figure 6.7 Effect of list length on ISR of lists of 1 through 13 words: human data and simulations.

of 7-item lists. Seven sets of bars are arrayed along the x-axis. Each set of bars represents a particular serial position in the target list (i.e., the presented list). The specific bars within each set indicate the frequencies of positions in which that target item was actually recalled. As can be seen, for each target position, the most probable recall position was the correct one. The adjacent positions were next highest in probability (denoting errors of $M = N \pm 1$), and the probability of the item being recalled further away than this was negligible. This profile of movement error gradients is qualitatively similar to that observed in analysis of human ISR performance (Henson et al., 1996).

Another classic characteristic of human ISR performance is the inverse-sigmoidal decrease in proportion of lists correctly recalled, as a function of list length. Figure 6.7 plots the proportion of lists correctly recalled as a function of list length, for both human performance (solid line) and simulated performance (dashed line). As can be seen, the list length effect observed in simulated ISR in the model is qualitatively similar to that observed empirically.

It is perhaps worth noting once again that the model's ability to perform both nonword repetition and immediate serial recall entails addressing the issue of serial ordering at multiple levels of representation. This difficult issue has not to our knowledge previously been addressed in an implemented computational model (but see Gupta, 1996). The two tasks are simulated, moreover, in a single model, with the identical architecture and long-term knowledge, and with identical parameter settings employed for both tasks. The ability to simulate both these tasks in a single model is therefore in itself of some interest as a computational demonstration. Going beyond this, however, the model achieves qualitatively humanlike performance in simulated nonword repetition and immediate serial recall, by a number of measures, thus providing support for the general theoretical ideas incorporated in the model. This led to the next phase in the present work: employing the model, as described thus far, to investigate the empirically observed relationships between immediate serial recall and nonword repetition.

The correlation between nonword repetition and immediate serial recall

One of the earliest and most influential indications of a relationship between ISR and NWR ability came from the finding of correlations between performance in these tasks. These correlations have now been documented across a variety of ages and populations (e.g., Gathercole & Baddeley, 1989; Gathercole, Willis, Emslie, & Baddeley, 1992; Gathercole, Hitch, Service, & Martin, 1997; Gathercole et al., 1999; Gupta, 2003; Gupta, MacWhinney, Feldman, & Sacco, 2003). For instance, Gathercole et al. (1992) reported significant correlations between performance in NWR and ISR of .52, .67, and .45 respectively, for 4-, 5-, and 8-year-old children, Gathercole et al. (1999) reported a significant correlation of .32 in 13-year-old children, and in two experiments, Gupta (2003) reported significant correlations of .41 and .36 in adults.

Why do these correlations arise? Answers to this question have hitherto been offered only in rather general terms. The hypothesis incorporated in the present work is more specific: nonword repetition and immediate serial recall would be expected to be correlated, because the same serial ordering mechanism operates over both word form and syllable levels of representation. Given that the model incorporates this hypothesis, and yields credible simulations of both nonword repetition and immediate serial recall, we are in a position to test whether correlations between NWR and ISR do indeed fall out of a dependence on the same serial ordering mechanism.

Another question arises at this point, however: Why are the correlations in human performance not higher than have been reported? The correlations between NWR and ISR, as summarized above, are mostly in the range of .4 to .5 for older children and adults, indicating shared variance of .16 to .25. If the same mechanism does indeed provide for serial ordering in both NWR and ISR, why is the correlation between performance in these tasks not considerably higher? Perhaps the model can shed light on this question as well?

To examine whether NWR and ISR performance would, in fact, be correlated, and to seek insight into the magnitudes of the correlations, several simulated "subjects" were created. The rationale here was to create a number of instantiations of the model incorporating the kind of variability that would certainly be present across human subjects – i.e., to simulate individual differences. Examining the correlation between

ISR and NWR performance across these instantiations of the model (the simulated subjects) would then be analogous to examining the correlation between ISR and NWR in the performance of a group of human subjects.

Each simulated subject was defined as a set of values of the parameters of the model. For all simulated subjects, this set of values was identical to that used in the simulations described above, except with regard to two parameters. One was a parameter governing the Hebbian learning rate in the connections from the serial ordering mechanism to the word form and syllable levels. This parameter can be thought of as a critical determinant of the efficacy of the serial ordering mechanism. The second parameter was one governing the learning rate between localist and distributed representations at the word form and syllable levels. This parameter can be thought of as affecting the efficiency of lexical and sublexical processing in the model. For each of these parameters, a range of parameter values was created, centered around the value that had enabled the model to yield the ISR and NWR performance described above. A value was picked randomly from each of these two parameter ranges, and this pair of parameter values was then taken to define one simulated subject. Seventy-five such pairs were chosen, thus creating 75 simulated subjects. Thus the simulated subjects incorporated individual differences in the efficiency of serial ordering and lexical/sublexical processing, but in all other respects were identical to each other and to the model that yielded the simulations described above. A simulation of ISR was then run using the parameter values of a particular "subject", and a simulation of NWR was also run using these same parameter values. This procedure was repeated for each of the 75 subjects. Thus each simulated subject was "tested" on both ISR and NWR.

For the purposes of assessing the correlation between ISR and NWR, each simulated subject's performance was gauged by a summary measure. Following the procedure adopted in empirical studies (e.g., Gupta, 2003; Gupta et al., 2003), ISR performance was measured in terms of list span, defined as the longest list length at which 50% or more of the presented lists were recalled correctly, and NWR performance in terms of the proportion of 2-, 4-, and 7-syllable nonwords correctly repeated. The correlation between these pairs of measures, derived from the 75 simulated subjects, was $r = .423$, $p < .01$. This is very close to the correlations observed in older children and adults.

The correlation arises in the model as a direct consequence of the engagement of the serial ordering mechanism at both the word form and syllable levels. To see why the correlation is not higher, it is useful to keep in mind what is involved in performance of ISR and NWR. The interaction of the long-term and short-term memory aspects of the system is particularly relevant here. As the model helps to make clear, although overall performance in ISR and NWR does depend on serial ordering mechanisms, it *also* depends on numerous other aspects of processing, including lexical and sublexical processing. This highlights the indubitable (but perhaps sometimes overlooked) fact that measures of ISR and NWR performance in humans are obtained from participants who vary not just in their verbal STM mechanisms, but in multiple other performance characteristics that are separate from verbal STM. The correlation between performance in ISR and NWR in humans is thus computed across variance in these multiple different performance characteristics, and this is one reason why the correlation can be expected to be less than perfect. This is concretized in the model, in which the measures of ISR and NWR performance from the various simulated subjects are obtained across variation in the efficacy of serial ordering *and* of lexical/sublexical processing. As a result of the differing sources of variance, the correlation between NWR and ISR is not perfect, even though the model employs precisely the same serial ordering mechanism for both ISR and NWR. A cautionary note here is that there are other variables that in human performance would be expected to introduce uncorrelated variance in performance of ISR and NWR, and thus provide similar explanations for why the correlations are of only moderate magnitude. For instance, the serially ordered constituents of nonwords (i.e., syllables) carry coarticulatory information and a linguistic stress contour, whereas the serially ordered elements of lists (i.e., words) do not carry coarticulatory information, and typically have monotone stress. Moreover, lists contain pauses whereas nonwords do not. These diffferences are likely to affect performance in NWR and ISR in ways that reduce covariance in the tasks. In addition, human performance in NWR and ISR tasks is quite variable, with imperfect test–retest reliability, offering another possible reason for the observed magnitudes of correlations. For these reasons, the present simulations should be viewed more as a demonstration of the general point that variables that reduce covariance between NWR and ISR are certainly operative in performance of these tasks, and will lead to the correlation between these tasks being less than perfect even if their performance is dependent on the same serial ordering mechanism – rather than as a demonstration that lexical processing ability necessarily is the specific or sole variable that accounts for the modest magnitude of correlation.

While keeping these caveats in mind, it is nevertheless the case that the correlation between NWR and ISR performance in the model is qualitatively similar to that documented in human behavior. The emergence of this correlation in the model supports the present account of NWR and ISR performance, and in particular, the hypothesis that human performance in both tasks may depend on the same serial ordering mechanisms. The present account also offers an explanation of why these correlations are not higher. But are the correlations in the model really emergent, or has the model simply been "fitted" to yield them? In considering this question, it is worth emphasizing once again that the development and calibration of the model described in the preceding sections of this chapter attempted only to achieve NWR and ISR performance that was qualitatively humanlike.

There was no attempt to tailor the model or adjust parameters to yield correlation between performance in different tasks. In the present creation of simulated subjects, all except two parameter values were identical to those employed for calibrating the model in the first place. Moreover, the values of the remaining two parameters were highly constrained (being centered around their original values); and furthermore, the variation in these two parameter values across "subjects" was random. The procedure employed for *examining* correlations in the model was therefore not at all one of *adjusting* the model's parameters so as to *yield* correlations between NWR and ISR. The correlations observed between NWR and ISR performance in the model were thus not simply a consequence of parameter fitting. In a real sense, they fell out of the model, and thus offer some genuine insight into why these abilities may be related in humans.

The "pure STM" deficit and word and nonword processing

Another very influential indication of a relationship between ISR and the processing of nonwords has come from the study of a neuropsychological syndrome termed the "pure STM" deficit. Patients with this deficit have dramatically impaired ISR span, but largely spared language comprehension and production, and other cognitive abilities (hence the name for the syndrome). As part of their generally spared language ability, such patients have little difficulty in repeating real words they know (Vallar & Baddeley, 1984). However, such patients present with great difficulty in repeating new words or nonwords (i.e., novel word forms), and also in learning them[4] (Baddeley, Papagno, & Vallar, 1988; Baddeley, 1993). This finding has been regarded as additional evidence for a relationship between ISR and NWR (e.g., Baddeley et al., 1988; Vallar & Baddeley, 1984).

This pattern (impaired ISR and NWR but preserved word repetition) has previously been addressed in computational work by Burgess and Hitch (1999), who described a simulation in which complete removal of a particular component of the model did lead to preserved word repetition coupled with a complete inability to perform ISR and NWR. As the authors noted, their model's *complete* inability to perform ISR and NWR was an exaggeration of the observed behavioral results. Although this was not explored further, it appears likely that partial (rather than complete) removal of the same component of the model would have achieved the desired pattern. Recall, however, that the Burgess and Hitch (1999) model (like all other computational models) did not address serial ordering at multiple levels of representation, and thus did not simulate serial ordering *within word forms*, which is a primary focus of the present work. The present simulations were thus aimed at investigating the pure STM pattern of impairment where serial ordering is computed both across word forms and within word forms.

To investigate the present model's ability to account for this pattern of results (viz., impaired ISR and NWR but preserved word repetition), its

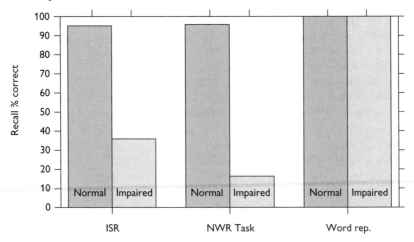

Figure 6.8 Simulation exhibiting a performance profile characteristic of a "pure STM" deficit.

performance was examined under "impairment" of serial ordering. A "lesion" of the serial ordering mechanism was simulated using the parameter that governs the rate of Hebbian learning in connections from this mechanism to the word form and syllable levels. Recall that this parameter was also one of the two varied in the creation of the 75 simulated subjects described in the previous section. However, in the previous simulations, variation of this parameter was in a relatively narrow range around the mean value (i.e., within a "normal" range). In the present simulations, the parameter was set to a much lower value (i.e., to a "pathological" value, outside the "normal" range).

The model's performance was examined in three tasks. Each task was simulated both in an unimpaired state of the model, and under a lesion to the serial ordering mechanism (a "pure STM lesion"). The unimpaired state was identical to the set of parameter values used in establishing the basic simulations of humanlike NWR and ISR discussed earlier. The lesioned state differed from this only in the value of the one parameter discussed above. The three tasks examined were: (1) ISR of lists of 4 known monosyllabic words, (2) NWR of 4-syllable nonwords, and (3) Immediate repetition of known 4-syllable words. Figure 6.8 shows the model's accuracy in each of these tasks, both with and without the pure STM lesion. The y-axis shows the proportion of lists/nonwords/words correctly recalled. Even with the lesion, the model remained structurally able to perform tasks of ISR and NWR, but its performance on both was severely impaired by the lesion. Repetition of known words, however, was unaffected by the lesion.

To understand how these results arise, it may be helpful to recapitulate certain aspects of the functioning of the model. Recall that the model incorporates learning in both its long-term components and its short-term components. Presentation of a polysyllabic novel word form (such as a new word or nonword – say, of three syllables) leads to short-term learning in the connections from the serial ordering mechanism to the word form and syllable levels, and thus to short-term encoding by the sequencing mechanism of the sequences of activations that occurred at the word form and syllable levels (see Figure 6.1). The sequence of activations that occurred at the word form level during presentation is simply a sequence of one activation – that of the newly created word form representation. The sequence of activations that occurred at the syllable level during presentation is the sequence of three syllables that comprise the word form. In addition to this short-term learning, exposure to the word form is also accompanied by long-term learning in the connections between and within the semantic, word form, syllable, and phoneme levels.

Immediate repetition of the just-presented novel word form requires re-creation of the sequences of activation that occurred at the word form and syllable (and, ultimately, phoneme) levels. This is initiated by the serial ordering mechanism, which had encoded the sequence of one word form at the word form level, and the sequence of three syllables at the syllable level, and now reactivates these sequences. A crucial distinction between known words and nonwords arises here. For a known word, reactivation of the appropriate word form level representation is all that is needed to repeat the word, because there are strong long-term weights from the word form level representation to the appropriate sequence of syllables (these have come to be encoded, through many exposures, in the middle SRN – see Figure 6.2). Following a single exposure to a novel word form, however, the long-term weights from the new word form level representation to the appropriate syllable level sequence are not strong enough for activation of the word form representation to produce the correct syllable sequence. Successful repetition of a novel word form (but not a known word form) is thus crucially dependent on the short-term encoding of the sequence of syllables. This is why NWR and ISR were both impaired by the lesion of the serial ordering mechanism in the previous simulation: both are crucially dependent on the maintenance of a sequence of activations (at the syllable level for NWR and at the word form level for ISR) by the serial ordering mechanism. For repetition of a known word, by contrast, the serial ordering mechanism need only recreate a single activation at the word form level. Once this word form level representation is activated, the long-term weights can do the rest; the short-term serial ordering mechanism's encoding of the syllable level sequence is not needed. Repetition of a known word requires the serial ordering mechanism only to recreate a single word form level representation, and this is feasible even under considerable impairment.

In summary, the model exhibits a pattern of impairment qualitatively similar to that observed in pure STM patients. This result provides additional support for the present characterization of NWR and ISR and their relationship, and of how the pure STM deficit may arise in human patients.

Verbal short-term memory and novel word learning

The discussion thus far has described a variety of ways in which the present model offers an answer to the question of why performance in nonword repetition and immediate serial recall are related, and of how it accounts for a variety of empirical results that bear on this relationship. According to the theoretical view incorporated in this model, NWR and ISR draw on the same serial ordering mechanism, and the model provides a concrete demonstration of how this might work. But what about the relationship between nonword repetition and word learning? At the beginning of this chapter, it was suggested that the existence of a relationship between nonword repetition and word learning appears fairly intuitive, because greater facility in processing nonwords would be expected to lead to greater facility in eventually learning them. How can this intuition be concretized in terms of the present model?

As reiterated in the preceding section, the model incorporates learning both in its long-term components and in its short-term components. Exposure to a novel word form leads to both short-term and long-term learning, with the long-term learning being in the connections between and within the semantic, word form, syllable, and phoneme levels. Although, as discussed above, the long-term learning that occurs during a single exposure to a novel word form does not suffice to "learn" it, multiple exposures to nonwords will lead to multiple instances of long-term learning in these connections, and over multiple exposures, a nonword will turn into a known word. Indeed, this is precisely what happens during the "pre-training" of the model. Initially, repetition of the form is dependent on the short-term weights from the serial ordering mechanism to the word form level and (crucially) the syllable level. Eventually, however, once the long-term connection weights have reached sufficient strength, short-term maintenance of the syllable sequence becomes redundant (although it still occurs, if the serial ordering mechanism is intact). The learning of a new word form thus represents a transition from dependence on short-term learning to long-term knowledge.

However, nothing in this description actually provides an account of why the accuracy of nonword repetition might be related to the efficacy of word learning. This is because learning in the model (both short-term and long-term) occurs during *exposure* to word forms. The short-term learning-dependent accuracy of word form repetition at *recall* does not impact long-term learning in the model as it has thus far been developed. How then might repetition accuracy for a novel word affect its long-term learning?

The current model does, in fact, provide a simple way of thinking about this question. In particular, let us suppose that long-term learning occurred not only at *exposure* to a word form, but also during *repetition* of the word form. At repetition, what was learned would be *the repetition itself*, errors and all. The efficacy of long-term learning would then be dependent on the accuracy of nonword (or novel word) repetition in a very direct manner. If repetition accuracy were high, the learning that occurred during repetition would supplement the learning that occurs during exposure. If repetition accuracy were low, however, the learning during repetition/recall would interfere with the learning at exposure. Although such learning-at-recall is not currently implemented in the model, the conceptualization offered by the model in this regard is fairly clear. The model thus helps concretize intuitions about *how* novel word learning may be related to nonword repetition (and thus to the serial ordering mechanism, or phonological short-term memory). It is also interesting that, in the domain of list recall, there is evidence for learning-at-recall: when specific to-be-recalled lists recur multiple times during a list recall session, facilitated performance on the repeating lists (the *Hebb effect*; e.g., Cumming et al., 2003; Hebb, 1961; Melton, 1963; Sechler & Watkins, 1991; Ward, 1937) is stronger if recall of the lists is overtly attempted than if there is no overt recall (e.g., Melton, 1963).

The question arises, of course, of whether the present hypothesis suggested by the model (i.e., that accuracy in learning-at-recall during novel word repetition will affect novel word learning) is a reasonable one for human performance. In fact, there is evidence to suggest that, at least in individuals with memory impairments, learning success may depend on the avoidance of performance errors – that is, on setting up an "errorless" training situation (e.g., Evans, Wilson, Schuri, Andrade, Baddeley, & Bruno, 2000; Glisky, 1995). The present hypothesis amounts to extension of these findings to normal word learning. The hypothesis also leads to testable predictions. According to the hypothesis, the greater the number of overt repetition errors made during the word learning process, the poorer the learning will be. What would affect the number of overt repetition errors made during word learning? Obviously, if overt repetition responses were not made at all during exposure events, this would limit the number of overt repetition errors made during learning. Therefore, according to the hypothesis under consideration, manipulating the presence or absence of overt repetition during word learning should affect the level of word learning obtained. However, such an effect will depend on the inherent level of accuracy of overt repetition. If this accuracy is high, then, even if overt repetitions are being made during exposure, there will be few inaccurate overt repetitions. Therefore, with high accuracy levels, the presence/absence of overt repetition during learning should make little difference to the ultimate word learning outcome. However, if the accuracy of overt repetition is low, then the presence of overt repetition during exposure will lead to many overt repetition errors, and the ultimate word learning outcomes should be lower than if there had been no overt repetition. Thus an interaction is predicted, such that the word learning outcome should be lower when overt repetitions are made during exposure than when they are not made – but only if the overt repetitions are inaccurate. What would affect the accuracy of overt repetitions? An obvious variable here is word length: overt repetition errors would be greater, for instance, for five-syllable novel names than for one-syllable novel names. It can therefore be predicted that word learning should be lower with than without overt repetition during learning, but only at higher word lengths.

This prediction receives some preliminary empirical support. In two experiments (Abbs, Gupta, & Khetarpal, 2007), participants engaged in a word learning task in which they were visually presented with a drawing of a novel object, together with an auditorily presented novel "name" for the object. These presentations were exposure trials. The participant's task was to learn the pairing so as to be able to produce the name when cued with the visual image (drawing) of the object, in test trials. Following the paradigm of Gupta (2003), the drawings depicted "space aliens", and the names were possible nonwords of English. The learning session contained several blocks of exposure and testing, for each of four name–picture pairs.

In each of the two experiments, half the participants were instructed to overtly repeat the name on each exposure trial, and half were instructed simply to listen to the name at each exposure trial, and not to repeat it overtly. Thus each experiment incorporated a 2 (between: overt repetition during exposure trials/no overt repetition) × 6 (within: exposure block 1/2/3/4/5/6) mixed factorial design, with 36 participants in each experiment (18 in each between condition). However, in Experiment 1, the names were 3-syllable nonwords while in Experiment 2 the names were 4-syllable nonwords. What varied between the two experiments was therefore word length, which was expected to affect the number of overt repetition errors during exposure trials. Such an effect was in fact obtained, with repetition accuracy in the overt repetition condition during exposure trials being 92.2% in E1 (3-syllable names) and 82.3% in E2 (4-syllable names). The difference was significant: F (1, 34) = 5.56, MSE = 9.93, p < .05.

Figures 6.9(a) and (b) show the proportion of names correctly recalled on the six test trials ("recaps") for E1 and E2 respectively. In E1 (3-syllable names), there was no significant difference in recall for the "repeat" versus "silent" conditions (p > .7). However, in E2, recall was worse in the repeat than in the silent condition, and the difference was very nearly significant (p = .054). It should be noted that these results are preliminary, requiring further investigation of both robustness and alternative explanations. Nevertheless, they are consistent with the somewhat counter-intuitive predictions derived from the current hypothesis, and thus provide some initial support for the model. Perhaps more importantly, they demonstrate the testability of the model.

Conclusions

The present model is to our knowledge the only current computational model to tackle the issue of serial ordering both across word forms (as in list recall) and within word forms (as in nonword repetition), and hence the

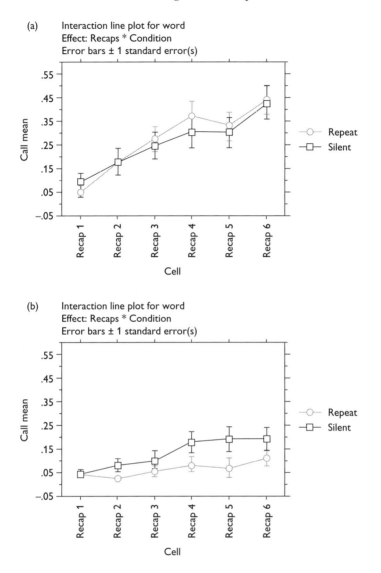

Figure 6.9 Effect of overt repetition of novel words during learning: (a) 3-syllable novel words; (b) 4-syllable novel words.

only current model that can offer an account of observed relationships between performance in these two tasks. Indeed, once the model had been set up to simulate performance in the two tasks, a number of patterns of relationship between performance in the tasks fell out of the model, including the well-documented correlation between performance in the tasks, and the profile of impairment in pure STM deficits. Additionally, the model generates a testable hypothesis regarding the relationship between nonword repetition and the long-term learning of novel words.

Of course, the model has many limitations. It currently addresses only a very few of the many and varied phenomena of immediate serial list recall that have been accounted for by a number of other computational models (e.g., Brown et al., 2000; Burgess & Hitch, 1992, 1999; Page & Norris, 1998). As noted in the introduction, such coverage is not the goal of the present work, but nevertheless it constitutes a limitation if the model is viewed as a model of list recall. As an account of linguistic processing also, the present model has many limitations. It does not, for instance, incorporate information about variables such as linguistic stress or coarticulation, to name just two, which are likely to impact processing. Despite these limitations, the model does provide a concrete, computationally rigorous, and empirically testable means of thinking about *relationships* between the domains of serially ordered memory and language processing, and in particular, between list recall and nonword repetition; it thus has the potential to play a useful role in investigation of these relationships.

Acknowledgments

The author thanks Jamie Tisdale and Tobe Hagge, who conducted the bulk of the computer programming underlying this work, and Gary Dell, Nadine Martin, and Myrna Schwartz for helpful discussion during its development. This research was supported in part by grants NIH NIDCD R01 DC006499 to Prahlad Gupta, and NIH NIDCD RO1 DC01924 to Nadine Martin, Prahlad Gupta, and others.

Notes

1 These hidden layer units have a one-to-one correspondence with the distributed semantic and distributed word form representations. As the localist word form units also have a one-to-one correspondence with the word form level distributed representations, the question arises of whether the model could be simplified by merging these two sets of localist units – that is, by making the localist word form units also serve as the hidden units between the semantics and word form levels. The reason for avoiding this merger was that sequencing at the word form level (via the avalanche) would then be equally influenced by semantic similarity and phonological similarity, which would be contrary to evidence suggesting that the effects of phonological similarity are much stronger than those of semantic similarity (e.g., Baddeley, 1968).

2 The patterns of activation at the syllable level in turn led to output of the appropriate phoneme sequences corresponding to the syllables.

3 Learning also occurred in all the long-term components of the model, but did not influence list recall, because the connection weights for the words had already been established during vocabulary pretraining.

4 It should be noted that they also do exhibit difficulty in certain other aspects of language processing such as repeating sentences longer than 8 syllables, and numeric sequences.

References

Abbs, B., Gupta, P., & Khetarpal, N. (2007). *Does overt repetition facilitate word learning?* Manuscript.

Baddeley, A. D. (1968). How does acoustic similarity influence short-term memory? *Quarterly Journal of Experimental Psychology, 20*, 249–264.

Baddeley, A. D. (1993). Short-term phonological memory and long-term learning: A single case study. *European Journal of Cognitive Psychology, 5*, 129–148.

Baddeley, A. D., Gathercole, S. E., & Papagno, C. (1998). The phonological loop as a language learning device. *Psychological Review, 105*, 158–173.

Baddeley, A. D., Papagno, C., & Vallar, G. (1988). When long-term learning depends on short-term storage. *Journal of Memory and Language, 27*, 586–595.

Botvinick, M., & Plaut, D. (2006). Short-term memory for serial order: A recurrent neural network model. *Psychological Review, 113*, 201–233.

Brown, G. D. A., & Hulme, C. (1996). Nonword repetition, STM, and word age-of-acquisition. In S. E. Gathercole (Ed.), *Models of short-term memory* (pp. 129–148). Hove, UK: Psychology Press.

Brown, G. D. A., Preece, T., & Hulme, C. (2000). Oscillator-based memory for serial order. *Psychological Review, 107*, 127–181.

Burgess, N., & Hitch, G. J. (1992). Toward a network model of the articulatory loop. *Journal of Memory and Language, 31*, 429–460.

Burgess, N., & Hitch, G. J. (1999). Memory for serial order: A network model of the phonological loop and its timing. *Psychological Review, 106*, 551–581.

Cumming, N., Page, M., & Norris, D. (2003). Testing a positional model of the Hebb effect. *Memory, 11*, 43–63.

Dell, G. S. (1986). A spreading activation theory of retrieval in sentence production. *Psychological Review, 93*, 283–321.

Elman, J. L. (1990a). Finding structure in time. *Cognitive Science, 14*, 179–211.

Elman, J. L. (1990b). Representation and structure in connectionist models. In G. P. Altmann (Ed.), *Cognitive models of speech processing: Psycholinguistic and computational perspectives.* Cambridge, MA: MIT Press.

Evans, J., Wilson, B., Schuri, U., Andrade, J., Baddeley, A., & Bruno, O. (2000). A comparison of errorless and trial-and-error learning methods for teaching individuals with acquired memory deficits. *Neuropsychological Rehabilitation, 10*, 67–101.

Gathercole, S. E., & Baddeley, A. D. (1989). Evaluation of the role of phonological STM in the development of vocabulary in children: A longitudinal study. *Journal of Memory and Language, 28*, 200–213.

Gathercole, S. E., Hitch, G. J., Service, E., & Martin, A. J. (1997). Short-term memory and new word learning in children. *Developmental Psychology, 33*, 966–979.

Gathercole, S. E., Service, E., Hitch, G. J., Adams, A.-M., & Martin, A. J. (1999). Phonological short-term memory and vocabulary development: Further evidence on the nature of the relationship. *Applied Cognitive Psychology, 13*, 65–77.

Gathercole, S. E., Willis, C., Emslie, H., & Baddeley, A. D. (1992). Phonological memory and vocabulary development during the early school years: A longitudinal study. *Developmental Psychology, 28*, 887–898.

Glisky, E. (1995). Acquisition and transfer of word processing skill by an amnesic patient. *Neuropsychological Rehabilitation, 5*, 299–318.

Grossberg, S. (1978). A theory of human memory: Self-organization and perform-ance of sensory-motor codes, maps, and plans. In R. Rosen, & F. Snell (Eds.), *Progress in theoretical biology* (Vol. 5). New York: Academic Press.

Grossberg, S. (1987). Competitive learning: From interactive activation to adaptive resonance. *Cognitive Science, 11*, 23–63.

Gupta, P. (1995). *Word learning and immediate serial recall: Toward an integrated account.* PhD thesis, Department of Psychology, Carnegie Mellon University, Pittsburgh, PA.

Gupta, P. (1996). Word learning and verbal short-term memory: A computational account. In G. W. Cottrell (Ed.), *Proceedings of the Eighteenth Annual Meeting of the Cognitive Science Society* (pp. 189–194). Mahwah, NJ: Lawrence Erlbaum Associates, Inc.

Gupta, P. (2002). Are nonwords lists? The effects of syllable serial position on repetition of individual nonwords. In *Abstracts of the Quebec'02 conference on short-term/working memory*. Quebec City, Quebec. Abstract.

Gupta, P. (2003). Examining the relationship between word learning, nonword repetition, and immediate serial recall in adults. *Quarterly Journal of Experimental Psychology (A), 56*, 1213–1236.

Gupta, P. (2005). Primacy and recency in nonword repetition. *Memory, 13*, 318–324.

Gupta, P., & Cohen, N. J. (2002). Theoretical and computational analysis of skill learning, repetition priming, and procedural memory. *Psychological Review, 109*, 401–448.

Gupta, P., Lipinski, J., Abbs, B., & Lin, P.-H. (2005). Serial position effects in nonword repetition. *Journal of Memory and Language, 53*, 141–162.

Gupta, P., & MacWhinney, B. (1997). Vocabulary acquisition and verbal short-term memory: Computational and neural bases. *Brain and Language, 59*, 267–333.

Gupta, P., MacWhinney, B., Feldman, H., & Sacco, K. (2003). Phonological memory and vocabulary learning in children with focal lesions. *Brain and Language, 87*, 241–252.

Hartley, T., & Houghton, G. (1996). A linguistically constrained model of short-term memory for nonwords. *Journal of Memory and Language, 35*, 1–31.

Hebb, D. O. (1961). Distinctive features of learning in the higher animal. In J. F. Delafresnaye (Ed.), *Brain mechanisms and learning* (pp. 37–46). Oxford: Blackwell.

Henson, R., Norris, D., Page, M., & Baddeley, A. (1996). Unchained memory: Error patterns rule out chaining models of immediate serial recall. *Quarterly Journal of Experimental Psychology, 49*, 80–115.

Houghton, G. (1990). The problem of serial order: A neural network model of sequence learning and recall. In R. Dale, C. Mellish, & M. Zock (Eds.), *Current research in natural language generation*. New York: Academic Press.

Jordan, M. I. (1986). *Serial order: A parallel distributed processing approach* (Report 8604). La Jolla, California: Institute for Cognitive Science, University of California, San Diego.

Levelt, W. J. M., Roelofs, A., & Meyer, A. S. (1999). A theory of lexical access in speech production. *Behavioral and Brain Sciences, 22*, 1–75.

McLeod, P., Plunkett, K., & Rolls, E. (1998). *Introduction to connectionist modeling of cognitive processes*. New York: Oxford University Press.

Melton, A. W. (1963). Implications of short-term mempry for a general theory of memory. *Journal of Verbal Learning and Verbal Behavior, 2,* 1–21.

Page, M. (2000). Connectionist modeling in psychology: A localist manifesto. *Behavioral and Brain Sciences, 24,* 443–512.

Page, M. P. A., & Norris, D. (1998). The primacy model: A new model of immediate serial recall. *Psychological Review, 105,* 761–781.

Rumelhart, D., Hinton, G., & Williams, R. (1986). Learning internal representations by error propagation. In D. Rumelhart, & J. McClelland (Eds.), *Parallel distributed processing, Vol. 1: Foundations* (pp. 318–362). Cambridge, MA: MIT Press.

Sechler, E. S., & Watkins, M. J. (1991). Learning to reproduce a list and memory for the learning. *American Journal of Psychology, 104,* 367–394.

Vallar, G., & Baddeley, A. D. (1984). Fractionation of working memory: Neuropsychological evidence for a phonological short-term store. *Journal of Verbal Learning and Verbal Behavior, 23,* 151–161.

Vousden, J. I., Brown, G. D. A., & Harley, T. A. (2000). Serial control of phonology in speech production: A hierarchical model. *Cognitive Psychology, 41,* 101–175.

Ward, L. B. (1937). Reminiscence and rote learning. *Psychological Monographs, 49,* 1–64.

7 Is there a common mechanism underlying word-form learning and the Hebb repetition effect? Experimental data and a modelling framework

Mike P. A. Page and Dennis Norris

Overview

The Hebb repetition effect (Hebb, 1961) is a phenomenon whereby performance on the immediate serial recall of a list of familiar items is seen to improve over unannounced repetitions of a given list. One possible real-world counterpart of this effect is the learning of phonological word-forms that are themselves sequences of familiar items, in this case phonemes or syllables. We discuss this hypothesis with reference to a variety of recent data, and propose a modelling framework, based on the primacy model of immediate serial recall (Page & Norris, 1998), that seeks to identify common underlying mechanisms.

Introduction

In this chapter, we will be exploring the possibility that the mechanism responsible for the Hebb repetition effect (Hebb, 1961) is essentially the same as that underlying the learning of phonological word-forms. In his influential paper, Hebb demonstrated that the immediate serial recall (ISR) of a given digit-list improved to the extent that that same list had been repeatedly presented (and recall attempted) on every third trial of a set of ISR trials. List repetition was unannounced, and Hebb showed that learning was seen regardless of whether subjects reported having noticed this manipulation. This latter finding has subsequently been supported by a number of other studies (e.g., McKelvie, 1987; Stadler, 1993). To this extent, it can be said that the Hebb repetition effect is sometimes implicit, even though it is manifested in the performance of an explicit serial recall task.

To those who are disposed to make the distinction, the Hebb repetition effect is a paradigmatic example of the transfer of information from short- to long-term memory. To be specific, the effect appears to involve the gradual development of a durable representation of the item and order information in a given list that can enable that list's subsequent recognition and enhanced recall. In recent years, a number of quantitative models of the ISR task have been developed (e.g., Brown, Preece, & Hulme, 2000; Brown,

Neath, & Chater, 2007; Burgess & Hitch, 1992, 1999; Farrell & Lewandowsky, 2002; Henson, 1998; Neath, 2000; Page & Norris, 1998) and we will discuss the Hebb effect here in relation to our own primacy model (Page & Norris, 1998). The primacy model can be thought of as an implementation of the phonological loop component of the working memory model (Baddeley, 1986; Baddeley & Hitch, 1974), inasmuch as it comprises a mechanism specialized in the ordered recall of speech-based material retained over the short term. Indeed, in recent work (Page, Madge, Cumming, & Norris, 2007), we have characterized both the phonological loop, and our model of it, as a system that permits the reproduction of a short portion of speech that has just been heard or, alternatively, that has just been recoded from the corresponding visual stimulus. In this conception, the phonological store is identified with a high-level utterance plan that, when executed, will result in the repetition of a stimulus list. In our model, the primacy gradient of activations that is instantiated across localist representations of list-items constitutes just such an utterance plan.

It is the identification of the phonological store/primacy gradient with a speech reproduction system that raises a question regarding the "ecological" counterpart of the Hebb repetition effect. Just as we presume that the phonological store is not available solely to enable laboratory performance of the ISR task, we can also presume that the learning processes seen in the Hebb repetition effect are not similarly confined to the laboratory conditions under which they have been demonstrated. Baddeley, Gathercole, and Papagno (1998) have drawn together data supportive of their view that the phonological store is a crucial component of the learning of phonological word-forms. They review evidence from a considerable variety of studies: neuropsychological work with the so-called "short-term memory patients", whose catastrophic performance on auditory ISR is invariably accompanied by a specific deficit in the learning of novel phonological forms; developmental research that shows that, at the early stages of word-learning, vocabulary size can be predicted by ability in ISR and in nonword repetition (NWR); research with gifted adults, which shows an association between language learning ability and immediate memory span, independent of IQ; and research with people with learning disabilities that suggests the same association. Given this proposed dependence of word-form learning on a mechanism that is able to retain sequence information in the short term, it is natural to go further and to suggest that the Hebb repetition effect is a laboratory analogue of word-learning. In naturalistic word-learning, repeated hearings of a novel word, that is a novel sequence of phonemes, can lead to the establishment of a new long-term representation of that sequence in memory. The result of this learning process would comprise the entry of that novel word-form into the mental lexicon.

A relationship between the Hebb repetition effect and the learning of phonological word-forms has, we think, surface plausibility. If the Hebb repetition effect were completely unrelated to word-form learning this would imply that there were two quite distinct mechanisms both of which used phonological short-term memory to learn new phonological sequences. This is particularly the case given the known association between short-term memory and word-form acquisition noted above. To give an example, in a reasonably typical Hebb-type experiment, using auditory letters rather than digits as list-items, one might be asked to recall the list "B J F M L". This would involve repeatedly hearing the sequence, perhaps some rehearsal of it, and repeated recall attempts. Is it likely that this process engages quite different mechanisms from those engaged when one is asked to learn the novel word "beejayeffemmelle", a task that is also facilitated by repeated presentation and (see later) repeated recall? We think not, though some might disagree. Of course, the learning of a novel word is not normally going to occur in isolation, being more likely to be encountered in, say, the learning of an object-name. However, as Baddeley et al. (1998) make clear with reference to such name-learning, it is the learning of the phonological word-form that correlates with short-term serial memory ability, rather than the secondary learning of the association between name and object.

In what follows, we will first supplement this intuition with data from a number of experiments that demonstrate that properties of the Hebb repetition effect align with a number of properties that one would expect to obtain for a word-form learning mechanism. While no amount of such evidence can *guarantee* the existence of a common mechanism, we will maintain that application of Occam's razor places the onus of proof on those who deny it. Then, in the latter part of the chapter, we will offer a qualitative framework, based around our model of short-term ordered memory, within which both Hebb repetition effects and the learning of phonological word-forms can be simulated.

Properties of the Hebb repetition effect

The Hebb repetition effect is not critically dependent on spacing

Following Hebb's (1961) finding of learning for repetitions spaced at every three trials, Melton (1963) claimed that the Hebb repetition effect was significantly reduced at spacings of every six trials and was not evident at all at spacings greater than this. Clearly this result is less than encouraging for our working hypothesis, as it would seem to imply that a novel word would need to be repeated at very short intervals for it to be incorporated into the lexicon. While it is possible that such massed presentation might well assist in the learning of a novel word, it would be preferable to our position if this were not a necessary requirement. In Cumming, Page, Norris, Hitch, & McNeil (2005), we decided to explore the issue further. In three experiments involving the recall of lists of seven or eight single-syllable words, we found an interaction between the spacing of list repetitions and the item-set from which the intervening, nonrepeating, "filler" lists were constructed. To be specific, when all lists (repeating and filler) were constructed by rearrangements of the same fixed set of items (in this case, words), repetition learning was present weakly, if at all, for spacings of either three or six lists. However, when filler lists were constructed from a different set of items from those used in the repeating lists, robust repetition learning was observed at spacings of three, six, nine and twelve lists, with no diminution of the learning effect with increasing spacing. Indeed, if anything, the repetition learning was stronger for 12-apart spacing than for the other spacing conditions.

How does this finding relate back to our working hypothesis regarding the learning of phonological word-forms? Certainly, the confirmation of repetition learning at 12-apart spacing, approaching the highest spacing that can reasonably be achieved in the Hebb (1961) paradigm while maintaining the good humour of participants, is encouraging. Had we found that 12-apart learning was never possible, then we would have had to consider rejecting the word-learning hypothesis. At the same time, the finding with respect to the composition of filler lists had the benefit of demonstrating consistency between our results and those of Melton (1963): in his experiments, Melton had used a closed set of list-items, namely, the digits 1–9, thus inadvertently reducing the extent to which learning could be seen at large spacings. With regard to word-learning, therefore, we predict that it will be difficult to learn, say, a novel word if repeated presentations of that word are spaced by "phonemic anagrams" of that word, that is, by other novel words comprising reorderings of the repeated word's constituent sounds. Given that the average word-length, in English at least, is in the region of 7 phonemes (this is the average over word types, the frequency-weighted token average is about 3.5 phonemes, Cutler, Norris, & Sebastián-Gallés, 2004) each drawn from a pool of around 45, it seems unlikely that the learning of any given novel word will be plagued by such a concentration of phonemic anagrams as are seen in the single-pool variant of the Hebb experiment. Notwithstanding Melton's work, therefore, the working hypothesis lives on.

Multiple lists can be learned simultaneously

In the traditional Hebb (1961) paradigm, learning is restricted to that of a single repeating list in a background of nonrepeating fillers. One would not be surprised, though, to find that learning could subsequently be found for a new repeating list in a fresh learning block, and this is indeed what is found (e.g., Cumming, Page, & Norris, 2003). Is it possible, though, to learn a number of interleaved but repeating lists at the same time? This would certainly be a desirable property if our word-learning hypothesis is to be maintained. The construction of a lexicon would be a rather pedestrian affair if each novel word had to be learned completely before one could begin to learn the next one. Fortunately, the third experiment in Cumming et al. (2005) permitted a clear response to that question. As noted above, repetition learning was demonstrated in that experiment for spacings of 6-apart, 9-apart and 12-apart. Moreover, the experimental design was such that at any given point, the learning of lists at the three different spacings was simultaneously under way. In other words, even though repetitions of the lists at the three different spacings were interleaved with each other and with nonrepeating fillers, robust learning was still observed. This result is self-evidently a good thing regarding our working hypothesis, but it is certainly not self-evident from all perspectives. For example, this finding is difficult to explain from the point of view of a position–item association account of Hebb repetition learning. In such an account (e.g., Burgess & Hitch, 1999), improved performance is explained by the strengthening of associations that are presumed to exist between representations of list-items and representations of the list positions in which they are repeatedly presented. This account has already fared badly in a number of subsequent tests (e.g., Cumming, et al. 2003; Hitch, Fastame, & Flude, 2005a) but its plausibility is weakened still further by simultaneous learning of several different lists. Indeed, in unpublished experiments, we have observed that five interleaved repeating lists can be learned simultaneously. This clearly poses major problems for any account based on learning position–item associations. Each position would have to be associated with multiple items, with no way of knowing which of the associated items should go with each list. This weakness is acknowledged in the latest version of the Burgess and Hitch model (Burgess & Hitch, 2006). In this modified model, multiple banks of positional context units compete for the representation of given lists, in much the same way as multiple, localist, chunk units compete for the same privilege in earlier models by Cohen and Grossberg (1987), Nigrin (1993) and Page (1994), as well as in the model described below. It is hard to see, though, how crosstalk between similar lists can be avoided unless parameters are set such that each list becomes associated with a different set of context units. In that case, though, one would wonder what was "positional" about the model at all, since each bank of context-units might just as well be represented by a localist unit exactly as in the earlier models. Note that one of the main pieces of data that drove the development of positional models was the finding that intrusion errors often involved the recall of an item that had appeared in the same position in a previous list (e.g., Henson, 1999). In a model in which every new list is associated to a novel set of positional-context units, one would not expect to see this form of positional error at all.

There is also a question, in any positional model that resorts to multiple banks of context units, of the account that it might offer of the relationship between immediate serial recall, nonword repetition and the learning of phonological word-forms. Burgess and Hitch (2006) are clear that their modified model only operates at the lexical level, that is, it represents sequences of words. And yet the relationship between ISR and word-form learning seems to call for a common ordering mechanism for words in lists and for sounds in words (see also Gupta, this volume). In our opinion, this calls for a class of model that can operate across the levels of a hierarchy, able to represent order across, say, phonemes, syllables, and words, as the need arises. Gupta's (this volume) model is certainly of this type, having a (single) bank of context units that connects to each of the model's hierarchical levels, driving serial recall at each. (Of course, this property of Gupta's model makes it less appropriate for modelling the Hebb effect.) For Burgess and Hitch, it is rather difficult to see how, say, phonemic associations with one of multiple banks of positional codes could ever constitute a content addressable entry in a mental lexicon, at least not in a manner consistent with the representation of lists of words that they themselves espouse. That is not to say that such a "hierarchically enabled" representation is impossible, but in our opinion it would need such modification (e.g., one context bank per word) as to make it functionally indistinguishable from prior localist, ordinal (i.e., completely nonpositional) models (e.g., Nigrin, 1993; Page, 1994) in which such a hierarchy has already been implemented.

Learning in the Hebb repetition effect is long term

Our word-learning hypothesis would certainly be corroborated if the benefits that accrue from repetition learning were seen to be longer lasting than is traditionally demonstrated. The Hebb repetition effect is usually seen in the context of a series of 20 or more ISR trials, perhaps with a final test at the end of the experiment. Less research has been conducted to investigate the longevity of the learning involved. Fendrich, Healy, and Bourne (1991) showed preserved sequence learning a month after the repeated typing of digit sequences, but conditions were rather different from those seen in the Hebb repetition effect. In the fourth experiment of Cumming et al. (2005), we looked at this directly. A large subset of the participants who had taken part in the experiment, in which they learned several interleaved lists, were unexpectedly asked back into the laboratory approximately 3 months later. They were tested on the recognition and recall of the lists they had previously seen repeatedly, compared with those of previous filler lists (presented once previously) and new recombinations of both Hebb lists and fillers (to control for item, as opposed to order, memory). The key finding was that lists that had been presented and recalled eight times in the prior experiment were both recognized as more familiar and better recalled than any of the controls. This benefit was not just a result of better item-memory, but was specific to the order in which the words had originally been presented. The learning that underlies the Hebb repetition effect is therefore very long-lasting indeed. Learning is of sufficient longevity to make it a suitable mechanism for word-form learning, and therefore consistent with our working hypothesis.

Learning in the Hebb repetition effect is relatively fast

Related to the longevity of Hebb-effect learning is the speed with which learning can proceed. Researchers such as Dollaghan (1985, 1987) have offered convincing evidence that word-learning among children is fast, with children learning both the form and meaning of novel words within a couple of presentations. Clearly, it is difficult to make quantitative comparisons between the learning of quite short, novel words, and the learning of word-lists of somewhat above span-length. Nonetheless, a number of observations can be made. First, it is a matter of logical necessity that the Hebb repetition effect must involve an element of learning on the very first exposure to a given list. If this were not the case, then there would be nothing to distinguish the second presentation of that list from the first presentation, and so on, with the result that learning could never "get started". In an unpublished experiment, we have found even this single-presentation learning to be relatively long-lasting. In a public event focusing on human memory, we exposed casual participants to a number of lists of letters for immediate serial recall. After this brief exposure to 10 or so lists, participants were given an envelope and asked to open it later in the event, after about 20 minutes had elapsed. When they opened the envelope, they were shown a number of lists and asked to rate them for familiarity. Some lists had been seen once previously, and others were entirely new. After they had completed their ratings, they were asked to hand them in to a collection point, together with an estimate of the time that had elapsed since the first part of the experiment. With a mean elapsed duration of over 20 minutes, participants rated lists that they had seen once previously as being more familiar than reordered lists of the same items. While such evidence for fast learning is more illustrative than definitive, it is consistent with observations of sustained improvements in mean recall performance of around 3–4% per repetition in traditional Hebb-effect experiments.

Similar results hold for the nonword repetition paradigm, although once again the relevant data have not often been collected. For example, in an experiment with children's nonword repetitions, we found that the 4/5-year-old participants could recognize, some 4 weeks later, a nonword that had been presented to them on a single occasion. Naturally, if our working hypothesis is correct, then we would expect more traditional Hebb repetition effects to be exhibited by such children too. It is to this issue that we now turn.

The Hebb effect is exhibited by young children

The learning of novel word-forms is clearly something that children do well. If word-form learning and the Hebb repetition effect share an underlying mechanism, we would therefore expect children to show Hebb repetition effects in the context of an ISR task. In a series of experiments, Hitch, McNeil, Page, Cumming, & Norris (2005b) showed that 5-,7- and 10-year old children do indeed show a Hebb repetition effect, although it was somewhat more difficult to find than had been anticipated. This weakness of the observed Hebb effects sometimes necessitated a reduction in the number of intervening filler lists, from Hebb's (1961) two, to one or even zero. Stronger effects were seen, too, when filler lists were taken from different categories (e.g., digits versus letters) from that of the repeating list, somewhat reminiscent of the experiments described above that showed stronger repetition effects for nonoverlapping filler-sets.

Finding Hebb effects in young children, even those young enough to be assumed not to be using strategies such as cumulative rehearsal, is a relief from our word-learning perspective. Nonetheless, the unexpected weakness of the effect might also serve to highlight an important issue in a framework such as ours (and, say, Gupta's, this volume) that assumes a common mechanism for word-learning and list-learning. The issue concerns the hierarchical level at which learning is presumed to take place. In word-learning, the sequence that is being learned is one of sublexical representations, be they phonemes or, for longer words, possibly syllables. These sequences are continuous, in the sense that they do not incorporate significant pauses in between sequence-items, and the sequence elements do not themselves have semantic or syntactic properties (assuming, of course, that they are not morphemes). Word-list learning is, however, somewhat different. The lists are typically punctuated by pauses during which strategic activity, such as rehearsal, might well take place, particularly for adult participants. Moreover, the list elements carry both meaning and syntactic information. Thus, while the data reviewed by Baddeley et al. (1998) strongly suggest a link between mechanisms underlying immediate serial recall and those engaged in word-form learning, we should not be blind to the different contexts in which this mechanism operates in the two tasks. The difference might be particularly important when considering word-learning in young children, for whom a list of words for immediate serial recall might lack the coherence of a novel word for repetition and/or learning. It is certainly possible that adult strategies such as list-rehearsal serve both to establish coherence across inter-word pauses and, of course, to provide additional list-repetitions, both of which would be either unavailable, or less available, to children. This would tend to weaken Hebb effects in children. It might also be that children are more adversely affected than are adults by the composition of the nonrepeating filler lists: this is certainly suggested by the manipulations of spacing and of filler-set. This factor might well interact with a lack of list-coherence, or a lack of focus at the whole-list level, to render the Hebb repetition effect still weaker in child participants. The fact that the Hebb repetition effect is seen at all is, however, consistent (though not exclusively so), with the idea of a mechanism shared with the word-learning process.

Partial lists can be learned

The issue of list-coherence also arises in relation to the learning of parts of lists. Schwartz and Bryden (1971) were the first to show that list-learning was prevented when the first two items of a list were changed on each "repetition". Hitch et al. (2005a) confirmed and extended these results. Together, these results have been used to falsify early positional models of the Hebb effect (e.g., Burgess & Hitch, 1999), and they are also uncomfortable for those that might want to look for an account of the effect based on associative chaining from one list-item to the next. From our perspective, these important results, together with others (e.g., Cumming et al , 2003; Page, Cumming, Norris, Hitch, & McNeil, 2006), suggest a chunking account of the Hebb repetition effect (see below), in which chunk access is conditional on the correctly ordered arrival of all list-items, with the consequence that it fails definitively if early list-items do not match. Nigrin (1993) and Page (1994) both published models of this kind. Moreover, this property is very reminiscent of (and, we will claim, functionally identical to) the well-known cohort effects seen in lexical access (Marslen-Wilson & Tyler, 1980).

Naturally, if list-learning is essentially chunk-learning, then it should be possible to learn partial lists provided the repeating portion is represented as somewhat distinct from the remainder of the list. Using Bregman's (1990) terminology, we should be able to find learning of partial lists that are *streamed* separately from other list-items. A number of preliminary results suggest that this is indeed the case. In two so-far unpublished sets of experiments, we investigated this issue in rather different ways. In the first, we showed that a sequence of 6 digits that appeared repeatedly within otherwise random longer 10-digit sequences was not well learned when the point at which the repeating portion began in the longer list varied between positions 2, 3 and 4: performance on the repeating portion never differed from that on the equivalent positions of nonrepeating lists. When, however, the repeating portion was presented in a different voice from the remainder of the list (i.e., it was streamed separately by voice), then learning of the repeating portion was evident, even when the entire 10-item list had to be recalled on each occasion. This is reminiscent of results from Hughes and Jones (2004), who showed that the Hebb repetition effect is abolished by having items within a given repeating list presented in different voices. In the second series of experiments, we showed that individual groups could be learned in an experiment in which word-lists were grouped by pauses. In these experiments, the repetition was that of individual groups rather than that of whole lists, and the relative position of repeating groups could vary from trial to trial. This is, perhaps, analogous to the appearance of a novel word in various different contexts over the course of learning. Overall, the results suggested that learning did indeed take place at the level of sublist chunks, where the chunk boundaries were circumscribed by the grouping structure of the overarching list. The learning of these sublist chunks did not seem to comprise the establishment of associations between list-items and either within-list or within-group positions. Nor did they appear to correspond to the learning of chains of associations, since the recall advantage accrued to all items in learned chunks including the first item, no matter where the chunk appeared in the overall structure of the list. We concluded that learning comprised the establishment of new chunks in longer-term memory, with the subsequent recognition of these chunks serving to assist in their recall. The idea of chunk boundaries aligning with group boundaries and, by extension, stream boundaries, is completely consistent with the early findings of Winzenz (1972), who showed, among other things, that list-learning by repetition did not extend to "repetitions" in which the ordering of items remained the same, but the grouping structure changed from trial to trial.

The Hebb effect does not require recall, but is strongest when recall is attempted

Past research (Cohen & Johansson (1967a, 1967b; Cunningham, Healy, & Williams, 1984) has appeared to show that a Hebb repetition effect only accrues when recall is attempted on each relevant trial of the learning phase. In Page, Cumming, Norris, Hitch, and McNeil (2005), we looked at this issue a little more closely, using a somewhat stronger manipulation of the Hebb effect, with more repetitions and a nonoverlapping filler-set. Our conclusion was somewhat different from that of prior work: while Hebb repetition effects were certainly stronger when recall was attempted, we did find evidence for both increased familiarity and better recall of lists that had been presented repeatedly but never recalled. In these experiments, covert recall of the auditorily presented stimulus lists was prevented (as far as was possible) by requiring the reading of another word-list from the screen during what would have otherwise been the recall phase of the trial. Using this design, we were additionally able to show that recall, and to a lesser extent recognition, was enhanced for a list that had been repeatedly read from the screen, but never heard as a stimulus list and, hence, never recalled.

   Finding significant Hebb repetition effects under presentation-only conditions is positive from the point of view of our working hypothesis. Word-form learning is clearly able to proceed in children too young to be able to produce the words themselves. If list-production were absolutely necessary in the Hebb repetition effect then we might be forced to explain the different pattern of results. Having said that, our experiments did clearly demonstrate that repetition effects were stronger when recall was attempted and that this was apparently not solely to do with the number of times a list, or a recalled approximation of it, were recalled overall. Do we see the corresponding effect in word-form learning? That is, are word-forms better learned if participants attempt to recall them overtly during learning? To us, the intuitive answer is yes. Casual observation suggests that infants often repeat a portion of what has been said to them, where that portion might correspond to the last word or, later, the last few words. But "data" is not the plural of "anecdote", and we have found it difficult to find any literature that answers the question directly. In a collaboration with Tania Zamuner, therefore, we have carried out some preliminary experiments to look at the matter. Over three such experiments with 4- to 5-year-old children, we did find that repetition of a novel word enhanced its subsequent recognition, even when overall frequency of occurrence (hearings plus recalls) was controlled.

A unified framework for modelling the Hebb repetition effect and word-form learning

In what remains of this chapter, we will outline a framework for modelling both the Hebb repetition effect and the learning of other sequences such as those corresponding to phonological word-forms. The framework is based on models going back to Grossberg (1978), via Cohen and Grossberg (1987), Nigrin (1993) and Page (1994), but departs from each of these in some important ways. Space forbids a detailed quantitative description of the mechanics of the model; rather we will outline the general principles underlying the operation of the model, relating them back to some of the issues covered above.

The model is a localist, connectionist model: that is to say, the presence of any item that can be said to have been learned by the model will be indicated in the model by the maximal activation of at least one connectionist unit, such that that unit does not respond maximally in the presence of any other item (see Page, 2000, for much more on the issue of localist representation in connectionist models). In the context of immediate serial recall of lists of letters, digits or familiar words, it will be assumed that the model already contains at least one localist representation of each list-item. That is what it means, in the model, to say that an item is familiar. In addition, it will be assumed that there are also individual units representing known sublexical items, such as phonemes (or, more accurately, allophones), and possibly syllables. Because their activation signals the occurrence of the corresponding item, these units will be known as "occurrence units", and the total collection of such units will be known as the "occurrence layer". The topology of the model is illustrated in Figure 7.1. Importantly, at any one time, there will be units available in the occurrence layer that have yet to be committed to the representation of any item; in line with the prior models mentioned above, these will be referred to as "uncommitted" occurrence units. There is only one layer of occurrence units, and that can contain within it, say, some units representing phonemes, some units representing syllables, some units representing words,

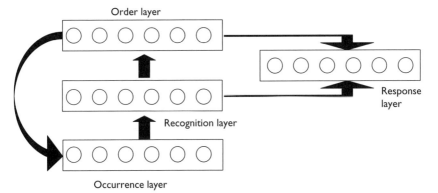

Figure 7.1 The topology of the model. Black arrows indicate one-to-one connections between layers. The order layer has excitatory within-layer connections; the recognition layer has inhibitory within-layer connections.

and some units representing familiar sequences of words (e.g., "The cat sat on the mat"). This single-layer structure is in contrast to the hierarchical structure seen in the predecessor models (e.g., Nigrin, 1993; Page, 1994). For our purposes, we will assume that the phoneme units are primary, in the sense that their activation is driven directly by pattern recognition processes exterior to the model; this assumption is founded on the idea that the recognition of phonemes does not constitute sequence recognition. By contrast, all the other occurrence units are secondary, in the sense that their activation is driven by the sequential activation of other units in the occurrence layer.

Immediately above the occurrence layer is another layer of units called the recognition units, each of which is in a one-to-one relationship with a corresponding occurrence unit. Strong activation of a recognition unit signals the recognition of the associated pattern within the model. Recognition units compete with each other to signal recognition in the same way as do masking field units in the model of Cohen and Grossberg (1987) and the later variants (Nigrin, 1993; Page, 1994), and in a manner that is commonly described as lexical competition in models such as the Shortlist model of word recognition from continuous speech (Norris, 1994). In order briefly to characterize the difference between the occurrence layer and the recognition layer, consider presentation of the stimulus "CAT". In the occurrence layer, five units will activate: those corresponding to the three phonemes (actually probably allophones) in the word and those corresponding to the familiar words CAT and AT, all of which are in some sense present in the stimulus signal. By contrast, at the recognition layer, competitive processes will ensure that only a single unit activates strongly, namely that corresponding to the word CAT. The competitive processes at the recognition layer therefore indicate the most likely lexical parsing, based on the entirety of the stimulus signal. Such processes have been described in great detail elsewhere, and will not be our focus here. In relation to this simple example, though, it is important to note that had the words CAT and AT not been familiar, then there would have been no such lexical entries to suppress activation of units corresponding to the word's constituent phonemes, and it would have been these three units that would have activated at the recognition layer. Suppression of "lower-level" representations (e.g., phonemes) by higher-level ones (e.g., words) is what constitutes chunking in this model and those from which it was developed.

There exists a third layer of units driven once again in a one-to-one and unidirectional fashion by the units in the recognition layer. This layer is called the "order" layer and it stores item and order information corresponding to the sequence of recognized words. The representation of serial order in our model is, unsurprisingly, the same as that in our primacy model of immediate serial recall (Page & Norris, 1998). (Indeed, the primacy model itself is based on elements of the earlier work mentioned above and, in particular, by Grossberg, 1978.) To be specific, the recognition of a sequence of familiar items at the recognition layer, be they phonemes/syllables in a previously unfamiliar word (as in the nonword repetition task) or familiar words (as in the ISR task), will result in a primacy gradient of activation at the order layer, such that units corresponding to items presented earlier in the sequence will have the higher activation. Once an item is represented at the order layer, its corresponding representation is reset at the recognition layer. Again, the details of the primacy model are described in sufficient detail elsewhere to preclude a reprisal here. Finally, each order-unit projects activation back down to its corresponding occurrence unit, and this information is used in the establishment of new occurrence units that come to represent sequences of "lower-level" items.

Before reflecting on some of the properties of the Hebb repetition effect and of word-form learning described above, we shall briefly outline the manner in which higher-order sequence representations can be learned. Again, space precludes a detailed quantitative account, but the qualitative account we offer here should be sufficient to elucidate the framework in which the model operates. As noted previously, the occurrence layer always contains a number of units that are uncommitted to any pattern. These uncommitted units are weakly connected to quite a large proportion of other occurrence units, but the "synaptic weights" on these connections are small and relatively homogeneous. These weights do not, therefore, strongly constrain the circumstances in which a given uncommitted unit activates (see below). By contrast, an occurrence unit that has learned to recognize a given sequence will have a pattern of weights on its input connections that is derived from the primacy gradient of activations representing that sequence. To give an abstract example, an occurrence unit that comes to encode the sequence ABCDE will have connections from the occurrence units for A, B, C, D and E, such that the weight on the connection from the A-unit to the

ABCDE-unit will exceed that from the B-unit, which in turn will be larger than that from the C-unit, and so on. There will thus be a primacy gradient in connection weights, which is essentially a scaled copy of the primacy gradient in activations across order-units that is repeatedly instated during repeated presentation of a novel word-form (where A, B, C, D and E represent, say, phonemes) or a new word-list (where the letters represent list-items).

The way in which occurrence units activate exclusively in response to their learned sequence is also different from that outlined in previous models of this class. In early work (e.g., Cohen & Grossberg, 1987), activation of a higher-level occurrence unit was a function of the dot product between the vector representing primacy-gradient activations and the vector representing that unit's incoming synaptic weights. So if the primacy gradient of activations across representations of the letters A, B and C was 5, 4.5 and 4 respectively, and the corresponding weights to the ABC-unit were 10, 9 and 8, the dot product would be equal to $(5 \times 10) + (4.5 \times 9) + (4 \times 8) = 122.5$, and the ABC-unit would activate as a function of this input. Later work (e.g., Nigrin, 1993; Page 1994) identified problems with the use of the dot product and more complex calculations were developed. All these calculations depended, however, on the combined presence of a set of synaptic weights and a primacy gradient of activations corresponding to the stimulus list. We now believe any such calculation to be unsustainable, at least in the framework we are proposing.

There are two main reasons. First, in the framework proposed above, for there to be a primacy gradient corresponding to each of the items A, B and C in that order, then each of them in turn must have won a competition for recognition at the recognition layer (since activation at the order-layer is contingent on such a sequence of recognitions having occurred). But if each of the constituent items (A, B and C) must already have been recognized before the (dot product) input to the ABC-unit can be calculated, there would no longer be any opportunity, at the recognition layer, for activation of the ABC-unit to suppress activation in the units corresponding to its constituent items. The only reason that previous versions of the model were able to avoid this problem was that they incorporated a hierarchical structure with units corresponding to, say, phonemes at one level, words at another, and word sequences at another. This causes its own problems, which are beyond the purview of this chapter.

Second, it will be a fundamental part of the framework that we are suggesting that so-called short-term memory patients, whose immediate serial recall, nonword recall and word-form learning are very poor, suffer from not being able to form a primacy gradient of activations in response to a stimulus sequence. However, it is well known that such patients are perfectly able to recognize sequences that they learned prior to their deficit. Ipso facto, such recognition cannot depend on the presence of a primacy gradient, or any dot product calculated using it. In short, in our framework, a primacy gradient in activations is necessary during sequence (word-form) learning, since the primacy gradient in synaptic weights is a learned version of the primacy gradient in activations, but is not necessary for subsequent sequence (word-form) recognition.

Our new mechanism for the activation of sequence-representing occurrence units does not, therefore, require the presence of a primacy gradient. It does, however, require the occurrence of each of the constituent items in the correct rank order. Again, a detailed mathematical exposition would be out of place here, but the essential idea can be summarized quite succinctly. Suppose that an ABC-unit (i.e., an occurrence unit representing the sequence ABC), has incoming weights equal to 10, 9 and 8 from the A, B and C units respectively. Assume also that when each of the units A, B and C is activated, each emits a pulse of activation of unit magnitude to all connected units, with that pulse's effect being modulated (multiplied) by the weight of the connection. Further suppose that the ABC-unit has a threshold, and that only incoming pulses above that threshold value can cause the ABC-unit itself to fire. Finally, assume that each time the ABC-unit fires, its threshold is lowered by a given value, say 1. If we assume that the resting threshold for the ABC-unit is, say, 9.5, then it is easy to see that the ABC-unit will only fire its maximum three times, if the items A, B and C, arrive in the rank order encoded in the primacy gradient of weighted connections. When A occurs, a unit pulse is sent from the A-unit to the ABC-unit, modulated by the connection weight 10 between the two. This signal 10 exceeds the threshold of 9.5, so the ABC-unit fires once and, as a consequence, its threshold is reduced to 8.5. When the B-unit fires, it causes a signal of strength 9 to arrive at the ABC-unit. This exceeds the new threshold, so the ABC-unit fires again and the threshold is accordingly lowered to 7.5. The arrival from a signal of strength 8 from the C-unit causes a third firing of the ABC-unit. In this way, the arrival of the items A, B and C in the correct order as specified by the ranking of incoming weights to the ABC-unit causes that unit to fire maximally. By contrast, applying the same procedure, the list ACB will only fire the ABC-unit once (in response to the A), and so on for other approximations to the learned list. In the full model, the firing is probabilistic, and there are multiple pulses per event, but the essential mechanism is the same.

Using this activation mechanism, it is clear that occurrence units that have learned a given sequence will activate whenever that sequence occurs in the input. Whether the sequences are fully recognized depends on the competitive processes at the recognition layer. These processes in turn influence what is stored at the order layer. For example, if the network has occurrence units for ABC, ABCD and DE, then it is perfectly possible that the stimulus ABCDE will be parsed as a recognition of ABC followed by a recognition of DE, which will be represented more compactly as a list of two familiar items (ABC followed by DE) at the order layer than the occurrence of the five items A, B, C, D and E would otherwise suggest. To reiterate, this is what is meant by chunking in this model. The competitive relationships that implement such a parsing at the recognition level are the subject of a good deal of previous work (e.g., Nigrin, 1993; Norris, 1994; Page 1994) and will not be discussed further here.

In outlining our framework, it only remains to specify the conditions under which learning of a new sequence will occur and of what that learning comprises. It will be simplest to use as an example the Hebb repetition-learning of a list of familiar items, say words. In this case, each ISR trial involves the presentation of a sequence of stimuli that is, in some sense, coherent. Sequence-items almost always come from a single spatial source and are presented in a common voice (for auditory) or format (for visual). In the absence of grouping cues, the boundaries of this coherent sequence are clearly delimited. In other words, if a sequence is to be learned at all, then it is very clear what that sequence comprises. Any such coherent sequence will be learned, to some extent, after a single presentation. This is because the system has no way of knowing whether the sequence is going to become frequent in the future (see above regarding the necessity of first-trial learning). It is for this reason that any novel coherent sequence in memory will get partially learned by the most active uncommitted unit that is available when the sequence ends. When partial learning has occurred, but before full commitment is achieved, a unit is said to be provisionally committed.

Because of the way uncommitted units respond to incoming sequences (i.e., sequences of firings of other occurrence units), there is always very likely to be at least one that is active at the end of any given sequence. As noted above, uncommitted units have low incoming weights, but remain responsive to incoming stimuli because they also have a low threshold of activation. Suppose, for example, that an uncommitted occurrence unit is widely (or even fully) connected to other occurrence units in the occurrence layer, with weights that are distributed randomly, but fairly tightly, around the value 1. If we assume also that the threshold is set to around 95% of the maximum weight (as it was for the committed unit discussed above) and that as the unit fires, the threshold reduces by appropriately scaled increments but does not drop below a minimum value of, say, 0.5. It should be clear that such an uncommitted unit will respond to a large variety of possible sequences. For this reason, at the end of any given coherent sequence, there will always be activated uncommitted occurrence units ready to learn the sequence. If the sequence is already (somewhat) familiar, however, there will also be an activated committed (or provisionally committed) unit. In order to prevent proliferation of units committed to the same sequence, a competitive mechanism is needed that will prevent learning at uncommitted units for sequences for which a committed unit already exists. Fortunately, there exists sufficient mechanism at the recognition layer, which is inherently geared towards competition. Essentially, for any coherent sequence for which there is no occurrence unit that spans the sequence, learning will accrue to the most active uncommitted/provisional unit. On the first presentation of a novel list, that will be an uncommitted unit; on the second and subsequent presentations it will be the same unit, which is now provisionally committed, until eventually the unit becomes fully committed to representing the given sequence. It is only at that point, when the unit becomes fully committed, that the unit will be enabled to suppress recognition of its constituent parts by competition at the recognition layer, and parse the sequence by its activation alone.

All this functionality can be achieved by ensuring that: uncommitted/provisional recognition units (i.e., those recognition units corresponding to uncommitted/provisional occurrence cells) can compete with each other; that their activation can be suppressed by competitive activation of other committed recognition units; but that they cannot suppress activation of those committed recognition units until they have accrued sufficient learning to become fully committed themselves. This asymmetric competitive arrangement between committed and uncommitted/provisional recognition units allows uncommitted units to activate when no other existing units better parse the sequence, but ensures that such activation does not prevent recognition of the sequence elements and the generation of the primacy gradient that the uncommitted unit needs to learn. When such an uncommitted unit sustains high activation at the recognition layer, its occurrence unit learns the primacy gradient that is projected down from the order layer to the occurrence units of the list-items that drove its activation. Over the course of several such learning trials, during which a primacy gradient builds up in the provisional unit's incoming weights, the previously uncommitted unit becomes specialized in the recognition and processing of the learned sequence.

How does the learned activation of a new occurrence unit enable progressively better recall of, say, a repeating list in a Hebb-type experiment? Each recognition unit is assumed to be connected to a production unit located in a fourth layer called the production layer. Each unit in the production layer is connected to the corresponding units in both the recognition layer and the order layer. For this reason, when a primacy gradient of activations is in place at the order layer, then the equivalent gradient is copied into the production layer (perhaps when a signal to recall is issued). Moreover, if a provisionally committed unit is active at the recognition layer (which it will be if the input stimulus is consistent with its provisionally learned pattern) then its corresponding production unit will also be active. Under these circumstances, this provisionally active production unit will learn the activation pattern across the other active production units. That is, it will learn a primacy gradient across its outgoing weighted connections that will enable it to produce the correct activation gradient across its constituent items, when it is activated as an isolated chunk. During this learning period, activation of the provisional production unit for an entire list, say ABCDE, will project its partially learned primacy gradient onto the production units of its list-constituents (i.e., the production units for A, B, C, D and E). This small learned gradient will add to that projected from the order layer, to produce a primacy gradient that is higher in activation, and steeper (in terms of activation step) than the primacy gradient corresponding to a list for which no provisional production unit exists. Given that a steeper primacy gradient will result in fewer order errors (when noise disrupts the correct rank order of gradient items) and a higher-activation gradient will result in fewer omission errors, the gradual learning of a primacy gradient in the outgoing weights of a provisionally committed production unit will result in the gradual recall improvement characteristic of the Hebb repetition effect. Once the unit is fully committed, activation of it alone will be sufficient to permit recall of its encoded list.

Finally, while we have described the model in terms of list recall, the same mechanism will apply to the learning of word-forms. Word-forms, in the conception presented here, are lists much like any other. The application to novel word-forms presented in isolation is straightforward. Slightly more involved is the application to word-forms presented in continuous speech. The principal issue here is what constitutes a coherent sequence (i.e., a possible word-form). Remember that in the context of the Hebb repetition effect, it is relatively clear where the boundaries of the to-be-learned list are located. In continuous speech the boundaries are less clear. That having been said, a good deal of research has shown that even quite young infants are sensitive to a variety of cues as to possible/likely word boundaries. These include pauses, lexical stress, lengthening, bigram probabilities, allophonic distinctions, etc. We suggest that the learning of such probabilistic cues, which has been shown both to precede and to influence word-form segmentation and learning, can permit good hypotheses to be made as to where coherent sequences begin and end. Regrettably, space restrictions forbid a more detailed exposition – this would probably require a chapter to itself.

Conclusion

To conclude, we will now briefly consider each of the properties of the Hebb effect and of word-form learning that were described in the first half of this chapter, and relate them to the model developed in the second half. The Hebb repetition effect was found not critically to depend on spacing; in our model, the learning carried out by a provisionally committed list-unit would be easily able to span any reasonable spacing. The use of filler lists all derived from a single-item pool shared with that of repeating lists will lead to a proliferation of units all provisionally committed to lists that are anagrams of each other. Simulations of the threshold-based activation mechanism have shown that in the early stages of learning, anagrams can cause inadvertent (though nonmaximal) activation of a given list-unit. Activation of a large number of provisional recognition units will slow down learning via the competitive relationships that exist between such units at the recognition layer. For this reason, Hebb repetition learning will be faster when filler lists are drawn from a separate item-pool. Multiple lists will be able to be learned simultaneously because, in the model, different units will come to represent those different lists. Given the properties of localist models, such learning can be either fast or slow, and can persist over long periods of time, without any risk of interference with previously stored knowledge. Hebb repetition effects will be found with young children, though the strength of these might be compromised to the extent that the children fail to perceive, say, word-lists as coherent streams. Moreover, partial lists will be learnable if factors relating to perceptual organization (e.g., grouping, streaming) permit somewhat distinct representation of the repeating parts. Finally, an attempt to recall a list will promote learning, not least because the recall attempt will constitute a second (and hopefully veridical) hearing.

In this chapter, we hope to have given some cause to believe that the Hebb repetition effect and the learning of phonological word-forms are related, and we have offered a qualitative description of a localist connectionist framework within which both might be modelled. The long-term viability of this framework will, of course, depend on its ability to furnish quantitative simulations of some of the data discussed above, and more. We are optimistic that it will be able to do so.

References

Baddeley, A. (1986). *Working memory*. New York: Clarendon Press/Oxford University Press.

Baddeley, A. D., & Hitch, G. J. (1974). Working memory. In G. H. Bower (Ed.), *Recent advances in learning and motivation* (Vol. 8, pp. 47–90). New York: Academic Press.

Baddeley, A., Gathercole, S., & Papagno, C. (1998). The phonological loop as a language learning device. *Psychological Review, 105*(1), 158–173.

Bregman, A. S. (1990). *Auditory scene analysis: The perceptual organization of sound.* Cambridge, MA: MIT Press.

Brown, G. D. A., Neath, I., & Chater, N. (2007). A temporal ratio model of memory. *Psychological Review, 114*(3), 539–576.

Brown, G. D. A., Preece, T., & Hulme, C. (2000). Oscillator-based memory for serial order. *Psychological Review, 107*(1), 127–181.

Burgess, N., & Hitch, G. J. (1992). Toward a network model of the articulatory loop. *Journal of Memory and Language, 31*(4), 429–460.

Burgess, N., & Hitch, G. J. (1999). Memory for serial order: A network model of the phonological loop and its timing. *Psychological Review, 106*(3), 551–581.

Burgess, N., & Hitch, G. J. (2006). A revised model of short-term memory and long-term learning of verbal sequences. *Journal of Memory and Language, 55*(4), 627–652.

Cohen, M. A., & Grossberg, S. (1987). Masking fields: A massively parallel neural architecture for learning, recognizing, and predicting multiple groupings of patterned data. *Applied Optics, 26*(10), 1866–1891.

Cohen, R. L., & Johansson, B. S. (1967a). Some relevant factors in the transfer of material from short-term to long-term memory. *Quarterly Journal of Experimental Psychology, 19*(4), 300–308.

Cohen, R. L., & Johansson, B. S. (1967b). The activity trace in immediate memory: A re-evaluation. *Journal of Verbal Learning and Verbal Behavior, 6*(1), 139–143.

Cumming, N., Page, M. P. A., & Norris, D. (2003). Testing a positional model of the Hebb effect. *Memory, 11*(1), 43–63.

Cumming, N., Page, M. P. A., Norris, D., Hitch, G., & McNeil, A. M. (2005). Repetition spacing and order competition effects in the Hebb repetition task. Paper submitted to the *Journal of Memory and Language.*

Cunningham, T. F., Healy, A. F., & Williams, D. M. (1984). Effects of repetition on short-term retention of order information. *Journal of Experimental Psychology: Learning, Memory, and Cognition, 10*(4), 575–597.

Cutler, A., Norris, D., & Sebastián-Gallés, N. (2004). *Phonemic repertoire and similarity within the vocabulary.* Paper presented at the 8th International Conference on Spoken Language Processing.

Dollaghan, C. (1985). Child meets word: "Fast mapping" in preschool children. *Journal of Speech and Hearing Research, 28*(3), 449–454.

Dollaghan, C. A. (1987). Fast mapping in normal and language-impaired children. *Journal of Speech and Hearing Disorders, 52*(3), 218–222.

Farrell, S., & Lewandowsky, S. (2002). An endogenous distributed model of ordering in serial recall. *Psychonomic Bulletin and Review, 9*(1), 59–79.

Fendrich, D. W., Healy, A. F., & Bourne, L. E. (1991). Long-term repetition effects for motoric and perceptual procedures. *Journal of Experimental Psychology: Learning, Memory, and Cognition, 17*(1), 137–151.

Grossberg, S. (1978). Behavioral contrast in short-term memory: Serial binary memory models or parallel continuous memory models. *Journal of Mathematical Psychology, 17*, 199–219.

Hebb, D. O. (1961). Distinctive features of learning in the higher animal. In J. F. Delafresnaye (Ed.), *Brain mechanisms and learning* (pp. 37–46). Oxford: Blackwell.

Henson, R. N. A. (1998). Short-term memory for serial order: The Start-End Model. *Cognitive Psychology, 36*(2), 73–137.

Henson, R. N. A. (1999). Positional information in short-term memory: Relative or absolute? *Memory and Cognition, 27*(5), 915–927.

Hitch, G. J., Fastame, M. C., & Flude, B. (2005a). How is the serial order of a verbal sequence coded? Some comparisons between models. *Memory, 13*(3–4), 247–258.

Hitch, G. J., McNeil, A. M., Page, M. P. A., Cumming, N., & Norris, D. (2005b). Do children show a Hebb effect? Paper submitted to the *Journal of Child Language.*

Hughes, R. W., & Jones, D. M. (2004) *Hebbian auditory sequence learning: The role of passive perceptual processes.* Poster presented at the 45th Annual Meeting of the Psychonomic Society. Minneapolis, USA.

Marslen-Wilson, W., & Tyler, L. K. (1980). The temporal structure of spoken language understanding. *Cognition, 8*(1), 1–71.

McKelvie, S. J. (1987). Learning and awareness in the Hebb digits task. *Journal of General Psychology*, *114*(1), 75–88.

Melton, A. W. (1963). Implications of short-term memory for a general theory of memory. *Journal of Verbal Learning and Verbal Behavior*, *2*, 1–21.

Neath, I. (2000). Modeling the effects of irrelevant speech on memory. *Psychonomic Bulletin and Review*, *7*(3), 403–423.

Nigrin, A. (1993). *Neural networks for pattern recognition*. Cambridge, MA: MIT Press.

Norris, D. (1994). Shortlist: A connectionist model of continuous speech recognition. *Cognition*, *52*(3), 189–234.

Page, M. P. A. (1994). Modelling the perception of musical sequences with self-organizing neural networks. *Connection Science*, *6*(2–3), 223–246.

Page, M. P. A. (2000). Connectionist modelling in psychology: A localist manifesto. *Behavioral and Brain Sciences*, *23*(4), 443–512.

Page, M. P. A., Cumming, N., Norris, D., Hitch, G. J., & McNeil, A. M. (2005). Exploring the importance of list recall in the Hebb repetition effect. Paper submitted to *Memory and Cognition*.

Page, M. P. A., Cumming, N., Norris, D., Hitch, G. J., & McNeil, A. M. (2006). Repetition learning in the immediate serial recall of visual and auditory materials. *Journal of Experimental Psychology: Learning, Memory, and Cognition*, *32*(4), 716–733.

Page, M. P. A., Madge, A., Cumming, N., & Norris, D. G. (2007). Speech errors and the phonological similarity effect in short-term memory: Evidence suggesting a common locus. *Journal of Memory and Language*, *56*(1), 49–64.

Page, M. P. A., & Norris, D. (1998). The primacy model: A new model of immediate serial recall. *Psychological Review*, *105*(4), 761–781.

Schwartz, M., & Bryden, M. P. (1971). Coding factors in the learning of repeated digit sequences. *Journal of Experimental Psychology*, *87*(3), 331–334.

Stadler, M. A. (1993). Implicit serial learning: Questions inspired by Hebb (1961). *Memory and Cognition*, *21*(6), 819–827.

Winzenz, D. (1972). Group structure and coding in serial learning. *Journal of Experimental Psychology*, *92*(1), 8–19.

8 Lexical and semantic influences on immediate serial recall: A role for redintegration

George P. Stuart and Charles Hulme

Overview

In this chapter we will consider the influence of a range of lexical and semantic variables on short-term memory (immediate serial recall) tasks. The term "lexical variables" refers to word properties, such as word frequency and concreteness, which reflect differences in the way in which words are represented in "long-term" or lexical memory. The fact that such lexical variables influence short-term memory tasks provides prima facie evidence that such tasks depend critically upon long-term memory representations, or more radically, that the fractionation of memory into short- and long-term stores may be unnecessary. We begin by describing the historical development of our own ideas, in the context of the trace decay models that have dominated the latter half of the twentieth century. Our primary aim is to show the influences and development of the redintegration model (Hulme, Roodenrys, Schweickert, Brown, Martin, & Stuart, 1997). However in the process, we will acknowledge parallel developments in other models. After outlining some of the major findings in the area, we draw out their theoretical implications and describe some of those models that have begun to take into account these findings.

A brief and partial history

The distinction between short- and long-term memory is one with a very long history, perhaps first brought to prominence in William James' (1890) distinction between primary and secondary memory. The field of cognitive psychology blossomed in the middle of the twentieth century. Cognitive psychology was heavily influenced by metaphors drawn from computer science. Expressions such as hardware and software, permanent memory vs. temporary memory and information processing from computer science were applied to the study of cognitive processes in people. Within the field of cognitive psychology, the study of memory is perhaps the area where the application of an information-processing approach, and computer metaphors in particular, seem most natural.

At the same time that computer programmers and computer scientists were developing and applying flow charts and Venn diagrams and sub-dividing the functions of random access memory and read only memory, so the pioneering cognitive psychologists were organizing mental representations into ordinate and super-ordinate categories and producing bisected models of human memory, represented in the classical flow chart style by boxes with connecting arrows. Indeed, so popular were these types of model that Broadbent would come to popularize one such model (Atkinson & Shiffrin, 1968) as representative of the whole class, labelling it the 'modal model'. Perhaps the most lasting influence of the modal model was its emphasis on the separation of short- and long-term memory. This dominance has remained in spite of subsequent processing accounts such as levels of processing (Craik & Lockhart, 1972) and transfer appropriate processing (Morris, Bransford, & Franks, 1977) and their derivatives, all of which have attempted to move the focus away from the underlying architecture and towards the underlying processes. While the modal model largely dominated thought on the issue of memory during the middle part of the twentieth century, its successor, the working memory model (Baddeley & Hitch, 1974), has dominated the latter decades of the twentieth and the beginning of the twenty-first century. For this reason, we will begin with a reappraisal of the working memory model and examine those findings that it can and cannot account for. We will go on to argue that any model that separates short- and long-term memory so completely will struggle to account for the ubiquitous effects of lexical variables on short-term memory tasks. In the light of such evidence that argument becomes not if, but in what ways, long-term memory influences short-term memory.

According to the working memory model, verbal short-term memory is constrained both by its limited storage capacity and by temporal constraints on rehearsal (e.g., Baddeley & Hitch, 1974; Baddeley, Lewis, & Vallar, 1984). A fundamental assumption of trace decay models is that the short-term memory trace is based on a phonological code. Without rehearsal, the phonological memory trace will decay and the memory will be lost in approximately 2 seconds. In this way trace decay models, epitomized by the phonological loop of the original working memory model (Baddeley & Hitch, 1974), may be seen as closed systems. Once the information to be retained has entered this system, the success or failure of retention and retrieval is determined exclusively by the intrinsic characteristics of the imported items. Loss from the system depends on temporal decay. The most salient and commonly cited stimulus properties that affect retention are phonological form and articulatory duration.

A classic finding relating to the importance of articulatory duration was reported by Baddeley, Thomson, and Buchanan (1975). In this paper serial recall of lists of 1-, 2-, 3-, 4- and 5-syllable words was assessed together with the maximal rate at which participants could read aloud lists of the memory items. When recall was plotted against maximal articulation rate (performance was averaged across participants) a striking pattern emerged with a linear relationship between recall and articulation rate. The slope of this function (which was about 1.8 seconds) was interpreted as an estimate of the decay time of the phonological loop. Thus recall was not limited in terms of the number of items that could be recalled (cf. Miller's, 1956, magical number 7) but rather in terms of the duration of a sequence of items, which in turn reflected the rate of decay, and the speed with which items could be rehearsed in order to overcome decay.

One other signature of the role of phonological coding comes from the phonological similarity effect (Conrad & Hull, 1964; Baddeley, 1966): the finding that serial recall of lists of phonologically similar letters (e.g., P D V C T) or words (e.g., mad, man, map, mat) is worse than the recall of phonologically dissimilar letters (e.g., K Y Z W R) or words (e.g., pen, rig, day, bar). The traditional explanation for the phonological similarity effect is that order confusions arise during maintenance of a phonological code (see Baddeley, 1986; Hulme & Mackenzie, 1992, for reviews); thus similar sounding items may be transposed or repeated. In a similar vein, since a memory trace is assumed to reflect the physical characteristics of the encoded words, both the word-length effect and the effect of speech rate are accounted for by the finite storage and rehearsal time available in which to maintain the to-be-remembered stimuli.

Problems with trace decay and rehearsal models

In this section, we review those findings that pose difficulties to trace decay models in the classical form of the articulatory (phonogical) loop model since it was such findings that led us to develop our own ideas on the influence of long-term memory. However, we acknowledge the parallel development of computational models of the phonological loop such as those proposed by Burgess and Hitch (1992) or Page and Norris (1998) that have at least the potential to account for some of these data, and we will return to these later.

Several findings pose problems for simple trace decay and rehearsal models such as the traditional phonological loop model (Baddeley & Hitch, 1974). For example, there are clear effects of semantic coding on short-term memory performance. In fact, semantic effects are easy to demonstrate with a simple thought experiment. It is clear that immediate serial recall of a random list of words such as "Bush, British, Measures, Today, Taxation, President, Imports, Against, Announced" is far less likely to be recalled accurately than the same words presented in a more contrived order, "Today, President, Bush, Announced, Taxation, Measures, Against, British, Imports". This is a simple yet important observation since, by the acknowledgement that semantic knowledge influences immediate recall, we are effectively acknowledging that long-term semantic memory is supporting our short-term phonological memory. Of course, the idea of a flow of information from semantic memory to episodic memory is not entirely new. Researchers investigating autobiographical memory have long been aware that schema are very often used to support episodic memory retrieval. For example, Linton (1978) describes two kinds of forgetting that she refers to as simple recall failure (complete loss of memory for an event) and loss of detail due to repetitions. To illustrate the point with one of Linton's own examples, a first parachute jump will contain a great deal of episodic information, with few established schemas, whereas memory for later jumps will rely far more heavily on established schemas for parachutes, landings, aeroplanes, etc. However, whereas schema research has largely been focused on the ways in which semantic memory can influence the retrieval of long-term memories, there has until recently been very little investigation of the effects of semantic memory on immediate recall. The idea of schematic representations in long-term memory being used to support episodic memory is important and we shall return to this later.

In recent years, there has been a small, but growing body of research findings indicating that the semantic properties of words influence immediate serial recall. For example, we now know that concrete words, such as Rhinoceros, are more likely to be recalled than abstract words, such as Phenomenon (Neath, 1997; Walker & Hulme, 1999). The effects of concreteness on recall are substantial. Using an immediate serial recall paradigm, Poirier and Saint-Aubin (1995) also showed that lists that contained words from the same semantic category were better recalled than lists containing words from different semantic categories. Finally, in the same class of findings, Hulme, Maughan, and Brown (1991) reported that meaningful words (e.g., hour, fear, view) were better recalled than meaningless nonwords (e.g., bim, fot, feg). If we accept that semantic information must necessarily depend upon long-term memory representations then the only logical conclusion is that such long-term memory representations play a critical role in immediate episodic memory.

Clearly there is a great deal of evidence to support the notion that at least semantic long-term memory can influence short-term memory performance. However, the information extracted from long-term memory need not necessarily be semantic in nature. Although simple linguistic usage may leave the physical word characteristics relatively unchanged, it too leaves a memorial impression that can influence subsequent short-term memory performance. Word usage effects of this type are demonstrated in the Hebb effect (Hebb, 1961). In Hebb's original experiment, participants were presented with a series of trials in which they were asked to memorize a string of digits, followed by immediate recall. Unknown to the participants, some of these digit strings were repeated throughout the experiment and with each repetition of a digit string, the participant's memory for that particular sequence improved. Furthermore, post-experimental questioning revealed that participants were apparently unaware of any of the sequences having been repeated. The implication is that the results are due to a change in long-term memory representation of the repeated string that in turn supports the short-term memory performance. Further evidence that a simple record of item repetition may be important comes from a study by Hulme, Roodenrys, Brown, and Mercer (1995) who demonstrated that nonword recall performance could be improved by familiarizing parti-cipants with the nonwords (a process in which participants simply repeated sequences of nonwords aloud). Hulme et al. (1995) suggested that this effect was attributable to participants gradually creating a phonological (lexical) representation of the nonwords that they were familiarized with.

Although our aim is primarily to discuss the experimental findings, we should also draw attention to a parallel neuropsychological literature in which the individual contributions of semantic and lexical processes have been identified in tasks such as memory span (N. Martin & Saffran, 1997; R. C. Martin, Shelton, & Yaffee, 1994), thus providing converging evidence in support of our argument. So where does this leave trace decay models and, in particular, how might the phonogical loop model of working memory deal with the findings described above. In short, the answer must be that it cannot, at least not in its orginal form. The failure of the original working memory model to account for or make predictions about any of the semantic or word usage effects described so far has been at least partly responsible for its recent modification. The episodic buffer (Baddeley, 2000; Allen & Baddeley, this volume) component was added to the working memory model as a means by which information from the other sub-systems could be bound together with information from long-term memory into a unitary episodic representation. Baddeley conceives of the episodic buffer as a limited capacity system that is able to provide temporary storage of information in an amodal code. However, until the means by which long-term memory might be accessed and processed are specified, it is difficult to fully acknowledge the operation of the working memory model as an open system. It is to the phonological loop component of the working memory model that we must turn our attention. Here we concentrate on one of the word characteristics described above, that of word frequency, and briefly examine how the effects of word frequency might fit with the phonological loop before going on to describe alternative accounts.

The effects of word frequency on immediate serial recall

High-frequency words are better recalled than low-frequency words in immediate serial recall tasks (e.g., Gregg, Freedman, & Smith, 1989). We began studying this effect (Hulme et al., 1997) in the belief that it reflects the availability of the long-term memory representations to support immediate serial recall. If the phonological loop model of short-term verbal memory is correct, then it must be able to account for the word-frequency effect. In order to do so, there must be some other means by which word frequency can affect short-term memory, other than by determining the ease with which information in long-term memory can be accessed. The most obvious suggestion is that the differences in articulatory duration for high- and low-frequency words are large enough to influence rehearsal. In other words, low-frequency words must occupy the rehearsal loop for significantly longer than high-frequency words in order that the former decays more rapidly. In order to overcome the potential confound of temporal differences between stimulus types, Hulme et al. (1997) had initially selected and matched their high- and low-frequency words for articulatory duration and still found a word-frequency effect. Moreover, in those experiments where articulatory duration was not equated for the participants involved, the word-frequency effect emerged even when the effects of articulatory duration were statistically partialled out using analysis of covariance. However, in order to strengthen the case, it would be useful to find some converging evidence. In fact, such evidence has been reported in experiments examining the effects of articulatory suppression. The effect of articulatory suppression on the word-length effect is often cited as one of the fundamental pieces of evidence in support of the phonogical loop model. Articulatory suppression (repeating one or more task-irrelevant words) is known to largely eliminate the word-length effect for visually presented words (Baddeley, 1986). Articulatory suppression is assumed to prevent visual material from being phonologically re-coded in the phonological loop and therefore any normal advantage of short words over long words is removed under such conditions (Baddeley, 1986; Neath & Nairne, 1995). Since high-frequency words are known, in general, to be articulated faster than low-frequency words (Wright, 1979), articulatory suppression might also be predicted to eliminate the word-frequency effect. In fact, this appears not to be the case (Tehan & Humphreys, 1988; Gregg, Freedman, & Smith, 1989; Roodenrys, Hulme, Alban, Ellis, & Brown, 1994 provide further evidence that the effects of word frequency on short-term memory span cannot be accounted for by speech rate differences).

These arguments satisfied us that it was not possible to explain the word-frequency effect in terms of rehearsal rate. It seemed that we needed a model in which stored long-term knowledge about items directly affected recall. To this end, we developed our own version of a redintegrative model. In fact, our interest in word frequency developed from studies of lexicality. Hulme, Maughan, and Brown (1991) had examined the lexicality effect in short-term memory and found that words were recalled substantially better than nonwords in a memory span task. However, for both types of stimuli, Hulme et al. (1991) also reported that short items that could be articulated more quickly were better recalled than long items. In other words, there was an equivalent relationship between articulation rate and memory span for both words and nonwords (this is illustrated in Figure 8.1). It is important to note that the words and nonwords in this experiment were deliberately selected to be articulated at equivalent rates (1-, 3- and 5- syllable words were compared with 1, 2- and 3-syllable nonwords). The very substantial

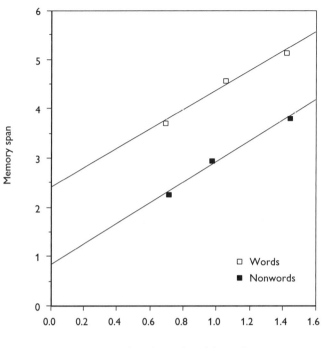

Figure 8.1 The relationship between speech rate and memory span for words and nonwords differing in syllable length. From Hulme et al. (1991). Reproduced with permission. Courtesy of Professor Jennifer Gourd.

recall advantage for words in this study therefore cannot be attributed to differences in articulation rate and clearly an additional mechanism was at work. Hulme et al. (1991) argued that whereas the positive relationship between speech rate and memory span was underpinned by a temporally-limited speech-based mechanism, of the type described in the phonological loop model, the lexicality effect reflected the presence or absence of a long-term memory representation of the phonological form. Further support for this idea came from Hulme, Roodenrys, Brown, and Mercer (1995), who demonstrated that participants' memory span for nonwords could be increased by pre-test familiarization with the nonwords. Since the familiarization method involved simple repetition of the stimuli, it was concluded that acquisition of phonological knowledge was sufficient to improve memory performance.

It was of considerable importance to discover that lexicality effects operate independently of articulatory duration, as it suggested that long-term memory representations directly support immediate serial recall. We argued that perhaps low-frequency words would also be less well recalled than high-frequency words, even when the articulatory duration of the stimuli was matched. The latter assumption was of particular importance in the case of word frequency since, as has already been mentioned, Wright (1979) had shown that even for items with equal numbers of letters, high-frequency words generally take less time to articulate than low-frequency words. Hulme et al. (1997) extended the work of Hulme et al. (1991) by examining the effects of word frequency on immediate serial recall. If, as Hulme et al. (1991) had suggested, lexical status was independently responsible for some of the memory span performance differences between words and nonwords, then it was likely that word frequency would have a similar effect on short-term memory. Surprisingly, this had received very little interest in the research literature. Though the investigation of word-frequency effects in long-term memory has a long and established history (see Gregg, 1976, for a review), very little regard had been paid to the effects of word frequency on short-term memory. At the time of these studies, we assumed that lexicality was simply one end of a continuum along which low- and high-frequency words assumed the middle and upper end positions respectively.

With this in mind, Hulme et al. (1997, following Schweickert, 1993) developed and tested a probabilistic model of redintegration in which word frequency plays a pivotal role. In the multinomial processing tree model, retrieval either occurs directly from the intact memory trace, as is commonly assumed in trace decay models, or indirectly through the retrieval of a lexical/phonological representation stored in long-term memory. This long-term lexical representation could then be used to repair a degraded short-term memory trace, the success of which would partially depend on the accessibility of the long-term memory information, and it is here that word frequency was thought to play a part. The representations of high-frequency words were thought to be more accessible than the representations of low-frequency words. The model was based on the assumption that during the recall of a list the memory traces of successive items would become increasingly degraded. This degradation, it was assumed, was largely due to output interference, and the greater the damage to the memory trace the more likely it was that redintegrative processes would be needed in order to repair it. In its simplest form redintegration involves a pattern-matching process in which stored phonology is retrieved from long-term memory and compared with the impaired phonological code in short-term memory. Once a suitable match is found, this stored phonology can be used to reconstruct the memory trace. Moreover, according to our particular conception of redintegration, the action is an automatic one and, as such, it utilizes those processes that are an integral part of the speech perception and speech production mechanisms (see also Hartley & Houghton, 1996; Page & Norris, this volume, for similar arguments). Indeed, there were already sufficient parallels in the literature to support the contention that the processes involved in speech perception and production could be co-opted for use in short-term recall tasks. For example, just as high-frequency words are better recalled than low-frequency words, so perceptual identification of high-frequency words is easier than for low-frequency words (Howes, 1957). Once again, this adds support to the notion that the phonological representations of high-frequency words are more accessible. In a more general sense, others have also argued explicitly that short-term memory involves processes common to speech perception and speech production (e.g., Ellis, 1980; Hulme et al., 1991; Schweickert, 1993) and that verbal short-term memory can be conceived of as a by-product of those processes. By way of circumstantial support for this idea, Hulme et al. (1997) also noted that participants occasionally produced non-experimental words during immediate serial recall. Of these extra-experimental intrusions, the majority were high-frequency word substitutions for phonologically neighbouring low-frequency word targets, for example, *list* as a substitute for *lisp*, *foul* substituted for *foal*, or *truth* for *truce*.

By making the assumption that the phonology of high-frequency words is more accessible than that of low-frequency words, the multinomial processing tree model could successfully account for the finding of superior immediate serial recall performance of high- over low-frequency words as well as the finding that the recall advantage for high-frequency words tended to increase from early to later serial position (see Figure 8.2, taken from Hulme et al., 1997, which illustrates the pattern obtained). The diverging serial position curves for high- and low-frequency words were interpreted in terms of the memory trace for later items becoming increasingly degraded (due to output interference from recalling earlier items), making the need for redintegration greater at later serial positions. In fact, these findings were accurately captured by a mathematical model developed from the one originally described by Schweickert (1993). In this model the probability of successful redintegration was higher for high-frequency words. Furthermore, Brown and Hulme (1995) described a series of simulations in which they demonstrated that the redintegration process was sufficient to account for the improved memory performance for nonwords.

In spite of its apparent success, there were problems in store for the multinomial processing tree model. Like many others, we had assumed that word frequency is a fixed stimulus attribute. However, we were soon to find evidence to the contrary. In the long-term memory literature, numerous studies have reported that lists composed only of high-frequency words are recalled significantly better than lists composed only of low-frequency words (DeLosh & McDaniel, 1996; Gregg, 1976; Tan & Ward, 2000; Ward, Woodward, Stevens, & Stinson, 2003; Watkins, LeCompte, & Kim, 2000). However, when high- and low-frequency words are mixed within the same list, the high-frequency word advantage very often disappears. Although high-frequency words are sometimes recalled better than low-frequency words in mixed lists (Balota & Neely, 1995), it has more often been reported that they are recalled equally well (e.g., Watkins et al., 2000; Ward et al., 2003) and sometimes low-frequency words are actually recalled better

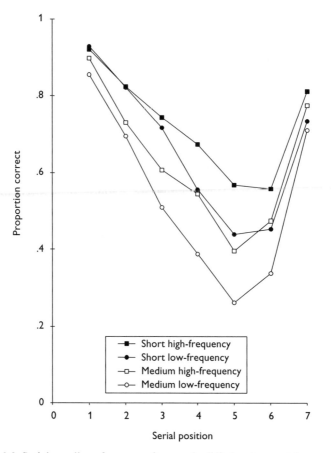

Figure 8.2 Serial recall performance for words differing in word-frequency and syllable length. From Hulme et al. (1997). Reproduced with permission.

than high-frequency words (DeLosh & McDaniel, 1996; Gregg, 1976; May & Tryk, 1970; Van Overschelde, 2002).

The multinomial processing tree model described by Hulme et al., (1997) predicted that word frequency effects should be preserved in immediate serial recall when high- and low-frequency words were mixed in the same list. The model predicted a sawtooth serial-position curve for the alternating lists, with the peaks touching the pure high-frequency word curves and the troughs touching the pure low-frequency word curves. Hulme, Stuart, Brown, & Morin (2003) tested this prediction in an experiment where participants recalled lists that consisted of either all high- or all low-frequency words (pure lists) or lists in which the frequency of words alternated between adjacent positions in the list (alternating lists). The results from this experiment are shown in Figure 8.3, and clearly refute the assumption that word frequency is an invariant factor within the multinomial processing tree

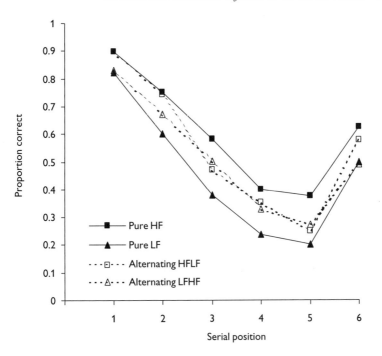

Figure 8.3 Serial recall performance for words of high and low frequency presented in either pure or alternating-mixed lists. From Hulme et al. (2003). Reproduced with permission.

model. For the recall of pure lists, the typical frequency effect was replicated, such that high-frequency words were recalled substantially better than low-frequency words. However, in the alternating list conditions, rather than finding the predicted sawtooth pattern, we found that high- and low-frequency words were recalled at identical levels and at levels intermediate between pure high- and pure low-frequency lists. This pattern is the same as typically found for the free recall of mixed-frequency lists reported in the long-term memory literature (Watkins et al., 2000; Ward et al., 2003).

In a third experiment in the series Hulme et al. (2003) examined the recall of pure and alternating lists of words and nonwords. As noted earlier, it was our assumption that nonwords were just one extreme of the word-frequency continuum. This time, as well as the predicted advantage of pure word lists over pure nonword lists (cf. Hulme et al., 1991), recall of the alternating lists followed the sawtooth pattern previously predicted (see Figure 8.4). Whereas the findings with alternating lists of words and non-words could easily be accommodated in the redintegration model, the findings for alternating word-frequency lists could not. The assumption on which we had previously worked was that the long-term memory representations of high-frequency words were simply more easily accessible than

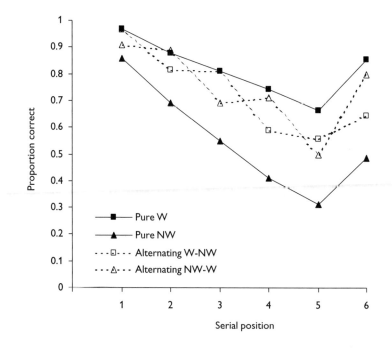

Figure 8.4 Serial recall performance for words and nonwords presented in either pure or alternating-mixed lists. From Hulme et al. (2003). Reproduced with permission.

those of low-frequency words, regardless of list construction, and that nonwords had no stored representation on which to rely. Although the nonword data fit this neatly, in order to support the redintegration model it would be necessary to change our conception of the way in which word frequency influences the accessibility of long-term memory representations.

Later in this chapter, we introduce our own interpretation of the alternating list findings. However, it is useful to begin by making a distinction between item-based and association-based accounts of the word-frequency and lexicality effects. Our own version of the redintegration model (Hulme et al., 1997) is an item-based account since word frequency is assumed to be an attribute of the items themselves. The multinomial processing tree model is not alone in this and many other memory models either explicitly or implicitly describe word frequency in terms of the pre-exposure to individual items (e.g., Farrell & Lewandowsky, 2002). One of the most common ways of describing the influence of word frequency is to conceptualize its effects in terms of baseline activation, with high-frequency words having a higher level of activation than low-frequency words (e.g., Henson, 1998; Morton, 1979). Alternatively, it has been described in terms of differential levels of output threshold (e.g., Page & Norris, 1998).

Item-based models can be contrasted with association-based accounts that acknowledge the importance of pre-experimental associations. These types of model have been particularly prominent in studies of long-term memory using free recall (e.g., Deese, 1960; Gillund & Shiffrin, 1984; Howard & Kahana, 2002a, 2002b; Raaijmakers & Shiffrin, 1981; see Crowder, 1976, for a review). Association-based accounts argue that the recall of high-frequency words will benefit from stronger pre-existing inter-word associations whereas these associations are weaker or absent among low-frequency words. Although the word-frequency data reported by Hulme et al. (2003) cannot be accounted for by an item-based model, these findings can be accounted for by suggesting that the availability of the long-term memory representation of an item is determined by the inter-item associations between items in a to-be-remembered set.

In deciding what kind of mechanism might best describe the alternating word-frequency list data reported by Hulme et al. (2003), one finding of particular importance must be considered. In an analysis of the types of errors made during recall, Hulme et al. reported that the recall differences between pure high- and pure low-frequency word lists were attributable to differences in item errors and not order errors. In other words, participants recalling low-frequency words were more likely to fail to recall the item itself, whereas confusions of the position in which a word appeared were similar for both word types. In alternating lists, the item errors were equated for high- and low-frequency words. This finding allows us to rule out at least one important account of the mixed-list word-frequency effect, the order-encoding hypothesis (DeLosh & McDaniel, 1996). DeLosh and McDaniel proposed a resource-sharing account in which limited attentional resources could be directed either to the to-be-remembered list items or to the links between them. According to this account, the pure list advantage for high-frequency words occurs because high-frequency words require fewer attentional resources than low-frequency words and therefore more resource capacity can be focused on the links between the items, aiding accurate reconstruction of order. When high- and low-frequency words are mixed within the same list, the low-frequency words require more attentional capacity to encode them and this, in turn, reduces the ability to encode order information for all items in the list.

The order-encoding account described above was clearly not applicable to the findings of Hulme et al. (2003) since there were no differences in order errors between the two types of words. Item-based accounts were also ruled out and so we turned our attention instead to developing an association-based account. For help in this, we looked back to the verbal learning literature from the mid-twentieth century. In particular, we re-examined the work of Deese (1959, 1960) who had challenged the traditional view of word frequency. Standard tabulations of word frequency are based on general tallies of word occurrence (Baayen, Piepenbrock, & van Rijn, 1995; Kucera & Francis, 1967) and as such, word frequency has proved to be a useful performance predictor in a number of paradigms, including recall. However, Deese suggested that such findings were coincidental and that it was actually the frequency of word co-occurrence, rather than frequency of occurrence, which determined the so-called word-frequency effect in free recall. Deese's arguments made intuitive sense, since we also know that high-frequency words are more likely to co-occur in natural language than low-frequency words (Howes, 1957). In order to provide support for his claims, Deese constructed a number of lists from randomly selected words and used free association to measure the inter-item association between the words in each list. He found that the index of inter-item association was significantly higher for lists of high-frequency words than for lists of low-frequency words. Using the same free-association technique, Deese (1960) went on to construct lists of high- and low-frequency words with zero inter-item association. When these lists were used as stimuli in a test of free recall, the word-frequency effect was eliminated. The importance of these findings is that they promote a view of word frequency that is not a fixed quantity. Rather, its value depends on the context in which a word is presented.

These ideas of Deese could have important implications for the findings of Hulme et al. (2003) and the redintegration model proposed by Hulme et al. (1997). In this view, the availability of the long-term memory representation of any particular item would be determined by the composition of the list in which it was presented. In an arbitrarily constructed list of high-frequency words, the high expected levels of inter-item association will mean that the long-term memory representation of any one word will be highly accessible. If, however, the same word appeared in a list of arbitrarily chosen high- and low-frequency words, the overall level of inter-item associations would be far lower and so the specific representation of that item would be less accessible. Stuart and Hulme (2000) followed up Deese's ideas by attempting to artificially create inter-item associations by mere exposure of word pairs. If high-frequency words were better recalled because they benefited from pre-existing associations between item representations in lexical memory, we argued that we may be able to artificially induce such associations for low-frequency words, simply by presenting pairs of low-frequency words repeatedly before assessing memory for them. We found that pre-exposing pairs of low-frequency words was sufficient to improve recall of those items to the same level as high-frequency words. Of particular importance, our paradigm allowed us to show that words presented in lists for which all consecutive items had been familiarized as pairs were significantly better recalled than lists constructed from the same familiarized words, but in which no consecutive pair of words had been familiarized. The combined findings of Deese (1960) and Stuart and Hulme (2000) were an important step in understanding the failure of the multinomial processing tree model, as described in Hulme et al. (1997), to account for the alternating list frequency experiments of Hulme et al. (2003). It appears that accessibility of the phonological representation of an item in long-term memory is determined by the list context in which it is retrieved.

Conclusions

We began by discussing trace decay models, and in particular the traditional phonogical loop model as the most popular model of this class. We considered how the working memory model can account for a range of short-term memory phenomena. We also pointed out, however, that the model as originally formulated has no natural way to deal with semantic influences, or the effects of word frequency, on immediate serial recall performance.

There are at least two possible reactions to the evidence we have considered here. The first is to modify trace decay and rehearsal models to accommodate new findings. This has been the dominant approach to date in this area. For example, Hulme et al. (1991) argued that the phonogical loop model needed to be broadened to encompass a critical role for redintegration. The same argument, essentially, was proposed for word-frequency effects (Hulme et al., 1997). Baddeley, Gathercole, and Papagno (1998) also pursued this approach, based partly on ideas put forward by Brown and Hulme (1996). Moreover, computational models of the phonological loop that developed in parallel to our own redintegration model (e.g., Burgess & Hitch, 1992; Page & Norris, 1998) give at least the potential for lexical and semantic memory influences in immediate recall by describing the representations underlying short-term memory as activated nodes in long-term memory. However, the precise mechanisms have yet to be described. In a recent review of the area, Burgess and Hitch (2005) concluded that "The interaction between working memory and LTM is a topic of much current interest, and computational models will be required for a quantitative understanding to emerge" (p. 539).

A second reaction to the evidence reviewed here (along with other evidence not dealt with, see e.g. Nairne, 2002; Hulme, Surprenant, Bireta, Stuart, & Neath, 2004) has been to suggest that the "standard model" as exemplified by trace decay and rehearsal models is beyond repair. In this view a very different theoretical framework is required. There is growing interest in what Nairne (2002) refers to as unitary models that assume that common representations and processes are responsible for remembering over both the long and short term. Models of this sort include the feature model (Nairne, 1990; Neath & Nairne, 1995), OSCAR (Brown, Preece, & Hulme, 2000) and SIMPLE (Brown, Neath, & Chater, 2007). In these models remembering in both short-and long-term memory tasks is cue driven, with retrieval depending on cue-overlap and item distinctiveness. Forgetting in such models is interference based, rather than dependent on decay.

What of the redintegration model? As we hinted earlier in this chapter, we believe that the redintegration model described by Hulme et al. (1997) is not irredeemable. In fact, it needs only the introduction of a mechanism by which word frequency is established as a dynamic rather than a torpid quantity. From the results of these and other findings, we tentatively suggest a modified version of the redintegration model in which long-term memory representations are dynamic and context dependent rather than fixed. Each time a stimulus is encountered, its level of activation is temporarily raised. However, if the item is presented as part of a list, activation spreads across the pathways connecting it to its activated cohort. We suggest that the degree of activation spread in this way is determined by the connection strength that in turn is determined by the degree to which the items have previously co-occurred. In this way, an activated sub-set of high-frequency word nodes are likely to offer maximal mutual support since the probability is that they have strongly established interconnections. On the other hand, a set of low-frequency word nodes will have relatively weak connections and therefore will offer little mutual support. Items presented in a mixed list will offer an intermediate level of support for all items, since they will consist of a mixture of high and low connection strengths. This hypothesis can also account for the sawtooth pattern for alternating words and nonwords reported by Hulme et al. (2003). Nodes for nonwords must first be established before pathways can in turn be established between them and existent word nodes and so we would expect words and nonwords presented in the same list to have no effect on one another, at least until the links become established.

In conclusion, the data reviewed in this chapter are amenable to a number of different interpretations either within a unitary cue-driven framework or within modified trace-decay and rehearsal frameworks such as the primacy model (Page & Norris, 1998) or the implemented phonological loop model (Burgess & Hitch, 1992). In our view the cue-driven unitary framework is gradually assuming dominance. However, we are, at the moment, a long way from a generally accepted account for the pervasive and powerful effects of lexical variables on immediate serial recall performance.

References

Atkinson, R. C., & Shiffrin, R.M. (1968). Human memory: A proposed system and its control processes. In K. W. Spence & J. T. Spence (Eds.), *The Psychology of learning and motivation: Advances in research and theory* (Vol. 2, pp. 89–195). New York: Academic Press.

Baayen, R. H., Piepenbrock, R., & van Rijn, H. (1995). *The CELEX lexical database, Release 2 (CD-ROM)*. Linguistic Data Consortium, University of Pennsylvania, Philadelphia, PA.

Baddeley, A. D. (1966). Short-term memory for word sequences as a function of acoustic, semantic and formal similarity. *Quarterly Journal of Experimental Psychology, 18*, 362–365.

Baddeley, A. (1986). *Working memory*. London: Oxford University Press (Clarendon).

Baddeley, A. D. (2000). The episodic buffer: A new component of working memory? *Trends in Cognitive Sciences, 4,* 417–423.

Baddeley, A. D., Gathercole, S. E., & Papagno, C. (1998). The phonological loop as a language learning device. *Psychological Review, 105,* 158–173.

Baddeley, A. D., & Hitch, G. J. (1974). Working memory, In G. A. Bower (Ed.), *Recent advances in learning and motivation* (Vol. 8, pp. 47–90). New York: Academic Press.

Baddeley, A. D., Lewis, V. J., & Vallar, G. (1984). Exploring the articulatory loop. *Quarterly Journal of Experimental Psychology: Human Experimental Psychology, 36*(A), 233–252.

Baddeley A. D., Thomson, N., & Buchanan, M. (1975). Word length and the structure of short term memory. *Journal of Verbal Learning and Verbal Behavior, 14,* 575–589.

Balota, D. A., & Neely, J. (1995). Test expectancy and word frequency effects in recall and recognition. *Journal of Experimental Psychology: Learning, Memory, and Cognition, 6,* 576–587.

Brown, G. D. A., & Hulme, C. (1995). Modelling item length effects in memory span: No rehearsal needed? *Journal of Memory and Language, 34,* 594–621.

Brown, G. D. A., & Hulme, C. (1996). Non-word repetition, STM and word age-of-acquisition: A computational model. In S. E. Gathercole (Ed.), *Models of short-term memory* (pp. 51–71). Hove, UK: Psychology Press.

Brown, G. D. A., Neath, I., & Chater, N. (2007). A temporal ratio model of memory. *Psychological Review, 114,* 539–576.

Brown G., Preece, T., & Hulme, C. (2000). Oscillator-based memory for serial order. *Psychological Review, 107,* 127–181.

Burgess, N., & Hitch, G. J. (1992). Towards a network model of the articulatory loop. *Journal of Memory and Language, 31,* 429–460.

Burgess, N., & Hitch, G. J. (1999). Memory for serial order: A network model of the phonological loop and its timing. *Psychological Review, 106,* 551–581.

Burgess, N., & Hitch, G. (2005). Computational models of working memory: Putting long-term memory into context. *Trends in Cognitive Sciences, 9,* 535–541.

Conrad, R., & Hull, A. J. (1964). Information, acoustic confusion and memory span. *British Journal of Psychology, 55,* 429–437.

Craik, F., & Lockhart, R. (1972). Levels of processing: A framework for memory research. *Journal of Verbal Learning and Verbal Behavior, 11,* 671–684.

Crowder, R. G. (1976). *Principles of learning and memory.* Hillsdale, NJ: Lawrence Erlbaum Associates, Inc.

Deese, J. (1959). Influence of inter-item associative strength upon immediate free recall. *Psychological Reports, 5,* 305–312.

Deese, J. (1960). Frequency of usage and the number of words in free recall: The role of association. *Psychological Reports, 7,* 337–344.

DeLosh, E. L., & McDaniel, M. A. (1996). The role of order information in free recall: Application of the word frequency effect. *Journal of Experimental Psychology: Learning, Memory, and Cognition, 22,* 1136–1146.

Ellis, A. W. (1980). Errors in speech and short-term memory: The effects of phonemic similarity and syllable position. *Journal of Verbal Learning and Verbal Behavior, 19,* 624–634.

Farrell, S., & Lewandowsky, S. (2002). An endogenous distributed model of ordering in serial recall. *Psychonomic Bulletin & Review, 9,* 59–85.

Gillund, G., & Shiffrin, R. M. (1984). A retrieval model for both recognition and recall. *Psychological Review, 91*, 1–67.

Gregg, V. (1976). Word frequency, recognition and recall. In J. Brown (Ed.), *Recognition and recall* (pp. 183–216). Chichester, UK: Wiley.

Gregg, V. H., Freedman, C. M., & Smith, D. K. (1989). Word frequency, articulatory suppression and memory span. *British Journal of Psychology, 80*, 363–374.

Hartley T., & Houghton G. (1996). A linguistically constrained model of short-term memory for nonwords. *Journal of Memory and Language, 35*, 1–31.

Hebb, D. O. (1961). Distinctive features of learning in the higher animal. In J. E. Delafreanaye (Ed.), *Brain mechanisms and learning* (pp. 37–46). London: Oxford University Press.

Henson, R. N. A. (1998). Short-term memory for serial order: The Start-End Model. *Cognitive Psychology, 36*, 73–137.

Howard, M. W., & Kahana, M. J. (2002a). A distributed representation of temporal context. *Journal of Mathematical Psychology, 46*, 269–299.

Howard, M. W., & Kahana, M. J. (2002b). When does semantic similarity help episodic retrieval? *Journal of Memory and Language, 46*, 85–98.

Howes, D. (1957). On the relation between the probability of a word as an association and in general linguistic usage. *Journal of Abnormal Psychology, 54*, 75–85.

Hulme, C., & Mackenzie, S. (1992). *Working memory and severe learning difficulties.* Hove, UK: Lawrence Erlbaum Associates, Inc.

Hulme, C., Maughan, S., & Brown, G. D. A. (1991). Memory for familiar and unfamiliar words: Evidence for a long-term memory contribution to short-term memory span. *Journal of Memory and Language, 30*, 685–701.

Hulme, C, Roodenrys, S., Brown, G. D. A., & Mercer, R. (1995). The role of long-term memory mechanisms in memory span. *British Journal of Psychology, 86*, 527–536.

Hulme, C, Roodenrys S., Schweickert, R., Brown, G. D. A., Martin, S., & Stuart, G. (1997). Word frequency effects on short-term memory tasks: Evidence for a redintegration process in immediate serial recall. *Journal of Experimental Psychology: Learning, Memory, and Cognition, 23*, 1217–1232.

Hulme, C., Stuart, G., Brown, G. D. A., & Morin, C. (2003). High- and low-frequency words are recalled equally well in alternating lists: Evidence for associative effects in serial recall. *Journal of Memory and Language, 49*, 500–518.

Hulme, C., Surprenant, A. M., Bireta, T. J., Stuart, G., & Neath, I. (2004). Abolishing the word length effect. *Journal of Experimental Psychology: Learning, Memory, and Cognition, 30*, 98–106.

James, W. (1890) *The principles of psychology.* New York: Holt.

Kucera, H., & Francis, W. N. (1967). *Computational analysis of present-day American English.* Providence, RI: Brown University Press.

Linton, M. (1978). Real world memory after six years: An in vivo study of very long term memory. In M. M. Gruneberg, P. E. Morris, & R. N. Sykes (Eds.), *Practical aspects of memory* (pp. 69–76). London: Academic Press.

Martin, N., & Saffran, E. M. (1997). Language and auditory-verbal short-term memory impairments: Evidence for common underlying processes. *Cognitive Neuropsychology, 14*, 641–682.

Martin, R. C., Shelton, J. R., & Yaffee, L. S. (1994). Language processing and working memory: Neuropsychological evidence for separate phonological and semantic capacities. *Journal of Memory and Language, 33*, 83–111.

May, R. B., & Tryk, H. E. (1970). Word sequence, word frequency and free recall. *Canadian Journal of Psychology, 24*, 299–304.

Miller, G. A. (1956). The magical number seven plus or minus two: Some limits on our capacity for processing information. *Psychological Review, 63*, 81–97.

Morris, C. D., Bransford, J. D., & Franks, J. J. (1977). Levels of processing versus transfer appropriate processing. *Journal of Verbal Learning and Verbal Behaviour, 16*, 519–533.

Morton, J. (1979). Word recognition. In J. Morton, & J. C. Marshall (Eds.), *Psycholinguistics Volume 2 – Structures and processes.* London: Paul Elek.

Nairne, J. S. (1990). A feature model of immediate memory. *Memory & Cognition, 18*, 251–269.

Nairne, J. S. (2002). Remembering over the short-term: The case against the standard model. *Annual Review of Psychology, 53*, 53–81.

Neath, I. (1997). Modality, concreteness, and set-size effects in a free reconstruction of order task. *Memory & Cognition, 25*, 256–263.

Neath, I., & Nairne, J. S. (1995). Word-length effects in immediate memory: Overwriting trace decay theory. *Psychonomic Bulletin & Review, 2*, 429–441.

Page, M. P. A., & Norris, D. (1998). The primacy model: A new model of immediate serial recall. *Psychological Review, 105*, 761–781.

Poirier, M., & Saint-Aubin, J. (1995). Memory for related and unrelated words: Further evidence concerning the influence of semantic factors on immediate serial recall. *Quarterly Journal of Experimental Psychology, 48A*, 384–404.

Raaijmakers, J. G. W., & Shiffrin, R. M. (1981). Search of associative memory. *Psychological Review, 88*, 93–134.

Roodenrys S., Hulme, C., Alban, J., Ellis, A. W., & Brown, G. D. A. (1994). Effects of word frequency and age of acquisition on short-term memory. *Memory & Cognition, 22*, 695–701.

Schweickert, R. (1993). A multinomial processing tree model for degradation and redintegration in immediate recall. *Memory & Cognition, 21*, 167–175.

Stuart, G., & Hulme, C. (2000). The effects of word co-occurrence on short-term memory: Associative links in long-term memory affect short-term memory performance. *Journal of Experimental Psychology: Learning, Memory, and Cognition, 26*, 796–802.

Tan, L., & Ward, G. (2000). A recency-based account of the primacy effect in free recall. *Journal of Experimental Psychology: Learning, Memory, and Cognition, 26*, 1589–1625.

Tehan, G., & Humphreys, M. S. (1988). Creating proactive interference in immediate recall: Building a dog from a dart, a mop and a fig. *Memory & Cognition, 26*, 477–489.

Van Overschelde, J. P. (2002). The influence of word frequency on recency effects in directed free recall. *Journal of Experimental Psychology: Learning, Memory, and Cognition, 28*, 611–615.

Walker, I., & Hulme, C. (1999). Concrete words are easier to recall than abstract words: Evidence for a semantic contribution to short-term serial recall. *Journal of Experimental Psychology: Learning Memory and Cognition, 25*, 1256–1271.

Ward, G., Woodward, G., Stevens, A., & Stinson, C. (2003). Using overt rehearsals to explain word frequency effects in free recall. *Journal of Experimental Psychology: Learning, Memory, and Cognition, 29,* 186–210.

Watkins, M., LeCompte, D. C., & Kim, K. (2000). Role of study strategy in recall of mixed lists of common and rare words. *Journal of Experimental Psychology: Learning, Memory, and Cognition, 26,* 239–245.

Wright, C. C. (1979). Duration differences between rare and common words and their implications for the interpretation of word frequency effects. *Memory & Cognition, 7,* 411–419.

9 Explaining phonological neighbourhood effects in short-term memory

Steven Roodenrys

Overview

Serial recall performance is influenced by the presence in long-term memory of words that sound similar to the word that is to be recalled. It is suggested that this influence occurs when degraded traces are retrieved from short-term memory (STM) and information in long-term memory is used to reconstruct the missing information. The history of this idea, and supporting evidence, are briefly reviewed in this chapter. An account of the reconstruction process is suggested in which the long-term memory influence is an inherent part of the recall process for all items, and how this might explain the influence of similar sounding words in long-term memory is described.

Introduction

This chapter reviews a small body of research that I and other researchers have been conducting in recent years which has examined whether serial recall is influenced by the presence in long-term memory of words that have not been presented but are phonologically similar to the presented items. I use the term "items" here because the to-be-recalled lists may comprise either words or nonwords, whereas the entries in the lexicon must be words by definition. In fact, the research has examined the recall of lists of words and lists of nonwords and so provides some information on whether the recall of these different types of items relies on the same processes. In this chapter I will review the precedents for the notion of redintegration that has been used to explain the influence of long-term knowledge on short-term recall, and suggest a possible mechanism for this process.

Conrad (1964) is often cited as an early demonstration of the phonological similarity effect on serial recall – the finding that performance is worse for lists of words that sound similar to each other than lists that do not. Conrad's (1964) methodology, however, mixed two sets of five similar sounding letters within the same lists, one set sharing the vowel and one a consonant, and examined errors in recall rather than overall levels of recall.

This paper is rightly cited as evidence for phonological coding in STM as it demonstrated that recall errors for visually presented letters in a serial recall task correlate with auditory identification errors of letter names presented in noise. The years immediately following saw the publication of a considerable number of research papers investigating the effect of phonological similarity, and probably the majority of these used two small sets of letters as the stimuli, one phonologically similar set and one dissimilar set. Conrad (1964) actually had the full set of stimuli available for the subjects to examine during recall in order to prevent intrusions from outside the set. In scoring the data only those lists which had a single item incorrect were included in the analysis. This procedure effectively makes all of the errors examined intrusions by letters in the set that were not presented in the list.

Along with Conrad (1964), Wickelgren (1965a) argued that the intrusion of similar sounding letters in recall suggested that it was possible to lose some of the information about an item. In one set of papers (Wickelgren, 1965b, 1965c) he presented lists of items that differed on only one phoneme and showed that confusions between items could be predicted by the overlap in the features of the phonemes that differed between the items. He argued that forgetting in STM is not all-or-none and that individual features of phonemes may be forgotten and others retained.

The redintegration concept

The finding that parts of words can be forgotten from short-term memory, whether they be phonemes or phonemic features, raises the question of whether the lost information might be reconstructed or replaced during recall on some occasions. In the current literature this has become known as the redintegration hypothesis (a term coined by Schweickert, 1993). In its most general form the redintegration hypothesis suggests that information in long-term memory can be used to reconstruct degraded traces retrieved from a short-term store. Variants of this idea differ in terms of the degree to which they specify the scale of the information in long-term memory that is used (e.g., lexical versus sublexical), and what particular type of information. For example, Nairne's (1990) feature model is a mathematical model that incorporates a process by which degraded short-term traces are compared against long-term traces of the items created during presentation. These long-term traces must be episodic but the model does not specify the nature of the "features" other than being in two classes, modality-dependent and modality-independent.

Almost since the initial papers on the phonological similarity effect were published there has been the suggestion of a phonologically based reconstruction process. Sperling and Speelman (1970) described a model of the recall of lists of letters in which phonemes could be "lost" from the trace independently of other phonemes. If a letter had lost one of its two phonemes the remaining phoneme was used to guess the letter from the set of letters that matched the remaining phoneme. One strong source of evidence for such a process is the nature of intrusions in recall.

Wickelgren (1965a) reported an experiment that contrasts with those described above in that it examined recall errors using a larger set of stimuli (the full alphabet and all nine digits) and included all extra-list intrusions. The results showed that the intrusions in recall were more likely than chance to share a phoneme with the item they replaced. This experiment convincingly demonstrated that phonological similarity was not just relevant to the order of recall of items within a list but also influences the process that gives rise to extra-list intrusions.

Drewnowski and Murdock (1980) reported a more substantial study that expanded the stimulus pool to over a thousand two-syllable words and examined a number of characteristics of the intruded words in recall and their overlap with the word presented in the list. In constructing the word lists they sampled with replacement and subjects were presented with on average around 500 words, so there would have been some small amount of unpredictable repetition of words. They examined the overlap in location of stress, the identity of the stressed vowel and the identity of the initial and final phonemes. When list presentation was auditory about 20% of the intrusions were words from the previous list while this figure was 40% for visually presented lists and the overlap on these features between the intrusion and the word that was replaced was largely not different from chance. In contrast, those intrusions that did not come from the preceding three lists showed more overlap than would be expected by chance on all of these features. The effect was strongest for the identity of the stressed vowel, showing that, under these conditions, the stressed vowel is less likely to be forgotten than other phonemes. These findings suggest that a large proportion of intrusions result from a redintegration process that works on phonological information producing the wrong word. They also suggest that the pool of items that take part in the redintegration process might be relatively unrestricted under the right conditions, such as a procedure where each word is used only once in the experiment. Drewnowski and Murdock's (1980) data approach this situation as they state that very few words were repeated for a subject.

In Sperling and Speelman's (1970) model of letter recall the likelihood of guessing (i.e., redintegrating) the correct letter from a single phoneme was a simple proportion of the number of letters that matched the remaining phoneme, so the mechanism would be a random choice. In Nairne's (1990) model the selection of a long-term trace to match the degraded short-term trace is based on a similarity choice rule, so the more similar the item is to the degraded trace the more likely it is to be selected. Both of these mechanisms predict that the more items there are in the comparison set the less likely it is that the degraded trace will be correctly redintegrated. My colleagues and I became interested in testing this prediction and specifying the nature of the redintegration process. Extra-list intrusion errors that are phonologically similar to the word they have replaced suggest that the redintegration process uses a comparison set that includes some subsection of the lexicon rather than being restricted to words in the list so it is possible to conceive of this set as the phonological neighbours of the presented word. There has been some study of the influence of phonological neighbours on other language tasks which might serve as an analogue for the redintegration process so it is worth reviewing some of these studies before describing our own studies on serial recall.

Phonological neighbourhood effects in language tasks

In order to investigate whether similar sounding words in long-term memory influence the recall of words in the serial recall task we need a metric of similarity. The metric that has been adopted in other language tasks comes from the literature on visual word recognition, where these effects have been more extensively investigated. Coltheart, Davelaar, Jonasson, and Besner (1977) described the visual neighbours of a word as being those words that differed from it by the substitution of a single letter. Thus defined, neighbourhoods can vary on a number of characteristics. Based on the number of reported effects in the literature, the size of the neighbourhood, that is the number of words that differ from the target word by a single letter, is probably the most crucial characteristic. However, as word frequency is such an important variable in determining performance in many tasks, the other characteristic that is often considered is the frequency of the neighbourhood. This is usually operationalized as the average frequency of the words in the neighbourhood. It is therefore possible to find words that have the same number of neighbours but differ in the average frequency of those neighbours, and vice versa.

Initially we thought of the process of redintegration as being akin to recognizing spoken words presented in a noisy background (Hulme, Roodenrys, Schweickert, Brown, Martin, & Stuart, 1997). Noise masks some of the information in the auditory speech signal that would be used to identify the word. Similarly, the degraded short-term trace is missing information about the word but we still need to identify it. So it seemed natural to look at research on neighbourhood effects in speech perception tasks.

Following the example of visual word recognition research, the phonological neighbours of a word can be defined as those that differ from it by the substitution of a single phoneme. In their research on neighbourhood effects in speech perception, Luce and his colleagues (e.g., Luce, Pisoni, & Goldinger, 1990) adopted a broader definition of a neighbour in assuming that a neighbour of a word might differ not just by a substitution of a phoneme but also by the addition or deletion of a phoneme. By this definition the words "tap" and "trap" are neighbours, as are "boy" and "boil". Calculations on the CELEX Lexical Database (Baayen, Piepenbrock, & Van Rijn, 1993) show that these two definitions produce neighbourhood counts that correlate extremely highly (.97 for both 3- and 4-phoneme words), so which definition is used in research may often be unimportant.

When the task is the perception of words spoken in a noisy background, neighbours compete in the process as words with more neighbours are less likely to be identified correctly than words with fewer neighbours at a given signal-to-noise ratio (Luce et al., 1990). In tasks in which the words were clearly presented, such as the auditory lexical decision task and a matching task, Vitevitch and Luce (1999) found that words with more neighbours were responded to more slowly than words with fewer neighbours and argued that this delay is due to competition from the neighbours.

Neighbourhood effects have been the subject of more extensive investigation in the area of visual word recognition, where the influence of orthographic neighbours has been the topic of research. In this field the findings have not been entirely consistent, although in reviewing the literature, Andrews (1997) argued that the inconsistency was more apparent than real. In her review Andrews observed that inhibitory effects of neighbourhood size were found in studies using perceptual identification tasks in which the stimulus was degraded in some way. In studies using the lexical decision task in which the word is clearly presented until the subject responds, neighbourhood size had a facilitative effect.

Recently, Yates, Lockyer, and Simpson (2004) have shown that phonological neighbours exert an influence on visual lexical decision even once the number of orthographic neighbours is controlled. They found that words with more phonological neighbours were responded to more quickly and accurately than words with fewer phonological neighbours. There are a number of possible explanations of how this effect might arise in models of visual word identification but the most relevant to effects of neighbourhood size in STM tasks is the notion of feedback activation coming from phonology. By this account once visual processing commences activation spreads to phonological representations of words that can then feed back into the visual system. However, the effect must occur within the phonological system as it occurs even when the words are matched on the number of orthographic neighbours (Yates et al., 2004, Experiment 2).

Studies of phonological neighbourhood effects on speech production tasks are consistent in showing facilitative effects of neighbourhood size on performance. Vitevitch (2002) found superior performance for words from large rather than small neighbourhoods in the speed of naming objects and Vitevitch and Sommers (2003) showed that performance on this task was also facilitated by higher neighbourhood frequency. Vitevitch (2002) also found that words with more neighbours were less likely to be pronounced incorrectly in a task designed to experimentally induce speech errors ("slips of the tongue"). Stemberger (2004) reported data showing that the neighbourhood effect in this induced speech error task was not due to the number of neighbours per se, but to the number of neighbours that shared the pair of phonemes in which the experimenter was attempting to induce an error.

The tip-of-the-tongue elicitation task requires subjects to generate a word from semantic information, usually a definition of the word. For some proportion of the words a subject will experience a "tip-of-the-tongue" state in which they are unable to produce the word but feel they know the word and can produce some information about the word, such as the initial letter or number of syllables. Studies by Harley and Brown (1998) and Vitevitch and Sommers (2003) have shown that words with more neighbours are less likely to suffer from the "tip-of-the-tongue" phenomenon. In one experiment, Vitevitch and Sommers (2003) also found that words with higher-frequency neighbourhoods were less likely to elicit tip-of-the-tongue states. These findings suggest that increasing neighbourhood size and neighbourhood frequency facilitates the production of spoken words.

To summarize, the evidence at present suggests that neighbours of the target word act as competitors for the target word in perception tasks, and particularly those that involve degraded presentation of the stimuli. Andrews' (1997) review suggests this is also true for visual word identification. In speech production tasks, however, neighbours facilitate output of the target word. Yates et al.'s (2004) finding of a facilitative phonological neighbourhood size effect in visual lexical decision suggests that if it is due to feedback from a phonological system then it is one involved in speech production rather than perception.

Phonological neighbourhood effects on serial recall

As described above, the basic conceptualization of the redintegration notion implies that words with more neighbours are less likely to be recalled correctly because the neighbours compete with the target word to be output in the redintegration process. For example, imagine that in an experiment using all consonant-vowel-consonant (CVC) words, the word *keg* was presented but at recall the trace retrieved from the short-term store included only the first consonant and vowel. There is only one other word that matches the fragment and so could compete in the redintegration process – *ketch* which is a word that may not be known by many subjects. Contrast that with the same situation following the presentation of *bug*. In this case there are several words that match the initial consonant and vowel, such as *bud*, *bung*, *buff*, *buck*, *bun* and *bus*. Of course the same applies for the loss of information from any part of the word with the result being that the more neighbours a word has the more likely it is that there will be other words which also match the information in the degraded trace retrieved from the short-term store.

Several prominent models of short-term memory and serial recall performance incorporate a process that is conceptually equivalent to the redintegration process and would make this same prediction (e.g., Burgess & Hitch, 1999; Nairne, 1990) of poorer recall for words with more neighbours. The assumption that the redintegration process is akin to reperceiving the words and makes use of the phonological system involved in speech perception would also lead to this prediction.

As is often the case in research, there appear to have been two research groups investigating this prediction at the same time, but unfortunately in this case finding opposite results. Both Roodenrys, Hulme, Lethbridge, Hinton, and Nimmo (2002) and Goh and Pisoni (2003) followed this line of reasoning and predicted that words from large neighbourhoods would be recalled more poorly than words from small neighbourhoods, all other things being equal. In Goh and Pisoni's (2003) data this prediction was upheld, whereas we found the exact opposite – poorer recall for words from small neighbourhoods. To foreshadow a more detailed discussion of our work, we argued that neighbours facilitate recall of the presented words and this effect arises from the involvement of speech production processes in the recall task. Before describing our results and suggesting a possible mechanism to explain them, however, I will discuss the study of Goh and Pisoni (2003) and some of our data to explain why they may have obtained the results that they did.

Goh and Pisoni (2003) compared serial recall performance for two sets of words that should differ in how easily they would be perceived in an auditory identification task, based on their phonological neighbourhood properties. The "easy" set had fewer neighbours and the average neighbourhood frequency was lower, whereas the "hard" set had more neighbours and a higher average neighbourhood frequency. They also compared performance when no items were repeated in the experiment against a condition in which a set of eight words was repeatedly sampled for each condition. Presentation of the stimuli was auditory and recall was written. Their results showed an advantage for the "easy' (small/low-frequency neighbourhood) words over the "hard" (large/high-frequency neighbourhood) but only in the non-repeating condition. They explain these results in terms of a redintegration process that uses speech perception mechanisms.

In selecting their stimuli Goh and Pisoni (2003) allowed neighbours of the words to occur in the same conditions. For example, the non-repeating, "hard" condition included the word *bead*, but also its neighbours *beak*, *bean*, *bed* and *seed*. They report that the non-repeating, "hard' and "easy" conditions did not differ significantly on the number of neighbours occurring within a condition with means of 2.61 and 2.21 respectively. Although this difference was not significant at the .05 level, the actual probability is .14 so the conditions are not as well matched as they might be. In addition the distribution of this variable is not equivalent between the two conditions. In the "hard" condition the median is three neighbours and the number of neighbours ranges from zero to five. The "easy" condition is more skewed such that the median is two neighbours and the range is zero to seven. After removing the two words from the "easy" condition that have six and seven neighbours, an independent samples t-test gives a two-tailed probability of .03. As the assignment of words to lists was random this means that the "hard" condition has a greater degree of phonological similarity than the "easy" condition if our measure of similarity is the number of words that share two phonemes with each other.

This conclusion is supported by another measure of similarity described by Mueller, Seymour, Kieras, & Meyer (2003). This measure, referred to as PSIMETRICA, breaks words down into separate syllables and then syllables into an onset, nucleus and coda and compares them on the number of matching phonetic features. In the case of CVC words this is simply the number of phonetic features that match in each of the three phonemes. By comparing each word in the stimulus set against all of the other words and then averaging we get a measure of how similar the word is to the rest of the set. These values can then be compared across the sets and show that the similarity within the "hard" condition is significantly greater than within the "easy" condition ($p < .00001$). Comparisons can be made at each phoneme position and these show significant differences in the similarity of the vowel and final consonant (both $p < .001$).

Although the sets of words in the repeating conditions in Goh and Pisoni's (2003) studies were matched on the number of neighbours, within the set of eight words the "hard" set could be considered more similar than the "easy" set as four of the eight words in the "hard" set shared the same vowel. Although the number of stimuli to be compared is small, the PSIMETRICA measure shows the two sets to be marginally different at the word level and on the first consonant ($p = .1$) and significantly different on the vowel ($p < .001$).

These differences in the phonological similarity of Goh and Pisoni's (2003) stimulus sets would act against any facilitative effect of neighbourhood size on recall and may be responsible for the pattern in their results. To test this explanation, Roodenrys (in preparation) used Goh and Pisoni's (2003) non-repeating stimuli but arranged the words into lists such that neighbours did not occur in the same or consecutive lists, and controlled for the level of within-list similarity. In three experiments varying presentation and recall modality I have failed to obtain a significant difference in recall between the "hard" (large/high-frequency neighbourhood) and the "easy" (small/low-frequency) words. This suggests that the confound with phonological similarity in Goh and Pisoni's (2003) experiments is partly responsible for the results that they obtained but it does not explain why I have as yet been unable to find a facilitative effect of neighbourhood size/frequency with these stimuli.

Another aspect of the stimuli that might explain why they do not produce a neighbourhood size/frequency effect is the manipulation of neighbourhood size itself. Goh and Pisoni (2003) report the average neighbourhood size for the "easy" condition to be 17.83 while it is 28.97 for the "hard" condition. Based on the nearly two thousand CVC words in the CELEX database these figures would correspond to roughly the 25th and the 60th percentiles of the distribution of neighbourhood sizes. This is not too surprising given the constraints of matching on other variables and our tendency to avoid using plurals, homophones or words with multiple meanings as stimuli (which seem to be more frequent at higher neighbourhood sizes). However, if neighbourhood size effects are similar to word frequency effects in other tasks it will follow a logarithmic curve, i.e., the effect of increasing the count by a constant number decreases as the count increases, then this manipulation of neighbourhood size might be expected to produce only a small effect. In comparison, for Experiment 1 of Roodenrys et al. (2002) the manipulation of neighbourhood size represented a comparison of the 3rd and 55th percentiles of the distribution of neighbourhood sizes and showed a significant facilitative effect of neighbourhood size on recall.

There is also a more interesting theoretical possibility for why I have been unable to obtain a neighbourhood size effect when neighbours of the list words are allowed to occur in other lists in the same experimental block. This relates to the finding in lexical access tasks that repeated presentation of the items not only increases the speed of performance on the items (the repetition priming effect) but it also reduces the frequency effect on performance (e.g., Scarborough, Cortese, & Scarborough, 1977). If the neighbourhood effect arises because the presence of a word in the list results in the activation of its phonological neighbours then the prior presentation of neighbours will "prime" the current list word and so might eliminate any effect of neighbourhood size. Alternatively, recently presented neighbours may compete more effectively in the redintegration process. This is consistent with the observation that many intrusions come from the previous list (e.g., Drewnoski & Murdock, 1980). Goh and Pisoni (2003) found more intrusions by neighbours in the "hard" (large/high-frequency neighbourhood) condition but did not report if these intrusions were the neighbours presented in earlier lists.

Roodenrys et al. (2002) examined the effect on serial recall performance of neighbourhood size, neighbourhood frequency and the frequency of the presented word. It was not possible to obtain stimuli to conduct a full factorial experiment on all three variables at once, partly because we avoided using neighbours in the experiments, so we measured memory span in a series of two-way experiments. The two experiments testing neighbourhood size showed a significant effect, although one of these was only marginal after covarying for differences in speech rate between the item sets. This was done to try and rule out differences in speech rate, and consequently potential differences in decay of the short-term trace, as a possible explanation of differences in memory span between conditions as speech rate was found to vary significantly between conditions. The two experiments manipulating neighbourhood frequency showed better recall for words from higher-frequency neighbourhoods; however, this effect was not significant after covarying for speech rate in one experiment. This finding was tempered by findings of an interaction between neighbourhood frequency and word frequency such that neighbourhood frequency affected recall of low-frequency words but not high-frequency words. On the whole, the interactions between the three variables were not consistent in the analyses with and without speech rate as a covariate. The main effects were fairly small and these experiments used only 24 subjects so experiments with more power should clarify the pattern of interactions between the variables.

Roodenrys et al. (2002) reported a final study using a different methodology to examine the effects of word frequency, neighbourhood size and neighbourhood frequency on serial recall. Subjects were presented with 90 lists of 6 words arranged pseudo-randomly for each subject such that each word occurred once in each position but no word occurred twice in the same list. The words covered a large range on the three variables that were used as predictors in a series of regression analyses using different dependent variables, such as proportion correct recall and number of intrusions by phonological neighbours. It is important to note that these analyses were predicting recall levels of the 90 words rather than the individual subjects. In addition, following the recommendations of Lorch and Myers (1990) this is done whilst considering variation within subjects. This is done to reduce the possibility of a Type I error due to variation in the effect across subjects and results in *r*-squared values that are extremely small as variation between subjects remains in the equation. Accordingly, it is more important to focus on whether predictors are significant or not.

The results of the regression analyses are extremely interesting because they suggest that neighbours both support the presented word and compete with it in recall. In brief, we found that word frequency, neighbourhood size and neighbourhood frequency all had significant effects on correct recall. That is, words were more likely to be recalled correctly if they were higher in frequency, came from larger neighbourhoods and their neighbourhood had a higher average frequency. However, all three variables were also significant predictors of the number of times a neighbour of the presented word intruded in recall. Higher-frequency words were less likely to be intruded upon by a neighbour but words with larger neighbourhoods or higher-frequency neighbourhoods were more likely to be intruded upon by a neighbour. The neighbour intrusions showed a strong tendency for the intruding word to be higher in frequency than the presented word with 60% being at least 10 words per million higher in frequency.

The method of analysis recommended by Lorch and Myers (1990) is more robust and conservative than the more traditional approach of collapsing the data across subjects but the outcome, in terms of understanding how influential these variables are on recall, is less helpful. Given that the more robust analysis has shown these effects to be significant it seems reasonable to use the more traditional approach to get an impression of the variance in performance that might be accounted for by these variables. This simply involves averaging the scores for each word across the subjects and is made more acceptable by the large number of subjects involved (*n* = 56). In all of the analyses reported below using this method the pattern of significant effects is the same as in the analyses using the more robust method reported by Roodenrys et al. (2002).

In predicting correct recall using this method the three main effects combined accounted for 30% of the variability in recall, but remember that this is collapsed across serial position and words were randomly allocated to lists. Independently, the frequency of the presented word accounted for approximately 24% of the variability, neighbourhood size for approximately 3%, and neighbourhood frequency for about 0.5%. In predicting intrusions by neighbours of the presented word they accounted for 23% of the variability in total, with word frequency accounting for approximately 12%, and neighbourhood size and neighbourhood frequency both accounting for 5–6% independently of the other variables.

The main conclusion we can draw from this is that the most important of these factors in determining recall is the frequency of the presented word, but neighbourhood size and frequency do play roles. The relatively greater influence of word frequency is more the case for correctly recalling the word than the likelihood of suffering a neighbour intrusion, whereas, the number and frequency of the neighbours is more influential in determining neighbour intrusions than the likelihood of correctly recalling the word. This suggests that when a word is in the serial recall task it activates its neighbours and this increases the likelihood of recalling the word but also increases the likelihood that a neighbour will intrude upon it in recall. Furthermore, it suggests that the neighbourhood effect in serial recall does not arise from the use of speech perception mechanisms in the redintegration process. Rather, the data are more consistent with the view that the effects arise from the use of speech production mechanisms in recall.

None of the interactions between frequency and the neighbourhood variables was a significant predictor in the regression study of Roodenrys et al. (2002), although the finding of intrusions tending to be higher in frequency than the word they have replaced is suggestive of an interaction. This may have been due to insufficient power as some of the interactions reached significance in the factorial experiments and 90 items is not a large number to try and examine interactions in regression (Aiken & West, 1991). This study is important though because it effectively rules out speech rate as a potential explanation of the effect. In the factorial experiments memory span was assessed for sets of words of a uniform neighbourhood size or frequency using an up-and-down method that ensures that 50% of the trials are recalled fully correctly. These sets of words were also found to vary in speech rate so according to a trace decay model the neighbourhood effects may have occurred because the differences in speech rate allowed more or less time for decay before recall. Speech rate was used as a covariate in the analyses to counter this suggestion. The methodology of the regression study refutes this suggestion even more clearly because the factors did not vary list-wise but randomly within lists. Thus if large neighbourhood words could be spoken more quickly, according to a trace decay model, this might affect the recall of subsequent words in the list (which varied randomly) but it would not affect recall of the word itself. This shows that the role of speech production processes in creating the neighbourhood effect is not restricted to facilitating the rate of overt recall.

Since we published the regression study in 2002 I have had the opportunity to rule out some other possible explanations for the effect. One of these was the possibility that the variables were confounded with concreteness. Walker and Hulme (1999) found that recall was better for lists of concrete words than lists of abstract words. I obtained concreteness ratings from 52 first-year psychology students at the same university where the regression study was run. These students rated 250 words in total, including all of the stimuli used in the regression study. These concreteness ratings did not correlate with the neighbourhood size or neighbourhood frequency of the words used in the study ($r = .03$ and $.05$, respectively) and only very weakly with word frequency ($r = .12$).

I have also examined the possibility of the variables of interest correlating with the phonological similarity of the words to all the other words in the set. Since assignment of words to lists was random every word should have occurred relatively equally often with every other word so the PSIMETRICA measure (Mueller et al., 2003) is an appropriate index of similarity. This measure was calculated by comparing each word with all of the other stimuli and averaging to get a value for each word that was then correlated with the neighbourhood variables and word frequency. None of these correlations was above an absolute value of .04.

I believe that the conclusion to be drawn from the studies reviewed above is that words with larger neighbourhoods and higher-frequency neighbourhoods are recalled better than words with smaller or lower-frequency neighbourhoods. The similarity of the effects observed with those seen in speech production tasks suggests that the redintegration process makes use of speech production rather than speech perception mechanisms. Before discussing the possible mechanism of the effect, however, it is worth describing evidence that the same effect of neighbourhood size occurs in the recall of CVC nonsense words.

The wordlikeness effect is the finding that repetition of nonwords is easier for those items rated as being more wordlike than those rated as less wordlike (Gathercole, Willis, Emslie, & Baddeley, 1991). This suggests a possible role in recall for phonological representations of words sounding similar to the nonword or common sublexical phonological patterns. Gathercole, Frankish, Pickering, and Peaker (1999) examined the possibility that the familiarity of sublexical phonology could influence nonword recall. They measured biphone frequency by counting how often each pair of phonemes (i.e., CV and VC from a CVC) occurred in monosyllabic words in the CELEX database. They found that lists of CVC nonwords with higher biphone frequencies were better recalled than lists of nonwords with lower biphone frequency. However, Roodenrys and Hinton (2002) showed that this measure was confounded with neighbourhood size and demonstrated that biphone frequency had no effect when neighbourhood size was controlled but neighbourhood size had a significant facilitative effect on recall when biphone frequency was controlled. More recently, Thorn and Frankish (2005) pointed out that Roodenrys and Hinton's (2002) manipulation of neighbourhood size while controlling biphone frequency was achieved by varying the number of neighbours that shared the two consonants with the nonword. They argued that this neighbourhood effect, based on differences in the number of C-C neighbours, could be masking a biphone frequency effect between conditions. They calculated biphone frequencies from all of the words in the CELEX database so that they could disconfound these variables and showed effects of both neighbourhood size and biphone frequency on the recall of CVC nonwords. This suggests a role for both lexical and sublexical phonological information in long-term memory in serial recall and that the lexical effect arises from a process that is common to word and nonword recall.

Explaining neighbourhood effects in serial recall

Roodenrys et al. (2002) discussed a few possibilities for how the neighbourhood effects might be accounted for in models of short-term memory and what follows below is the development of one of those possibilities, a conceptual account based on multiple levels of representation in an interactive network. The problem for most models of short-term memory that include a redintegration process that might explain the neighbourhood effects is that they are based on whole-item representations. Any redintegration process that involves a comparison against traces of the whole item and other items in long-term memory seemingly must predict a competitive action from phonological neighbours. This process can explain the increase in neighbour intrusions as neighbourhood size increases but it cannot explain the facilitative effect of larger neighbourhoods on correct recall.

One way of explaining the facilitative effect of neighbours on correct recall is if the redintegration process involves sublexical information represented separately from the lexical representations in an interactive network. Only two levels of information are necessary for the present discussion, a level representing the individual phonemes in the items and a level of word representations. There may be other levels of information within the system, such as the phonetic features that make up the phonemes or sublexical, multiple phoneme units such as rimes. Wickelgren's (1965b, 1965c) data suggest that information loss from the short-term trace occurs at the level of phonetic features but the general basis of the explanation may be better understood if the present discussion is restricted to phonemes and words.

In McClelland and Rumelhart's (1981) classic interactive activation model of visual word identification visual input results in the activation of units corresponding to the features of letters. These pass activation up to units corresponding to the letters containing those features, which in turn pass activation up to units representing words containing those letters. Units at the word level also pass activation back down to the letters. The model is inherently competitive as units at the word level are linked by inhibitory connections but the feedback of activation from word units to letters also allows it to produce facilitative neighbourhood effects ("gang" effects in their paper). If the phonemes in a degraded trace retrieved from the short-term store were used as input into such a network comprising phonemes and words it is possible to obtain the neighbourhood effects we have observed. The actual outcome for any word depends not just on how many neighbours it has but also on which parts of the trace are intact.

Consider a case where the word *gulf* has been presented but at retrieval from short-term store the initial consonant is missing, thus the remaining information uniquely specifies the correct word. This information is taken as the input to activate a set of phonemes which then activate words that they are consistent with, followed by a period in which activation flows through the connections in the model until a stable state is achieved. In the first stage of processing this would result in the activation of the phonemes for *u*, *l* and *f*. We need to assume that these phoneme representations are position specific and this might be achieved by something like the syllable template mechanism of Hartley and Houghton (1996). Once activated the phonemes activate words with which they are consistent, and words that contain more of the phonemes become more activated. This means that in this example the word *gulf* will be most activated, but words like *gold* and *gulp* will also be activated to a lesser degree. Each word unit will then start to feed this activation back down to the phonemes of which it is comprised. Thus all three of these words will activate the missing *g* phoneme. As *gold* and *gulp* are partially activated, *g* is activated more quickly than if they were not present in the network. So, in this case where the degraded input uniquely specifies a single word, the partially activated neighbours facilitate the identification/recall of the correct word. The more neighbours the word has the more activation the word will ultimately receive and the more likely it is that the missing information will be "filled in" correctly.

Now consider a situation in which the input does not uniquely specify a single word, for instance if *gulf* was presented but the identity of the vowel was lost. In this case the degraded information will activate the phonemes for *g*, *l* and *f*. This will in turn result in the activation of the words that are consistent with those phonemes in those positions in the word, such as *gulf* and *golf* and, to a lesser degree, *gulp* because it only contains two of the phonemes. In this case the input cannot resolve whether the presented word was *gulf* or *golf* and so the neighbour *golf* effectively competes with the presented word *gulf*. Whether it is recalled instead of the presented word will be determined by information other than the identity of the phonemes. If activation levels of words are related to frequency then the higher frequency word will tend to be produced in this situation. This is consistent with the data on intrusions from Roodenrys et al. (2002). It also means that the more neighbours a word has the more likely it is that a preserved fragment will not uniquely identify the word and so words with more neighbours will suffer from more neighbour intrusions in recall.

According to this account, redintegration operates at a phonemic level. The input to the process is the phonemes retrieved from the short-term store. The output, however, could be either at the phoneme or the word level as ultimately a stable state should exist across both the word and phoneme units. It would seem more parsimonious if the output is at the phoneme level as the studies on neighbourhood and phonotactic effects in the recall of nonwords show the same facilitative effects of lexical neighbours as our experiments with words. Schweickert (1993) suggested that there may be two redintegrative processes, one operating at a lexical level and one at the phonemic level. However, an interactive network approach like the one described can combine lexical and phonemic influences into one process. The phonotactic effect on the recall of nonwords suggests that information about typical phoneme pairings contributes to recall and this must occur at a sublexical level. It is interesting that in Thorn and Frankish's (2005) data the phonotactic and lexical neighbourhood effects on recall are of equivalent magnitude. It seems likely that when the stimuli are words the influence of a lexical representation would tend to reduce the influence of sublexical and neighbourhood effects. Consistent with this suggestion, the neighbourhood effects we have observed on the recall of words are quite small. However, it raises the question of whether phonotactic effects might also be seen in word recall.

If phonemes retrieved from the short-term store are used as input into an interactive activation network as I have described, where in the language processing system is this network located? As I have argued above, it seems unlikely that the phonological system underlying the influence of long-term phonological knowledge is part of the speech perception system as neighbours reduce performance in speech perception tasks. It seems more likely to be part of the speech production system, as neighbours have been shown to facilitate performance in speech production tasks, but this requires a flow of information from a store that takes its input from the auditory system into a production system at the lower end of the production process (i.e., the phonemes) rather than a higher level, such as via semantics. The fact that we can repeat nonwords at all suggests strongly that speech perception mechanisms are linked directly to production processes at a sublexical level.

Monsell (1987) argued for a theory of serial recall performance in which sublexical phonological input and output buffers were linked. The model described above would require only that activation of sublexical phonological representations used in production could spread to lexical representations, and in turn feed back to phonemes. Monsell (1987) also made this suggestion, but this was done to explain the lexical advantage in aphasia. Martin, Lesch, and Bartha (1999) also describe a model of the language system that explains serial recall performance by the use of phonological input and output buffers; however, in their model there is no direct link between the buffers. Instead, activity in the input buffer passes to the output buffer via phonological representations in long-term memory.

Schweickert's (1993) multinomial processing tree model of serial recall proposes that redintegration occurs only if an item is not intact in the short-term store, and potentially the phonological process may operate only after the lexical process has failed to produce the word. In the approach I have described above, phonological information is passed directly from the perceptual system to production mechanisms, regardless of the integrity of the information for any particular word. This means that all items would undergo some degree of "redintegration", making the long-term influences on recall an inherent part of a single process rather than a second or third stage process that operates only after the earlier stages have failed.

The account suggested here has in common with many models of short-term memory, the proposal that recall of a word will be determined by how degraded the trace retrieved from short-term memory is, and by how effective the redintegration process will be. For a given level of degradation, the effectiveness of the redintegration process is likely to be influenced by factors specific to that particular occasion, such as the similarity of the word to other words in the list, and the availability of semantic information that might contribute by restricting activation within the phonological system, such as when all the words in the list come from a single category (e.g., Poirier & Saint-Aubin, 1995). However, there are also factors that are not specific to that occasion but relevant every time that particular word is recalled, such as frequency and neighbourhood size. We can think of these factors as combining to provide a type of redintegrative factor for the word, an index of how readily it can be redintegrated. We might expect that words that are readily redintegrated will be less affected by degradation. That is, the likelihood of recalling them correctly stays high for longer in the face of increasing levels of degradation. At the other end of the scale, the recall of words that are difficult to redintegrate will be reduced more quickly by degradation. This type of relationship is captured by a sigmoidal function, $1/(1 + e^{-x})$, where the function has asymptotes of 0 and 1. If x is a function of two parameters, the degree of degradation of the short-term trace and how readily it can be redintegrated, it is possible to produce curves like those shown in Figure 9.1. The vertical axis represents the likelihood of recall, while the horizontal axis represents the degree of degradation of the trace. The separate curves are formed by different values denoting how readily redintegrated the word is: the more readily redintegrated the word the further to the right the transposition of the curve, and the greater the likelihood that the word will be recalled for any given level of degradation.

To test this type of approach it is necessary to obtain measures of recall for words that can reasonably be assumed to vary in how readily

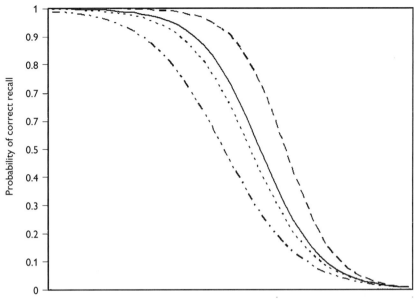

Figure 9.1 Recall level as a sigmoidal function of trace degradation for four hypothetical words varying in ease of redintegration.

redintegrated they are across varying levels of degradation. This would require a large study designed specifically for this purpose but if we assume that degradation increases across serial positions in a list then the data from the regression study of Roodenrys et al. (2002) can be used to provide a preliminary evaluation of this approach. In that study each word was presented once in each serial position to each subject, and the arrangement of words in lists was random, so other factors that might influence recall, such as phonological similarity, should be roughly equated across the different words and different positions. This means that for each position there should be a degree of degradation that is fairly consistent across the different words. It also means that how readily redintegrated a word is should not vary across serial positions (i.e., different lists) but will be a function of factors intrinsic to the word such as frequency and neighbourhood size. Thus, the recall of the same word in different serial positions should fall along a function like those in Figure 9.1.

Data for three sets of six words taken from the regressions study of Roodenrys et al. (2002) are shown in Figure 9.2. The three sets of words were selected based on elements that should represent different levels of ease of redintegration. One set are high frequency and generally have large neighbourhoods and therefore would be expected to be recalled better than average. Another set are low frequency and have few neighbours and would

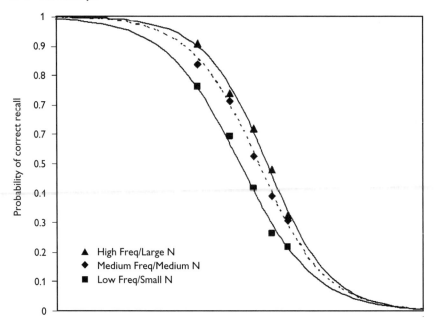

Figure 9.2 Recall level as a sigmoidal function of trace degradation and ease of redintegration of the word, showing example data for three sets of words from Roodenrys et al. (2002). N = Neighbourhood.

be expected to be relatively poorly recalled. The third set of words are moderate frequency and of varying neighbourhood sizes and should fall between the other two in terms of recall performance. Using the same function as in Figure 9.1 it is possible to plot the recall performance for these sets of words against the function using a single "ease of redintegration" value for each word set and a single degree of degradation value for each serial position. The results of half an hour's effort by trial and error are shown in Figure 9.2 and suggest that the approach may have some merit. Performance on positions 1 to 5 of the six-item lists is shown. Data from the final position could be included in this figure, and fit as well as the other positions, but the strong recency effect on this position would detract slightly from the very clear picture in Figure 9.2 of the relationships between serial position, the degree of degradation and recall performance. The suggestion that the last item in a list is less degraded than earlier items is not controversial and is assumed in some models (e.g., Nairne, 1990).

One interesting feature of the data fit in Figure 9.2 is that the words are already quite degraded in position 1. The exact function used to fit the data can be modified but adjusting the parameters will not result in zero degradation in the first position, and nor should it as performance in the first position is not perfect. To account for this we would have to assume that supra-span lists undergo some degradation before recall commences (and further degradation occurs during recall). This does not seem unreasonable when we consider that recall of shorter lists, such as three or four items, which fall within most subjects' span would fall to the left of the data points in Figure 9.2. Clearly, data from the recall of lists of different lengths is required to fully test this approach.

Summary

Phonological neighbourhood effects in serial recall demonstrate that words in long-term memory that sound similar to the presented word influence recall of that word. I argue that the evidence shows that neighbours support the correct recall of the presented word as well as potentially intruding on it in recall as a result of the redintegration of degraded phonological traces. This pattern can be explained if a degraded string of phonemes retrieved from an auditory-based store is taken as the input to an interactive phonological network involved in speech production with distinct representations of phonemes and words. An implication of this view of the redintegration process is that words can be distinguished in terms of their ease of redintegration and it is demonstrated how this factor, in combination with degradation of the memory trace, could be used to model recall.

References

Aiken, L. S., & West, S. G. (1991). *Multiple regression: Testing and interpreting interactions*. Thousand Oaks, CA: Sage.

Andrews, S. (1997). The effect of orthographic similarity on lexical retrieval: Resolving neighbourhood conflicts. *Psychonomic Bulletin & Review, 4*, 439–461.

Baayen, R. H., Piepenbrock, R., & Van Rijn, H. (1993). *The CELEX lexical database* [CD-ROM]. Philadelphia: Linguistic Data Consortium, University of Pennsylvania.

Burgess, N., & Hitch, G. J. (1999). Memory for serial order: A network model of the phonological loop and its timing. *Psychological Review, 106*, 551–581.

Coltheart, M., Davelaar, E., Jonasson, J. T., & Besner, D. (1977). Access to the internal lexicon. In S. Dornic (Ed.), *Attention and performance VI*. Hillsdale, NJ: Lawrence Erlbaum Associates, Inc.

Conrad, R. (1964). Acoustic confusions in immediate memory. *British Journal of Pyschology, 55*, 75–84.

Drewnowski, A., & Murdock, B. B. (1980). The role of auditory features in memory span for words. *Journal of Experimental Psychology: Human Learning and Memory, 6*(3), 319–332.

Gathercole, S. E., Frankish, C. R., Pickering, S. J., & Peaker, S. (1999). Phonotactic influences on short-term memory. *Journal of Experimental Psychology: Learning, Memory, and Cognition, 25*, 84–95.

Gathercole, S. E., Willis, C., Emslie, H., & Baddeley, A. D. (1991). The influences of number of syllables and wordlikeness on children's repetition of nonwords. *Applied Psycholinguistics, 12,* 349–367.

Goh, W. D., & Pisoni, D. B. (2003). Effects of lexical competition on immediate memory span for spoken words. *Quarterly Journal of Experimental Psychology, 56A,* 929–954.

Harley, T. A., & Brown, H. E. (1998). What causes a tip-of-the-tongue state? Evidence for lexical neighbourhood effects in speech production. *British Journal of Psychology, 89,* 151–174.

Hartley, T., & Houghton, G. (1996). A linguistically constrained model of short-term memory for nonwords. *Journal of Memory and Language, 35,* 1–31.

Hulme, C., Roodenrys, S., Schweickert, R., Brown, G. D. A., Martin, S., & Stuart, G. (1997). Word frequency effects on short-term memory tasks: Evidence for a redintegration process in immediate serial recall. *Journal of Experimental Psychology: Learning, Memory, and Cognition, 23,* 1217–1232.

Lorch, R. F., & Myers, J. L. (1990). Regression analyses of repeated measures data in cognitive research. *Journal of Experimental Psychology: Learning, Memory, and Cognition, 16,* 149–157.

Luce, P. A., Pisoni, D. B., & Goldinger, S. D. (1990). Similarity neighbourhoods of spoken words. In G. T. M. Altmann (Ed.), *Cognitive models of speech processing: Psycholinguistic and computational perspectives.* Cambridge, MA: MIT Press.

Martin, R. C., Lesch, M. F., & Bartha, M. C. (1999). Independence of input and output phonology in word processing and short-term memory. *Journal of Memory and Language, 41,* 3–29.

McClelland, J. L., & Rumelhart, D. E. (1981). An interactive activation model of context effects in letter perception: Part 1. An account of basic findings. *Psychological Review, 88*(5), 375–407.

Monsell, S. (1987). On the relation between lexical input and output pathways for speech. In *Language and perception.* London: Academic Press.

Mueller, S. T., Seymour, T. L., Kieras, D. E., & Meyer, D. E. (2003). Theoretical implications of articulatory duration, phonological similarity, and phonological complexity in verbal working memory. *Journal of Experimental Psychology: Learning, Memory, and Cognition, 29*(6), 1353–1380.

Nairne, J. S. (1990). A feature model of immediate memory. *Memory and Cognition, 18*(3), 251–269.

Poirier, M., & Saint-Aubin, J. (1995). Memory for related and unrelated words: Further evidence on the influence of semantic factors in immediate serial recall. *Quarterly Journal of Experimental Psychology, 48A*(2), 384–404.

Roodenrys, S. (in preparation). Similarity and lexical neighbourhood effects on verbal short-term memory.

Roodenrys, S., & Hinton, M. (2002). Sublexical or lexical effects on serial recall of nonwords? *Journal of Experimental Psychology: Learning, Memory, and Cognition, 28,* 29–33.

Roodenrys, S., Hulme, C., Lethbridge, A., Hinton, M., & Nimmo, L. M. (2002). Word frequency and phonological neighborhood effects on verbal short-term memory. *Journal of Experimental Psychology: Learning, Memory, and Cognition, 28,* 1019–1034.

Scarborough, D. L., Cortese, C., & Scarborough, H. S. (1977). Frequency and repetition effects in lexical memory. *Journal of Experimental Psychology: Human Perception and Performance, 3,* 1–17.

Schweickert, R. (1993). A multinomial processing tree model for degradation and redintegration in immediate recall. *Memory & Cognition, 21,* 168–175.

Sperling, G., & Speelman, R. G. (1970). Acoustic similarity and auditory short-term memory: Experiments and a model. In D. A. Norman (Ed.), *Models of human memory* (pp. 152–202). New York: Academic Press.

Stemberger, J. P. (2004). Neighbourhood effects on error rates in speech production. *Brain and Language, 90,* 413–422.

Thorn, A. S. C., & Frankish, C. R. (2005). Long-term knowledge effects on serial recall of nonwords are not exclusively lexical. *Journal of Experimental Psychology: Learning, Memory, and Cognition, 31*(4), 729–735.

Vitevitch, M. S. (2002). The influence of phonological similarity neighborhoods on speech production. *Journal of Experimental Psychology: Learning, Memory, and Cognition, 28,* 735–747.

Vitevitch, M. S., & Luce, P. A. (1999). Probabilistic phonotactics and spoken word recognition. *Journal of Memory and Language, 40,* 374–408.

Vitevitch, M. S., & Sommers, M. S. (2003). The facilitative influence of phonological similarity and neighborhood frequency in speech production in younger and older adults. *Memory & Cognition, 31*(4), 491–504.

Walker, I., & Hulme, C. (1999). Concrete words are easier to recall than abstract words: Evidence for a semantic contribution to short-term serial recall. *Journal of Experimental Psychology: Learning, Memory, and Cognition, 25,* 1256–1271.

Wickelgren, W. A. (1965a). Acoustic similarity and intrusion errors in short-term memory. *Journal of Experimental Psychology, 70*(1), 102–108.

Wickelgren, W. A. (1965b). Distinctive features and errors in short-term memory for English consonants. *Journal of the Acoustical Society of America, 39*(2), 388–398.

Wickelgren, W. A. (1965c). Distinctive features and errors in short-term memory for English vowels. *Journal of the Acoustical Society of America, 38,* 583–588.

Yates, M., Lockyer, L. J., & Simpson, G. B. (2004). The influence of phonological neighborhood on visual word perception. *Psychonomic Bulletin & Review, 11*(3), 452–457.

10 The influence of long-term knowledge on short-term memory: Evidence for multiple mechanisms

Annabel S. C. Thorn, Clive R. Frankish and Susan E. Gathercole

Overview

Whilst significant advances in understanding of the contribution of long-term knowledge to verbal short-term memory have been made in recent years, the mechanisms underpinning the effects of permanent representations on temporary memory processes are not yet fully specified. The main theoretical accounts advanced to date differ principally with respect to the stage in the memory process at which long-term knowledge is proposed to interact with the temporary trace. Common to all accounts, though, is the assumption that the influence of long-term knowledge on short-term memory occurs at a single point in the memory system. In this chapter we will argue that this assumption is incorrect. Instead, on the basis of recent empirical work, we will suggest that long-term knowledge contributes to short-term memory at more than one point in the memory process, and in more than one way.

Introduction

A number of sources of evidence point to the view that verbal short-term memory operates on the basis of transient phonological representations: intrusion errors tend to be phonologically similar to the original memory item (Conrad, 1962; Sperling, 1963) and immediate memory is substantially worse for verbal information that is phonologically similar than for information that is phonologically distinct (e.g., Conrad, 1964; Conrad & Hull, 1964). Despite this reliance on a phonological coding system, it has recently become clear that stable lexical and semantic attributes of memory items influence their memorability. One of the most widely documented examples of this is the lexicality effect, which refers to the superior levels of recall accuracy found for familiar words compared with unfamiliar non-words (e.g., Hulme, Maughan, & Brown, 1991). Other linguistic factors found to influence the memorability of verbal information include word frequency (e.g., Gregg, Freedman, & Smith, 1989; Hulme, Roodenrys, Schweickert, Brown, Martin, & Stuart, 1997), imageability (Bourassa &

Besner, 1994), language familiarity (Thorn & Gathercole, 1999, 2001) and semantic similarity (Poirier & Saint-Aubin, 1995; Saint-Aubin, Ouellette, & Poirier, 2005). In addition to these lexical factors, sublexical variables such as lexical neighbourhood size (the number of words that share a close phonological structure with the memory item) and constituent phonotactic frequency (the frequency of occurrence of component phoneme combinations) have also been shown to impact on our ability to remember over the short term (Goh & Pisoni, 2003; Roodenrys & Hinton, 2002; Thorn & Frankish, 2005). Taken together, these phenomena indicate a pervasive impact of stable knowledge on ostensibly temporary memory processes.

Investigations of the impact of long-term knowledge on short-term memory indicate that long-term knowledge specifically influences the retention of information concerning the identity of a memory item rather than its ordinal position in a memory sequence (see Majerus, this volume). For example, Saint-Aubin and Poirier (1999) showed that both semantic similarity and word frequency influence the number of item errors produced, but have little effect on order errors (see also Murdock, 1976; Poirier & Saint-Aubin, 1996). Similarly, we have shown that, when compared with serial recall, the effects of lexicality, word frequency and language familiarity are greatly diminished in an order serial recognition task in which participants hear a target memory list and are required to judge whether or not a second list presented immediately after contains an order transposition of two adjacent list items (Gathercole, Pickering, Hall, & Peaker 2000; Thorn, Gathercole, & Frankish, in prep, a). It appears that the effects of long-term knowledge variables on memory performance are reduced in this task as a consequence of the minimal demands placed on the retention of item information. Consistent with this interpretation, when demands on the retention of item information are increased in the serial recognition task by the requirement to identify an item rather than order change, beneficial effects of long-term knowledge are observed (Jefferies, Frankish, & Lambon Ralph, 2006; Thorn et al., in prep, a).

Theoretical accounts of long-term knowledge effects

Theoretical accounts of the interaction between long-term knowledge and short-term memory aim to model the impact of permanent memory representations on the retention and retrieval of item information in the temporary memory trace. Broadly, these accounts fall into two categories.

Redintegration

One class of account attributes long-term knowledge effects to a process termed "redintegration", in which established phonological representations are used to reconstruct information in the temporary memory trace at the point at which information in the trace is accessed, typically at retrieval

(Botvinick & Bylsma, 2005; Brown & Hulme, 1995, 1996; Hulme et al., 1997; Schweickert, 1993; Sperling & Speelman, 1970). A reconstruction process of this type is incorporated in many recent models of immediate recall (Botvinick & Plaut, 2006; Brown, Preece, & Hulme, 2000; Burgess & Hitch, 1999; Lewandowsky, 1999; Lewandowsky & Farrell, 2000; Nairne, 1990; Page & Norris, 1998). By a redintegration account, long-term knowledge effects on short-term memory arise through differences in the accessibility of long-term representations which influence the degree to which the reconstruction process is successful (see Roodenrys, this volume). For example, according to the redintegration view, the lexicality effect reflects the fact that long-term representations are available for the reconstruction of degraded traces of words, but no such representations exist for the reconstruction of nonword memory traces (Hulme et al., 1991; Hulme, Newton, Cowan, Stuart, & Brown, 1999). Similarly, the recall advantage for high compared with low frequency words is proposed to reflect differences in the accessibility of long-term representations of high and low frequency words, with greater accessibility facilitating the reconstruction process leading to a recall advantage for high frequency words (Hulme et al., 1997). One suggestion is that permanent representations of high frequency words are more readily accessible because their representations co-occur more regularly than those of low frequency words (e.g., Stuart & Hulme, 2000, this volume), although this proposal is currently the subject of some debate (see Saint-Aubin & Leblanc, 2005; Saint-Aubin & Poirier, 2005).

A number of variants of the basic redintegration mechanism have been proposed in the literature. One elegant instantiation is provided by Schweickert's multinomial processing tree model of degradation and redintegration (Schweickert, 1993; see also Batchelder & Riefer, 1986; Chechile & Meyer, 1976). In a multinomial processing tree model, branches of the tree represent successive cognitive processes applied to achieve a particular goal. The outcome of the attempt to achieve the goal is dictated by the path from the root of the tree to a terminal node. Gathercole and colleagues (Gathercole, Frankish, Pickering, & Peaker, 1999) proposed an adaptation of Schweickert's (1993) model which formalises features of Schweickert's account that were implicit in his exposition but were not explicitly addressed in the model (Figure 10.1). The model represents a two-stage recall process, according to which there are two possible routes to achieving correct recall of a memory item. Branches leading from the root of the tree represent the initial state of the temporary memory trace, which could be either intact, partially degraded or completely degraded to the point of being unidentifiable. If intact, the item can be recalled directly from memory. If partially degraded, a second stage of the recall process may be invoked in which redintegration may reconstruct the item: completely successful reconstruction will result in correct recall of the memory item, and unsuccessful redintegration will generate a recall error. Implicit in Schweickert's (1993) analysis is the notion that redintegration cannot take

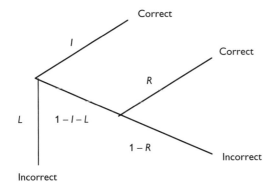

Figure 10.1 A multinomial processing tree model of the redintegration process proposed by Gathercole et al. (1999) based on Schweickert's (1993) multinomial processing tree model of degradation and redintegration. This extension of Schweickert's model incorporates the notion that a degraded trace might be lost entirely and that such a trace could not be subject to redintegration. I = probability that the representation for a given item is intact and that the item can be recalled directly and correctly. R = probability that a degraded item can be successfully redintegrated. L = probability that a degraded trace is lost entirely. From "Phonotactic influences on short-term memory" by S. E. Gathercole et al., 1999, *Journal of Experimental Psychology: Learning, Memory, and Cognition*, p. 93. Copyright 1999 by the American Psychological Association, Inc. Adapted with permission.

place when there is nothing left in the memory trace on which to base a reconstruction attempt. Accordingly, Gathercole et al.'s (1999) revision of Schweickert's (1993) model incorporates a branch representing completely lost traces that originates from the root of the tree and, unlike the branch for partially degraded traces, does not have a redintegration pathway leading from it. Note that the central tenet of this model of the redintegration process is that redintegration is restricted to memory items for which the memory trace contains partial but incomplete information.

Other models of redintegration do not restrict the reconstruction process to partial memory traces, but propose instead that redintegration is applied to all memory items irrespective of their initial encoding status. In their connectionist model of short-term recall Lewandowsky and Farrell (2000) implement redintegration as a process involving the matching of a memory vector to an "attractor", with attractors selected from the set of items in the input memory list, plus some spurious items arising from extra-list intrusions. Redintegrative effects of long-term knowledge are attributed in this model to differences in the strengths of the potential attractors, reflecting differences in the probability of successful redintegration. A similar implementation of redintegration is incorporated in Nairne's feature model of immediate memory (Nairne, 1990), in which all memory items are "assembled" at recall by reference to a set of long-term representations activated during input of the memory list. Redintegrative effects of long-term knowledge on short-term recall arise in this model by affecting the probability of trace interpretation and consequently the success of the assembling process. Importantly, although differing in detail, both of these models propose that the redintegration process is applied to all memory traces irrespective of their state following encoding and/or degradation.

The models of redintegration reviewed above represent varying implementations of the basic redintegration process. All instantiations of the redintegration process, though, work on the thesis that verbal material is first encoded into short-term memory, with the temporary memory representation subsequently being subjected to a reconstruction process. An important implication of this view is that factors whose influence on short-term memory is mediated by the redintegration process should not affect the initial retention of the memory trace. Consequently, if long-term knowledge effects are mediated exclusively by a redintegration type process, the initial retention of the memory trace should be independent of the linguistic properties of the memory item.

Pre-retrieval accounts

An alternative class of accounts that have been advanced to explain long-term knowledge influences on short-term memory locates the interaction between temporary and permanent memory representations earlier, during the encoding and/or storage of verbal material in short-term memory. By these accounts verbal short-term memory representations are based in some direct way on the long-term representation of verbal information and consequently reflect not only the phonological structure of the memory item but the lexical and semantic properties of that item too (see Martin, this volume).

One influential theory of this type has been developed from neuro-psychological observations of impaired short-term memory functioning. On the basis of evidence from patients presenting with dissociable impairments for the phonological and lexical-semantic features of memory items, R. Martin and colleagues propose that short-term recall performance is supported by multiple temporary buffers, including one specialised for the retention of phonological information and one which retains lexical-semantic information (Martin, 2006; Martin & Lesch, 1996; Martin, Lesch, & Bartha, 1999; Martin, Shelton, & Yaffee, 1994). Martin and colleagues propose that this model accounts for long-term knowledge phenomena in short-term recall in terms of the relative strength of representations within the buffers and the strength of connections between buffers: the lexicality effect arises because of the additional availability of lexical-semantic representations for word but not nonword memory traces, while the recall advantage obtained for high frequency words can be explained in terms of stronger connections between semantic and phonological representations for high than for low frequency memory items (Martin et al., 1999).

A second set of theories that view long-term knowledge influences as occurring during encoding/storage are those that ultimately view short-term memory as a state of activated long-term memory. For example, Ruchkin and colleagues (Cameron, Haarmann, Grafman, & Ruchkin, 2005; Ruchkin, Grafman, Cameron, & Berndt, 2003) propose that long-term memory systems provide the representational basis for short-term memory, and Cowan (1988, 1995) proposes that short-term memory is the activated portion of long-term memory. By this type of view, temporary memory representations necessarily embody the properties of the permanent knowledge base and consequently long-term knowledge effects in short-term memory can be viewed as simply a by-product of the representational system used in short-term memory. Note that the view that short-term memory is simply a state of activated long-term memory does not readily account for the temporary retention of novel verbal information, something that has been proposed to be a central function of short-term memory (Baddeley, Gathercole, & Papagno, 1998). Cowan & Chen (this volume) attempt to address this issue.

Although the "pre-retrieval" accounts of long-term knowledge effects in short-term memory reviewed above differ in the extent to which a role for a separable temporary memory system is assumed, all consider that the linguistic properties of memory items influence the retention of those items during the storage stage of remembering over the short term. Consequently, and contrary to the redintegration view, by these accounts memory items cannot be retained and processed independently of their linguistic properties.

Dissociating between pre-retrieval and redintegration accounts

The restriction of the redintegration process to a post-storage stage in the memory system clearly differentiates the redintegration account from those accounts which view long-term knowledge effects as arising during encoding and/or storage. An appropriate starting point for any attempt to validate redintegration as the process responsible for long-term knowledge influences on short-term memory is therefore analysis of the retrieval process involved in verbal short-term memory functioning.

Reducing retrieval demands

One way to assess the importance of retrieval processes in mediating the benefits of long-term knowledge on short-term memory is to observe the effects of long-term knowledge variables in paradigms that place relatively reduced demands on the retrieval of information from short-term memory. One such paradigm that reduces demands on the retrieval of detailed item information, but retains the requirement for retrieval of order information, is serial order reconstruction. In this task, memory items are presented sequentially as in serial recall but, in contrast to serial recall, presentation of the list is shortly followed by the simultaneous visual presentation of all items in the memory list. These are presented in a randomised array, and the task is simply to recall the order in which the items were presented. Both serial recall and serial order reconstruction require information about the ordering of the memory items to be recalled, but only serial recall places significant demands on the retrieval of detailed item information; because the memory items are provided at test, serial order reconstruction requires relatively little item information to be retrieved. As such, serial order reconstruction might be expected to bypass the redintegration process that is proposed to take place during the retrieval of item information from short-term memory. This reasoning predicts that factors whose impact on short-term memory is mediated exclusively by the redintegration process will make relatively little impact on performance in the serial order reconstruction task.

To evaluate this prediction we have compared the impact of a series of long-term knowledge variables on serial recall and on serial order reconstruction (Thorn, Gathercole, & Frankish, in prep, b). In two initial experiments we looked at the effect of lexicality on the two tasks. To establish task sensitivity, we also manipulated the phonological similarity of the memory items in these experiments. The effect of phonological similarity on serial recall – better performance for lists containing items which are phonologically distinct than phonologically similar – is specifically thought to influence memory for order information (Henson, Norris, Page, & Baddeley, 1996) and hence this variable might be expected to make a comparable impact on serial recall and serial order reconstruction performance since both tasks require the retrieval of detailed order information. In our experiments, both tasks involved the auditory presentation of memory lists, but whereas for serial recall this was followed by a prompt for immediate spoken recall of the memory list, in the serial order reconstruction task, all memory items were presented in a randomised array on a card at the end of presentation and participants were required to read off the items in the order in which they occurred in the original list.

The mean performance levels on the serial recall and serial order reconstruction tasks are provided in Table 10.1. In serial recall the standard beneficial effects of lexicality and detrimental effects of phonological similarity were observed. In contrast, the effect of phonological similarity persisted in the serial order reconstruction task, but compared to serial recall, the effect of lexicality was greatly reduced in serial order reconstruction. The contrasting impact of the lexicality and phonological similarity variables on the two short-term memory tasks can be assessed more directly by calculation of partial eta squared (partial η^2), a measure of the proportion of variability in memory performance that is accounted for by each of the experimental variables at a given level of the experimental design. This analysis indicated comparable effects of phonological similarity in serial

Table 10.1 Mean proportion (standard deviation) correct item recall on the serial recall and serial order reconstruction tasks as a function of lexicality and phonological similarity

	Serial recall		Serial order reconstruction	
	Words	Nonwords	Words	Nonwords
Distinct	.85 (.07)	.60 (.08)	.96 (.03)	.95 (.02)
Similar	.68 (.06)	.53 (.08)	.88 (.03)	.86 (.04)

Data from Thorn, Gathercole, & Frankish (in prep, b), Experiments 1 and 2.

recall (partial $\eta^2 = .82$) and serial order reconstruction (partial $\eta^2 = .91$), but whereas the impact of lexicality on serial recall performance was also sizeable (partial $\eta^2 = .94$), the effect of this variable was greatly reduced in serial order reconstruction (partial $\eta^2 = .38$).

The greatly diminished impact of lexicality on serial order reconstruction compared with serial recall is consistent with the view that the lexicality effect is mediated by the redintegration process, and that this process is bypassed in serial order reconstruction as a consequence of the reduced demands on the retrieval of detailed item information. Note that the effect of lexicality was not entirely removed in this task. In fact, this is consistent with other data we have indicating that the effect of lexicality is diminished but not completely removed in serial recognition too (Gathercole et al., 2000). Our preferred interpretation of this finding is that the effect of lexicality in these tasks (and maybe at least part of the effect in serial recall) arises from the additional use of semantic properties to encode words, whereas encoding of nonwords necessarily relies exclusively on phonological properties. Semantic properties are known to affect serial recall accuracy (Poirier & Saint-Aubin, 1995) and the use of semantic rather than (or in addition to) phonological properties has been previously observed in serial recall, particularly when the memory load is heavy (Gathercole & Baddeley, 1990; Salamé & Baddeley, 1986). The remaining effect of lexicality on serial order reconstruction could therefore reflect the use of a semantic coding strategy in this task.

To determine whether the reduced impact of lexicality on serial order reconstruction extends to other types of long-term knowledge we conducted two further experiments in which we manipulated a further two long-term knowledge variables, word frequency and nonword phonotactic frequency, and compared their effects in serial recall and serial order reconstruction. In these experiments, following auditory presentation of memory lists, participants were required to either verbally recall the memory items immediately in strict serial order (serial recall) or to read off the items in their order of presentation from a randomised computer display (serial order reconstruction).

The mean performance levels on the serial recall and serial order reconstruction tasks in these experiments are provided in Table 10.2. Replicating

Table 10.2 Mean proportion (standard deviation) correct item recall on the serial recall and serial order reconstruction tasks as a function of stimulus type

	Word frequency		Phonotactic frequency	
	High	Low	High	Low
Serial recall	.90 (.08)	.79 (.13)	.57 (.14)	.49 (.15)
Serial order reconstruction	.61 (.13)	.58 (.12)	.51 (.14)	.45 (.12)

Data from Thorn, Gathercole, & Frankish (in prep, b), Experiments 3 and 4.

standard findings, both word frequency and nonword phonotactic frequency made a significant impact on serial recall performance: high frequency words were significantly better recalled than low frequency words and high phonotactic frequency nonwords were significantly better recalled than low phonotactic frequency nonwords. In contrast, beneficial effects of word frequency were greatly diminished in serial order reconstruction (consistent with our earlier lexicality findings), but the effect of phonotactic frequency persisted in this task. This pattern of reduced effects of word frequency on serial order reconstruction compared with serial recall, but comparable influence of phonotactic frequency on the two tasks is confirmed by the effect sizes: for word frequency partial $\eta^2 = .63$ for serial recall and partial $\eta^2 = .13$ for serial order reconstruction, and for phonotactic frequency partial $\eta^2 = .36$ in serial recall and partial $\eta^2 = .29$ in serial order reconstruction.

These findings clearly indicate that, like lexicality in the previous experiments, the effects of word frequency are diminished in serial order reconstruction. Critically though, the findings indicate that the effect of phonotactic frequency is not reduced in this task. Note that speeded articulation measures for the high and low phonotactic frequency nonword sets indicated no significant difference in the rate at which nonwords from the two sets could be articulated (mean articulation rate = 2.46 nonwords per second for the high phonotactic frequency stimuli compared with mean articulation rate = 2.31 nonwords per second for the low phonotactic frequency stimuli), suggesting that the persistent phonotactic frequency effect obtained in the serial order reconstruction task cannot be attributed to articulation rate differences for high and low phonotactic frequency stimuli. Further, reading latency data indicated no significant difference in the rate at which nonwords from the two sets could be read from the visual display (mean naming latency = 707 ms for the high phonotactic frequency stimuli and 715 ms for the low phonotactic frequency stimuli), suggesting that the effect also cannot be attributed to differences in the speed with which the unfamiliar orthographic forms of the high and low phonotactic frequency nonwords were read, which might have resulted in differences in the extent of output delay during the reconstruction of memory sequences and consequent effects on memory performance (Cowan, Day, Saults, Keller, Johnson, & Flores, 1992).

Table 10.3 Mean proportion (standard deviation) correct item recall on the serial recall and serial order reconstruction tasks as a function of stimulus type

	Words		Nonwords	
	High frequency	Low frequency	High frequency	Low frequency
Serial recall	.80 (.13)	.59 (.15)	.35 (.10)	.29 (.10)
Serial order reconstruction	.83 (.13)	.80 (.10)	.70 (.14)	.61 (.14)

Data from Thorn, Gathercole, & Frankish (in prep, b), Experiments 5 and 6.

We have since replicated our serial order reconstruction findings in a second set of experiments, which also addressed possible ceiling effects for the lexicality variable in the serial order reconstruction task in our original experiments. For comparison, the results from these experiments are provided in Table 10.3. In serial recall, significant beneficial effects of word frequency (high compared with low frequency words), lexicality (low frequency words compared with high phonotactic frequency nonwords), and phonotactic frequency (high compared with low phonotactic frequency nonwords) were found. In line with the findings of our original experiments, the effects of word frequency and lexicality were greatly reduced in serial order reconstruction compared with serial recall (partial η^2 .84 in serial recall and .12 in serial order reconstruction for word frequency, and .90 in serial recall and .58 in serial order reconstruction for lexicality). In contrast, and replicating our original findings, the benefits of phonotactic frequency persisted in serial order reconstruction (partial η^2 of .38 in serial recall and .34 in serial order reconstruction).

The results of this series of experiments clearly demonstrate dissociable influences of lexicality, word frequency and phonotactic frequency on serial order reconstruction. What can this tell us about the mechanisms mediating each of these long-term knowledge effects? Recall that central to the concept of redintegration is the notion that reconstruction of memory items takes place at a post-storage stage in the memory process, when the memory trace is accessed, typically at retrieval. In serial recall successful performance requires each item in the memory list to be fully and correctly retrieved from memory. In serial order reconstruction, however, demands on the retrieval of item information are minimal because the items themselves are represented at test. In this case, serial order reconstruction can effectively bypass the redintegration process and consequently is likely to be much less sensitive than serial recall to variables whose influence on short-term memory is mediated exclusively by redintegration: provided that at least some item information is present in the memory trace, the complete item can be identified from the potential candidates that are provided at test.

By this analysis, the greatly diminished impact of lexicality and word frequency in serial order reconstruction compared with serial recall is consistent with a redintegration account of the influence of these variables on short-term recall. In contrast, the finding that the nonword phonotactic frequency effect persists in serial order reconstruction suggests that the effect of this variable on temporary memory performance is not mediated exclusively by the redintegration process. Instead, this finding suggests that phonotactic frequency influences the memory process at an earlier stage, possibly by determining the strength or quality of the initial memory trace. At the extreme of poor trace strength or quality the memory trace will contain no usable information about the identity of the original memory item. In serial recall this will directly result in reduced recall accuracy due to item loss. In serial order reconstruction, where nothing remains of a memory item in the memory trace there will be nothing to guide the identification of that item from the response set presented at test, resulting in a consequent detrimental effect on memory performance. By this reasoning, the persistence of the phonotactic frequency effect in serial order reconstruction arises because high phonotactic frequency memory items are less likely to be lost from the memory trace completely and are consequently more likely to be correctly identified from the display of memory items at test, leading to a recall advantage in serial order reconstruction.

We believe that the findings from this series of experiments comparing the effects of long-term knowledge variables on two tasks which place contrasting demands on the retrieval of item information from short-term memory, serial recall and serial order reconstruction, thereby provide important evidence concerning the mechanisms mediating these effects. Specifically, the observation of persistent or diminished effects of long-term knowledge variables in a paradigm like serial order reconstruction which reduces the demands on the retrieval of item information from short-term memory suggests that long-term knowledge effects on the temporary memory system are not mediated by a single mechanism, but rather can be attributed to the functioning of more than one mechanism operating at more than one stage in the memory process.

Observing effects limited to retrieval processes in the serial recall task

Alternative evidence in support of the notion that long-term knowledge effects on short-term memory operate through multiple mechanisms might be provided if we are able to observe dissociable effects of long-term knowledge variables within a single paradigm, and specifically within a task that requires all of the component processes of short-term memory (encoding, storage and retrieval of both item and order information), such as the serial recall task.

In our laboratory we have conducted an experiment with just this aim. From nearly all accounts of the effects of long-term knowledge on short-term memory it is possible to derive very specific predictions concerning how the amount of information that might be recalled about a given memory item in the serial recall task might be affected by long-term knowledge. In particular, both redintegration and pre-retrieval accounts of long-term knowledge effects on short-term recall make very specific predictions about the likelihood of making a completely incorrect recall attempt with respect to an input memory item.

Consider first the redintegration account. In many models of redintegration the reconstruction process is proposed to operate on all memory traces, irrespective of their encoding/storage status. By this view of redintegration, all variables whose effect on immediate memory is mediated exclusively by the redintegration process should make a significant impact on the production of completely incorrect recall responses. For example, a "response selection" model of redintegration proposes that the reconstruction process operates on the basis of pooled information about the entire memory list, with long-term knowledge biasing the selection of response items (e.g., Lewandowsky & Murdock, 1989). A "response selection" model of redintegration predicts that variables whose impact is mediated by the redintegration process should reduce the likelihood of making a completely incorrect recall attempt, because for these variables possible responses are more likely to be readily available for selection, increasing the likelihood of a completely correct recall being made and reducing the likelihood of any other type of response (i.e., a response that is either partially correct or completely incorrect) being produced. Similarly, those models that view long-term knowledge effects as residing in the encoding and/or retention of memory items also predict that long-term knowledge variables will reduce the production of completely incorrect recalls, in this case by affecting the strength of the temporary memory trace. For example, in the dual-buffer model (Martin, 2006) connections between lexical-semantic and phonological representations increase the strength of the temporary trace, and hence militate against the loss of information and ultimately against the complete loss of a memory item.

An alternative prediction about the impact of long-term knowledge variables on the production of completely incorrect recalls can be derived from Schweickert's multinomial processing tree model of redintegration (Schweickert, 1993; see adaptation by Gathercole et al., 1999, Figure 10.1). By Schweickert's (1993) model, memory traces containing a complete memory item can be recalled directly from memory; redintegration is only necessary for traces containing partial but incomplete item information. Assuming that existing information in the trace is not altered or erased by the reconstruction process (an assumption implicit in Schweickert's original formulation of the model), the model predicts that redintegration will only influence the production of completely incorrect recall attempts if the redintegration process can use sub-phonetic features to guide reconstruction. In this case, a degraded trace that contains sub-phonetic features only but no whole phonemes would be output as a completely incorrect (null) response without redintegration, but could be converted to a partially correct or fully accurate recall through successful redintegration. Importantly though, the model predicts that if, in line with Sperling and Speelman's (1970) proposal, redintegration requires complete phonemes on which to build a reconstruction attempt, factors whose influence on immediate memory is mediated exclusively by the redintegration process will not affect the production of completely incorrect recalls. This is because in this case the reconstruction process would not be able to operate on traces containing no whole phonemes and consequently will not affect the production of completely null responses.[1] Moreover, a completely incorrect recall could not result from unsuccessful redintegration because the process does not alter existing information in the trace and so any existing phonemes would persist in the recall attempt resulting in a response that is partially correct with respect to the input memory item.

To investigate the influence of long-term knowledge on the production of completely incorrect recalls we conducted an error analysis of adults' serial recall protocols (Thorn, Gathercole, & Frankish, 2005). The serial recall performance of adult monolingual speakers of English was assessed for four types of stimuli (all with a consonant-vowel-consonant (CVC) structure) presented in English: high and low frequency words and high and low phonotactic frequency nonwords, providing a test of the impact of word frequency (high vs. low frequency words), lexicality (low frequency words vs. high phonotactic frequency nonwords) and phonotactic frequency (high vs. low phonotactic frequency nonwords). In addition, a group of native French bilingual adults who spoke English fluently as a second language also completed the serial recall task, to assess the influence of language familiarity on memory performance for all four stimuli types. Following auditory presentation of memory lists, participants performed spoken serial recall. Their recall protocols were recorded and phonemically transcribed. The number of occasions on which memory items were recalled completely correctly (all three phonemes correct), partially correctly (one or more but not all phonemes correct) or completely incorrectly (none of the constituent phonemes from the target item recalled correctly, including any combination of omitted and/or incorrect recall of the three target phonemes) was scored for both groups for all four stimuli types.

The profiles of recall responses obtained in this analysis are provided in Table 10.4. Replicating standard findings, all four knowledge variables had a beneficial impact on immediate recall accuracy. However, consideration of the recall errors underpinning these effects, and in particular those errors that reflect responses that were completely incorrect with respect to the input memory item, reveals strikingly different response profiles. For lexicality, the number of occasions on which none of the phonemes from the target item were recalled correctly was equivalent for words and nonwords. This finding of equivalent rates of completely incorrect recalls for word and nonword memory items replicates other work we have done with children (Gathercole et al., 1999). In clear contrast, the three remaining variables –

Table 10.4 Mean proportion (standard deviation) of items recalled completely correctly, partially correctly and completely incorrectly in serial recall, as a function of language group and stimulus type

Response type	Words		Nonwords	
	High frequency	Low frequency	High frequency	Low frequency
Monolingual group				
Completely correct	.90 (.10)	.77 (.13)	.50 (.19)	.42 (.20)
Partially correct	.03 (.03)	.08 (.05)	.34 (.13)	.38 (.12)
Completely incorrect	.07 (.08)	.15 (.11)	.16 (.10)	.20 (.12)
Bilingual group				
Completely correct	.71 (.15)	.50 (.18)	.25 (.12)	.25 (.12)
Partially correct	.11 (.07)	.23 (.12)	.46 (.13)	.44 (.13)
Completely incorrect	.18 (.11)	.27 (.15)	.29 (.13)	.31 (.14)

Adapted from Thorn, A. S. C., Gathercole, S. E., & Frankish, C. R. (2005). Redintegration and the benefits of long-term knowledge in verbal short-term memory: An evaluation of Schweickert's (1993) multinomial processing tree model. *Cognitive Psychology*, *50*, 133–158.

word frequency, nonword phonotactic frequency and language familiarity – all influenced the production of completely incorrect recall attempts: both groups made fewer completely incorrect responses for the high frequency than the low frequency words (word frequency manipulation), the monolingual group produced fewer completely incorrect responses for low compared with high phonotactic frequency nonwords[2] (phonotactic frequency manipulation) and the monolinguals (recalling in their first language) produced fewer completely incorrect responses than the bilinguals (recalling in their second language) for all four stimuli types.

It is clear from these data that long-term knowledge variables do not make a consistent impact on the production of completely incorrect recall attempts. The reduced proportions of completely incorrect recalls for high compared with low frequency words, high compared with low phonotactic frequency nonwords and first compared with second language memory performance is consistent with many of the accounts of long-term knowledge effects on short-term recall reviewed above. Importantly, though, the lexicality data cannot be accommodated by these accounts: equivalent rates of completely incorrect recalls are not consistent with a redintegration process that applies to all memory traces irrespective of their encoding/storage status, nor with any model in which the influence of lexicality on short-term memory is proposed to occur prior to retrieval during the encoding and/or storage of memory items. The equivalent rates of completely incorrect recalls for words and nonwords can, though, be accommodated by Schweickert's multinomial processing tree model of redintegration, if the redintegration process specified in the model uses a phoneme-based reconstruction procedure (Sperling & Speelman, 1970). When operating only on the basis of whole phonemes, such a process predicts that redintegration-mediated effects will only influence the conversion of traces containing some but not all of the target item phonemes to completely correct recalls. By this account traces containing none of the target item phonemes cannot be reconstructed and so will not be affected by factors mediated by the redintegration process. In addition, unsuccessful redintegration will not result in a completely incorrect recall attempt because phonemes present in a partially complete memory trace will not be altered or erased by the redintegration process and so will persist in any recall response that is produced. Consequently, if Schweickert's (1993) redintegration process requires whole phonemes on which to base a reconstruction attempt, redintegration-mediated effects will not impact on the proportions of completely incorrect recalls made.

The equivalent rates of completely incorrect recalls for memory items varying in lexical status can accordingly be accounted for by a redintegration mechanism of the type specified in Schweickert's (1993) multinomial processing tree model of the immediate recall process, requiring whole phonemes on which to build a reconstruction attempt. If such a process were exclusively responsible for all long-term knowledge effects, though, the other three knowledge variables considered here – word frequency, nonword phonotactic frequency and language familiarity – should all also make no impact on the production of completely incorrect recalls. By the same token, and as we have argued above, the finding of non-equivalent rates of completely incorrect recalls for these three knowledge variables could be attributed to any mechanism whereby long-term knowledge determines the strength of or is applied to all items in the memory trace, but if such a process were exclusively responsible for the effects of all long-term knowledge variables in immediate recall then lexicality should also influence the proportions of completely incorrect recalls that are made. Consequently, the contrasting impact on completely incorrect recalls of lexicality on the one hand and word frequency, nonword phonotactic frequency and language familiarity on the other is not consistent with the view that long-term knowledge effects are mediated by a single mechanism operating at a single point in the memory process.

A multiple-mechanism account

The data we have presented suggest that long-term knowledge effects in immediate recall are mediated by more than one mechanism. Elsewhere we have proposed that a multiple-mechanism account could be readily instantiated in Schweickert's (1993) multinomial processing tree model of immediate serial recall (Thorn et al., 2005). The starting point for Schweickert's (1993) model of redintegration is the state of the temporary memory trace following encoding of a memory list. In the two-stage recall process described by the model, redintegration is a process applied to those traces that are partially degraded at the point at which information is retrieved from the trace. Hence long-term knowledge influences that operate through the redintegration process will have their effect at this retrieval-stage of the memory process. Our suggestion is that long-term knowledge could also influence recall accuracy at an earlier stage in Schweickert's (1993) recall process too, by affecting the initial state of the temporary memory trace.

We suggest that the contents of the temporary memory trace can be conceived of as patterns of activation across a network of phonological units. By this analysis, the representational strength of a memory trace reflects the level of activation that an item is able to achieve during temporary storage. In this type of system, long-term knowledge could influence the strength of the temporary representation through top-down interactive activation of elements in the network from stored phonological knowledge (Gathercole, 1997; Gathercole & Martin, 1996; Gupta & MacWhinney, 1997; Thorn & Gathercole, 1999; see also McClelland, Mirman, & Holt, 2006). Advocates of the multiple-buffer account of short-term memory (Martin, 2006) might argue that an influence on the state of the memory trace is readily accommodated by their system, in which both the quality of the representation and the strength of connections between buffers determine the integrity of the trace for a given memory item. Note, though, that in the multiple-buffer system there is no opportunity for selectively influencing the state of the trace. That is, the trace cannot be independent of any long-term knowledge influences. This account is therefore unable to accommodate our key experimental findings, which clearly suggest that the benefits of lexicality are attributable to a separable retrieval-stage redintegration process. Theoretical accounts that view short-term memory as a state of activated long-term memory (Cowan, 1988, 1995; Ruchkin et al., 2003) face similar difficulties in accommodating this finding.

Note that the suggestion that long-term knowledge might influence short-term recall at both redintegration and some other stage in the recall process is not new. In their connectionist model of short-term recall, Lewandowsky and Farrell (2000) found that in order to produce a sufficiently large lexicality effect, it was necessary to adjust a parameter of their model to reflect a disadvantage at encoding for nonwords compared with words. In direct contrast, our data point towards lexicality having its effect exclusively through a redintegration process of the type specified in Schweickert's (1993) model.

By our multiple-mechanism account long-term knowledge variables influence immediate memory at two points in the memory process: during the retention of the temporary trace and during the reconstruction of partially degraded memory traces on the basis of remaining whole phonemes. Our data suggest that phonotactic frequency impacts on the retention of the trace: beneficial effects of phonotactic frequency persist in serial order reconstruction, a task that plausibly bypasses the redintegration process, and phonotactic frequency also influences the proportions of completely incorrect recalls that are made in the serial recall task. Plausibly, phonotactic frequency could also influence the redintegration process applied to the memory trace at retrieval. In contrast, our data suggest that the benefits of lexicality in immediate recall are mediated exclusively by the redintegration process: the effect of lexicality is greatly reduced in serial order reconstruction and lexicality makes no impact on the production of completely incorrect recalls. Is it plausible that the benefits of phonotactic frequency could be mediated by more than one mechanism, but the influence of lexicality is mediated by a single mechanism? Our proposal that an influence on the state of the initial trace be conceived of in terms of patterns of activation across a phonological network provides a relatively straightforward account of this. Lexicality and phonotactic frequency are qualitatively different knowledge variables: whereas phonotactic frequency is a continuous dimension, representing the frequency of occurrence of given sound combinations in words in the language, lexicality is a dichotomous variable referring to whether or not a stable whole-item representation of a given memory item exists. Activation networks readily embody statistical frequencies, but words do not have to be encountered very often to be incorporated in our mental lexicon (Carey, 1978; Dickinson, 1984; Taylor & Gelman, 1988). So words that give rise to a recall advantage over nonwords will not necessarily have been encountered very often and hence what is essentially a relatively small difference in the frequency of occurrence of patterns corresponding to words compared with nonwords may well not be embodied by the activation network. In contrast, it seems plausible that the redintegration process could be sensitive to statistical frequencies such as the frequency of occurrence of particular phoneme combinations but is likely to be even more sensitive to the availability of exact matches for the reconstruction of memory items, matches that can be provided for word but not nonword stimuli.

The account advanced here proposes that long-term knowledge can influence immediate recall in two ways: through an effect on the state of the initial trace and through the reconstruction of degraded information in the temporary trace. We have developed this account on the basis of key findings from a series of experimental studies which indicate that not all long-term knowledge variables operate in the same way. From these studies one further point needs considering, which relates to our findings for word frequency. Word frequency significantly influenced the production of completely incorrect serial recall responses, suggesting that this variable impacts on the state of the initial trace. If so, beneficial effects of word frequency might, like those of phonotactic frequency, be expected to persist in serial order reconstruction. Our data clearly indicate that the effects of word frequency are almost completely removed in serial order reconstruction. How might these competing findings be reconciled? One possibility is that the serial order reconstruction task is sensitive to differences in trace strength only at the lower end of the range of trace integrity. To successfully identify an item from the response set presented at test in this task requires the retention of at least some information; although overall less information may have been retained for low than high frequency memory items, plausibly sufficient information was retained for low frequency words to be identified from the display at recall. By this reasoning, the effects of word frequency on short-term memory are mediated by both of the mechanisms we propose here, but this is not observable in the serial order reconstruction task for reasons of task sensitivity. This nuance of the data underscores the importance of using more than one approach to fully understand the impact of long-term knowledge on short-term memory.

Summary and conclusions

The evidence we have presented calls into question previous accounts that have attributed the effects of long-term knowledge variables to a single mechanism operating at a single point in the temporary memory process. Firstly, our data indicate that not all long-term knowledge effects are subject to reduction in a serial order reconstruction task which minimises demands on the retrieval of item information from short-term memory. Secondly, our data indicate that not all long-term knowledge variables produce the same profiles of response errors in serial recall. Specifically these data indicate that the influence of long-term knowledge on the production of responses that are completely incorrect with respect to the input memory item varies across knowledge variables. These data are difficult to accommodate within a single-mechanism account of the effects of long-term knowledge on short-term memory. Instead, we suggest that long-term knowledge impacts on immediate recall accuracy in two ways: by influencing the quality or strength of representations in the short-term store and subsequently by influencing the likelihood of success of a reconstruction process that attempts to rebuild memory traces that have become degraded on the basis of remaining information in the trace. We propose that these two processes can be readily implemented in Schweickert's (1993) multinomial processing tree model of immediate recall (see adaptation proposed by Gathercole et al., 1999). In this model long-term knowledge can affect the initial state of the memory trace, specifically whether the trace for a given memory item is complete, partially degraded or degraded to the point of being unidentifiable. In addition, long-term knowledge can also facilitate a subsequent redintegration process that converts partially degraded traces to full recalls on the basis of remaining whole phonemes in the temporary trace.

Acknowledgements

The empirical work reported in this chapter was supported by ESRC grants R000222737 and R000239113.

Notes

1 If nothing remains in the memory trace of the original memory item, participants might plausibly guess at the identity of the target item, but the probability of guessing correctly would be independent of the redintegration process proposed in the model.
2 Interestingly the bilinguals did not show a nonword phonotactic frequency effect in their recall performance, suggesting that they were unable to access or did not have available appropriate long-term knowledge to aid the recall of second language nonword memory items.

References

Baddeley, A. D., Gathercole, S. E., & Papagno, C. (1998). The phonological loop as a language learning device. *Psychological Review, 105*, 158–173.

Batchelder, W. H., & Riefer, D. M. (1986). The statistical analysis of a model for storage and retrieval processes in human memory. *British Journal of Mathematical & Statistical Psychology, 39*, 129–149.

Botvinick, M., & Bylsma, L. M. (2005). Regularization in short-term memory for serial order. *Journal of Experimental Psychology: Learning, Memory, and Cognition, 31*, 351–358.

Botvinick, M., & Plaut, D. C. (2006). Short-term memory for serial order: A recurrent neural network model. *Psychological Review, 113*, 201–233.

Bourassa, D. C., & Besner, D. (1994). Beyond the articulatory loop – a semantic contribution to serial order recall of subspan lists. *Psychonomic Bulletin & Review, 1*, 122–125.

Brown, G., & Hulme, C. (1995). Modeling item length effects in memory span: No rehearsal needed? *Journal of Memory and Language, 34*, 594–621.

Brown, G., & Hulme, C. (1996). Nonword repetition, STM, and word age-of-acquisition: A computational model. In S. E. Gathercole (Ed.), *Models of short-term memory* (pp. 129–148). Hove, UK: Psychology Press.

Brown, G., Preece, T., & Hulme, C. (2000). Oscillator-based memory for serial order. *Psychological Review, 107*, 127–181.

Burgess, N., & Hitch, G. J. (1999). Memory for serial order: A network model of the phonological loop and its timing. *Psychological Review, 106*, 551–581.

Cameron, K. A., Haarmann, H. J., Grafman, J., & Ruchkin, D. S. (2005). Long-term memory is the representational basis for semantic verbal short-term memory. *Psychophysiology, 42*, 643–653.

Carey, S. (1978). The child as word learner. In M. Halle, J. Bresnan, & G. Miller (Eds.), *Linguistic theory and psychological reality*. Cambridge, MA: MIT Press.

Chechile, R., & Meyer, D. L. (1976). A Baysean procedure for separately estimating storage and retrieval components of forgetting. *Journal of Mathematical Psychology, 13*, 269–295.

Conrad, R. (1962). An association between memory errors and errors due to acoustic masking of speech. *Nature, 193*, 1314–1315.

Conrad, R. (1964). Acoustic confusion in immediate memory. *British Journal of Psychology, 55*, 75–84.

Conrad, R., & Hull, A. J. (1964). Information, acoustic confusion and memory span. *British Journal of Psychology, 55*, 429–432.

Cowan, N. (1988). Evolving conceptions of memory storage, selective attention, and their mutual constraints within the human information processing system. *Psychological Bulletin, 104*, 163–191.

Cowan, N. (1995). *Attention and memory: An integrated framework*. Oxford Psychology Series, No. 26. New York: Oxford University Press.

Cowan, N., Day, L., Saults, J. S., Keller, T. A., Johnson, T., & Flores, L. (1992). The role of verbal output time in the effects of word length on immediate memory. *Journal of Memory and Language, 31*, 1–17.

Dickinson, D. K. (1984). On words gained from a single exposure. *Applied Psycholinguistics, 5*, 359–373.

Gathercole, S. E. (1997). Models of verbal short-term memory. In M. A. Conway (Ed.), *Cognitive models of memory* (pp. 13–45). Hove, UK: Psychology Press.

Gathercole, S. E., & Baddeley, A. D. (1990). Phonological memory deficits in language-disordered children: Is there a causal connection? *Journal of Memory and Language, 29*, 336–360.

Gathercole, S. E., Frankish, C. R., Pickering, S. J., & Peaker, S. (1999). Phonotactic influences on short-term memory. *Journal of Experimental Psychology: Learning, Memory, and Cognition, 25*, 84–95.

Gathercole, S. E., & Martin, A. J. (1996). Interactive processes in phonological memory. In S. E. Gathercole (Ed.), *Models of short-term memory* (pp. 73–100). Hove, UK: Lawrence Erlbaum Associates Ltd.

Gathercole, S. E., Pickering, S. J., Hall, M., & Peaker, S. (2000). Dissociable lexical and phonological influences on serial recognition and serial recall. *Quarterly Journal of Experimental Psychology, 53A*, 1–30.

Goh, W. D., & Pisoni, D. B. (2003). Effects of lexical competition on immediate memory span for spoken words. *Quarterly Journal of Experimental Psychology, 56A*, 929–954.

Gregg, V. H., Freedman, C. M., & Smith, D. K. (1989). Word-frequency, articulatory suppression and memory span. *British Journal of Psychology, 80*, 363–374.

Gupta, P., & MacWhinney, B. (1997). Vocabulary acquisition and verbal short-term memory: Computational and neural bases. *Brain & Language, 59*, 267–333.

Henson, R. N. A., Norris, D. G., Page, M. P. A. & Baddeley, A. D. (1996). Unchained memory: Error patterns rule out chaining models of immediate serial recall. *Quarterly Journal of Experimental Psychology, 49A*, 80–115.

Hulme, C., Maughan, S., & Brown, G. (1991). Memory for familiar and unfamiliar words: Evidence for a long-term memory contribution to short-term memory span. *Journal of Memory and Language, 30*, 685–701.

Hulme, C., Newton, P., Cowan, N., Stuart, G., & Brown, G. (1999). Think before you speak: Pauses, memory search, and trace redintegration processes in verbal memory span. *Journal of Experimental Psychology: Learning, Memory, and Cognition, 25*, 447–463.

Hulme, C., Roodenrys, S., Schweickert, R., Brown, G., Martin, S., & Stuart, G. (1997). Word frequency effects on short-term memory tasks: Evidence for a redintegration process in immediate serial recall. *Journal of Experimental Psychology: Learning, Memory, and Cognition, 23*, 1217–1232.

Jefferies, E., Frankish, C. R., & Lambon Ralph, M. A. (2006). Lexical and semantic influences on item and order memory in immediate serial recognition: Evidence from a novel task. *Quarterly Journal of Experimental Psychology, 59*, 949–964.

Lewandowsky, S. (1999). Redintegration and response suppression in serial recall: A dynamic network model. *International Journal of Psychology*, *34*, 434–446.

Lewandowsky, S., & Farrell, S. (2000). A redintegration account of the effects of speech rate, lexicality and word frequency in immediate serial recall. *Psychological Research*, *63*, 163–173.

Lewandowsky, S., & Murdock, B. B. (1989). Memory for serial order. *Psychological Review*, *96*, 25–57.

Martin, R. C. (2006). Semantic short-term memory, language processing and inhibition. In A. Meyer, L. Wheeldon, & A. Krott (Eds.), *Automaticity and control in language processing*. London: Routledge.

Martin, R. C., & Lesch, M. F. (1996). Associations and dissociations between language impairment and list recall: Implications for models of STM. In S. Gathercole (Ed.), *Models of short-term memory* (pp. 149–178). Hove, UK: Psychology Press.

Martin, R. C., Lesch, M. F., & Bartha, M. C. (1999). Independence of input and output phonology in word processing and short-term memory. *Journal of Memory and Language*, *41*, 3–29.

Martin, R. C., Shelton, J. R., & Yaffee, L. S. (1994). Language processing and working-memory – neuropsychological evidence for separate phonological and semantic capacities. *Journal of Memory and Language*, *33*, 83–111.

McClelland, J. L., Mirman, D., & Holt, L. L. (2006). Are there interactive processes in speech perception? *Trends in Cognitive Sciences*, *10*, 363–369.

Murdock, B. B. (1976). Item and order information in short-term serial memory. *Journal of Experimental Psychology: General*, *105*, 191–216.

Nairne, J. S. (1990). A feature model of immediate memory. *Memory & Cognition*, *18*, 251–269.

Page, M. P. A., & Norris, D. (1998). The primacy model: A new model of immediate serial recall. *Psychological Review*, *105*, 761–781.

Poirier, M., & Saint-Aubin, J. (1995). Memory for related and unrelated words: Further evidence on the influence of semantic factors in immediate serial recall. *Quarterly Journal of Experimental Psychology*, *48A*, 384–404.

Poirier, M., & Saint-Aubin, J. (1996). Immediate serial recall, word frequency, item identity and item position. *Canadian Journal of Experimental Psychology*, *50*, 408–412.

Roodenrys, S., & Hinton, M. (2002). Sublexical or lexical effects on serial recall of nonwords. *Journal of Experimental Psychology: Language, Memory, and Cognition*, *28*, 29–33.

Ruchkin, D. S., Grafman, J., Cameron, K., & Berndt, R. S. (2003). Working memory retention systems: A state of activated long-term memory. *Behavioural and Brain Sciences*, *26*, 709–777.

Saint-Aubin, J., & LeBlanc, J. (2005). Word frequency effects in immediate serial recall of pure and mixed lists: Tests of the associative link hypothesis. *Canadian Journal of Experimental Psychology*, *59*, 219–227.

Saint-Aubin, J., Ouellette, D., & Poirier, M. (2005). Semantic similarity and immediate serial recall: Is there an effect on all trials? *Psychonomic Bulletin & Review*, *12*, 171–177.

Saint-Aubin, J., & Poirier, M. (1999). The influence of long-term memory factors on immediate serial recall: An item and order analysis. *International Journal of Psychology*, *34*, 347–352.

Saint-Aubin, J., & Poirier, M. (2005). Word frequency effects in immediate serial recall: Item familiarity and item cooccurrence have the same effect. *Memory, 13*, 325–332.

Salamé, P., & Baddeley, A. D. (1986). Phonological factors in STM: Similarity and the unattended speech effect. *Bulletin of the Psychonomic Society, 24*, 263–265.

Schweickert, R. (1993). A multinomial processing tree model for degradation and redintegration in immediate recall. *Memory & Cognition, 21*, 168–175.

Sperling, G. (1963). A model for visual memory tasks. *Human Factors, 5*, 19–31.

Sperling, G., & Speelman, R. G. (1970). Acoustic similarity and auditory short-term memory: Experiments and a model. In D. A. Norman (Ed.), *Models of human memory* (pp. 152–202). New York: Academic Press.

Stuart, G., & Hulme, C. (2000). The effects of word co-occurrence on short-term memory: Associative links in long-term memory affect short-term memory performance. *Journal of Experimental Psychology: Learning, Memory, and Cognition, 26*, 796–802.

Taylor, M., & Gelman, S. A. (1988). Adjectives and nouns: Children's strategies for learning new words. *Child Development, 59*, 411–419.

Thorn, A. S. C., & Frankish, C. R. (2005). Long-term knowledge effects on serial recall of nonwords are not exclusively lexical. *Journal of Experimental Psychology: Learning, Memory, and Cognition, 31*, 729–735.

Thorn, A. S. C., & Gathercole, S. E. (1999). Language-specific knowledge and short-term memory in bilingual and non-bilingual children. *Quarterly Journal of Experimental Psychology, 52A*, 303–324.

Thorn, A. S. C., & Gathercole, S. E. (2001). Language differences in verbal short-term memory do not exclusively originate in the process of subvocal rehearsal. *Psychonomic Bulletin & Review, 8*, 357–364.

Thorn, A. S. C., Gathercole, S. E., & Frankish, C. R. (2005). Redintegration and the benefits of long-term knowledge in verbal short-term memory: An evaluation of Schweickert's (1993) multinomial processing tree model. *Cognitive Psychology, 50*, 133–158.

Thorn, A. S. C., Gathercole, S. E., & Frankish, C. R. (in prep, a). Long-term knowledge influences on item and order information in short-term memory: Evidence from serial recognition.

Thorn, A. S. C., Gathercole, S. E., & Frankish, C. R. (in prep, b). Dissociable lexical and phonotactic influences on serial recall and serial order reconstruction.

11 The roles of semantic and phonological processing in short-term memory and learning: Evidence from aphasia

Nadine Martin

Overview

In this chapter, I review evidence from normal and language-impaired (acquired aphasia) populations that bears on the role of language processes in short-term memory (STM) and learning. Along with other mechanisms such as rehearsal, processes that activate and maintain activation of the lexical-semantic and phonological representations of a single word support the maintenance of multiple words held in a short-term buffer. Moreover, evidence from aphasia suggests that activation of semantic representations and phonological representation of words differentially support items at the beginning and end of a sequence. Impaired access to semantic representations affects maintenance of items in early serial positions and impaired phonological processing affects maintenance of items at the end of a sequence. A model is proposed to account for the contributions of word processing systems to verbal STM.

Introduction

Verbal short-term memory (STM) and language processing have been studied extensively as unique systems. In the last few decades, interest in the relations between these two systems and their integrated roles in verbal learning has increased substantially. The integrity of language processes influences STM and learning in a seemingly straightforward manner: if verbal information cannot be adequately encoded, it cannot be learned. And yet, the relationship is more complex, because encoding verbal information requires that we maintain activation of linguistic representations for a certain period. However brief that period may be, this maintenance is a form of short-term memory. An account of the conjunction of language, memory and verbal learning processes is fundamental to theories of these systems and will inform our models of treatment of acquired word retrieval deficits.

There is now converging evidence from normal adult, brain-damaged adult, and developmental populations that verbal short-term memory, as measured in an immediate serial recall task, is not fixed in its capacity, but rather, varies based on the characteristics of the items to be recalled. Verbal span has long been known to be greater for digits than for familiar words (Brener, 1940), which in turn is greater than span for nonwords (Hulme, Maughan, & Brown, 1991). Content words (e.g., nouns, verbs) are better recalled than function words (e.g., articles, conjunctions), and these are both better recalled than pseudowords (Caza & Belleville, 1999). Moreover, performance on verbal span tasks is influenced by a number of different linguistic variables. Phonological factors such as phonological similarity (Conrad & Hull, 1964), pronunciation time (Baddeley, Thomson, & Buchanan, 1975) and probability of phonotactic segments (Gathercole, Frankish, Pickering, & Peaker, 1999) all affect span performance. Additionally, span is influenced by lexical factors such as word frequency (Hulme, Roodenrys, Schweickert, Brown, Martin, & Stuart, 1997; Watkins & Watkins, 1977) and semantic factors such as semantic similarity (Crowder, 1979; Poirier & Saint Aubin, 1995; Shulman, 1971) and category membership (Brooks & Watkins, 1990). There is even evidence of a conceptual level of short-term memory that supports recall of language input that cannot be reproduced verbatim (Potter, 1993; R. C. Martin & Romani, 1996; Saffran & Martin, 1999).

How are these lexical and semantic influences accounted for in models of verbal STM? The influential working memory model proposed by Baddeley and Hitch (1974) assumes a phonological short-term store separate from long-term memory. In this model, lexical and semantic influences on short-term memory are attributed to articulatory rehearsal processes that access long-term memory and refresh the contents of the short-term store. However, increasing evidence of direct influences of linguistic variables other than phonology on short-term memory has inspired the idea that the contents of verbal STM are not just represented as a phonological trace supported by articulatory rehearsal, but rather that all levels of word representation are stored temporarily during encoding and decoding of single and multiple words (as in a span task) and phrase/sentence level utterances. Models of verbal STM have accounted for these influences in several ways. A more recent version of the working memory model (Baddeley, 2001) includes an "episodic buffer", a short-term store of events that serves as an interface between other short-term stores (phonological, visual spatial) and long-term memory (see Allen & Baddeley, this volume). Another influential model based on Schweickert's (1993) model is the "redintegration" model of Brown and Hulme (1995; Hulme et al., 1997; Saint-Aubin & Poirer, 1999). This model hypothesizes that the influences of long-term knowledge on verbal short-term memory are mediated via a process that restores a degraded phonological trace at output.

R. C. Martin and colleagues have proposed a model (Martin & Lesch, 1996) that closely links word processing and temporary storage mechanisms with multiple buffers that temporarily store representations (the "knowledge structure") generated by the word processor. As levels of linguistic representation in the knowledge structure interact, representations in the buffer reflect the integrity of those interactions. Recent versions of this model describe this relationship as a reverberatory circuit that maintains activation of the knowledge representations (R. C. Martin & Freedman, 2001). They propose that linguistic knowledge is represented in temporal areas (Patterson, Graham, & Hodges, 1994) and that the "buffer" part of the circuit resides in prefrontal cortex and inferior parietal areas, keeping active semantic and phonological representations respectively (Fiez, 1997; Vallar & Papagno, 1995). More recent research suggests that the inferior parietal cortex supports more general executive processes (Majerus et al., 2006; Ravizza, Delgado, Chein, Becker, & Fiez, 2004) and in the ventral part, supports phonological encoding and recoding processes (Ravizza et al., 2004). Nonetheless, efforts to identify neural substrates of temporary storage functions follow cognitive models of STM that propose the role of attentional systems is to temporarily activate long-term representations in STM (e.g., Cowan, 1997; Cowan & Chen, this volume; Gupta, 1996; Ruchkin, Grafman, Cameron, & Berndt, 2003). On this view, performance of verbal STM tasks depends on the integrity of long-term representations, the efficiency of their activation and the integrity of attentional control processes. Although the role of attentional processes in verbal STM is not fully understood, its end result is a coordinated temporary activation of long-term representations in the posterior cortex that form the representational basis of verbal STM (Ruchkin et al., 2003).

This chapter will provide a review of evidence from aphasia in support of a multiple-store model of verbal STM that depends in part on the integrity of processes responsible for activating and maintaining activation of language representations in verbal tasks, including those used to measure verbal span. These "activation maintenance" processes are viewed as one component of the mechanism that enables temporary storage of language representations as well as their integration into long-term memory. They could be termed the "linguistic" component of temporary storage as they enable the "linguistic content" of verbal STM to be available for storage, but, as the evidence presented here will suggest, these processes may do more than just provide the "content" of verbal STM. They also can account for part of a mechanism responsible for maintaining serial order in verbal STM.

Temporary storage of verbal information requires processes other than those which activate and maintain activation of linguistic representations. It is assumed that the linguistic components of verbal short-term memory work in tandem with "nonlinguistic" control processes such as rehearsal (Atkinson & Shriffin, 1968; Baddeley, 1986) and some mechanism that is specialized to encode and retain serial order (e.g., Gupta, 1996). Retrieval from short- and long-term memory also depends on both linguistic and nonlinguistic processes: the integrity of language-specific activation processes and a selection mechanism (Thompson-Schill et al., 2002) that is in some way sensitive to the activation levels and availability of language representations.

This chapter will focus on the linguistic component of verbal STM with the understanding that the activation processes that play a role in maintaining information in STM could be dissociable from other components of temporary storage such as rehearsal and sequencing. Such dissociations ultimately could distinguish a language-based impairment of STM from a pure STM deficit. However, if such dissociations are to be revealed, it is critical to know what characterizes a "language"-based STM deficit and how this can be differentiated from a "non-language"-based short-term memory deficit. This chapter aims to make this characterization. Although the implications of the model presented here should extend to sentence processing, the review and discussion will focus primarily on short-term maintenance of semantic and phonological representations of words during single and multiple word processing tasks and the effect of impairments to this ability on long-term learning. The following points will be emphasized:

(1) Word processing deficits in aphasia reflect an impairment of the ability to maintain activation of semantic and phonological representations of words. This deficit lies at the lower end (i.e., the more severe end) of a severity continuum.

(2) At least some cases of so-called pure verbal STM impairment in the absence of language impairment reflect a milder impairment of this same activation maintenance deficit. Although there may exist a pure STM deficit affecting the nonlinguistic components of verbal STM, the characteristics of such impairment that distinguish it from a language-based STM impairment remain to be determined.

(3) The activation maintenance deficit can affect the ability to maintain activation of semantic and/or phonological representations of words over the course of the time it takes to perform single or multiple word processing tasks.

(4) When this deficit affects maintenance of semantic representations of words, learning new words or encoding new verbal information into long-term memory is impeded.

(5) An interactive spreading activation model of word processing can account for this "linguistic" contribution to verbal STM.

Verbal STM deficits in aphasia: Evidence for a multi-store, language-based model of verbal short-term memory

Verbal STM deficits are pervasive in aphasia, and so, this disorder has provided an opportunity to identify co-occurring deficits that reflect links between STM and language processing. Cognitive neuropsychological studies have revealed associations and dissociations of language and memory deficits in aphasia that have furthered our understanding of linguistic and nonlinguistic components of verbal STM (Berndt & Mitchum, 1990; Hamilton & Martin, 2002; N. Martin & Saffran, 1997; N. Martin, Saffran, & Dell, 1996; R. C. Martin & Lesch, 1996; R. C. Martin, Shelton, & Yaffee, 1994; Saffran, 1990; Saffran, & Martin, 1990). Neuropsychological data such as these and other studies of language and short-term memory impairment in aphasia reveal effects of variables on short-term memory that are not often observable in normal speakers. For example, imageability of words, a semantic factor, can have a powerful effect on repetition and span performance of an aphasic speaker that is readily apparent in the accuracy and types of error that are produced (Hanley & Kay, 1997; N. Martin, 2000; N. Martin & Saffran, 1997). Additionally, errors produced in repetition tasks indicate levels of representation available to support language and verbal STM by virtue of their relationship with the target words. Individuals with phonological impairment tend to make semantically related errors or produce paraphrases of utterances that they cannot repeat verbatim (e.g., N. Martin & Saffran, 1992; R. C. Martin, Lesch, & Bartha, 1999; Saffran & Marin, 1975; Trojano, Stanzione, & Grossi, 1992). The examples of sentence repetition, (1) and (2) below from a person with aphasia, IL, reported by Saffran and Marin (1975) illustrate this pattern in sentence repetition.

(1) Target sentence: The automobile narrowly avoided the obstruction on the highway.
    IL: The automobile narrowly escaped the barricade in the road.
(2) Target sentence: The residence was located in a peaceful neighborhood.
    IL: The residence was situated in a quiet district.

In contrast, when semantic processing is impaired, errors are scarce in repetition of a single word, but emerge when a word string exceeds the subject's span, and tend to be phonologically related word and nonword errors. The examples of sentence repetition, (3) and (4), below, from a person with aphasia, VP, reported in Martin (2000) illustrate this pattern.

(3) Target sentence: The automobile narrowly avoided the obstruction on the highway.
    VP: The arrow but . . . the decision ah, no . . . the arrow doesn't the . . . I can't.
(4) Target sentence: The residence was located in a peaceful neighborhood.
    VP: The /ɛz ə dənt/ of /lo pɛɪ təd/ in a peaceful neighborhood.

Saffran and Marin's (1975) study noted above was one of the first to show that in aphasia, a deficit in retaining the verbatim phonological representation of a sentence does not preclude access to the semantic representations of the words in the sentence and the ability to maintain and report in the short term the gist of the sentence. This was followed by other reports of patients who showed lexical and semantic influences in their performance of verbal STM tasks (Berndt & Mitchum, 1990; N. Martin & Saffran, 1990; Saffran & Martin, 1990). In 1994, R. C. Martin, Shelton and Yaffee reported two patients, EA and AB, who demonstrated contrasting patterns of verbal STM performance. EA's pattern showed reduced effects of phonological variables (reduced word length effect, no recency effect) on span, better recall of word than nonword lists and better performance on a task probing short-term maintenance of semantic information than one that probes STM of phonological information. This pattern indicated a reliance on lexical and semantic information to perform these STM tasks. AB demonstrated the opposite pattern of performance, indicating a reliance on maintaining activation of phonological information to perform STM tasks. Following this seminal study, R. C. Martin and colleagues and others have reported a number of studies indicating involvement of semantic processes in STM tasks, lending support to a multi-store model of verbal STM (Hamilton & Martin, 2002; R. C. Martin & Freedman, 2001; R. C. Martin & Lesch, 1996).

Concurrent with this line of research, Saffran (1990) and N. Martin & Saffran (1990, 1997) provided evidence to support a model of verbal STM in which temporary storage of verbal information *depends in part* on activation processes that support comprehension, repetition and production of single words. N. Martin, Saffran and colleagues offered several sources of evidence indicating that performance on word processing tasks are related systematically to verbal STM abilities: co-recovery of short-term memory and word processing ability, correlation of severity of word processing and verbal STM abilities, and variability of span size depending on word processing demands of the span task. These studies are reviewed below.

Co-recovery of word processing and verbal STM

N. Martin and colleagues (Martin, Dell, Saffran, & Schwartz, 1994; Martin, Saffran, & Dell, 1996) conducted a longitudinal study of an individual with deep dysphasia. Early in the course of his recovery from a stroke, NC presented with the following error pattern: formal, semantic and phonemic paraphasias in naming and in single word repetition and a severely restricted STM span (single item only in repetition or pointing span tasks). The occurrence of semantic errors in single word repetition is the feature that led to the diagnosis of deep dysphasia. Examples of NC's errors in repetition, (5)–(8), are provided below:

(5) unicorn → horse
(6) cactus → desert
(7) muzzle → muscles
(8) racquet → /graek/

As NC recovered, his span increased to 2–3 items and, importantly, his error pattern changed as well. In single word repetition, he no longer made semantic errors, but continued to make formal and phonological paraphasias. However, when asked to repeat two words in sequence, semantic errors re-emerged in his error pattern, particularly in recalling the second word (Examples (9)–(11) below):

(9) officer liquor → officer alcohol
(10) picture cattle → picture saddle
(11) piano dollar → piano money

NC's pattern of repetition/recall error had initially been characterized on an interactive activation model of word retrieval as an increase in the rate at which activated nodes decay in the lexical network (N. Martin et al., 1994). His recovery pattern (decrease in semantic errors in repetition, but emergence once again in repeating two words) was simulated in this same model by reducing decay rate towards a more normal level (N. Martin et al., 1996).

NC's recovery pattern and the computational study of that pattern suggest that the processes which maintain activation of semantic and phonological representations of words in single word repetition are the same processes which maintain activation of two words that are to be repeated in sequence. The behavioral and computational data from this study support the view that interactive activation in the lexical system is the basis for maintaining information over time in the lexical system (via persistence of the activation of representations). From this perspective, this maintenance function of interactive activation is a form of STM. Although other factors, such as auditory rehearsal contribute to the maintenance of verbal representations in STM, the interactive activation processes that mediate single and multiple word processing are clearly involved, and their integrity is critical to performance of verbal STM tasks.

A severity continuum affecting word recognition, word retrieval, and single word and multiple word repetition/recall

Models that postulate common processes mediating word processing and verbal STM receive some support from studies of these two domains in aphasia. N. Martin and Gupta (2004) examined the relationship of two abilities that engage both semantic and phonological processing, word recognition (auditory lexical decision) and word production (picture naming) with four span measures (pointing and repetition span for digits and for words). Fifty individuals with aphasia (representing a variety of aphasic syndromes and severity levels) were administered the four span tasks, the auditory lexical decision task (N. Martin & Saffran, 1992) and the picture naming task (Philadelphia Naming Test, Roach, Schwartz, Martin, Grewal,

& Brecher, 1996). Span size correlated positively with word recognition. Not surprisingly, the associations between word recognition and span were more robust for words ($p < .01$) than digits ($p < .05$). Also, correlations were more robust for concrete words ($p < .01$) than abstract words (pointing: $p < .05$, repetition span: not significant). This pattern could be due to the fact that the span task used in this study included only high frequency concrete words.

To examine associations between naming and span, two measures of performance on the Philadelphia Naming Test were used: percent correct and percentage of "no response" errors. These measures are, respectively, the extreme of success and failure in the picture naming task. Positive associations between span and percent correct indicate that better naming is associated with greater span. Negative associations between span and "no responses" indicate that better naming is associated with fewer of these responses. We found that both measures robustly correlated ($p < .01$) in the predicted directions with all four span measures (see N. Martin & Gupta, 2004 for data).

These associations indicate a close relation between verbal STM capacity and word processing ability. However, individual case studies of apparent dissociations of word retrieval ability and verbal STM impairments (e.g., Warrington & Shallice, 1969) argue against such a link between the two systems. These seemingly contrasting phenomena may reflect a severity continuum of impairment to processes that maintain activation of linguistic representations over the course of speech processing (connection strength and decay as described above). In such a model, mild impairments to these processes would not affect maintenance of a single word's representations but do affect that of multiple words, resulting in the semblance of a storage capacity separate from the word processor. In the case of more severe impairment, processing of multiple *and* single words is affected, leading to a more apparently aphasic profile.

Severity continuum of semantic STM deficits

The studies described above indicate a severity continuum relationship between word processing and span size. The language-based multiple-store model of verbal STM would predict that an impairment of activation maintenance processes could be specific to a particular level of a word's representation. That is, if aphasic impairment affects primarily processing and maintenance of semantic representations, for example, there should be evidence of a severity continuum that affects performance on semantic short-term span tasks as well as language tasks that require maintaining activation of semantic representations. Some evidence for this relationship was found in a recent study (N. Martin, 2005) that examined performances of 35 aphasic individuals on verbal and nonverbal association judgment tasks in relation to their word span and nonverbal spatial span (Corsi Block Spatial Span Task, De Renzi & Nichelli, 1975) The premise of the study was a need to explain the nature of "semantic" impairment in aphasia. Traditionally, it has been viewed as a difficulty in accessing semantic representations and is differentiated from a "semantic knowledge" deficit in dementia that affects integrity of semantic representations themselves (Hodges, Patterson, Oxbury, & Funnell, 1992). The distinction between semantic access and semantic knowledge deficits has been most reliably manifested in performances on tests of verbal and nonverbal semantics. If semantic knowledge is degraded, performance on both verbal and nonverbal semantic tasks should be impaired. If knowledge is preserved, but access to that knowledge through language is somehow disrupted, performance on nonverbal tests should be preserved even when performance on verbally mediated semantic tasks is impaired. A classic test of verbal and nonverbal semantics is the Pyramids and Palm Trees Test (Howard & Patterson, 1992). This test involves choosing one of two pictured objects that is most associated with a third pictured object (e.g., a pyramid is matched to either a fir tree or a palm tree). In another version, these judgments are made with written (and simultaneously spoken) names of the objects. Presumably, the picture triads probe conceptual semantic knowledge and the word triads measure the ability to access that knowledge from words. These association judgment tasks require activation and maintenance of semantic representations to compare the meanings of words or concepts depicted in pictures and judge relative closeness of association. The expected pattern is that semantic knowledge deficits will lead to poor performance on both versions and semantic access deficits will yield better performance with pictures than with words.

Of the 35 aphasic individuals reported by N. Martin (2005), 9 performed poorly on both verbal and nonverbal versions of the Pyramids and Palm Trees Test. Nickels and Howard (1994) have also reported this pattern in some aphasic individuals. These reports could be interpreted as evidence that conceptual semantics is not intact in all aphasic individuals. N. Martin (2005) proposed an alternative account that the apparent deficit in conceptual semantics was related instead to a difficulty maintaining activation of semantic representations sufficiently in order to perform the judgments involved in the Pyramids and Palm Trees Test. In support of this proposal, N. Martin (2005) provided two pieces of evidence. First, the performance of the subset of 9 participants on tasks of lexical-semantic processing was more variable than that of the other 26 participants, and that variability was linked to the "ease" of the semantic task itself with respect to its content (characteristics of words probed such as imageability) and the degree to which a task stressed the limits of short-term memory. Second, the verbal span capacities of the two groups differed in a way that suggested a severity continuum of impairment. The digit and word spans as well as nonverbal spatial spans of the 9 individuals who performed poorly on both verbal and nonverbal semantic judgment tasks were significantly lower than those of the rest of the subjects in the study. The results of this study were interpreted as evidence that the nature of semantic impairment in aphasia is one of impaired access to semantic representations rather than a deficit of semantic knowledge. That access, however, depends on the integrity of activation maintenance processes which support performance on single and multiple word tasks (including the Pyramids and Palm Trees Test and verbal span tasks).

This study is provocative in that it suggests that apparent conceptual-semantic impairments could be due to a difficulty maintaining activation of conceptual-semantic representations or links between lexical and semantic representations. However, questions remain about the exact nature of the severity continuum of impairment to activation of conceptual and lexical-semantic representations. Does it affect activation that links lexical and conceptual semantics? Or are the lexical and conceptual semantics represented, activated and maintained separately? These and other questions remain to be investigated, but should provide insight into the organization of lexical-semantics and conceptual-semantics.

Effects of task and source of word processing impairment on verbal STM

N. Martin & Ayala (2004) investigated the possibility that span size would vary depending on the task that was used to assess span. This hypothesis was based on the idea that span tasks are language tasks and will vary depending on the components of the language system that are deployed in performance of the task and the components of the language system that are impaired in aphasia. N. Martin and Ayala observed differences in span size on two tasks used to assess digit and word span that differ with respect to the language processes they engage. In a pointing span task, the subject hears a sequence of digits or words and points to pictures that correspond to the items in the sequence (from a field of nine choices). This task requires activation of input phonological and semantic representations of the words in the sequence. In a repetition span task, the subject hears a sequence of words or numbers and immediately repeats the words in that same sequence. At minimum, this task involves access to input phonological representations and corresponding output phonological representations, followed by enactment of articulatory sequences. N. Martin and Ayala found that measures of phonological ability (e.g., phoneme discrimination and rhyming ability) correlated positively with pointing span and repetition span. This finding makes sense because each of these span paradigms engages phonological processes. In contrast, measures of lexical-semantic processing correlated only with pointing span. Pointing span engages semantic processes. Essentially, it is a word-to-picture matching task, but one that requires matching a series of words to pictures. Repetition span does not *require* activation of semantic representations. Although it can be assumed that activation will spread to lexical and semantic representations if access to these levels is intact, repetition can proceed without support of lexical or semantic representations. These results are consistent with the processes that are exploited in each span measure and indicate that span size varies depending on the task used to assess span.

The studies reviewed thus far provide support for a model in which those processes which maintain activation of single words in language tasks also support activation of these same representations in verbal span tasks. This conclusion might seem somewhat trivial and not necessarily evidence that these word activation processes are part of what we call verbal STM. They could, in theory, be dissociable from other nonlinguistic components of temporary storage such as rehearsal and sequencing. However, if such dissociations are valid, we need to know what constitutes a "language"-based STM deficit and how this can be differentiated from a "non-language"-based "pure" short-term memory deficit. What these studies *do* indicate is that language-based STM impairments can appear to be "pure" STM deficits when in actuality they are mild impairments of the processes by which language representations are activated and maintained in single word processing and multiple word processing tasks such as short-term span tasks. Such mild impairments mimic isolated STM deficits because they do not affect single word processing tasks such as picture naming or word-to-picture matching comprehension tasks.

Word processing and serial position effects

In the next section, I review evidence from aphasia indicating that the same word activation maintenance processes contribute to another property of short-term storage, the maintenance of serial order of representations within STM. Here again, it is important to stress that this evidence does not preclude the involvement of a nonlinguistic mechanism that maintains serial order, but rather indicate a contribution of the activation processes that make available the *content* of verbal STM, the semantic and phonological representations of words, to serial order. This mechanism is presumed to work in tandem with rehearsal and other attentional mechanisms (e.g., Ruchkin et al., 2003) that likely also contribute to serial order.

Semantic and phonological influences on serial position effects

How we maintain serial order of the contents of STM is an important and yet not fully understood problem. Serial order information is inherent in language. Words are sequences of phonemes, sentences are sequences of words, stories are sequences of ideas and so on. Processing and temporary storage of language requires some means of encoding and maintaining the serial order of the units of language being encoded. Studies of serial position effects, primacy and recency, reveal both linguistic and nonlinguistic factors that play a role in this process. Articulatory rehearsal, the process of silently repeating a sequence before recall, influences the recall of items early in a sequence (primacy) (Campbell & Dodd, 1984; Posner, 1964).

Linguistic factors are involved as well. Phonological factors have long been linked to performance on verbal span tasks. Phonological similarity effects are present in all serial positions (Henson, Norris, Page, & Baddeley, 1996). Lexical factors such as word frequency have been shown to influence primacy (Watkins & Watkins, 1977) with more high frequency items recalled at the early part of the lists than low frequency items. Other studies have shown no particular effect for frequency on order recall (Poirier & Saint Aubin, 1996). Primacy has also been shown to be sensitive to semantic factors such as category similarity. Brooks and Watkins (1990) conducted several experiments that varied the category relationships of items in the first half (related) and second half (unrelated) of lists to be recalled. Span was larger when the same category words were in the first half of the list. This suggests that initial items had support from semantic processes over and above phonological support.

Neuropsychological evidence also indicates a linguistic contribution to serial position effects. The evidence from language-impaired individuals shows loss of primacy or recency effects when semantic or phonological processing is impaired. In 1990, N. Martin and Saffran studied the repetition and span abilities of an individual, ST, with transcortical sensory aphasia. Typical of this syndrome (Berthier, 1999), ST was able to repeat short sequences of digits and short-sentences, but was impaired on tests of word comprehension (e.g., word-to-picture matching tasks) and production. Errors in production included related and unrelated word substitutions and neologisms. Also, ST's ability to recognize words and nonwords (auditory lexical decision) was only mildly impaired. This pattern indicates that although input and output pathways between phonological and lexical representations are relatively intact, input and output pathways between lexical and semantic systems are impaired. On word span tasks, ST could repeat two words, but when asked to repeat three or more words, she consistently repeated the last few items correctly followed by a production of neologisms made up in part from phonemes of other words in the input string. This pattern occurred despite the fact that she overtly rehearsed each item as it was presented. ST's inability to maintain activation of initial items in a sequence of words led N. Martin and Saffran to hypothesize that her impaired ability to access semantic representations reduced the support of semantic processes to maintaining the primacy portion of a sequence of words, leaving her dependent on the short-lived phonological trace of the most recently presented words.

ST's pattern and the opposite pattern (impaired phonological processes leading to a reliance on semantic processes to retain information in short-term memory) were observed in a study of 15 individuals with aphasia and accompany span impairments (N. Martin & Saffran, 1997). Subjects were asked to repeat single words and word pairs which were varied for frequency and imageability. Although repeating two words might seem an easy "span" to manage, for the aphasic individuals in this study, two word strings were sufficiently taxing to their spans to reveal primacy and recency effects as well as their associations with semantic and phonological processing ability. N. Martin and Saffran (1997) found that performance on measures of lexical-semantic processing correlated positively with primacy in retrieval of (1) phonemes within a single word and (2) words within a two-word string. They also found that performance on measures of phonological processing correlated with retrieval of the final phoneme within a word and the second word within a word pair. This finding was later replicated with a larger group of aphasic subjects that sampled a wider range of span capacity (1–4 items) and aphasia severity (N. Martin, Ayala, & Saffran, 2002). The associations of primacy with lexical-semantic processing and recency with phonological processing were observed in repetition of two-, three-, and four-word strings but were most evident when the span length tested was close to the actual span of the individual. For example, individuals with spans between 2 and 3.5 demonstrated the associations of semantic and phonological abilities with primacy and recency when tested on strings of three words but not when tested on strings of four or five words.

In a second experiment, N. Martin et al. (2002) showed that these same effects varied depending on the ease of the span task. The words used in the first experiment varied in frequency and imageability and were two or three syllables in length. When the span task was made easier by using concrete, one- and two-syllable words from a finite set of nine items, robust correlations between serial position and lexical-semantic and phonological ability emerged at longer string lengths than in the first experiment. For example, those subjects who did not demonstrate the associations on three-word strings in the "harder" span task of the first experiment did so in the second experiment. Martin et al. concluded that making the span task easier increased the "functional" span of the individuals.

Together, these two studies indicate that (1) associations of primacy with lexical-semantic processing and recency with phonological processing are most apparent when a span task taxes the limits of span capacity and (2) that this span capacity varies based on task factors such as item characteristics.

A model of the contribution of word activation processes to verbal short-term memory

On the basis of the studies reviewed above, N. Martin and Saffran (1997) proposed a language-based model of verbal STM that attempted to account for the linguistic contribution to verbal STM and serial order that was later elaborated in N. Martin et al. (2002) and N. Martin and Gupta (2004). They proposed that the linguistic influences on serial order are due to the time course at which phonological and semantic representations are activated in a repetition span task and its effect on the probabilities that words from different serial positions will be recalled. Their account is based on an interactive activation model proposed by Dell and O'Seaghdha (1992) which has been used elsewhere to account for the naming and repetition patterns observed in aphasic speakers (Dell, Martin, & Schwartz, 2007; Dell, Schwartz, Martin, Saffran, & Gagnon, 1997; Schwartz, Dell, Martin, Gahl, & Sobel, 2006). This is a competitive activation model with two parameters that contribute to activation levels of words in a "winner-takes-all" retrieval process: connection weight and decay rate. Connection weight refers to the strength of activation spread between levels of representation. Decay rate refers to the rate at which activation of a representation decays after it has been contacted by spreading activation. In naming, activation spreads forward through the network from semantic to lexical to phonological representations and feeds back activation at each level to refresh primed representations that begin to decay as soon as they are activated. The word intended to be spoken receives the most activation while representations of words related semantically or phonologically to the target are primed to a lesser degree with spreading activation. When a word needs to be retrieved for production, the word node with the highest level of activation is retrieved. In repetition, the sequence of spreading activation begins with phonological representations and spreads to lexical and semantic representations. Patterns of error in aphasic naming and repetition were modeled by lesioning the connection weight and/or decay rate parameters globally, that is, affecting the entire semantic-lexical-phonological network (Dell et al., 1997). Distinct error patterns were accounted for by reducing the connection weights, leading to weaker spread of activation throughout the network, or increasing the decay rate, leading to normal, but short-lived activation of representations.

Dell and colleagues' model was later modified in two ways by Foygel and Dell (2000). First, lesions to the model were made to affect connection weight only. Second, the model allowed for separate lesions of the connection weight parameter that could selectively affect mappings between semantic and lexical representations or between lexical and phonological representations. N. Martin and Gupta's (2004) account of linguistic influences on serial order, although based on Foygel and Dell's interactive model, departs from that model in that it attributes deficits in processing to accelerated decay rate rather than reduced connection weight. Figure 11.1 depicts the structure of an interactive activation model of single word repetition and Figure 11.2 shows an extension of the model to accommodate repetition of multiple words. In the model of single word repetition, there are four levels of word representation: conceptual (nonverbal) semantics, lexical (verbal) semantics, word form and phonological. Retrieving names in production (e.g., picture naming) involves output pathways from conceptual to phonological representations. When repeating a single word, auditory input initiates spreading activation to all levels of representation. Nonetheless, repetition of a single word or nonword can proceed when there is damage to the lexical, semantic or conceptual levels of representation by

Conceptual

Semantic

Lexical

Phonological

Input   Output

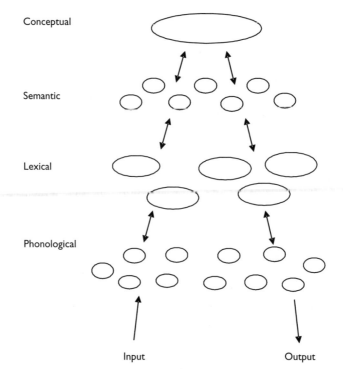

Figure 11.1 A model of single word repetition with four levels of word representation depicted: phonological, lexical, semantic and conceptual. Bidirectional arrows indicate feedforward–feedback spreading activation between levels of representation.

activating phonological representations and using these as the basis of output. When there is damage at the phonological level, repetition of a single word is impaired but supported in part by higher levels of representation (via feedback activation).

As activation spreads between levels of representations, a series of feedforward–feedback cycles of priming activation and decay is set in motion. This serves to maintain activation of a word's lexical representation over the course of speech comprehension or production. Phonological representations are activated first, followed by lexical and semantic representations. A number of interactive activation cycles precede retrieval, allowing time for representations to accumulate activation.

Repetition of multiple words, as in a verbal span task, requires maintaining activation of all levels of each word's representations in the sequence. Figure 11.2 shows the predicted activation strengths of connections between semantic and lexical representations and lexical and phonological representations of each word in a four-item span task at the point in time when recall of a span of words begins. (Conceptual levels of representation are

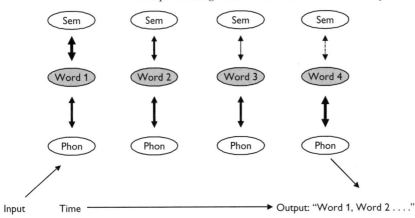

Figure 11.2 A depiction of the activation levels of semantic, lexical and phonological representations of each of four words in a multiple word repetition span task at time of recall. Bold arrows indicate greater levels of activation. Semantic representations of words heard early are more strongly activated at time of recall because they have more time to receive feedforward and feedback spreading activation than words heard later.

not shown in this model, but it is assumed that this level is also activated in multiple-word repetition.) This model is meant to account for the "language" contribution to maintenance of items in STM. It is similar in principle to activation-based models such as the primacy model (e.g., Page & Norris, 1998) but does not address contributing factors included in other models such as the inter-item associations (e.g., Lewandowsky & Murdock, 1989).

As each word in the string is heard (INPUT), activation spreads up through the lexical network from phonological to lexical to semantic representations. Once activated, representations begin to decay, but are refreshed by feedback from subsequently activated representations. Phonological and semantic representations are primed by spreading activation at different points in time leading to differential activation strengths of the semantic and phonological representations of words. The importance of this temporal differential is that the accumulated activation and support of each word differs across the sequence. *All other factors being equal*, the first word in a sequence receives the greatest amount of semantic activation over the course of the span task. This increases its relative probability of being recalled (the primacy effect). Semantic impairment in aphasia is characterized as diminished ability to access semantic representations. In this model, that difficulty is attributed to too-fast decay of representations. If this impairment is present, initial words in the input string will not benefit from accumulating semantic activation because at each time step when feedback activation replenishes activation support to the word, the activation decays too rapidly. The net effect is to make the items in initial positions less accessible at recall. If activated phonological representations decay too quickly, feedback from activated semantic representations will still be available to support their activation, but this support is *weakest at the end of the list*. This reduces the probability of recalling final words in a string which are supported by weak semantic activation and recently activated but rapidly decaying phonological representations.

This variability in activation strength is related to the temporal course of activation, and decay of semantic and phonological representations of words is presumed to be one mechanism that works in concert with others such as rehearsal or inter-item associations to maintain serial order of language content in verbal STM. One piece of anecdotal evidence that is consistent with multiple contributions was noted in the earlier discussion of ST, the individual with transcortical sensory aphasia who only repeated the last few items in a string of words. Despite her inability to retain initial items in a sequence, ST always rehearsed each item as it was heard. This pattern has been observed in other aphasic individuals with semantically based anomia or transcortical sensory aphasia, but has not yet been investigated systematically.

Effects of semantic and phonological impairments on verbal learning

The integrity of verbal STM systems is important not just for remembering in the short term, but also, learning language and encoding knowledge conveyed via language into long-term memory. If word activation processes are an integral part of verbal STM systems, as proposed here, impairments to those processes should impact learning. Early studies of learning in aphasia focused on the influences of verbal STM capacity on learning (Basso, Spinnler, Vallar, & Zanobio, 1982; Warrington, Logue, & Pratt, 1971; Warrington & Shallice, 1969) and often included subjects who demonstrated phonological STM deficits with minimal language impairment. One particularly well-studied case was PV (Baddeley, Papagno, & Vallar, 1988; Basso et al., 1982; Vallar & Baddeley, 1984) who, despite an impaired phonological STM, demonstrated an ability to learn words, but not nonwords in a paired associate paradigm. Trojano et al. (1992) reported another case, SC, who demonstrated a pattern of short-term memory performance that was consistent with a phonological STM deficit. They investigated influences of word length, concreteness and word category on short-term list learning and found that SC's performance was affected by word category, but not word length. That is, more items in a list were learned for concrete nouns than for function words. This suggested a role of lexical-semantic coding in verbal learning and that some learning can occur in the presence of a phonological STM impairment.

What would be the effect of a semantic STM deficit on verbal learning? Martin and Saffran (1999) investigated factors affecting word-list learning in 18 aphasic individuals. They used a standard word-list learning paradigm in which the participant hears a supraspan list of words and recalls as many items as he/she can. The list is repeated again and the participant once again attempts to recall as many items as possible. Typically, more items are recalled with each presentation. Martin and Saffran found that short-term learning of word lists is affected by semantic factors (imageability and semantic relatedness) and that both phonological and semantic impairment impede performance on verbal learning tasks. Freedman and Martin (2001) investigated learning of new words in aphasia examined with a paired associates paradigm. They found that semantic memory was a critical factor and that deficits in semantic processing were detrimental to learning. Finally, a recent study by Gupta, Martin, Abbs, Schwartz, and Lipinski (2006) examined new word learning ability in 21 individuals with aphasia. Subjects were trained on names of "aliens" through repetition priming alone in one condition (phonological learning) and through priming of the name in the presence of the picture of the alien (recognition learning). Learning performance in each of these tasks was correlated with a composite lexical-semantic score and a composite phonological score each based on a battery of relevant measures. The results indicated a double dissociation between receptive recognition and phonological learning. Lexical-semantic measures correlated significantly and positively with receptive recognition but not with phonological learning and measures of phonological ability correlated positively with phonological learning, but not with receptive recognition learning.

There is still much to learn about how semantic and phonological processing and STM affect the ability to gain long-term knowledge via language or to learn new words. Phonological impairment has been shown to impair new word learning, although it does not seem to preclude learning verbal material altogether. Furthermore, under conditions of phonological impairment, learning that does occur is modulated by the nature of the verbal input (e.g., concreteness and word category effects). In contrast, lexical-semantic impairment consistently has been shown to impair short- and long-term learning. This difficulty is also seen in treatment of aphasia. N. Martin and Laine and colleagues (Martin, Fink, & Laine, 2004; Martin, Fink, Renvall, & Laine, 2006; Renvall, Laine, Laakso, & Martin, 2003) have shown that treatment of word retrieval deficits with repetition priming is successful when the aphasic impairment spares access to semantic representations.

Summary and conclusions

In this chapter, I have reviewed studies of language impairment carried out in recent years that support a model of verbal STM and learning that incorporates a definitive role of word processing beyond that of providing the content of verbal STM and learning. In a very real sense, the overall message here is that word processing deficits in aphasia *are* short-term memory impairments, or they are at least impairments to one mechanism that contributes to our ability to keep verbal information active in consciousness for short periods. Word processing deficits in aphasia reflect an impairment of the mechanism that serves to maintain activation of semantic and phonological representations of words over the course of any language task whether it involves processing single or multiple words.

It is important to reiterate that this deficit does not preclude the possibility of a pure STM deficit as has been reported in several cases in the last few decades (e.g., Warrington & Shallice, 1969). However, it is also important to note that some cases of impairments to a "selective" STM may have actually been instances of a mild impairment of the "activation maintenance" deficit proposed in this chapter. The studies reported in this paper provide some indication of the character of the language-based verbal STM deficit: varied performance on span tasks based on lexical and semantic factors (e.g., imageability) and on the task used to assess span, differential associations with semantic and phonological processing and primacy and recency, respectively, and differential effects of semantic and phonological STM deficits on short- and long-term learning. Future studies should aim to precisely characterize the language and STM patterns associated with pure STM deficits and identify characteristics that differentiate them from language-based STM deficits.

The evidence presented here also indicates that the activation maintenance deficit can adversely affect activation of either or both semantic and/or phonological representations of words. Although more research in this area is needed, studies to date indicate that when the deficit affects the ability to maintain activation of semantic representations of words, learning new words or encoding new verbal information into long-term memory is impeded. This indication has both theoretical and clinical implications and, therefore, it is of great importance that we find more and better ways to investigate the relationships among word processing, STM and learning abilities.

Acknowledgments

The preparation of this chapter was supported by grants from the National Institutes of Health (Deafness and other Communication Disorders), DC 01924-11 (PI: N. Martin) granted to Temple University and DC00191-21 (PI: M. Schwartz) granted to Moss Rehabilitation Research Institute. I am grateful to my colleagues, Gary Dell, Matti Laine, Myrna Schwartz, Prahlad Gupta and Randi Martin, for the many helpful discussions over the years, which have contributed in important ways to the development of the ideas put forth in this chapter. I am especially indebted to my mentor for many years, Eleanor Saffran, who inspired me and encouraged me to pursue this most intriguing line of research.

References

Atkinson, R. C., & Shiffrin, R. M. (1968). Human memory: A proposed system and its control processes. In K. W. P. Spence & J. T. Spence (Eds.), *The psychology of learning and motivation* (Vol. 2, pp. 89–195). New York: Academic Press.

Baddeley, A. D. (1986). *Working memory*. Oxford: Clarendon Press.

Baddeley, A. D. (2001). Is working memory still working? *American Psychologist, 56*, 851–864.

Baddeley, A. D., & Hitch, G. J. (1974). Working memory. In G. H. Bower (Ed.), *The psychology of learning and motivation* (Vol. 8). New York: Academic Press.

Baddeley, A. D., Papagno, C., & Vallar, G. (1988). When long term learning depends on short-term storage. *Journal of Memory and Language, 27*, 586–595.

Baddeley, A. D., Thomson, N., & Buchanan, M. (1975). Word length and the structure of short-term memory. *Journal of Verbal Learning and Verbal Behavior, 14*, 575–589.

Basso, A., Spinnler, H., Vallar, G., & Zanobio, M. E. (1982). Left hemisphere damage and selective impairment of auditory verbal short-term memory: A case study. *Neuropsychologia, 20*, 263–274.

Berndt, R. S., & Mitchum, C. C. (1990). Auditory and lexical information sources in immediate recall: Evidence from a patient with deficit to the phonological short-term store. In G. Vallar & T. Shallice (Eds.), *Neuropsychological impairments of short-term memory*. Cambridge: Cambridge University Press.

Berthier, M. (1999). *Transcortical aphasias*. Hove, UK: Psychology Press.

Brener, R. (1940). An experimental investigation of memory span. *Journal of Experimental Psychology, 26*, 467–482.

Brooks III, J. O., & Watkins, M. J. (1990). Further evidence of the intricacy of memory span. *Journal of Experimental Psychology: Learning, Memory, and Cognition, 16*(6), 1134–1141.

Brown, G. D. A., & Hulme, C. (1995). Modeling item length effects in memory span: No rehearsal needed? *Journal of Memory and Language, 34*, 594–621.

Campbell, R., & Dodd, B. (1984). Aspects of hearing by eye. In H. Bouma & D. G. Bouwhuis (Eds.), *Attention and performance X* (pp. 300–311). Hillsdale, NJ: Lawrence Erlbaum Associates, Inc.

Caza, N., & Belleville, S. (1999). Semantic contributions to immediate serial recall using an unlimited set of items: Evidence for a multi-level capacity view of short-term memory. *International Journal of Psychology, 34*, 334–338.

Conrad, R., & Hull, A. J. (1964). Information, acoustic confusion and memory span. *British Journal of Psychology, 55*, 429–432.

Cowan, N. (1997) *Attention and memory: An integrated framework*. Oxford: Oxford University Press.

Crowder, R. G. (1979). Similarity and order in memory. In G. H. Bower (Ed.), *The psychology of learning and motivation: Advances in research and theory* (Vol. 13, pp. 319–353). New York: Academic Press.

Dell, G. S., Martin, N., & Schwartz, M. F. (2007). A case-series test of the interactive two-step model of lexical access. Predicting word repetition from picture naming. *Journal of Memory and Language, 56*, 490–520.

Dell, G. S., & O'Seaghdha, P. G. (1992). Stages in lexical access in language production. *Cognition, 42*, 287–314.

Dell, G. S., Schwartz, M. F., Martin, N., Saffran, E. M., & Gagnon, D. A. (1997).

Lexical access in aphasic and non-aphasic speakers. *Psychological Review, 104*(4), 801–838.

De Renzi, E., & Nichelli, P. (1975). Verbal and non-verbal short-term memory impairment following hemispheric damage. *Cortex, 11*, 341–354.

Fiez, J. (1997) Phonology, semantics and the role of the left inferior prefrontal cortex. *Human Brain Mapping, 5*, 79–83.

Foygel, D., & Dell, G. S. (2000). Models of impaired lexical access in speech production. *Journal of Memory and Language, 43*, 182–216.

Freedman, M. L., & Martin, R. C. (2001). Dissociable components of short-term memory and their relation to long-term learning. *Cognitive Neuropsychology, 18*, 193–226.

Gathercole, S. E., Frankish, C. R., Pickering, S. J., & Peaker, S. H. (1999). Phonotactic influences on serial recall. *Journal of Experimental Psychology: Learning, Memory, and Cognition, 25*, 84–95.

Gupta, P. (1996) Word learning and verbal short-term memory: A computational account. In *Proceedings of the 18th Annual Conference of the Cognitive Science Society* (pp. 189–194). Hillsdale, NJ: Lawrence Erlbaum Associates, Inc.

Gupta, P., Martin, N., Abbs, B., Schwartz, M. F., & Lipinski, J. (2006). New word learning in aphasic patients: Dissociating phonological and semantic components. *Brain and Language, 99*, 8–9.

Hamilton, A. C., & Martin, R. C. (2002). Inhibition and proactive interference effects in impaired semantic short-term memory of aphasic patients. *Brain and Language, 83*, 9–224.

Hanley, J. R., & Kay, J. (1997). An effect of imageability on the production of phonological errors in auditory repetition. *Cognitive Neuropsychology, 14*(8), 1065–1084.

Henson, R. N. A., Norris, D. G., Page, M. P. A., & Baddeley, A. D. (1996). Unchained memory: Error patterns rule out chaining models of immediate serial recall. *Quarterly Journal for Experimental Psychology, 49A*, 80–115.

Hodges, J., Patterson, K., Oxbury S., & Funnell, E. (1992). Semantic dementia, *Brain, 115*, 1783–1806.

Howard, D., & Patterson, K. (1992). *The Pyramids and Palm Trees Test: A test of semantic access from words and pictures.* Bury St Edmunds, UK: Thames Valley Test Company.

Hulme, C., Maughan, S., & Brown, G. (1991). Memory for familiar and unfamiliar words: Evidence for a long-term memory contribution to short-term span. *Journal of Memory and Language, 30*, 685–701.

Hulme, C., Roodenrys, S. Schweickert, R., Brown, G. D., Martin, S., & Stuart, G. (1997). Word frequency effects on short-term memory tasks: Evidence for redintegration process in immediate serial recall. *Journal of Experimental Psychology: Learning, Memory, and Cognition, 23*, 1217–1232.

Lewandowsky, S., & Murdock, B. B., Jr (1989). Memory for serial order. *Psychological Review, 96*(1), 25–57.

Majerus, S., Poncelet, M., Van der Linden, M., Albouy, G., Salmon, E., Sterpenich, V., et al. (2006). The left intraparietal sulcus and verbal short-term memory: Focus of attention or serial order? *NeuroImage, 32*, 880–891.

Martin, N. (2000). Repetition in aphasia: Theoretical and clinical implications. In R. S. Berndt (Ed.), *Handbook of Neuropsychology*, (2nd ed.), (Vol. 3, pp. 137–155). Elsevier.

Martin, N. (2005). Verbal and nonverbal semantic impairment in aphasia: An activation deficit hypothesis. *Brain and Language*, *95*, 251–252.

Martin, N., & Ayala, J. (2004). Measurements of auditory-verbal STM in aphasia: Effects of task, item and word processing impairment. *Brain and Language*, *89*, 464–483.

Martin, N., Ayala, J., & Saffran, E. M. (2002). Lexical influences on serial position effects in verbal STM span in aphasia. *Brain and Language*, *83*, 92–95.

Martin, N., Dell, G. S., Saffran, E. M., & Schwartz, M. F. (1994). Origins of paraphasias in deep dysphasia: Testing the consequences of a decay impairment in an interactive spreading activation model of language. *Brain and Language*, *47*, 609–660.

Martin, N., Fink, R., & Laine, M. (2004). Treatment of word retrieval with contextual priming. *Aphasiology*, *18*, 457–471.

Martin, N., Fink, R., Renvall, K., & Laine, M. (2006). Effectiveness of contextual repetition priming. Treatments for anomia depends on intact access to semantics. *Journal of International Neuropsychological Society*, *12*, 853–866.

Martin, N., & Gupta, P. (2004) Exploring the relationship between word processing and verbal STM: Evidence from associations and dissociations. *Cognitive Neuropsychology*, *21*, 213–228.

Martin, N., & Saffran, E. M. (1990). Repetition and verbal STM in transcortical sensory aphasia: A case study. *Brain and Language*, *39*, 254–288.

Martin, N., & Saffran, E. M. (1992). A connectionist account of deep dysphasia: Evidence from a case study. *Brain and Language*, *43*, 240–274.

Martin, N., & Saffran, E. M. (1997). Language and auditory-verbal short-term memory impairments: Evidence for common underlying processes. *Cognitive Neuropsychology*, *14*(5), 641–682.

Martin, N., & Saffran, E. M. (1999). Effects of word processing and short-term memory deficits on verbal learning: Evidence from aphasia. *International Journal of Psychology*, *34*(5/6), 330–346.

Martin, N., Saffran, E. M., & Dell, G. S. (1996). Recovery in deep dysphasia: Evidence for a relation between auditory-verbal STM capacity and lexical errors in repetition. *Brain and Language*, *52*, 83–113.

Martin, R. C., & Freedman, M. L. (2001). Neuropsychology of verbal working memory: Ins and outs of phonological and lexical-semantic retention. In H. L. Roediger, J. S. Nairne, I. Neath, & A. M. Suprenant (Eds.), *The nature of remembering: Essays in honor of Robert G. Crowder*. Washington, DC: American Psychological Association.

Martin, R. C., & Lesch, M. F. (1996). Associations and dissociations between language impairment and list recall: Implications for models of STM. In S. E. Gathercole (Ed.), *Models of working memory* (pp. 149–178). Hove: Psychology Press.

Martin, R. C., Lesch, M., & Bartha, M. C. (1999). Independence of input and output phonology in word processing and short-term memory. *Journal of Memory and Language*, *40*, 1–27.

Martin, R. C., & Romani, C. (1996). Remembering stories but not words. In R. Campbell & M. Conway (Eds.), *Broken memories*. Cambridge, UK: Blackwell.

Martin, R. C., Shelton, J., & Yaffee, L. (1994). Language processing and working memory: Neuropsychological evidence for separate phonological and semantic capacities. *Journal of Memory and Language*, *33*, 83–111.

Nickels, L., & Howard, D. (1994). A frequent occurrence? Factors affecting the production of semantic errors in aphasic naming. *Cognitive Neuropsychology, 11,* 289–320.

Page, M. P. A., & Norris, D. G. (1998). The primacy model: A new model of immediate serial recall. *Psychological Review, 104,* 761–781.

Patterson, K. E., Graham, N., & Hodges, J. R. (1994). The impact of semantic memory loss on representations. *Journal of Cognitive Neuroscience, 6*(1), 57–69.

Poirier, M., & Saint Aubin, J. (1995). Memory for related and unrelated words: Further evidence on the influence of semantic factors immediate serial recall. *Quarterly Journal of Experimental Psychology, 48A,* 384–404.

Poirier, M., & Saint Aubin, J. (1996). Immediate serial recall, word frequency, item identity and item position. *Canadian Journal of Experimental Psychology, 50,* 408–412.

Posner, M. I. (1964). Rate of presentation and order of recall in immediate memory. *British Journal of Psychology, 55,* 303–306.

Potter, M. C. (1993). Very short-term conceptual memory. *Memory & Cognition, 21*(2), 156–161.

Ravizza, S. M., Delgado, M. R., Chein, J. M., Becker, J. T., & Fiez, J. A. (2004). Functional dissociations within the inferior parietal cortex in verbal working memory. *NeuroImage, 22,* 562–573.

Renvall, K., Laine, M. Laakso, M., & Martin, N. (2003). Anomia rehabilitation with contextual priming: A case study. *Aphasiology, 17,* 305–308.

Roach, A., Schwartz, M. F., Martin, N., Grewal, R. S., & Brecher, A. (1996). The Philadelphia naming test: Scoring and rationale. *Clinical Aphasiology* (Vol. 24, pp. 121–134). Austin: Pro-Ed.

Ruchkin, D., Grafman, J., Cameron, K., & Berndt, R. (2003). Working memory retention systems: A state of activated long-term memory. *Behavioral and Brain Sciences, 26*(6), 709–777.

Saffran, E. M. (1990). Short-term memory impairment and language processing. In A. Caramazza (Ed.), *Advances in cognitive neuropsychology and neurolinguistics.* Hillsdale, NJ: Lawrence Erlbaum Associates, Inc.

Saffran E. M., & Marin, O. S. M. (1975). Immediate memory for word lists and sentences in a patient with deficient auditory short-term memory. *Brain and Language, 2,* 420–433.

Saffran, E. M., & Martin, N. (1990). Neuropsychological evidence for lexical involvement in short-term memory. In G. Vallar and T. Shallice (Eds.), *Neuropsychological impairments of short-term memory.* Cambridge: Cambridge University Press.

Saffran, E. M., & Martin, N. (1999). Meaning but not words: Neuropsychological evidence for very short-term conceptual memory. In V. Coltheart (Ed.), *Fleeting memories.* Cambridge, MA: MIT Press.

Saint-Aubin, J., & Poirier, M. (1999). The influence of long-term memory factors on immediate serial recall: An item and order analysis. *International Journal of Psychology, 34,* 347–352.

Schwartz, M. F., Dell, G. S., Martin, N., Gahl, S., & Sobel, P. (2006). A case series test of the two-step interactive model of lexical access: Evidence from picture naming. *Journal of Memory and Language, 54,* 228–264.

Schweickert, R. (1993). A multinomial processing tree model for degradation and redintegration in immediate recall. *Memory & Cognition, 21,* 168–175.

Shulman, H. G. (1971). Similarity effects in short-term memory. *Psychological Bulletin, 75*, 399–415.

Thompson-Schill, S. L., Jonides, J., Marshuetz, C., Smith, E. E., D'Esposito, M., Kan, I., et al. (2002). Effects of frontal lobe damage on interference effects in working memory. *Cognitive, Affective and Behavioral Neuroscience, 2*, 109–120.

Trojano, L., Stanzione, M., & Grossi, D. (1992). Short-term memory and verbal learning with auditory phonological coding defect: A neuropsychological case study. *Brain and Cognition, 18*, 12–33.

Vallar, G., & Baddeley, A. D. (1984). Phonological short-term store, phonological processing and sentence comprehension: A neuropsychological case study. *Cognitive Neuropsychology, 1*, 121–141.

Vallar, G., & Papagno, C. (1995). Neuropsychological impairments of short-term memory. In A. D. Baddeley, B. A. Wilson, & F. Watts (Eds.), *Handbook of memory disorders* (pp. 135–165). Chichester, UK: Wiley.

Warrington, E. K., Logue, V., & Pratt, R. T. C. (1971). The anatomical localisation of selective impairment of short-term memory. *Neuropsychologia, 9*, 377–387.

Warrington, E. K., & Shallice, T. (1969). The selective impairment of auditory verbal short-term memory. *Brain, 92*, 885–896.

Watkins, O. C., & Watkins, M. J. (1977). Serial recall and the modality effect. *Journal of Experimental Psychology: Human Learning and Memory, 3*, 712–718.

12 Verbal short-term memory and temporary activation of language representations: The importance of distinguishing item and order information

Steve Majerus

Overview

This chapter presents developmental, neuropsychological and neuroimaging arguments in favour of a position considering that short-term storage of item information is intimately related to temporary activation of the language network. On the other hand, I will argue that short-term storage of serial order information is a specific function of a dedicated short-term memory system. I will conclude by proposing a short-term memory framework that integrates language processing and serial order processing modules, and which is supported by a common but flexible pool of attentional resources.

Introduction

Let us begin with a concrete example of an everyday life situation involving verbal short-term memory processing: taking the order in a restaurant. When an experienced waiter in a restaurant takes the order and is told "soda, beer, glass of red wine, and crisps", he will temporarily store the words he heard in verbal short-term memory (STM), but he will also activate at the same time semantic knowledge about these words and all other information and scripts necessary for the execution of the order. It would be somewhat absurd to imagine that the waiter would just store the chain of sounds "[səʊdə bɪəʳ glaːs ɒv red waɪn ænd krɪsps]" without accessing lexical and semantic knowledge associated with the sound sequence.

Although an extreme idea, this is a caricature of the situation that has characterized the verbal short-term memory (STM) literature for many years. When the first patients with selective STM deficits were described, most emphasis was put on the fact that their STM deficit was independent from deficits in episodic long-term memory or receptive and productive language pathology (e.g., Saffran & Marin, 1975; Warrington, Logue, & Pratt, 1971; Warrington & Shallice, 1969). This approach was of important heuristic value, as it permitted a better demarcation of the verbal STM system from other cognitive functions, and contributed to the development of one of the most influential STM models, the working memory model by Baddeley and Hitch (1974). However, the corollary of this approach was a certain tendency to neglect the fact that verbal STM primarily serves to store *language-based* representations and that as such, it is very likely to interact with sublexical and lexical phonological and semantic language representations. About 20 years later, models taking into account the linguistic nature of verbal STM tasks slowly began to receive more attention. One of the most extreme linguistic models of STM that appeared during this period was the interactive activation model proposed by N. Martin and Saffran (1992); in this model, verbal STM does not exist as an independent system, but STM is merely the emergent property of the temporary activation of phonological, lexical and semantic language representations of the language network.

In the present chapter, I will review evidence that supports language-based STM models and I will argue that temporary activation of language representations determines verbal STM processing to a much greater extent than is commonly accepted. However, I will also argue that verbal STM cannot be reduced only to activation of language representations, but that one of the specific properties of a verbal STM store may be the encoding and storage of sequence information, i.e. the serial and temporal order of items that were presented in a list. I will discuss this hypothesis in the light of recent computational models of verbal STM, and I will review convergent evidence from recent experimental, developmental, neuropsychological and neuroimaging studies. Finally, I will present a hybrid theoretical framework of verbal STM that is rooted within language processing but which includes specific serial order processing/short-term storage systems.

Verbal STM as activation of language representations

Experimental studies in adults and children

There is now a substantial body of research showing that the availability of rich and easily accessible language representations enhances immediate serial recall of lists of verbal items in healthy adults: (1) recall of lists of words yields significantly higher performance levels than recall of lists of nonwords (e.g., Hulme, Maughan, & Brown, 1991; Poirier & Saint-Aubin, 1996), (2) words of high lexical frequency are more likely to be recalled than words of low lexical frequency (Roodenrys, Hulme, Alban, & Ellis, 1994; Roodenrys & Quinlan, 2000; Watkins & Watkins, 1977), (3) recall of concrete words is superior to recall of abstract words (Caza & Belleville, 1999; Walker & Hulme, 1999). These lexicality, word frequency and word imageability effects on immediate serial recall performance suggest that lexical and semantic language knowledge, when available, actively contribute to STM recall. These effects have been most often interpreted as reflecting access to language representations at the moment of retrieval of information in STM:

the decayed STM trace is reconstructed via the selection of representations in the language knowledge base that provide the best fit with the STM trace (Hulme et al., 1991; Schweikert, 1993). This process, called "redintegration" of STM traces, is assumed to be more successful for words than nonwords as nonwords, by definition, have no matching lexical representations in the language knowledge base; this redintegration process will also be easier for high frequency words as their lexical representations are more familiar and can be retrieved more quickly (e.g., Poirier & Saint-Aubin, 1996; Saint-Aubin & Poirier, 2005; however, see Stuart & Hulme, 2000, and Hulme, Stuart, Brown, & Morin, 2003, for inter-item associative accounts of the word frequency effect). Finally, high imageability, concrete words will be reconstructed more easily than abstract words because they have more unique and stable representations at the semantic level (Walker & Hulme, 1999).

However, there is no compelling evidence for a position that considers that activation of language representations occurs only at the moment of retrieval and output in STM. First, even nonword recall is influenced by subtle sublexical phonotactic knowledge. Gathercole, Frankish, Pickering, and Peaker (1999) showed that immediate serial recall performance for nonword lists is higher for nonwords containing phoneme combinations that are frequent in the native language of the participants. Although this effect could also be explained by redintegration processes at a sublexical level consisting in access to statistical knowledge relative to phoneme co-occurrence probabilities (Gathercole et al., 1999; Thorn & Frankish, 2005), we should note that phonotactic frequency effects are present in many speech perception tasks such as minimal pair discrimination and rhyme judgment (e.g., Vitevitch & Luce, 1998, 1999) and thus are likely to facilitate not only retrieval, but also encoding of high phonotactic frequency nonwords. Thorn, Gathercole, and Frankish (2005) reached a similar conclusion, based on the fact that not only partially correct, but also completely incorrect items recalled in a STM task, are influenced by word frequency and phonotactic frequency effects. The redintegration hypothesis would only predict an influence of these variables on partially correct items or the proportion of items correctly recalled.

Second, the influence of language knowledge on list recall seems to be a highly automatic and obligatory phenomenon. We recently showed that recall of nonwords is influenced by a new phonotactic grammar that was learned via a 30-minute incidental learning paradigm just prior to the nonword recall task. In a first phase of our experiment, we exposed 8-year-old children and adults to a 30-minute auditory continuous sequence of CV-syllables (e.g., *pumotitalapimulamutilomotulopipumulapimo* . . . ; Majerus, Van der Linden, Mulder, Meulemans, & Peters, 2004a; see also Botvinick & Bylsma, 2005, for similar results). The combination of phonemes and syllables within the sequence was not random but rather was governed by an artificial phonotactic grammar the participants ignored. The participants were even encouraged not to listen actively to the sequence of CV-syllables but to concentrate on a complex colouring task they had to perform while they were exposed to the CV-syllable sequence presented via headphones. After this incidental learning condition, the participants were presented a nonword repetition task including nonwords that were either legal (e.g., *pimutalopupi*) or illegal (e.g., *lutomapoluli*) with respect to the artificial phonotactic grammar. We observed that nonword recall was significantly higher for legal than illegal nonwords, despite the fact that the participants were not aware of the artificial phonotactic grammar. Furthermore, the advantage of legal over illegal nonwords was equivalent for both the children and adults. This study shows that verbal STM performance directly reflects very subtle changes that occur in the sublexical network of input phonological representations.

Third, there is now considerable evidence that lexical and sublexical language knowledge influences verbal STM performance at a very early stage of cognitive development. Brock and Jarrold (2004) as well as Majerus, Poncelet, Greffe, and Van der Linden (2006c) showed significant lexicality effects already in 4-year-old children using either recognition or immediate serial recall tasks. Furthermore, these effects seem to be stable across ages: Majerus and Van der Linden (2003) showed that lexicality, phonotactic frequency, word frequency and word imageability effects in immediate serial recall tasks are of comparable size in 6-year-olds, in 8-year-olds, in 10-year-olds, in adolescents and in adults.

In sum, the experimental and developmental data presented here show that language knowledge influences verbal STM performance in a very direct, automatic, obligatory and developmentally invariant way. Temporary activation of the language knowledge base during verbal STM tasks should be considered as a fundamental property of verbal STM processing.

Neuropsychological data

At the neuropsychological level, deep dysphasia, a severe form of repetition-type conduction aphasia, is probably the most spectacular illustration of the complex interplay between temporary activation of language representations and verbal STM capacity.

Deep dysphasia is characterized by severely impaired digit span (often less than 3), and difficulties in single word repetition, with marked lexicality and word imageability effects. Deep dysphasia occurs as a result of lesions to the left temporo-parietal junction, in the context of a cerebral vascular accident (CVA) or a neurodegenerative disease (e.g., Majerus, Lekeu, Van der Linden, & Salmon, 2001; N. Martin & Saffran, 1992). The most characteristic feature is the appearance of semantic paraphasias in single word repetition; for example, the patient may repeat "Tuesday" or "tomorrow" when presented with the target stimulus "Monday". Although the impairment of these patients can be interpreted as resulting from the conjunction of a verbal STM impairment and multiple impairments of lexical and sublexical repetition routes (e.g., Katz & Goodglass, 1990), a very elegant interpretation forwarded by N. Martin and Saffran (1992) relates deep dysphasia to a pathologically increased decay rate of activated phonological, lexical and semantic language representations. Following this model, in repetition tasks for auditorily presented verbal information, phonological levels of representations are activated earlier than lexical and semantic representations, and so they have more time to decay; in the case of a pathologically increased decay rate, the phonological representations may have decayed almost completely at the moment of response output; in that case, response selection will be based on those levels of representations that are still somewhat active at the moment of recall, i.e. lexical and semantic representations. This is then supposed to lead to semantic paraphasias as well as to marked lexicality and word imageability effects in single word repetition, as well as to difficulties in other single word processing tasks such as picture naming and auditory lexical decision.

Hence, the theoretical framework forwarded by N. Martin and Saffran (1992) relates the spectacular single word processing impairments observed in deep dysphasia to an STM impairment. More generally, for N. Martin and Saffran (1992), verbal STM is simply the emergent property of the temporary activation and decay of representations within a language network including sublexical (phonemic), lexical and semantic levels of representation. For example, during an immediate serial recall task for word lists, upon presentation of the list, the different words will successively activate their corresponding phonological, lexical and semantic levels of presentation. This activation will last for a short time (e.g., several seconds), and then decay. The longer the list, the higher the probability the temporary activation will have decayed completely at the moment of recall, leading to poor performance for long STM lists. One might expect in that case that the first items of the memory list should be most decayed, leading to especially poor recall of first items. This is contrary to the standard primacy effects observed in immediate serial recall. N. Martin and Saffran have accounted for the presence of primacy effects by deeper and stronger semantic processing for first relative to later presented items, while recency effects are related to greater reliance on phonological levels of activation which have decayed to a lesser extent for later than earlier presented items (see also later section on the "item–order" distinction for further discussion on serial order processing within language-activation-based STM models).

If the decay rate is pathologically increased, the duration of temporary activation of language representations will be much shorter, and activation for most of the words will have decayed at the moment of recall, even for short STM lists. Similarly, if the stimulus lists contain items with weak or no lexical and semantic representations, such as nonwords, STM performance will also be drastically reduced as performance will rely only on activation of the phonological (phonemic) level of representation which will decay very fast if it does not receive stabilizing feedback from lexical levels of representation.

One of the most obvious arguments commonly invoked against language-based STM models such as the N. Martin and Saffran model is that language impairments and STM impairments should necessarily co-occur, given that both are determined by the same cognitive substrate. In that case, the many patients presenting apparently selective verbal STM impairments but no (at least measurable) language impairments should in principle invalidate such unitary frameworks (e.g., Basso, Spinnler, Vallar, & Zanobio, 1982; McCarthy & Warrington, 1987; Silveri & Cappa, 2003; Vallar & Baddeley, 1984). However, given the gradual and dynamic nature of the N. Martin and Saffran model, it is possible to consider a wide range of pathological decay rates, with only the severest ones affecting performance in both single word and STM processing tasks. With milder increases in decay rate, temporary activation could last long enough to maintain relatively normal single word processing performance but could yet lead to significant verbal STM impairments as here information has to be maintained longer than in single word processing tasks. However, if this is true there should be at least a correlation between the severity of span impairment and the presence of single word processing difficulties in patients with STM deficits. In other words, following the N. Martin and Saffran framework, the patients with the most severe STM impairments should also show difficulties at the level of single word processing.

In order to check this prediction, I reviewed STM and single word processing performance for published STM patients where sufficient data were available with respect to single word processing tasks. The publications I examined are presented in Table 12.1. For single word processing measures, I included single word repetition, object naming and auditory lexical decision. I also checked for single nonword repetition and perceptual-phonological processing abilities. As can be seen in Table 12.1, patients with the lowest digit and word spans were more likely to present naming and single word repetition deficits. Similarly, difficulties in phoneme perception and discrimination were more likely in patients with the lowest STM spans. Finally, single (short) nonword repetition was preserved only in some patients with a digit span of 3 or higher. In order to provide a more thorough analysis of these descriptive data, I conducted Spearman rank order correlations between the span and language measures. As shown in Table 12.2, these correlations were all significant, except those between word span and picture naming. Thus, overall, this pattern of results is generally consistent with the hypothesis that the severity of the STM impairment reflects the severity of a decay impairment of temporary language activation, and that single word and nonword processing is affected in the cases with the most important STM impairment, i.e. those with the greatest pathological increase in decay rates of the activation of language representations.

Table 12.1 Digit/word span and single word processing abilities in published cases with selective STM deficits

Patient	Lesion	Digit span	Word span	Single word repetition	Single nonword repetition	Phonological discrimination/ identification	Object naming
NC (N. Martin & Saffran, 1992)	Temporo-parietal L	< 2	< 2	–	–	+ (– after delay)	–
MC (Caramazza et al., 1981)	Temporo-parietal L	< 2	< 2	–	?	?	+
RAN (McCarthy & Warrington, 1987)	Parietal L	2	2	–	?	?	–
ER (Vallar et al., 1990)	Temporo-parietal L; insula L	2	2	–	–	–	–
SC (Trojano et al., 1992)	Temporo-parietal L	2	2	–	–	–	–
NHA (McCarthy & Warrington, 1987)	L middle cerebral artery territory	2	2	+	?	?	+
LS (Strub & Gardner, 1974)	Parieto-occipital L	2	2	+	–	–	–
EA (Friedrich et al., 1984)	Posterior temporal, superior and inferior parietal L	2	2	+	–	–	+
WH (Warrington et al., 1971)	Temporal and inferior parietal L	3	2	?	?	?	+
TI (Saffran & Martin, 1990)	Temporo-parietal L; inferior frontal R	3	2	+	?	–	+
EDE (Berndt & Mitchum, 1990)	Temporo-parietal R	3	2	+	–	+	(–)
IL (Saffran & Marin, 1975)	Posterior parietal L	3	2	+	+	+	?
ML (Freedman & Martin, 2001)	Frontal and parietal operculum; temporal operculum L	?	2	?	–	+	?

Patient	Lesion location						
AK (Freedman & Martin, 2001)	Lacunar infarct L	?	3	?	−	+	?
GR (Freedman & Martin, 2001)	Fonto-temporo-parietal L	?	3	?	+	+	?
AB (Freedman & Martin, 2001)	Frontal L	?	3	?	−	−	?
RR (Bisiacchi et al., 1989)	Temporo-parietal L	3	3	+	−	+	?
KF (Warrington et al., 1971)	Superior and inferior parietal L	3	3	?	?	?	(−)
CN (Saffran & Martin, 1990)	Inferior, middle and superior temporal L	4	2	+	+	+	+
JB (Warrington et al., 1971)	Posterior temporal and inferior parietal L	4	3	?	?	?	+
PV (Basso et al., 1982)	Inferior frontal, parietal and superior temporal L	4	3	+	?	?	+
DC (Majerus et al., 2004b)	Superior temporal L	4	3	+	−	+	+
SR (Baddeley, 1993)	?	4	4	+	+[a]	?	+
JPH (Majerus et al., 2004b)	Superior temporal L	4	3	+	−	+	+
MS (R. C. Martin et al., 1999)	Temporal L	?	4	+	+	+	− −
Case (Takayama et al., 2004)	Posterior superior temporal L	4	?	+	?	+	+
TG (Majerus et al., 2004b)	Superior temporal LR	5	4	+	+	+	+

[a] Perfect for short nonwords, but severely deficient for nonwords longer than 3 syllables.

+ Normal performance; − impaired performance; − − severely impaired performance; ? no information available.

Table 12.2 Spearman rank order correlations between STM and single word processing measures for STM patients reported in Table 12.1

	Word repetition	Nonword repetition	Phonological discrimination	Picture naming
Digit span	**.69**	**.86**	**.83**	**.53**
Word span	**.58**	**.61**	**.53**	.18

Significant correlations ($p < .05$) in bold font.

However, our analysis does not rule out the possibility of an alternative interpretation. It could also be the case that the very low spans in patients with a digit span of 2 or less are in fact due to the conjunction of an STM impairment and perceptual deficits as all these patients have impaired performance on phoneme categorization or discrimination tasks. On the other hand, one could argue that the difficulties in the perceptual tasks are in fact due to very fast decay rates of perceptual-phonological representations: even a minimal pair discrimination or phoneme categorization task requires that the perceptual representation is maintained for a small amount of time, the time necessary to reach a match–mismatch decision between two phonological representations. We know that at least in one case, NC, the perceptual problems could be related to a phonological decay impairment as NC's performance in perceptual tasks was most impaired when inserting a delay between the stimulus and the response (N. Martin & Saffran, 1992). We also know that patient NC (N. Martin, Saffran, & Dell, 1996), who initially presented a pattern of deep dysphasia (difficulties in single word repetition and naming), showed no single word processing difficulties anymore after 2 years of recovery, despite still having an impaired verbal STM span. However, when the delay between the stimulus and the response was increased, difficulties in single word repetition and naming reappeared, with marked lexicality effects.

Finally one could argue that the correlation between STM and language impairments in STM patients is simply the consequence of the overall extent of the brain lesion and the anatomical proximity of language processing areas in the posterior superior temporal lobe and STM storage areas in the inferior parietal lobe, leading to a co-occurrence of language and STM processing deficits in the case of larger lesions. Unfortunately, lesion reports for many of the published cases are not very detailed. Nevertheless we can see in Table 12.1 that some patients with very low spans and associated language disorders, for example RAN, have a relatively focalized lesion only in the left parietal lobe while other patients presenting much larger spans and no associated language impairments have much more extensive lesions (e.g., PV, JB, CN; Table 12.1).

In any case, this review of the co-occurrence of STM and single word processing deficits shows that there is a very intimate relationship between the severity of the STM impairment and single word processing abilities.

Most importantly, this association is much stronger than the isolated presentation of the different STM patients might suggest: while single word processing and STM processing can appear to dissociate in a single patient, single word processing impairments are nevertheless most likely in the patients with the lowest STM spans, and much less likely in patients with higher spans. This is most apparent when considering the different published single case studies of STM patients at a group level.

Neuroimaging data

Recent neuroimaging data also suggest a close relationship between neural substrates implicated in verbal STM and phonological processing. Using positron emission tomography (PET) brain imaging, Collette et al. (2001) showed that middle temporal gyri are more activated when four words have to be maintained in STM and then repeated relative to a control condition where the same words are repeated using a single word repetition procedure. These data suggest that middle temporal gyri implicated in lexical phonological processing are actively recruited during verbal STM tasks. Furthermore, in STM patients DC and JPH reported earlier (Table 12.1), we observed decreased metabolism in right or bilateral superior temporal cortex during a verbal STM task (immediate serial recall of 4-word sequences) (Majerus et al., 2003).

However, we should note that the recruitment of brain areas in the temporal lobe is not the only cortical activation during verbal STM tasks. In accordance with patient lesion data, different sites of activation within the left inferior parietal lobes have indeed been documented in brain imaging studies in healthy adults, although their respective function in verbal STM tasks still remains uncertain. A more dorsal region, buried deep into the intraparietal sulcus (IPS), has been shown to respond to STM load effects (i.e., greater activation for greater STM load) (e.g., Becker, MacAndrew, & Fiez, 1999; Ravizza, Delgado, Chein, Becker, & Fiez, 2004). Activation of a more inferior and ventral region, closer to the damaged region reported in verbal STM patients, has been observed less consistently and seems not to respond to verbal STM load (e.g., Paulesu, Frith, & Frackowiak, 1993; Paulesu et al., 1996; Ravizza et al., 2004; Salmon et al., 1996; Zatorre, Evans, Meyer, & Gjedde, 1992). Finally, activation in inferior prefrontal areas is also commonly observed and has been ascribed to articulatory rehearsal of STM traces (Paulesu et al., 1993; Salmon et al., 1996). I will come back to this issue later.

The item–order distinction

In sum, there is a vast amount of experimental, neuropsychological and brain imaging data suggesting that verbal STM and language processing are intimately related. In the light of the data presented as so far, we could easily deduce that, *ultimately*, verbal STM is simply and only temporary activation of language representations. However, such a strong version of the "STM as temporary language activation" hypothesis probably does not hold. In verbal STM tasks, decay of temporarily activated language representations can explain difficulties at the level of the retention of phonological and semantic information. However, phonological and semantic information is not the only kind of information that has to be retained: in STM tasks, items are typically presented in an ordered sequence and they have to be recalled in the same order. Hence retention of order information is also a critical component of verbal STM performance. Language activation and decay frameworks, such as discussed here, do not include a precise mechanism that would allow the encoding of serial order presentation, i.e. the association of each item with a given list position, even if these models propose a mechanism accounting for more general primacy and recency effects, by attributing a recall advantage for earlier presented items to more prolonged and deeper semantic processing and an advantage for later presented items to a lesser extent of phonological decay. Furthermore, brain imaging findings suggest the systematic recruitment of brain regions outside the language processing areas during verbal STM tasks, showing once again that immediate serial recall cannot be reduced only to temporary activation of language representations. But that does not mean that temporary activation of language representations is not involved in STM processing. This is precisely the point of the current argument. In the following sections, I will argue that short-term storage of sequences of verbal items is best explained by a hybrid model, where a significant part of STM storage is related to temporary activation of language representations, while the other part takes place in a dedicated STM system storing mainly serial order information. Before considering the data that support such a position, I will briefly review recent theoretical models that distinguish item and order processing modules. A more detailed presentation of these models can also be found in the chapters by Gupta and by Page and Norris (this volume).

A brief overview of theoretical models distinguishing item and order information

A number of recent computational models of STM consider distinct processes for coding and storing serial order and item information. For example, Burgess and Hitch (1999) proposed a model in which item information is directly coded within the language network, via activation of lexical and phoneme nodes. These nodes are connected to a context system whose state changes over time and which is implicated in encoding serial order information: each item activated in the language network is associated with a different state of the context system. At the moment of recall, the different states are reactivated, as well as the different items that were associated with each state. Similar models, although varying with respect to the precise mechanisms that instantiate coding and storage of serial order information, have been proposed and share a common property: distinct codes for item and serial order information (e.g., Burgess & Hitch, 2005; Brown, Preece, & Hulme, 2000; Henson, 1998; Gupta, 2003). These models are in line with the more general idea that during immediate serial recall, list and order information is encoded in a specialized STM system while codes for item information are directly implemented as temporary activation of language representations. However, not all models share this view. Some computational models of immediate serial recall assume that storage of serial order information is intrinsic to the activation strength of the item representations themselves (e.g., Farrell & Lewandowsky, 2002, 2004). For example, Farrell and Lewandowsky (2002) showed that the serial order for item sequences can be represented within an auto-associative network in which successive items are encoded with decreasing associative strength and recalled items are suppressed. In this type of model, no external coding mechanism is needed to represent serial order information. Page and Norris (1998) also proposed a similar primacy gradient governing the activation level of successive item representations for simulating the encoding of serial order information in immediate serial recall tasks. It should be noted that the latter model is nevertheless closer to the first line of models, distinguishing order and language processing mechanisms, given that Page and Norris's primacy gradient is considered an external mechanism, contrary to Farrell and Lewandowsky's framework. In the following sections, I will report experimental, developmental, and neuropsychological evidence that favours the separation of codes and capacities implicated in STM for item information and STM for serial order information. I will also show that these capacities have distinct relationships with language knowledge and language learning.

Item/order: Recent data from experimental and developmental studies

A number of experimental studies suggest that codes for item and serial order information are indeed distinct. Some of these studies have shown that recall of item and order information is differentially affected by phonological similarity of the items within a STM list. For example, Fallon, Groves, and Tehan (1999) decomposed immediate serial recall performance for rhyming and non-rhyming word lists as a function of item and order errors. They observed that item recall (i.e., the number of items recalled independently of correct serial position) was highest for rhyming lists while order accuracy (i.e., the number of items recalled in correct serial position as a proportion of items recalled regardless of position) was highest for non-rhyming lists (for similar findings see also Bjork & Healy, 1974; Nairne & Kelley, 2004; Nimmo & Roodenrys, 2004; Wickelgren, 1965). Nairne and Kelly, using estimates of item and order recall based on the process dissociation procedure developed by Jacoby (1991, 1998), also confirmed these results, obtaining highest estimates for item recall for phonologically similar word lists while the highest estimates for order recall were observed for phonologically dissimilar word lists. Thus phonological similarity enhances item recall but decreases recall of serial order information. Further evidence stems from studies that have dissociated STM for item and serial order information, by using tasks designed to specifically measure the retention of these two different types of information. For example, Henson, Hartley, Burgess, Hitch, and Flude (2003) used serial order and item probe recognition tasks. The serial order probe recognition task was similar to tasks previously used by Allport (1984) as well as Gathercole, Service, Hitch, Adams, and Martin (1999) and comprised a sequential presentation of a list of letters, followed by the simultaneous presentation of a new list containing the same letters. If the second list differed from the original list, it was only by the inversion of two adjacent items. For the item probe recognition task, a list of letters was presented sequentially, and was followed by a single probe item that either was or was not part of the list. Henson et al. showed that articulatory suppression and the presence of irrelevant speech during the tasks had a greater detrimental effect on the serial order probe recognition task than on the item probe recognition task. Related findings were observed by McElree and Dosher (1993), using a judgment of recency probe recognition task and an item probe recognition task, both for visually presented letter sequences. The authors showed that a slow, serial process characterized retrieval dynamics (as measured by a speed–accuracy trade-off analysis of response accuracy and timing) during probe recognition for order information. On the other hand, retrieval dynamics for recognition of item information were characterized by a fast, parallel process (see also Murdock & Franklin, 1984, for similar results).

If we consider that item information is supposed to be stored primarily via temporary activation of language representations, then we can also make a prediction with respect to the influence of psycholinguistic factors on immediate serial recall performance. We should expect that linguistic variables such as word frequency, word imageability or lexicality should influence primarily item recall but not order recall. There are a number of experimental data suggesting that this is indeed the case. For example, Saint-Aubin and Poirier (1999) showed that during immediate serial recall of words with varying degrees of semantic similarity and word frequency, only item recall was influenced by semantic similarity and lexical frequency. No effect of linguistic variables was observed for order recall. These data suggest that lexical and semantic knowledge mainly supports item recall, but much less order recall (see also Murdock, 1976; Poirier & Saint-Aubin, 1996; Saint-Aubin & Poirier, 2000). Similarly, the item recall advantage for phonologically similar word lists mentioned above can also be interpreted within language-based accounts of item STM. Many psycholinguistic studies suggest that representations for phonologically similar words tend to be grouped together in the space of lexical phonological representations (the so-called phonological neighbourhood effect; Vitevitch & Luce, 1999). Due to lexical co-activation of similar sounding words and their sharing of a number of phonological segments (see, e.g., Dell, 1986), retrieval of phonologically similar item representations will be facilitated. However, the encoding and storage process of serial order information will be somewhat blurry precisely due to the phonological proximity of the words: the serial order mechanisms will have difficulty clearly associating a unique serial position to a word that shares many phonological segments with other words presented at earlier and later serial positions (see Gupta & MacWhinney, 1997, for a similar explanation).

Further evidence for a distinction between STM for item and serial order information can also be derived from recent studies examining the relationship between STM for item and STM for serial order information and learning of new word forms. It is widely accepted that there is a strong relationship between verbal STM capacity and vocabulary development or novel word learning (e.g., Gathercole, Hitch, Service, & Martin, 1997; Gupta, 2003; Papagno & Vallar, 1995). However, the question whether this relationship is specific to STM for serial order or item information has not yet been specifically explored. Furthermore, there is still controversy whether the relationship between verbal STM capacity and vocabulary development in children reflects a causal relationship (i.e., verbal STM capacity determines vocabulary development) or whether the relationship is simply an epiphenomenon of the fact that performance in verbal STM and vocabulary tasks is determined by a common factor (i.e., the level of segmentation and the precision of phonological representations of the language network) (e.g., Bowey, 1996; Brown & Hulme, 1996; Fowler, 1991; Metsala, 1999). In a first developmental study, we presented to 60 typically developing children (aged 4 to 6 years) a serial order reconstruction task and a delayed single nonword repetition task, as well as a receptive vocabulary measure (French version of the Peabody Picture Vocabulary Test, Dunn, Thériault-Whalen, & Dunn, 1993) (Majerus et al., 2006c). The serial order reconstruction task had been designed to maximize retention capacities for serial order information: the stimulus pool consisted of seven highly familiar monosyllabic animal names presented in sequences ranging from two to seven items. After the auditory presentation of each sequence, the children received cards on which only those animals that had been presented in the auditory sequence were displayed. The children had to reconstruct the order of presentation of the animals using the cards. A second task maximized retention of item information: single nonwords (syllable structure: CVC) were presented and had to be repeated after a filled delay. This task maximized processing and storage of phonological item information as each item was new and unfamiliar on any trial. Serial order requirements were kept to a minimum in that only a single item had to be repeated; however, they were not completely abolished given that retention of order information at the phoneme level was necessary. They nevertheless were minimized in the sense that the phoneme sequence was predictable because all items had the same monosyllabic CVC structure – beginning with a consonant, followed by a vowel, and ending with another consonant – so mainly phoneme identity had to be retained to "fill in" the different consonant and vowel positions.

Correlation analysis showed that both item and order STM measures were associated with vocabulary knowledge (after partialling out age and estimates of non-verbal intelligence). Multiple regression analysis revealed that the serial order STM measure was an independent predictor of vocabulary knowledge in 4- and 6-year-olds, while the item STM measure was an independent predictor in 5-year-olds. These results suggest that there is a specific association between serial order retention capacities and vocabulary development at least in 4- and 6-year-olds. The absence of a specific relationship in 5-year-olds should, however, be considered with caution due to the reduced sample sizes when considering the three age groups separately ($n = 20$). An additional interesting result was that item and order STM followed different developmental trajectories: while there was a linear increase in performance for the serial order STM measures between 4 and 6 years of age, performance for the delayed item repetition task was stable at ages 4 and 5, and then sharply increased between ages 5 and 6 (Figure 12.1). In sum, all these data confirm that item and order STM reflect distinct capacities with different maturational rates and independent relations with vocabulary development.

Similar data were obtained in a sample with adult participants. Majerus, Poncelet, Elsen, & Van der Linden (2006b) examined the relationship between serial order and item retention capacities and novel word learning in 60 adults. Serial order STM was assessed using a serial order reconstruction task very similar to the task described in the previous paragraph. Digit sequences were used as stimulus material. In order to diminish item processing requirements as far as possible, the digits that were to be presented were known in advance: for sequences of length 4, only the digits 1, 2, 3 and 4 were presented; for sequences of length 5, only the digits 1, 2, 3, 4 and 5 were presented, and so forth for the higher list lengths. At recall, the participants received cards on which the digits that had been presented were printed, and they just had to put the digits in the order they had been presented using the cards provided. Item STM was assessed using an item probe recognition task: word lists of increasing length were presented, followed by a probe word. The participants had to decide whether the probe word shared the rhyme with one of the words in the list or not. We also computed the number of item errors from an immediate serial recall task in order to obtain an additional estimate of item STM performance. The version of the immediate serial recall task we used in this study maximized item retention requirements since the lists were constructed by sampling items from an open pool without replacement. The novel word

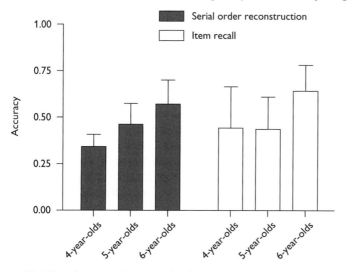

Figure 12.1 Developmental trajectories for performance on serial order reconstruction and item recall STM tasks. Note the linear increase in performance for recall performance on the serial order reconstruction task in the three age groups. By contrast, performance for the item recall task (single nonword delayed repetition) is stable at ages 4 and 5 and then suddenly increases at age 6 (adapted from Majerus et al., 2006c).

learning task was a paired associate word–nonword learning task: four word–nonword pairs were presented; the participants had to learn the nonword associated with each cue word in 5 trials. We observed a significant correlation between performance on the serial order reconstruction task and novel word learning capacity (number of correct novel words recalled over the 5 learning trials); no significant correlation was obtained between novel learning capacity and either the item probe recognition measure or the item error measure of the word list recall task. These results once again support the role of STM capacities for sequence information in learning new phonological information. More generally, they support the specificity of STM for serial order and item information.

Our data are in accordance with the theoretical models mentioned above, distinguishing separate mechanisms for order and item encoding (e.g., Burgess & Hitch, 1999; Gupta, 2003; Page & Norris, 1998). Gupta (2003) proposed that, when learning new word forms, it is the serial order information stored in the STM system that makes it possible to reactivate and "re-play" the sequence of phonemes of the new word form, gradually leading to a stable long-term phonological representation (via Hebbian adjustments between the phoneme nodes and a new lexical node). Hence, the fact that we observed a specific correlation between serial order STM capacity and vocabulary development in children as well as novel word learning in adults supports this position, suggesting that there is a causal relationship between serial order STM measures and language learning. On the other hand, the specific correlation observed between item STM capacity (single nonword repetition) and vocabulary development in children could reflect the common dependence upon activation of lexical and sublexical representations in the language network, as well as the degree of segmentation of these representations. However, in order to provide even stronger arguments in favour of this position, we need to use longitudinal study designs in future studies and to show that serial order but not item STM capacity at age T predicts vocabulary performance at age T + 1 and that vocabulary performance at age T predicts item but not serial order STM performance at age T + 1. Meanwhile, the present data clearly indicate that the distinction of item and order recall capacities could help to clarify the question of the causal nature of verbal STM capacity with regard to vocabulary development.

Item/order: Recent neuropsychological data

There are also recent neuropsychological data supporting a distinction between processes involved in STM for item and serial order information, while demonstrating at the same time the strong dependency of item STM upon language activation. In a first study, Majerus, Glaser, Van der Linden, and Eliez (2006a) showed that children (aged 8–12 years) presenting with a 22q11.2 chromosomal microdeletion (a major aetiology of velo-cardio-facial syndrome) had chronological age-appropriate performance in immediate serial recall tasks when counting the number of items recalled independently of correct serial position. However, when using a strict serial recall criterion, seven of the eight children we studied presented impaired performance, due to an abnormally high rate of order errors. Half of the children were also impaired on a serial order short-term recognition task (digit sequences of increasing length were presented, followed by a probe sequence containing the same digits in the same order, except for two digits whose position was exchanged in 50% of the trials). In a second study, we re-explored serial order and item STM capacities in a sample including this time both children and adults ($N = 11$) with a 22q11.2 microdeletion (Majerus, Van der Linden, Braissand, & Eliez (2006c). We also included control groups individually matched for verbal mental age (younger typically developing children). The serial order STM tasks included a serial order reconstruction task for digit sequences (same task as above) and a serial order recognition task for word sequences.[1] Item STM was measured using a single nonword delayed repetition task (as previously described) and a nonword probe recognition task.[2] Relative to the matched control groups, all participants with a 22q11.2 deletion (except one) showed preserved performance for both item STM measures. However, for the serial order STM measures, all participants (except two) with a 22q11.2 deletion showed impaired performance.

A reverse dissociation has been observed in patients suffering from semantic dementia, a neurodegenerative disease affecting primarily the temporal lobes. By conducting a case study in two patients with semantic dementia, we observed a very unusual profile in immediate serial recall of word lists: the vast majority of errors were item errors (ranging from 41% to 90%) while order errors were virtually non-existent (range: 0–8%) (Majerus, Norris, & Patterson, 2007b). This profile in error percentages was in striking contrast to performance observed in controls. Here, order errors were predominant (range: 16–83%) while item errors were much less frequent (range: 0–33%). In other words, nearly everything the patients recalled was recalled in correct serial position, but they recalled fewer correct items. Item errors were intrusions and phonologically related nonword errors. The increased rate of item errors was most likely due to loss of lexical and semantic knowledge: the neurodegenerative process in semantic dementia starts by affecting semantic representations, leading to progressive loss of word knowledge. Hence, for the patients with semantic dementia, the word items were likely to be less familiar than for control participants, and in some cases, they were probably more like nonwords than words. In that case, language support from lexical and semantic levels of language representations will be less efficient during STM tasks. In sum, the results observed in these two patients with semantic dementia provide further evidence for the strong interaction between language representations and item recall in verbal STM.

Item/order: Recent neuroimaging data

Finally, neuroimaging studies also begin to hint at distinct cerebral correlates underlying processing of serial order and item information. Following the theoretical framework outlined here, STM for phonological item information should recruit language processing areas given that we consider that storage of item information is related to temporary activation of language representations. With respect to STM for serial order, a potential candidate region could be the left inferior parietal lobe; this region has been considered to support the function of a dedicated STM storage system, is impaired in most patients with selective STM deficits and should, in our theoretical view, mainly serve to store serial order information.

With respect to language activation during STM tasks, I have already mentioned the PET study by Collette et al. (2001) showing that an area in the left middle temporal gyrus and the posterior part of the superior temporal gyrus, close to the angular gyrus, are significantly more activated when comparing word list to nonword list recall, relative to single word versus single nonword repetition. A number of studies have shown that these areas underlie phonological, lexical and semantic processing of speech stimuli (Binder et al., 2000; Demonet et al., 1992; Demonet, Price, Wise, & Frackowiak, 1994; Howard et al., 1992). This increased activation of a region supporting lexical and/or semantic language processing, during a verbal STM task, is in line with our hypotheses that consider temporary activation of language representations as being a major determining factor of STM performance. Similarly, Majerus et al. (2005b) also showed that the posterior superior temporal gyrus is involved in processing and temporarily holding unfamiliar phonological information, such as implicated in repeating single nonwords. Studies using different techniques and methodologies (event-related potentials, EEG coherence analysis) also showed the implication of language-related areas during the retention interval of STM tasks. For example, Ruchkin, Grafman, Cameron, and Berndt (2003) showed a persistence of EEG activity during the retention interval in posterior temporo-parietal cortex that is also involved in the initial perception and comprehension of the verbal stimuli. This maintenance of activation in language processing areas during the retention interval was furthermore driven by activation in the prefrontal cortex.

However, the results of these studies have to be considered with caution as they do not allow ascribing the activation of language processing during verbal STM tasks specifically to item STM. Other studies have tried to distinguish more specifically neural networks implicated in STM for item and serial order information. Using fMRI, Marshuetz, Smith, Jonides, DeGutis, and Chenevert (2000) and Henson, Burgess, and Frith (2000) compared short-term probe recognition for item and order information for short lists of visually presented consonants. Relative to short-term item recognition, both studies obtained greater activation in the bilateral intraparietal sulcus (as well as in premotor frontal areas) during short-term recognition of order information. No differential brain activation was observed for the short-term item recognition condition, relative to the order condition. It must be noted that there were a number of differences between the item and order STM conditions that make the interpretation of these results uncertain. In the study of Marshuetz et al., the item condition yielded significantly higher behavioural performance levels than the order condition. In the Henson et al. (2000) study, the item and order probe stimuli were not perfectly comparable as the probe array contained a probe sequence of the same length as the target sequence (6 consonants) while in the item condition, the probe array consisted of one single item (we should note that Henson et al.'s study design was motivated by slightly different theoretical questions than those of interest here). Hence, we cannot exclude the possibility that the differential activation observed in the intraparietal sulcus for the order STM condition in both studies actually might have reflected greater attentional load or executive demands rather than order processing. Finally, as I have already noted, neither of these two studies observed greater activation in language processing areas for the item STM condition relative to the order STM conditions. This negative finding could, however, be related to the fact that consonant lists were used in the two studies: the very simple phonological structure and the poor semantic content of single consonants does not put very high demands on phono-logical and semantic item retention processes.

In the light of these results, we recently re-explored the neural substrates of the item–order distinction in STM by using an fMRI task design that maximized retention requirements for both item and order information (Majerus et al., 2006d). As in Henson et al. (2000) and Marshuetz et al. (2000), we used probe recognition STM tasks implying the visual presentation of lists of verbal stimuli (four items in our case), immediately followed by probe stimuli probing either order or item information. However, unlike these studies, we used word stimuli instead of letters in order to be able to manipulate the phonological/orthographic proximity between the probe and the target stimuli and thus increase the difficulty of the item STM recognition condition. For the item condition, negative probes consisted of the presentation of a probe word which differed from the target item by a single consonant in the middle portion of the word (e.g., "poste" versus "porte"). For the order condition, probes consisted of the presentation of two adjacent items of the target list, either in the same order as in the target list, or in a reversed order. Behavioural data showed that task difficulty was fairly matched between the item and order conditions, as a mean level of accuracy of .87 was obtained for both conditions. We observed that both the order and item STM conditions activated the left intraparietal sulcus. When comparing the order and item STM conditions, the order condition yielded greater activation in the right intraparietal sulcus, right cerebellum and bilateral premotor cortex while the item condition activated more the superior temporal gyrus (superior temporal sulcus) and the left fusiform gyrus, these regions being associated, respectively, with phonological and orthographic processing (e.g., Binder et al., 2000; Bolger, Perfetti, & Schneider, 2005; Scott, Blank, Rosen, & Wise, 2000). Most importantly, functional connectivity analysis showed that during the order STM condition, the left intraparietal sulcus was functionally connected to the right intraparietal sulcus, the bilateral dorsal premotor cortex, the insula and the right cerebellum, while during the item STM condition the same region in the left intraparietal sulcus was functionally connected to the superior temporal gyrus, bilaterally. The results suggest that different cortical networks are implicated in STM for item and serial order information, but that the left intraparietal sulcus is equally involved in serial order and item recognition when the level of task difficulty is matched between both conditions. Overall, the data also confirm the implication of language processing areas in the temporal lobe during STM for item information.

More specifically, the parieto-fronto-cerebellar network implicated in STM for order information is likely to support a number of sub-processes necessary for encoding, maintenance and recognition of serial order information. The right and left parietal sulci have been involved in processing magnitude codes in number processing tasks (e.g., Chochon, Cohen, van de Moortele, & Dehaene, 1999). At a behavioural level, judgement of magnitude gives rise to distance effects (i.e., reaction times are shorter when the two items to be compared are more distant as in 56 vs. 19, as compared to 56 vs. 53) and is comparable to judgement of sequential order in verbal STM tasks. When judging which of two items A and B occurred first in an STM list, reaction times are also faster when the two items are more distant in the list (Henson et al., 2003; Marshuetz et al., 2000). Marshuetz et al. proposed that number and order processing share common representational codes, coding for magnitude, and that the IPS is the neural substrate of this cognitive process. Other neuroimaging data on time processing and episodic memory have also implicated the right IPS in retrieval of temporal order (Cabeza et al., 1997; Rao, Mayer, & Harrington, 2001). The prefrontal areas that were found to be functionally connected to the left IPS in the order STM condition were all dorsal premotor areas that had also been found active in the order conditions in the Marhshuetz et al. and Henson et al. studies. In the Henson et al. study, this was in fact the only region that remained significant when comparing the order probe recognition STM task to a different order probe recognition STM task that included a grouped presentation of the stimulus sequence.[3] With reference to the Burgess and Hitch (1999) model, Henson et al. (2000) had interpreted the activation of the left premotor cortex in the first order STM condition as underlying a regular timing signal that could store temporal order information; this regular timing signal was supposed to have been interrupted during the second, grouped order STM condition.

More generally, the role of the dorsolateral premotor areas as underlying the maintenance of sequential verbal information is also supported by a recent fMRI study from Cairo, Liddle, Woodward, & Ngan (2004) showing that these regions are active not only during the encoding phase, but also during the maintenance phase of a verbal STM paradigm (see also Fiez et al., 1996). Due to technical constraints, the studies by Majerus et al. (2006d), Henson et al. (2000) and Marshuetz et al. (2000) all used a blocked design, confounding brain activity for encoding, maintenance and retrieval phases. Future studies need to separate these different stages of STM processing, in order to show that the activity in the right IPS and the dorsal premotor cortex is specifically related to encoding and maintenance of serial order information, and that it does not reflect only serial order comparison processes at the stage of retrieval of information in STM.

Overall, the brain imaging data I have reviewed suggest that there are distinct neural substrates involved in STM for item and STM for serial order information, with a significant implication of language processing areas in the temporal lobe during STM for item information, and the recruitment of prefrontal and right parietal regions during STM for serial order information. Our study also suggests that the left intraparietal sulcus plays a more general role, intervening during both item and order STM. The possible role of the left intraparietal sulcus during STM tasks will be discussed in the Conclusions section.

Conclusions

The data presented in this chapter can be summarized in the following way: (1) experimental, developmental, neuropsychological and neuroimaging data show that STM for item information and STM for order information rely on distinct cognitive processes, on distinct capacities and on distinct neuro-anatomical substrates; (2) STM for item information shares many processes with language processing and reflects the organization of the semantic, lexical and sublexical networks that underlie language representations; (3) STM for item information includes temporary activation of language representations in the temporal lobes; (4) STM for order information is supported by a distinct network distributed over right fronto-parieto-cerebellar areas (although the relative specificity of these areas for serial order processing and their possible association with time encoding and magnitude processing await further empirical investigation).

However, although I have tried to convince the reader that item and order information rely on a subset of specific processes, our message should not be mistaken as implying that STM for item and order information would be two entirely independent systems. On the contrary, in order to be fully operational, all the different processes and networks have to work in close interaction, so that both types of information can be recalled in typical STM tasks. In order to make our perspective more explicit, I provide a graphical illustration of our perspective of the interplay between STM for item and order information in Figure 12.2. In accordance with other recent STM models, the core of our STM architecture is based on sublexical, lexical and semantic language representations (e.g., Brown et al., 2000; Burgess & Hitch, 1999; Gupta, 2003). Upon presentation of a list of words, these different levels of representations will be activated, maintain their activation over some small amount of time, and decay (very similar to the interactive spreading activation model of N. Martin and Saffran, 1992). This temporary activation of language representations ensures the encoding of sublexical and lexical phonological as well as semantic item information associated with the items presented. At the same time, word order information is encoded in a different system which is closely connected to language representations and which keeps track of the sequence of activation events in the sublexical, lexical and semantic networks (this system is conceptually similar to the phonological store component in the model by Gupta and MacWhinney (1997) or the context node system in the Burgess and Hitch (1999) model). In the case of nonwords, this interaction will be restricted to the sublexical network containing sublexical phonological information, such as phonemes and statistical knowledge about legal and frequent phoneme combinations (phonotactic knowledge). At this stage, our framework can be considered as a hybrid architecture between the interactive spreading activation model of N. Martin and Saffran (taking into account the strong interactions between language activation and item

(A) Attentional modulation directed towards order STM

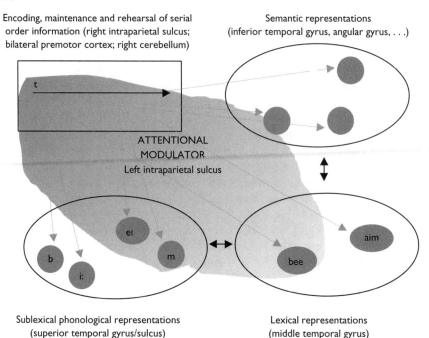

Encoding, maintenance and rehearsal of serial
order information (right intraparietal sulcus;
bilateral premotor cortex; right cerebellum)

Semantic representations
(inferior temporal gyrus, angular gyrus, . . .)

ATTENTIONAL
MODULATOR
Left intraparietal sulcus

Sublexical phonological representations
(superior temporal gyrus/sulcus)

Lexical representations
(middle temporal gyrus)

Figure 12.2 Schematic representation of components involved in STM for item and STM for order information and their possible neural substrates. Figure A represents STM functioning for tasks with explicit requirements on serial order recall. Figure B represents STM functioning for tasks with explicit requirements on item recall. In both cases, items are encoded via temporary activation phoneme nodes (sublexical phonological representations), lexical nodes and semantic nodes. Feedback activation between the different levels of language representation contributes to maintaining the initial activation for a short amount of time; this activation will then decay if not refreshed via articulatory rehearsal mechanisms (not represented here). In addition, upon presentation of each item (two in this illustration), item nodes activated in the language system and separated by a certain amount of time will be associated with a different timing signal, ensuring the encoding of serial order information (see, for example, Brown et al., 2000, and Burgess & Hitch, 1999, for a precise implementation of these timing signals). If task demands for serial order information are increased, then an attentional modulator (represented by the shaded cloud-like form) will increase allocation of attentional resources to the temporal order encoding mechanism; given that attentional resources are limited, a lesser amount of attentional resources will be available for the encoding of item information (Figure A). The situation is reversed when the task is more demanding at the level of item encoding and storage. This model assumes a trade-off between item and serial order short-term retention capacities, due to a common pool of limited attentional resources.

(B) Attentional modulation directed towards item STM

Encoding, maintenance and rehearsal of serial
order information (right intraparietal sulcus;
bilateral premotor cortex; right cerebellum)

Semantic representations
(inferior temporal gyrus, angular gyrus, . . .)

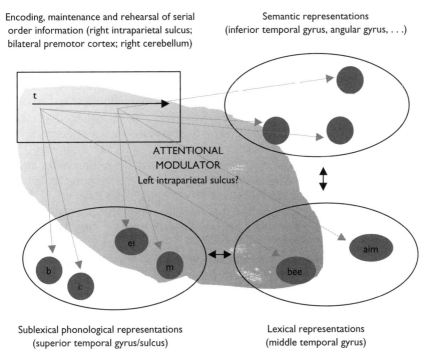

ATTENTIONAL
MODULATOR
Left intraparietal sulcus?

Sublexical phonological representations
(superior temporal gyrus/sulcus)

Lexical representations
(middle temporal gyrus)

STM), and the serial order STM models of Burgess and Hitch (1999) and
Gupta and MacWhinney (1997). However, relative to these models, a distinctive feature of our framework is the proposal of an attentional modulator. The role of this attentional modulator is to selectively or globally
"energize" the different systems involved in encoding and storing order and
item information. Hence, depending on task requirements, the attentional
modulator can selectively steer attentional resources towards either language representations and item processing (Figure 12.2B) or serial order
components and processing (Figure 12.2A) or both. This differential allocation of attentional resources will tend to privilege either item or order
STM performance, depending on task requirements.

Why do I propose this attention modulating component, in addition to
separate STM systems implicated in item and serial order processing? A first
argument can be derived from the neuroimaging results I have reported. We
did observe that a specific region in the inferior parietal lobe, the left
intraparietal sulcus, is activated in both order and item STM conditions. A
first straightforward explanation of this activation could be that this region
subtends a general phonological STM system, such as the phonological store
component of the Baddeley and Hitch (1974) working memory model, which
would store both item and order information. However, as we have seen, the

behavioural, neuropsychological and neuroimaging data presented in this chapter rather support a position that distinguishes separate STM capacities for item and order information. A further major argument against the position of the left intraparietal sulcus being the neural substrate of a general phonological store is that this region is also activated in visuo-spatial STM tasks, indicating that this region exerts a more general role than verbal STM storage (e.g., Becker et al., 1999; Ravizza et al., 2004). A number of recent studies have indeed suggested that this region is involved in attentional control (e.g., Collette et al., 2005; Ravizza et al., 2004) during STM tasks. The fact that this region also showed differential functional connectivity with distant brain regions during item and order STM conditions as a function of task instruction further strengthens our suggestion of an attentional control function: language processing areas in the temporal lobes were connected to this region during the item STM condition while regions in the right intraparietal sulcus, the premotor cortex and the cerebellum were functionally connected to the left intraparietal sulcus in the order STM condition.

Further supportive data for this interpretation of attentional control in the intraparietal sulcus can also be derived from recent fMRI studies by Todd, Fougnie, and Marois (2005) and Todd and Marois (2004) in the visual STM domain. The authors showed that activity in the right intraparietal sulcus increased with visual STM load while activity in the right temporo-parietal junction was suppressed by STM load. Todd et al. (2005) suggested that the role of the intraparietal sulcus is to enhance task-driven attention (which is necessary during STM tasks where multiple items have to be retained in an ordered sequence or in their respective spatial locations). This notion of task-related attentional control processes can also be compared to the concept of "focus of attention" proposed by Cowan (1995, 1999); within Cowan's framework, the "focus of attention" allows a limited number of activated long-term memory representations to remain available to consciousness for further use in a given STM task.

Finally, we recently reproduced our results on differential functional connectivity patterns for the left intraparietal sulcus with distant brain regions as a function of task instruction using a visual STM task (unfamiliar face sequences), showing preferential functional connectivity with a fronto-parieto-cerebellar network when encoding the order of presentation of the face stimuli, and preferential functional connectivity with a temporo-parietal network involved in face identity processing, when encoding item information (Majerus et al., 2007a).

Perspectives for future research

One remaining important question pertains to the patients with selective STM impairments and the nature of their verbal STM impairment. In the light of the distinction between STM for item and order information, it is currently not clear whether these patients present a specific deficit at the level of item retention capacities, order retention capacities or both. Given that most of these patients present lesions in the left temporo-parietal area close to the language processing areas (see Table 12.1), it is possible that these patients mainly have difficulties at the level of item retention. Furthermore, nearly all of these patients were initially aphasic, suggesting that their STM impairment is not completely independent from their language processing abilities. In this context, we recently completed a detailed cognitive neuropsychological analysis of a patient with a selective STM impairment related to a focal lesion in the posterior part of the superior temporal gyrus. The patient's STM impairment could indeed be related to difficulties at the level of item retention capacities, given that she had significant difficulties in maintaining single items in STM (Majerus, Van der Kaa, Renard, Poncelet, & Van der Linden, 2005a). A rehabilitation strategy aiming at increasing the duration of temporary activation of language representations for single items (via an intensive training pro- gramme based on delayed repetition of word or nonword stimuli) led to a significant improvement of digit span (from 3 to 5) and nonword span (from <1 to 3). However, our patient is certainly not representative of all STM patients, given that the lesions can be quite extensive, and include the left intraparietal sulcus or connections with the left intraparietal sulcus. Hence it could be very productive at both the empirical and theoretical levels to conduct a large-scale study examining item and order STM in patients with selective STM deficits. The possibility of attentional impair- ments in STM patients with lesions concerning more specifically the left intraparietal sulcus or superior parietal cortex should also be investigated.

Finally, we also need more detailed knowledge of how serial order is stored in verbal STM, how it is processed in the brain and how it is related to other cognitive domains such as number and time processing as well as learning of new verbal sequences. In this respect, the recent computational models of serial order STM that inspired a significant portion of this chapter should provide excellent starting points for guiding further experimental, neuropsychological and neuroimaging research on STM, serial order and their roots within language processing. The developmental studies presented in this chapter provide a very compelling illustration of how important it is to make a distinction between processes implicated in item and order STM, and how this distinction could lead to a better understanding of the complex relationships between verbal STM processing and language processing.

Acknowledgements

Steve Majerus is a postdoctoral researcher supported by the Fonds National de la Recherche Scientifique, Belgium.

Notes

1 In order to minimize item retention capacities, the words used were very familiar (e.g., tree, house, flower) and were repeatedly sampled from a highly restricted pool of items.
2 Nonword sequences ranging from two to five nonwords were presented, followed by probe stimuli; for each probe stimulus, the participants had to decide whether it had occurred in the nonword list or not; in order to increase task difficulty, the foils differed from the target nonword by a single phoneme.
3 In the first order STM condition, Henson et al. (2000) presented the six items of the STM list at regular inter-stimulus intervals, while in the grouped condition, there was a much larger inter-stimulus interval between the third and fourth items, giving an impression of grouped presentation of the first three items and grouped presentation of the last three items.

References

Allport, D. A. (1984). Auditory verbal short-term memory and conduction aphasia. In H. Bouma & D. G. Bouwhuis (Eds.), *Attention and performance X: Control and language processes* (pp. 351–364). Hillsdale, NJ: Erlbaum.

Baddeley, A. D. (1993). Short-term phonological memory and long-term learning: A single case study. *European Journal of Cognitive Psychology*, 5, 129–148.

Baddeley, A. D., & Hitch, G. J. (1974). Working memory. In G. H. Bower (Ed.), *The psychology of learning and motivation* (pp. 47–90). San Diego, CA: Academic Press.

Basso, A., Spinnler, H., Vallar, G., & Zanobio, M. E. (1982). Left hemisphere damage and selective impairment of auditory verbal short-term memory: A case study. *Neuropsychologia*, 20, 263–274.

Becker, J. T., MacAndrew, D. K., & Fiez, J. A. (1999). A comment on the functional localization of the phonological storage subsystem of working memory. *Brain and Cognition*, 41, 27–38.

Berndt, R. S., & Mitchum, C. C. (1990). Auditory and lexical information sources in immediate recall: Evidence from a patient with deficit to the phonological short-term store. In G.Vallar & T. Shallice (Eds.), *Neuropsychological impairments of short-term memory* (pp. 115–144). New York: Cambridge University Press.

Binder, J. R., Frost, J. A., Hammeke, T. A., Bellgowan, P. S. F., Springer, J. A., Kaufman, J. N., et al. (2000). Human temporal lobe activation by speech and nonspeech sounds. *Cerebral Cortex*, 10, 512–528.

Bisiacchi, P. S., Cipolotti, L., & Denes, G. (1989). Impairment in processing meaningless verbal material in several modalities: The relationship between short-term memory and phonological skills. *Quarterly Journal of Experimental Psychology*, 41A, 293–319.

Bjork, E. L., & Healy, A. F. (1974). Short-term order and item retention. *Journal of Verbal Learning and Verbal Behavior*, 13, 80–97.

Bolger, D. J., Perfetti, C. A., & Schneider, W. (2005). Cross-cultural effect on the brain revisited: Universal structures plus writing system variation. *Human Brain Mapping*, 25, 92–104.

Botvinick, M., & Bylsma, L. M. (2005). Regularization in short-term memory for serial order. *Journal of Experimental Psychology: Learning, Memory, and Cognition*, 31, 351–358.

Bowey, J. A. (1996). On the association between phonological memory and receptive vocabulary in five-year-olds. *Journal of Experimental Child Psychology*, *63*, 44–78.

Brock, J., & Jarrold, C. (2004). Language influences on verbal short-term memory performance in Down syndrome: Item and order recognition. *Journal of Speech, Language and Hearing Research*, *47*, 1334–1346.

Brown, G. D. A., & Hulme, C. (1996). Nonword repetition, STM, and age-of-acquisition: A computational model. In S. E. Gathercole (Ed.), *Models of short-term memory* (pp. 129–148). Hove, UK: Psychology Press.

Brown, G. D. A., Preece, T., & Hulme, C. (2000). Oscillator-based memory for serial order. *Psychological Review*, *107*, 127–181.

Burgess, N., & Hitch, G. J. (1999). Memory for serial order: A network model of the phonological loop and its timing. *Psychological Review*, *106*, 551–581.

Burgess, N., & Hitch, G. (2005). Computational models of working memory: Putting long-term memory into context. *Trends in Cognitive Sciences*, *9*, 535–541.

Cabeza, R., Mangels, J., Nyberg, L., Habib, R., Houle, S., McIntosh, A. R., et al. (1997). Brain regions differentially involved in remembering what and when: A PET study. *Neuron*, *19*, 863–870.

Cairo, T. A., Liddle, P. F., Woodward, T. S., & Ngan, E. T. (2004). The influence of working memory load on phase specific patterns of cortical activity. *Cognitive Brain Research*, *21*, 377–387.

Caramazza, A., Basili, A. G., Koller, J. J., & Berndt, R. S. (1981). An investigation of repetition and language processing in a case of conduction aphasia. *Brain and Language*, *14*, 235–271.

Caza, N., & Belleville, S. (1999). Semantic contribution to immediate serial recall using an unlimited set of items: Evidence for a multi-level capacity view of short-term memory. *International Journal of Psychology*, *34*, 334–338.

Chochon, F., Cohen, L., van de Moortele, P. F., & Dehaene, S. (1999). Differential contributions of the left and right inferior parietal lobules to number processing. *Journal of Cognitive Neuroscience*, *11*, 617–630.

Collette, F., Majerus, S., Van der Linden, M., Dabe, P., Degueldre, C., Delfiore, G., et al. (2001). Contribution of long-term memory to verbal short-term memory tasks: A PET activation study. *Memory*, *9*, 249–259.

Collette, F., Van der Linden, M., Laureys, S., Delfiore, G., Degueldre, C., Luxen, A., et al. (2005). Exploring the unity and diversity of the neural substrates of executive functioning. *Human Brain Mapping*, *25*, 409–423.

Cowan, N. (1995). *Attention and memory: An integrated framework*. New York: Oxford University Press.

Cowan, N. (1999). An embedded-processes model of working memory. In A. Miyake & P. Shah (Eds.), *Models of working memory: Mechanisms of active maintenance and executive control* (pp. 62–101). Cambridge: Cambridge University Press.

Dell, G. S. (1986). A spreading activation theory of retrieval in sentence production. *Psychological Review*, *93*, 283–321.

Demonet, J. F., Chollet, F., Ramsay, S., Cardebat, D., Nespoulous, J. L., Wise, R. J. S., et al. (1992). The anatomy of phonological and semantic processing in normal subjects. *Brain*, *115*, 1753–1768.

Demonet, J. F., Price, C., Wise, R. J. S., & Frackowiak, R. S. J. (1994). Differential activation of right and left posterior sylvian regions by semantic and phonological tasks: A positron emission tomography study in normal human subjects. *Neuroscience Letters, 182,* 25–28.

Dunn, L. M., Thériault-Whalen, C. M., & Dunn, L. M. (1993). *Echelle de vocabulaire en images Peabody: Adaptation française du Peabody Picture Vocabulary Test.* Toronto, Canada: Psycan.

Fallon, A. B., Groves, K., & Tehan, G. (1999). Phonological similarity and trace degradation in the serial recall task: When CAT helps RAT, but not MAN. *International Journal of Psychology, 34,* 301–307.

Farrell, S., & Lewandowsky, S. (2002). An endogenous distributed model of ordering in serial recall. *Psychonomic Bulletin and Review, 9,* 59–79.

Farrell, S., & Lewandowsky, S. (2004). Modelling transposition latencies: Constraints for theories of serial order memory. *Journal of Memory and Language, 51,* 115–135.

Fiez, J. A., Raife, E. A., Balota, D. A., Schwartz, J. P., Raichle, M. E., & Petersen, S. E. (1996). A positron emission tomography study of the short-term maintenance of verbal information. *Journal of Neuroscience, 16,* 808–822.

Fowler, A. E. (1991). How early phonological development might set the stage for phonological awareness. In S. Brady & D. P. Shankweiler (Eds.), *Phonological processes in literacy: A tribute to Isabelle Y. Liberman* (pp. 97–117). Hillsdale, NJ: Lawrence Erlbaum Associates, Inc.

Freedman, M. L., & Martin, R. C. (2001). Dissociable components of short-term memory and their relation to long-term learning. *Cognitive Neuropsychology, 18,* 193–226.

Friedrich, F. J., Glenn, C. G., & Marin, O. S. (1984). Interruption of phonological coding in conduction aphasia. *Brain and Language, 22,* 266–291.

Gathercole, S. E., Frankish, C. R., Pickering, S. J., & Peaker, S. (1999). Phonotactic influences on short-term memory. *Journal of Experimental Psychology: Human Learning and Memory, 25,* 84–95.

Gathercole, S. E., Hitch, G. J., Service, E., & Martin, A. J. (1997). Phonological short-term memory and new word learning in children. *Developmental Psychology, 33,* 966–979.

Gathercole, S. E., Service, E., Hitch, G. J., Adams, A. M., & Martin, A. J. (1999). Phonological short-term memory and vocabulary development: Further evidence on the nature of the relationship. *Applied Cognitive Psychology, 13,* 65–77.

Gupta, P. (2003). Examining the relationship between word learning, nonword repetition and immediate serial recall in adults. *Quarterly Journal of Experimental Psychology, 56A,* 1213–1236.

Gupta, P., & MacWhinney, B. (1997). Vocabulary acquisition and verbal short-term memory: Computational and neural bases. *Brain and Language, 59,* 267–333.

Henson, R. N. A. (1998). Short-term memory for serial order: The start-end model. *Cognitive Psychology, 36,* 73–137.

Henson, R. N. A., Burgess, N., & Frith, C. D. (2000). Recoding, storage, rehearsal, and grouping in verbal short-term memory: An fMRI study. *Neuropsychologia, 38,* 426–440.

Henson, R., Hartley, T., Burgess, N., Hitch, G., & Flude, B. (2003). Selective interference with verbal short-term memory for serial order information: A new paradigm and tests of a timing-signal hypothesis. *Quarterly Journal of Experimental Psychology, 56A,* 1307–1334.

Howard, D., Patterson, K., Wise, R. J. S., Brown, W. D., Friston, K. J., Weiller, C., et al. (1992). The cortical localization of the lexicons. *Brain, 115,* 1769–1782.

Hulme, C., Maughan, S., & Brown, G. D. (1991). Memory for familiar and unfamiliar words: Evidence for a long-term memory contribution to short-term memory span. *Journal of Memory and Language, 30,* 685–701.

Hulme, C., Stuart, G., Brown, G. D. A., & Morin, C. (2003). High- and low-frequency words are recalled equally well in alternating lists: Evidence for associative effects in serial recall. *Journal of Memory and Language, 49,* 415–584.

Jacoby, L. L. (1991). A process dissociation framework: Separating automatic from intentional uses of memory. *Journal of Memory and Language, 30,* 513–541.

Jacoby, L. L. (1998). Invariance in automatic influences of memory: Toward a users guide for the process-dissociation procedure. *Journal of Experimental Psychology: Learning, Memory, and Cognition, 24,* 3–26.

Katz, R. C., & Goodglass, H. (1990). Deep dysphasia: An analysis of a rare form of repetition disorder. *Brain and Language, 39,* 153–185.

Majerus, S., Bastin, C., Poncelet, M., Van der Linden, M., Salmon, E., Collette, F., & Maquet, P. (2007a). The intraparietal sulcus and short-term memory: Focus of attention? Further evidence from a face short-term memory fMRI paradigm. *NeuroImage, 35,* 351–367.

Majerus, S., Glaser, B., Van der Linden, M., & Eliez, S. (2006a). A multiple case study of verbal short-term memory in velo-cardio-facial syndrome. *Journal of Intellectual Disability Research, 50,* 457–469.

Majerus, S., Laureys, S., Collette, F., Del Fiore, G., Degueldre, C., Luxen, A., et al. (2003). Phonological short-term memory networks following recovery from Landau and Kleffner syndrome. *Human Brain Mapping, 19,* 133–144.

Majerus, S., Lekeu, F., Van der Linden, M., & Salmon, E. (2001). Deep dysphasia: Further evidence on the relationship between phonological short-term memory and language processing impairments. *Cognitive Neuropsychology, 18,* 385–410.

Majerus, S., Norris, D., & Patterson, K. (2007b). What do patients with semantic dementia remember in verbal short-term memory? Sounds and order but not words. *Cognitive Neuropsychology, 24,* 131–151.

Majerus, S., Poncelet, M., Elsen, B., & Van der Linden, M. (2006b). Exploring the relationship between verbal short-term memory for serial order and item information and new word learning in adults. *European Journal of Cognitive Psychology, 18,* 848–873.

Majerus, S., Poncelet, M., Greffe, C., & Van der Linden, M. (2006c). Relations between vocabulary development and verbal short-term memory: The importance of short-term memory for serial order information. *Journal of Experimental Child Psychology, 93,* 95–119.

Majerus, S., Poncelet, M., Van der Linden, M., Albouy, G., Salmon, E., Sterpenich, V., et al. (2006d). Parieto-fronto-cerebellar and parieto-temporal networks centered around the left intraparietal sulcus differentiate verbal short-term memory for word order and word identity. *NeuroImage, 32,* 880–891.

Majerus, S., Van der Kaa, M. A., Renard, C., Van der Linden, M., & Poncelet, M. (2005a). Treating verbal short-term memory deficits by increasing the duration of temporary phonological representations: A case study. *Brain and Language, 95,* 174–175.

Majerus, S., & Van der Linden, M. (2003). The development of long-term memory effects on verbal short-term memory: A replication study. *British Journal of Developmental Psychology*, *21*, 303–310.

Majerus, S., Van der Linden, M., Braissand, V., & Eliez, S. (2007c). An investigation of verbal short-term memory in children and adults with a 22q11.2 deletion: A specific deficit for the retention of serial order information? *American Journal on Mental Retardation*, *112*, 79–93.

Majerus, S., Van der Linden, M., Collette, F., Laureys, S., Poncelet, M., Degueldre, C., et al. (2005b). Modulation of brain activity during phonological familiarization. *Brain and Language*, *92*, 320–331.

Majerus, S., Van der Linden, M., Mulder, G., Meulemans, T., & Peters, F. (2004a). Verbal short-term memory reflects the sublexical organization of the phonological language network: Evidence from an incidental phonotactic learning paradigm. *Journal of Memory and Language*, *51*, 297–306.

Majerus, S., Van der Linden, M., Poncelet, M., & Metz-Lutz, M. N. (2004b). Can phonological and semantic short-term memory be dissociated? Further evidence from Landau-Kleffner Syndrome. *Cognitive Neuropsychology*, *21*, 491–512.

Marshuetz, C., Smith, E. E., Jonides, J., DeGutis, J., & Chenevert, T. L. (2000). Order information in working memory: fMRI evidence for parietal and prefrontal mechanisms. *Journal of Cognitive Neuroscience*, *12*, 130–144.

Martin, N., & Saffran, E. M. (1992). A computational account of deep dysphasia: Evidence from a single case study. *Brain and Language*, *43*, 240–274.

Martin, N., Saffran, E. M., & Dell, G. S. (1996). Recovery in deep dysphasia: Evidence for a relation between auditory-verbal STM capacity and lexical errors in repetition. *Brain and Language*, *52*, 83–113.

Martin, R. C., Lesch, M. F., & Bartha, M. C. (1999). Independence of input and output phonology in word processing and short-term memory. *Journal of Memory and Language*, *41*, 3–29.

McCarthy, R. A., & Warrington, E. K. (1987). The double dissociation of short-term memory for lists and sentences. *Brain*, *110*, 1545–1563.

McElree, B., & Dosher, B. A. (1993). Serial retrieval processes in the recovery of order information. *Journal of Experimental Psychology: General*, *112*, 291–315.

Metsala, J. L. (1999). Young children's phonological awareness and nonword repetition as a function of vocabulary development. *Journal of Educational Psychology*, *91*, 3–19.

Murdock, B. B. (1976). Item and order information in short-term serial memory. *Journal of Experimental Psychology: General*, *105*, 191–216.

Murdock, B. B., & Franklin, P. E. (1984). Associative and serial-order information: Different modes of operation? *Memory and Cognition*, *12*, 243–249.

Nairne, J. S., & Kelley, M. R. (2004). Separating item and order information through process dissociation. *Journal of Memory and Language*, *50*, 113–133.

Nimmo, L. M., & Roodenrys, S. (2004). Investigating the phonological similarity effect: Syllable structure and the position of common phonemes. *Journal of Memory and Language*, *50*, 245–258.

Page, M. P. A., & Norris, D. (1998). The primacy model: A new model of immediate serial recall. *Psychological Review*, *105*, 761–781.

Papagno, C., & Vallar, G. (1995). To learn or not to learn: Vocabulary in foreign languages and the problem with phonological memory. In R. Campbell & M. A. Conway (Eds.), *Broken memories: Case studies in memory impairment* (pp. 334–343). Malden, MA: Blackwell Publishers Inc.

Paulesu, E., Frith, C. D., & Frackowiak, R. S. J. (1993). The neural correlates of the verbal component of working memory. *Nature, 362*, 342–345.

Paulesu, E., Frith, U., Snowling, M., Gallagher, A., Morton, J., Frackowiak, R. S. J., et al. (1996). Is developmental dyslexia a disconnection syndrome? Evidence from PET scanning. *Brain, 119*, 143–157.

Poirier, M., & Saint-Aubin, J. (1996). Immediate serial recall, word frequency, item identity and item position. *Canadian Journal of Experimental Psychology, 50*, 408–412.

Rao, S. M., Mayer, A. R., & Harrington, D. L. (2001). The evolution of brain activation during temporal processing. *Nature Neuroscience, 4*, 317–323.

Ravizza, S. M., Delgado, M. R., Chein, J. M., Becker, J. T., & Fiez, J. A. (2004). Functional dissociations within the inferior parietal cortex in verbal working memory. *NeuroImage, 22*, 562–573.

Roodenrys, S., Hulme, C., Alban, J., & Ellis, A. W. (1994). Effects of word frequency and age of acquisition on short-term memory span. *Memory and Cognition, 22*, 695–701.

Roodenrys, S., & Quinlan, P. T. (2000). The effects of stimulus size and word frequency on verbal serial recall. *Memory, 8*, 73–80.

Ruchkin, D. S., Grafman, J., Cameron, K., & Berndt, R. S. (2003). Working memory retention systems: A state of activated long-term memory. *Behavioral and Brain Sciences, 26*, 709–728.

Saffran, E. M., & Marin, O. S. M. (1975). Immediate memory for word lists and sentences in a patient with deficient auditory short-term memory. *Brain and Language, 2*, 420–433.

Saffran, E. M., & Martin, N. (1990). Neuropsychological evidence for lexical involvement in short-term memory. In G. Vallar & T. Shallice (Eds.), *Neuropsychological impairments of short-term memory* (pp. 428–447). London: Cambridge University Press.

Saint-Aubin, J., & Poirier, M. (1999). Semantic similarity and immediate serial recall: Is there a detrimental effect on order information? *Quarterly Journal of Experimental Psychology, 52A*, 367–394.

Saint-Aubin, J., & Poirier, M. (2000). Immediate serial recall of words and nonwords: Tests of a retrieval-based hypothesis. *Psychonomic Bulletin and Review, 7*, 332–340.

Saint-Aubin, J., & Poirier, M. (2005). Word frequency effects in immediate serial recall: Item familiarity and item co-occurrence have the same effect. *Memory, 13*, 325–332.

Salmon, E., Van der Linden, M., Collette, F., Delfiore, G., Maquet, P., Degueldre, C., et al. (1996). Regional brain activity during working memory tasks. *Brain, 119*, 1617–1625.

Schweickert, R. (1993). A multinomial processing tree model for degradation and redintegration in immediate recall. *Memory and Cognition, 21*, 168–175.

Scott, S. K., Blank, C., Rosen, S., & Wise, R. J. S. (2000). Identification of a pathway for intelligible speech in the left temporal lobe. *Brain, 123*, 2400–2406.

Silveri, M. C., & Cappa, A. (2003). Segregation of the neural correlates of language and phonological short-term memory. *Cortex, 39*, 913–925.

Strub, R. L., & Gardner, H. (1974). The repetition defect in conduction aphasia: Mnestic or linguistic? *Brain and Language, 1*, 255.

Stuart, G., & Hulme, C. (2000). The effects of word co-occurrence on short-term memory: Associative links in long-term memory affect short-term memory performance. *Journal of Experimental Psychology: Learning, Memory, and Cognition, 26,* 796–802.

Takayama, Y., Kinomoto, K., & Nakamura, K. (2004). Selective impairment of the auditory-verbal short-term memory due to a lesion of the superior temporal gyrus. *European Neurology, 51,* 115–117.

Thorn, A. S., & Frankish, C. R. (2005). Long-term knowledge effects on aerial recall of nonwords are not exclusively lexical. *Journal of Experimental Psychology: Learning, Memory, and Cognition, 31,* 729–735.

Thorn, A. S., Gathercole, S. E., & Frankish, C. R. (2005). Redintegration and the benefits of long-term knowledge in verbal short-term memory: An evaluation of Schweickert's (1993) multinomial processing tree model. *Cognitive Psychology, 50,* 133–158.

Todd, J. J., Fougnie, D., & Marois, R. (2005). Visual short-term memory load suppresses temporo-parietal junction activity and induces inattentional blindness. *Psychological Science, 16,* 965–972.

Todd, J. J., & Marois, R. (2004). Capacity limit of visual short-term memory in human posterior parietal cortex. *Nature, 428,* 751–754.

Trojano, L., Stanzione, M., & Grossi, D. (1992). Short-term memory and verbal learning with auditory phonological coding defect: A neuropsychological case study. *Brain and Cognition, 18,* 12–33.

Vallar, G., & Baddeley, A. D. (1984). Fractionation of working memory: Neuropsychological evidence for a phonological short-term store. *Journal of Verbal Learning and Verbal Behavior, 23,* 151–161.

Vallar, G., Basso, A., & Bottini, G. (1990). Phonological processing and sentence comprehension: A neuropsychological case study. In G. Vallar & T. Shallice (Eds.), *Neuropsychological impairments of short-term memory* (pp. 448–476). New York: Cambridge University Press.

Vitevitch, M. S., & Luce, P. A. (1998). When words compete: Levels of processing in perception of spoken words. *Psychological Science, 9,* 325–329.

Vitevitch, M. S., & Luce, P. A. (1999). Probabilistic phonotactics and neighborhood activation in spoken word recognition. *Journal of Memory and Language, 40,* 374–408.

Walker, I., & Hulme, C. (1999). Concrete words are easier to recall than abstract words: Evidence for a semantic contribution to short-term serial recall. *Journal of Experimental Psychology: Learning, Memory, and Cognition, 25,* 1256–1271.

Warrington, E. K., Logue, V., & Pratt, R. T. C. (1971). The anatomical localisation of selective impairment of auditory verbal short-term memory. *Neuropsychologia, 9,* 377–387.

Warrington, E. K., & Shallice, T. (1969). The selective impairment of auditory verbal short-term memory. *Brain, 92,* 885–896.

Watkins, O. C., & Watkins, M. J. (1977). Serial recall and the modality effect: Effects of word frequency. *Journal of Experimental Psychology: Human Learning and Memory, 3,* 712–718.

Wickelgren, W. A. (1965). Acoustic similarity and intrusion errors in short-term memory. *Journal of Experimental Psychology, 70,* 102–108.

Zatorre, R. J., Evans, A. C., Meyer, E., & Gjedde, A. (1992). Lateralization of phonetic and pitch discrimination in speech processing. *Science, 256,* 846–849.

13 From auditory traces to language learning: behavioural and neurophysiological evidence

Elisabet Service

Overview

This chapter tries to find explanations for the often-replicated statistical relationship between performance in phonological short-term memory tasks and learning of new vocabulary in both laboratory and real-world settings. First, the contribution of sensory memory to phonological short-term memory is explored by discussing a set of event-related potential data. Those results were formerly interpreted to show better auditory discrimination between minimally different syllables by a group of children who also were better at pseudoword repetition and at learning novel word forms.

Next, data that show correlated performance in non-phonological sensory memory tasks and traditional phonological short-term memory tasks in a group of adults with dyslexia, as well as a group of fluently reading adults, are presented. These data are taken to suggest that the ability to keep several representations active at the same time, whether these are phonological or not, may be of crucial importance for reading ability as well as phonological short-term memory tasks. Further data are described suggesting that there are individual differences in the encoding of phonological representations. These are argued to result in correlated performance in immediate recall of pseudoword lists and incidental learning of the phonotactic structure of new words.

Finally, data bearing on the neural substrate of phonological short-term memory are discussed. It is concluded that brain areas supporting working memory processes, such as attention and rehearsal, appear to play a role in the learning of new words. However, a clearly distinct area supporting a temporary phonological store appears not to have been found outside the language and memory areas in the left temporal lobe. It is concluded that the link between phonological short-term memory performance and word learning is likely to be in the representational efficiency of the neural language networks that encode and maintain complex phonological stimuli.

Introduction

In the late 1980s, three data sets collected in the working memory framework developed by Baddeley and Hitch (1974) suggested that long-term phonological learning depended on short-term phonological memory. Two longitudinal studies, one on first-language development in young children (Gathercole & Baddeley, 1989) and one on second-language learning in school (Service, 1989, 1992), found that the ability to repeat auditorily presented unfamiliar pseudowords predicted development of first- and second-language vocabulary (see also Service & Kohonen, 1995), respectively. Both studies interpreted pseudoword repetition to be a measure of phonological working memory capacity. An experimental study testing a brain-damaged patient (Baddeley, Papagno, & Vallar, 1988) was, however, the most significant for theory development. It investigated new word learning in a case of verbal short-term memory impairment with preserved long-term memory. The patient PV was reported to have a highly restricted span of about two letter names or words. She was able to repeat disyllabic pseudowords but began making mistakes when a third syllable was added. Yet, she performed at the same level as control subjects on paired-associate and word list learning. When the familiar words to be recalled in the association pairs were replaced by pronounceable pseudowords PV's performance fell to floor as, after 10 auditory trials repeating the same pairs, she was unable to recall a single pseudoword when cued with its word pair. In contrast to the typical pattern in unimpaired subjects, she performed clearly better, although not at the level of the control group, when the pseudowords were presented visually. The authors of all three studies concluded that phonological short-term storage is important for the learning of new phonological material. Findings supporting this conclusion have since been reported in numerous studies (for a review, see Baddeley, Gathercole, & Papagno, 1998). The present chapter discusses possible sources of individual variation in phonological short-term memory (STM) tasks that could explain the relationship between immediate recall of auditorily presented language material and long-term learning of wordlike forms.

In the Baddeley and Hitch framework (Baddeley, 1986, 2003), working memory supports temporary activation of information that is needed in a current task as well as the processes manipulating it. The architecture is based on the idea of a central control component and slave systems that are subordinate to it. The *central executive* component is an attentional resource that organizes behaviour as well as delegates the resources of the modality-specific slave systems to specific tasks. The *visuo-spatial sketchpad* records and stores visual and spatial information in working memory. This system may consist of one or more components (Logie, 1995). Verbal working memory is served by the *phonological loop*, consisting of a *phonological store* and an active *articulatory rehearsal process*. The phonological store was originally described as a passive store, automatically accessed by auditory verbal material (Baddeley, 1986; Vallar & Baddeley, 1984). The articulatory rehearsal process is thought to be an active process, coming under strategic control in development around the age of 7 (Gathercole & Hitch, 1993). Recently, Baddeley (2000; see also chapter by Allen & Baddeley) has introduced a third slave system, the *episodic buffer*, which is proposed to bring together information maintained in different modalities as well as, for instance, semantic information in long-term memory (LTM).

The relationship between phonological STM tasks, such as pseudoword repetition, pseudoword span, as well as digit span, and language learning has mostly been investigated within the Baddeley and Hitch working memory framework. Most studies have speculated that the component explaining both individual differences in word learning and impaired learning in some special populations is the phonological store (Baddeley et al., 1998; Brock & Jarrold, 2004; Gathercole & Baddeley, 1990; Service, 1992) although the articulatory rehearsal process has also been proposed to play a role, at least when the new word can be mapped onto a sufficiently specified articulatory representation to allow inner or outer speech (Baddeley, 2003). However, there is no consensus to date on the exact mechanism that could explain why performance in phonological STM tasks predicts vocabulary learning. This chapter will follow an information processing path from auditory sensory processing to phonetic and phonological encoding, and subsequently to retention and recall. The aim is to probe stages possibly involved in the relationship between STM and LTM learning of new phonological material.

Does the learning of new words depend on the strength of sensory traces, representations based on phonetic features, or encoding in terms of phonological categories?

A recurring question in connection with various verbal-domain learning disorders, such as specific language impairment, developmental dyslexia, or dominant symptomatology in Down syndrome, has been whether some low-level sensory or motor impairment could explain the higher-level difficulties. Rita Čeponienė and I (Čeponienė, Service, Kurjenluoma, Cheour, & Näätänen, 1999) decided to ask a similar question about individual differences in pseudoword repetition and new word learning, using an electric brain response recorded on the scalp as the criterion measure. This response, the *mismatch negativity* or *MMN*, is a so-called event-related potential (ERP), i.e. a fluctuation in the electroencephalogram (EEG) related to a specific stimulus event and seen when EEG is averaged over numerous trials. It was first recorded as an increased negativity to a deviant sound in a sequence of repeating (so-called standard) tone stimuli (Näätänen, Gaillard, & Mäntysalo, 1978). Intensive study of this response has shown that it occurs whenever there is a change of any kind in the auditory scene (for a review, see Näätänen, 1992), even when the sounds are not actively attended to or this change consciously noticed. Moreover, it is sensitive to familiarity; for instance, in the context of semi-synthetic phoneme sounds, a deviant speech sound belonging to the native language of the listener gives rise to a larger MMN than an unfamiliar deviant even when the latter is acoustically more salient (Näätänen et al., 1997; Winkler et al., 1999).

In order to find out whether both pseudoword repetition and pseudo-word learning performance are related to better speech sound discrimination, we first presented 24 Finnish children, aged 7–9 years, with a pseudoword pair repetition task. As a simulation of word learning, we then asked them to memorize 8 word–pseudoword pairs, repeated four times (cf. Baddeley et al., 1988; Papagno & Vallar, 1992; Service & Craik, 1993). We used written pairs in order to exclude the involvement of auditory perception in the learning process. We also tested the children on phoneme discrimination with 12 minimal pseudoword pairs differing in one consonant phoneme in the second syllable of the three-syllable items. Based on the pseudoword repetition results, we selected the 9 best repeaters (high repeaters) and the 9 poorest repeaters (low repeaters) for MMN recording. The children had no active task but were watching a silent movie while we played them sequences of /baka/ and /baga/ stimuli as well as sequences of 1000 and 1100 Hz tones. In the sequences, the infrequent (deviant) stimulus occurred on 10% of the trials. We had chosen the speech stimuli to be semi-familiar. The /k/ vs. /g/ contrast is not used in original Finnish words but occurs in a number of loan words. Unlike the speech sounds in previous MMN experiments, our pseudoword stimuli had been edited from digitized natural speech. The critical difference in voice onset time, i.e., the silence before the vocal cords start to vibrate after an initial noise burst in stop consonants, was only 15 ms between our /k/ and /g/ sounds, a smaller difference than reported for typical English speakers, and, thus, providing a potentially challenging discrimination task. Our hypothesis was that the high repeaters would show a larger MMN to the speech but not the tone stimuli than the low repeaters.

All the children performed well (range 8–11 correct out of 12 pairs) on the behavioural phoneme discrimination task with minimal pairs, distinguished by a single phonetic feature, and there was no difference between the high and the low repeaters. However, the group of high repeaters were able to orally recall more pseudowords (a mean of 4.83 of 8) on the fourth trial than the low repeaters (a mean of 2.5). We also found that there was no statistically significant difference in the MMN to the relatively easy tone contrast between the two groups. In contrast, the amplitude of the MMN to deviant speech sounds was significantly higher in the high repeater compared to the low repeater group. Thus, our high repeater group was better at repeating back pairs of four- and five-syllable pseudowords, learning pronounceable written pseudowords, and their brain responses suggested that they discriminated a semi-familiar, acoustically small, consonant contrast better than the low repeater group. We originally interpreted this to be consistent with the conclusion that better sensory memory for speech sounds results in better phonological STM and possibly also better learning of new phonological material. How does this interpretation stand up some 10 years later?

First, how good were our data? On testing more children with the same tasks, we found a correlation of $r(41) = .60$, $p < .0001$, between repetition of pseudoword pairs and learning of written pseudowords. Thus, the connection between pseudoword repetition and learning seems robust even though the learning task had no auditory component. In contrast, there was no connection between pseudoword repetition and auditory discrimination of consonants embedded in pseudowords ($r(34) = -.06$), although this may have been concealed by the near-ceiling performance in the discrimination task. In the original experiment, we also found a correlation between pseudoword repetition and the amplitude of the MMN response on the electrode that showed the largest response, ($r(16) = .47$, $p < .05$. However, the correlation between MMN amplitude and pseudoword learning did not reach significance, $r(16) = .39$, $p = .1096$. We explored this further by dividing the subjects into high learners and low learners by a median split. It looked like the better learners had a relationship between learning and MMN amplitude, $r(7) = .60$, $p = .0881$, whereas the low learners did not, $r(7) = .31$, $p = .4348$ (Figure 13.1). We thought that this pattern of results might have been a consequence of some of the children, perhaps the low learners, finding it very hard to concentrate on looking at the screen during the presentation of the word–pseudoword learning pairs. However, we did not have enough statistical power in our experiment to back up our speculation. Thus, evidence for a direct link between MMN amplitude and pseudoword learning remains only suggestive.

Our interpretation of the original experiment was based on the then dominant view of the MMN response as being, above all, dependent on sensory traces. Since our study, an increasing number of experiments have suggested that the MMN is not just a measure of sensory trace quality, but also of the learnability and maintainability of the critical features separating the repeating standard stimuli from the infrequent deviants. The response is not only a signature of a sensory discrimination but is conditional on the formation of a template of the standard stimulus that can be compared with the incoming deviants. This template incorporates not only the recently heard standard stimulus residing in echoic memory but also past events in the auditory stream (e.g., a past standard stimulus in a situation in which the standard has been changed to a new sound). Thus, one interpretation of the MMN is that it is a representation building process that dynamically keeps

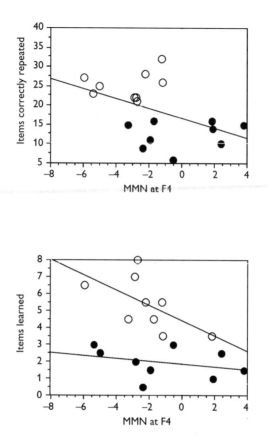

Figure 13.1 Mismatch negativity (MMN) peak amplitude at electrode F4 (frontal right) as a function of pseudoword pair repetition performance (upper panel) and word–pseudoword recall on 4th trial (lower panel). In the upper panel, unfilled circles show responses for high repeaters and filled circles responses for low repeaters. In the lower panel, unfilled circles show the response for high learners and filled circles the response for low learners (based on a median split).

track of the changing auditory environment (Winkler, Karmos, & Näätänen, 1996). The response is enhanced in situations, in which the standard (e.g., Cowan, Winkler, Teder, & Näätänen, 1993; Jacobsen, Schröger, Winkler, & Horváth, 2005) and the deviant (Jacobsen et al., 2005) stimuli are supported by existing LTM representations, i.e., when these have been previously encoded or have some degree of familiarity.

MMN responses have been recorded not just to auditory differences but also to breaches of abstract rules (e.g., rare ascending tone pairs among frequent descending ones) creating expectations in a sound sequence (for a review see, e.g., Näätänen, Tervaniemi, Sussman, Paavilainen, & Winkler, 2001). Moreover, not only is the MMN sensitive to the familiarity of prototypical speech sounds (with bigger responses to more familiar sounds) (Cheour et al., 1998; Näätänen et al., 1997), it also detects a situation when a collection of standard sounds form a phoneme category whereas a collection of rare sounds are all part of a different phoneme category (Phillips et al., 2000), and responds to members of the two categories in a dichotomous manner, at the same time as it ignores acoustic differences within the two categories. The MMN response to tones peaks ~100–200 ms after stimulus onset, somewhat later for more complex stimuli and speech sounds. Its main neural generators have been found in the auditory cortex, in the supratemporal plane (Alho, 1995).

What we currently know about the MMN response is consistent with multiple alternative hypotheses of why our high pseudoword repeaters had larger-amplitude responses to the /baka/–/baga/ contrast. The simplest one is that they were better able to discriminate between the stimuli. This was not supported by the two groups' similar performance on an embedded speech sound discrimination task or the zero correlation between the MMN amplitude and behavioural phoneme discrimination. If pure discrimination is not the explanation it is likely that the quality of the traces being compared, that of the standard and the deviant, varied between the two groups. This could have been purely in terms of auditory features – our original conclusion. If this was the case, one possible inference is that better quality sensory traces underlie individual differences in phonological short-term memory, or at least pseudoword repetition.

However, the two groups may instead have differed based on the quality of the representations for the particular phonetic prototype sounds for /k/ and /g/ – a rare contrast in Finnish. Experimental work with synthetic native and foreign speech sounds has shown that both auditory and phonetic representations affect MMN amplitude (Winkler et al., 1999). Another possibility is that the high repeater group identified the critical sounds as belonging to two exclusive categories (with the labels /k/ and /g/) whereas the low repeater group may have processed them on the basis of proximity to one familiar prototype (e.g., a typical /k/ and an atypical /k/) or in terms of acoustic distance from each other.

One reason to favour explanations based on phonetic prototypes or phonological categories is that the critical contrast was embedded in natur-ally spoken pseudowords. However, phonetic and phonological accounts come with a disturbing element of circularity: maybe the high repeaters were better language learners in general. They may have had larger vocabularies and better established representations for rare phoneme categories. Both factors could have affected their ability to repeat complex pseudowords as well as to memorize new pseudowords. To get away from the circle, two studies will be reported below, one that concentrated on the connection between phonological STM and sensory processing and another that investigated the relationship between immediate recall from STM and learning of the phonological structure of novel words (pseudowords).

Evidence from developmental dyslexia

During the 1990s, explanations in terms of sensory processing deficits became popular for two developmental disorders typically associated with poor phonological STM: specific language impairment (SLI) and developmental dyslexia. Tallal and Piercy (1974) originally suggested that a subgroup of children with SLI were impaired in processing rapid changes in the auditory signal, which led to poor phoneme discrimination and other language problems. The findings were later generalized to children with dyslexia (Tallal, 1980). The account attracted considerable attention after the publication of results suggesting that abnormal language development could be corrected by training the perception of fast auditory transitions (Merzenich, Jenkins, Johnston, Schreineer, Miller, & Tallal, 1996).

Partly inspired by this work, Marja Laasonen, Veijo Virsu, and I conducted a number of studies to investigate the hypothesis that developmental dyslexia is caused by a core deficit in the processing of rapid stimulus changes. Our psychophysical experiments were concerned with the temporal acuity of sensory processing in Finnish adult individuals with normal or above normal intelligence but a history of developmental dyslexia. In addition to our results concerning sensory processing we also found that Finnish individuals with dyslexia as a group have poor phonological STM (Laasonen, Service, & Virsu, 2001, 2002) as well as, for instance, delayed learning of morphological word inflections (Service & Tujulin, 2002). They are, therefore, a potentially interesting group also from the point of view of the link between phonological STM and language learning.

In the psychophysical part of our work we found that a group of readers with dyslexia were less accurate at performing comparisons that involved fast trains of auditory (tones), visual (light flashes) or tactile (solenoid indentations on fingertips) stimuli (Laasonen et al., 2001, 2002; Laasonen, Tomma-Halme, Lahti-Nuuttila, Service, & Virsu, 2000). They also performed more poorly than fluent readers in a number of phonological tasks as well as in digit and nonword span tasks. However, there was no direct correlation between their temporal processing acuity and reading performance. We, therefore, set out to explore the possibility that their problems with reading and phonology were caused by an STM deficit that encompassed both sensory and phonological levels of memory. To investigate this hypothesis, we gave them serial recognition tasks with sensory stimuli in three modalities and their combinations (Laasonen, Virsu, Oinonen, Sandbacka, Vedenpää, & Service, 2006). The subjects were presented with pairs of sequences consisting of binary stimuli: tones of two pitches, light flashes from two adjacent LEDs, solenoid indentations on forefinger and middle finger. Their task was to say whether the sequences with a growing number of items were the same or not (matching span). Sequences that were different had the order of two stimuli transposed. In another condition, the sequences were all of a set length but the time interval between the items grew as the subject responded correctly. We found that the dyslexic subjects had shorter matching spans and needed shorter pauses between the items for successful matching responses. We also found compound variables based on the sensory matching span tasks to be correlated with a phonological memory construct (based on pseudoword pair repetition, digit span forwards and backwards, pseudoword span and pseudoword matching span) in both the dyslexic and the fluent readers.

These data led us to conclude that the STM deficit observed in persons with developmental dyslexia is general, affecting both phonological and sensory, non-verbal, material. One parsimonious explanation is that the neural networks that have to simultaneously represent multiple stimuli for immediate recall/recognition are less well specified in dyslexic individuals. STM tasks are good indicators of the quality of the neural representations because multiple items, as well as long pauses between items that belong together in a memory episode, put the neural network under maximal strain. Other work that is consistent with this hypothesis showed that dyslexic readers had equal MMN amplitudes in an experiment in which the standard and deviant stimuli were tone pairs with a short (50 ms onset to onset) vs. a longer (150 ms) pause between the tones (Kujala, Myllyviita, Tervaniemi, Alho, Kallio, & Näätänen, 2000). When these same tone pairs were embedded in four-tone sequences the dyslexic readers showed no detectable MMN before 400 ms from stimulus onset whereas fluent readers responded with significant early negativities to the embedded tone pair difference. Performance in a behavioural task in which the subjects were instructed to press a button when they heard a deviance in the stimulus sequence paralleled the MMN results: both groups had near-ceiling hit rates in the tone pair condition, with hit rate falling to just below 75% for the fluent readers and to about 30% for the dyslexic readers when the tone pair was embedded in a four-tone sequence. Thus, it seemed that the neural networks of the dyslexic subjects were unable to support complex four-tone template representations in the MMN recording situation and the behavioural task although both brain and behavioural responses to simple tone pairs were similar to those of the fluent readers.

We propose that the same neural networks that support online processing and STM are also responsible for encoding material for long-term storage. This would explain why individuals who perform better in STM tasks are also better learners: better-specified representations are easier (and faster) to recall later on. If we accept the idea that similar factors may explain individual differences between more and less efficient vocabulary learners as between individuals with or without dyslexia we can present the more general hypothesis that word learning depends on the ability of neural networks to represent multiple stimuli consisting of overlapping elements (e.g., phonetic features; in binary sequences: repeated whole items). The variability in representational capacity is best tested in STM tasks, and the aspect of it affecting phonological material could be termed *phonological store capacity*. However, the expression *phonological encoding capacity* would be a more accurate label for our view. At the moment we do not know whether the phonological aspect always covaries with the capacity to represent other types of stimuli. An individual-differences study in a typically performing population will be reviewed below to demonstrate how STM performance and phonological learning could both reflect the quality of representations, at least for phonological material.

Factors affecting phonological encoding capacity

In their influential article, Baddeley et al. (1998) proposed that the phonological loop component of working memory acts as a language learning device. Their view is essentially a gateway view: novel language material gets represented first in the phonological loop and then in LTM. The role of the phonological store was especially emphasized. In later writings, Baddeley (2003) has argued that representations in the phonological store are not affected by top-down repair processes and that the articulatory rehearsal process may play a role in learning by providing rehearsal of top-down repaired representations. A consequence of the *gateway hypothesis* is that whatever can be easily represented in the phonological loop should also be better remembered in the long term. However, commonly used STM measures do not make it easy to distinguish between "pure" phonological store capacity for unfamiliar material, the effect of existing knowledge in LTM and a potential contribution from rehearsal.

Top-down influences on phonological STM have mostly been modelled in terms of repair processes, so-called redintegration, active at the recall stage (e.g., Hulme, Maughan, & Brown, 1991; Schweickert, 1993). According to these views, more or less degraded traces can be restored at output on the basis of pre-existing material in LTM, for example known words. However, Thorn and her colleagues (Thorn, Gathercole, & Frankish, 2005) recently found evidence consistent with top-down effects at different stages in memory. Some factors, such as the lexical status of the stimuli, appear to affect the recall stage only, as evidenced by effects on partly and fully recalled items but no effect on totally incorrectly recalled items (which presumably cannot be affected by repair processes as there is nothing correct left in them to trigger successful top-down repair). Other factors, such as word frequency, nonword phonotactic frequency and language familiarity, appear to strengthen or repair traces already at the encoding and/or storage stages of STM tasks. According to the gateway hypothesis, if top-down influences have an impact on phonological store representations they may also affect learning. In addition, top-down influences available for trace repair at the recall stage may also be able to clean up representations fed back to the rehearsal system over one or more cycles and may, thus, add to a learning enhancing effect of rehearsal.

An alternative to the gateway hypothesis is provided by the proposal above that the same neural networks that encode phonological stimuli for immediate recall also encode permanent traces. According to this *trace quality hypothesis*, a phonological representation is as good as its initial encoding (plus possible subsequent top-down repair) whether it is tested in an immediate recall task or at a later time. In exceptional cases, no new phonological representations may be encoded at all but familiar words can be activated in LTM. This could be how STM patients, such as PV, are able to later recall familiar words but not pseudowords.

We explored the trace quality hypothesis in the context of individual differences in auditory pseudoword memory (Service, Maury, & Luoto-niemi, 2007). We first tested a group of Finnish university students on immediate serial recall of consonant-vowel-consonant-vowel-consonant-vowel (CVCVCV) pseudowords. Based on the number of correctly recalled pseudoword lists of growing length in an initial test, we selected the best and the poorest third for our good and poor phonological memory groups. We then presented the poor group with 32 lists consisting of 3 pseudowords (span + 1) and the good group with 24 lists consisting of 4 pseudowords, for immediate recall. All list items were drawn from a pool of 12 pseudowords, each of which occurred 8 times during the experiment. The immediate memory performance in terms of items correctly recalled was similar for both groups. However, in a surprise test, the good group remembered a greater number of the pseudowords that had made up the stimulus pool in a free recall, a cued recall (completion of a missing syllable in each item) and recognition (picking out each pool item from a set including 6 phonological neighbours) test. Thus, although the poor and the good group had equal immediate recall performance for the pool items in the STM task, the good group had learnt more of the phonological structure of the stimulus items during the experiment.

On the basis of these results, we argue that the good group were able to initially create better specified traces for the individual stimulus items. As a result, they could repeat back a longer sequence of such items in an immediate recall task because the traces were supposedly more resistant to interference from each other than those of the poor group. We also propose that greater specification at encoding is the explanation for the better incidental learning of the items. Note that we equated phonological store trace quality in the STM task by forcing the good group to keep more material simultaneously activated (longer strings), thereby pushing the representational limits of both groups to an equal extent. However, what determined incidental memory for the stimuli appeared to be the individual differences in the ability of the relevant neural networks to initially encode highly specified (=strong, good-quality) representations of the material, not the actual traces in the phonological store during the STM task.

In a subsequent study with different participants (Vuorivirta, 2006), incidental learning of the phonological composition of the pseudoword stimulus pool was significantly correlated with learning of written word–pseudoword pairs. Thus, we have some tentative evidence for our hypothesis that the initial quality of representations encoded into the phonological store is related to the probability of phonological long-term learning and that this in turn is related to the most commonly used laboratory task simulating word learning: word–pseudoword cued recall.

The evidence reviewed so far can be summarized by saying that the MMN results allow both sensory and phonological explanations of individual differences in both phonological short-term memory and new word learning. Data from a study with dyslexic adults suggest that it may be the ability of neural networks to support multiple representations of the same kind at the same time that is important for phonological memory as well as tasks like reading. The experiment controlling for short-term memory performance and, yet, finding individual differences in incidental learning of phonological items, pointed to the potentially crucial role of the quality of initial encoding, before interference from other short-term memory items takes effect. In the next section, we will examine evidence for a neurally distinct phonological working memory store that would support temporary activation as well as learning.

The neural substrate of phonological STM: What supports encoding?

One way of constraining different hypotheses about how phonological STM is related to phonological LTM is to see on which parts of the brain the performance in STM and LTM tasks depends. To our knowledge, no studies have been conducted combining phonological STM tasks and learning of new vocabulary in one brain imaging experiment. We, therefore, have to make inferences from studies targeting language processing, phonological working memory (WM) or phonological LTM, separately.

Nearly, if not absolutely, all studies that have reported a relationship between phonological loop performance and language learning used auditory presentation to test phonological STM. The most common task has been pseudoword repetition. Less frequently reported tasks have included immediate serial recall, or recognition, of sequences of digits, words or pseudowords. A substantial lesion literature has shown that a functioning left temporal cortex is critical for the processing of spoken language (see, e.g., Caplan, 1987). More recent neuroimaging studies have confirmed that left temporal areas are active during the phonological encoding and processing of material (e.g., Bonte, Parviainen, Hytönen, & Salmelin, 2006; Helenius, Salmelin, Service, Connolly, Leinonen, & Lyytinen, 2002; Kujala, Alho, Service, Ilmoniemi, & Connolly, 2004; Scott, Blank, Rosen, & Wise, 2000).

The time course of phonological encoding can be traced in event-related EEG and MEG (magnetoencephalography) investigations. A brain response occurring in the context of word recognition, and first dissociated from semantic responses by Connolly and Phillips (1994), emerges approximately 200 ms after the onset of a spoken stimulus and peaks at 250–300 ms past stimulus onset. This phonological mismatch negativity (PMN; recently renamed phonological mapping negativity, Steinhauer & Connolly, in press) response is most easily seen in auditory word (or pseudoword) recognition when a condition with a strong but not fulfilled phonological expectation is compared with one where the expectation is met by the first sound (as well as the subsequent sounds) of a heard word. Based on MEG, the response appears to be (predominantly) generated in the left temporal cortex, anterior to auditory areas linked to acoustic analysis (Kujala et al., 2004). Another localization study (D'Arcy, Connolly, Service, Hawco, & Houlihan, 2004), using high-resolution ERPs, found one source in the left inferior frontal cortex (Broca's area, BA 44/45) and another in the left inferior parietal cortex (BA 39/40). MEG and ERP allow the localization of temporally specified activation components. However, the spatial resolution based on the inverse solutions from these methods is not as good as that of haemodynamic methods, measuring changes in blood flow and oxygenation. A positron emission tomography (PET) study by Scott and her colleagues (Scott et al., 2000) suggests that the auditory processing of incoming speech moves from posterior sites towards anterior sites with activation elevated for recognizable speech in the left superior temporal sulcus, anterior to primary auditory cortex.

Two MEG studies provide information on the time course of top-down influences on language reception. Bonte and her colleagues (Bonte et al., 2006) studied the passive perception of CV syllables either in isolated blocks or blocks also containing word and sentence stimuli. The brain activations, with probable bilateral sources in the posterior superior temporal gyrus area, were similar for isolated syllables and syllables mixed with other language stimuli up to approximately 200 ms after stimulus onset. After that, the responses to identical syllables presented together with words and sentences gave rise to stronger activation, the difference peaking at ~280 ms post-onset in both hemispheres. The superior temporal gyrus response also lasted longer for the syllables in context with other language stimuli than for the isolated syllables. The same response (but only in the left hemisphere) was sensitive to whether the syllable was one that had been originally spoken in isolation or had been spliced from a sentence context. Although syllables originally spoken in context were reduced in length (212 vs. 129 ms), they probably included phonetic cues to the context they had originally occurred in and gave rise to stronger responses. Thus top-down information affects syllable encoding starting at ~200 ms post-onset, more or less at the time when the PMN response, thought to reflect phonological encoding, emerges.

As encoding to phonological memory is thought to involve an abstract code, shared by auditory and written stimuli, it is of interest to compare the time course of encoding stimuli in the two modalities. This was done in a study by Marinkovic, Dhond, Dale, Glessner, Carr, & Halgren (2003). Subjects were instructed to indicate the size of an animal, object or body part denoted by a spoken or written word, presented in separate sessions. Ten words were repeated on half of the trials whereas the other half of the trials had non-recurring word stimuli.

In both modalities, activation was first seen in modality-specific areas and then spread anteriorly via ventral streams. After ~250 ms, both modalities were associated with activation in the superior temporal sulcus and left anterior temporal areas. In addition, the anterior left inferior prefrontal cortex as well as the bilateral ventromedial prefrontal cortex were recruited in both tasks. The left inferior prefrontal activation started earlier and was sustained longer for the auditory words. Modality-specific sustained activations were seen in the perisylvian area for auditory words and inferotemporal and posteromedial areas for visual words. Repetition affected both early, modality-specific, stages of processing and later supramodal processing. The supramodal stage, possibly including encoding into phonological STM, was seen as attenuated activation between 300 and 500 ms post-stimulus onset in the anterior temporal area, including the temporopolar area, and in the anterior superior temporal sulcus, after ~350 ms, as well as in the anterior left inferior prefrontal area, and in a left prefrontal area superior to the anterior left inferior prefrontal region after ~400 ms. Interactions between modality and repetition suggested that auditory effects were bilateral whereas the visual effects were left-lateralized. Although a task involving a semantic judgement of meaningful words cannot dissociate phonological processing from semantic processing, the study suggests that priming (or learning) affecting supramodal representations is detectable from ~350 ms after visual word presentation and the onset of the first phoneme in auditory presentation. The areas involved have been linked with both semantic search and phonological processing. To summarize, various lines of evidence: the PMN response, progress of auditory word identification and supramodal effects of word processing all suggest that anterior and possibly posterior temporal areas as well as some left-lateralized frontal areas contribute to word recognition, with activation beginning ~200 ms after hearing the first sound of a word. This is, therefore, probably the earliest stage at which phonological encoding can occur.

The neural substrate of phonological STM: Lesion studies

The section above concentrated on what we know about brain processes related to auditory word recognition, possibly including encoding of STM representations. Another source of knowledge are so-called STM patients, individuals without obvious aphasia but a highly restricted STM span for verbal material. In an early description, the Russian pioneer of cognitive neuropsychology, Luria (1973), characterizes *acoustico-mnestic aphasia* as a disturbance in audio-verbal memory, affecting the retention of word series in the absence of impairments in phonemic hearing or auditory analysis. Luria continues to describe the disorder as "not so much an instability of audio-verbal traces themselves as a pathologically increased inhibitability of the audio-verbal traces" (p. 144), which he proposes arises from the competition between the traces or other interfering factors, affecting selectively verbal traces. According to Luria, who also cites an unpublished dissertation by Klimkovsky (1966), acoustico-mnestic aphasia is seen in connection with "lesions of the middle zones of the left temporal region or in lesions lying in the depths of the left temporal lobe" (p. 143).

Western descriptions (Vallar & Shallice, 1990) of critical lesion sites causing phonological STM impairment have concentrated on a shared lesion area between patients in the left inferior parietal lobe bordering on the temporal lobe (supramarginal gyrus, angular gyrus). A recent study of patients with conduction aphasia (a selective disorder of verbal repetition) (Bartha & Benke, 2003) describes a number of acute cases with symptoms resembling previously described phonological STM impairment. In a group of 17 patients with forward digit span ≤ 4, computer tomography performed in the acute stages of the brain trauma revealed lesions in the posterior sections of the left middle, the left inferior, and the left fourth temporal gyrus (Brodmann's area, BA, 37) in all cases. Most patients (12/17) also had a lesion in the posterior part of the left medial temporal gyrus (BA 21), 9 out of 17 in the left posterior superior gyrus (BA 22) and 8 out of 17 in the temporo-occipital junction (BA 19). Only a small number of patients had lesions near inferior parietal regions: 4 out of 17 in the supramarginal (BA 40) and 4 in the angular (BA 39) gyrus. All participants also had damage of the underlying white matter. The patients were not tested for long-term learning of novel language material. However, the study suggests that phonological STM impairment in association with a repetition disorder may be more closely related to left temporal lobe damage than inferior parietal area damage, consistent with the early observations of Luria and his colleagues.

The neural substrate of phonological STM: Neuroimaging studies

A considerable number of neuroimaging studies have investigated verbal working memory. In a theoretical review, Chein and his colleagues (Chein, Ravizza, & Fiez, 2003) mention that nearly a hundred studies had been reported at the time of writing. The early PET work (e.g., Paulesu, Frith, & Frackowiak, 1993) established a network of brain areas active in a letter memory task: Broca's area and its right homologue (BA 44), superior temporal gyri (BA 22/42), supramarginal gyri (BA 40), insulae, supplementary motor area, cerebellum and primary cortical areas of mouth and larynx. When activation in a task thought to depend on the articulatory rehearsal process only, i.e., rhyming judgements of visually presented words, was subtracted out, only one area remained above threshold: the left supramarginal gyrus (BA 40). This was concluded to be the home of the phonological store, especially, as the area is part of the left inferior parietal lobule that had previously been described to be damaged in STM patients.

A number of other studies have used the so-called *n*-back task to dissociate different working memory components (for a review, see Smith & Jonides, 1997). In the *n*-back task, stimuli are presented in a continuous stream and the task is to make decisions as to whether probe stimuli, presented at unpredictable intervals, are identical to the stimulus processed *n* positions back in the stream. Typically, load is manipulated by comparing an easy decision (does probe equal last experienced stimulus? –1-back) with a difficult decision (does probe equal the stimulus before the last two stimuli? –3-back). This task requires constant updating of working memory contents and activates areas (especially dorsolateral prefrontal cortex) associated with the executive component of working memory (for a review of prefrontal WM activation, see Kane & Engle, 2002).

The *n*-back task has also been found to activate posterior parietal brain areas. In a comparison of parietal activation areas reported in different studies, Becker et al. (Becker, MacAndrew, & Fiez, 1999) argued that two different but adjacent parietal areas in the left hemisphere were being repeatedly reported in the literature as the locus of the phonological store. The authors suggested that one of the areas was more dorsal and was also active in studies of visual attention. The other area, the one reported in the studies by Paulesu and colleagues, has more ventral coordinates and had consistently been found to be activated in a verbal item memory task but had not been reported in studies varying load in the *n*-back task.

A subsequent functional magnetic resonance imaging (fMRI) study by the same research group (Ravizza, Delgado, Chein, Becker, & Fiez, 2004), systematically varied working memory task (*n*-back vs. item recognition) and type of information (familiar letters vs. Korean letters). Activation in the ventral vs. dorsal inferior parietal areas did, indeed, show different patterns. The more dorsal area was sensitive to *n*-back load but not to the distinction between English and Korean letters. In the English conditions, load also affected areas thought to reflect executive functions (left and right dorsolateral prefrontal cortex) and the articulatory rehearsal process (the supplementary motor area, the left premotor cortex, Broca's area and the cerebellum).

The more ventral left inferior parietal area was not sensitive to *n*-back load. In the high-load condition of the item recognition task, participants had to indicate whether a probe stimulus had been part of a set of six serially displayed stimuli or not. In the low-load condition, they were shown the target stimulus before the set of six stimuli. Neither parietal region showed an activation difference related to this type of load although the more dorsal region was more active in the high-load condition than in a simple visual fixation condition. A comparison of English and Korean letters in high-load conditions revealed an activation increase for English stimuli in the dorsal inferior parietal area in the *n*-back but not the item memory task. A left inferior parietal/superior temporal gyrus area was more activated for familiar letters in both tasks. The pattern of results is compatible with the interpretation that the activation in the more dorsal inferior parietal area – in both hemispheres – is directly linked to the attentional demands of a task, perhaps providing the neural substrate for a focus of attention in working memory (Cowan, 1995, 2005). The activation of the more ventral left inferior parietal region, bordering on the posterior superior temporal gyrus, was enhanced by stimulus familiarity/phonological codability but was also high in a simple fixation situation and during matching of a single Korean letter to subsequently shown Korean letters. The authors concluded that this area did not fit the description of the phonological store because it was insensitive to working memory load. Presently, any conclusion about the functional specialization of this area, activated in many language tasks (for a discussion, see Ravizza et al., 2004), can only be based on speculation. Although it did not respond to attentional load, or number of items to be searched in an STM probe matching task, it is not impossible that it is sensitive to phonological load, i.e., the amount of phonological material that has to be encoded and kept in mind in a verbal STM task. Thus, it could still play an important role in processing of the kind associated with the WM component called the phonological store in the Baddeley and Hitch framework.

Neuroimaging studies that have investigated verbal LTM have mostly concentrated on word lists, making it difficult to distinguish between episodic memory and learning of phonological forms. One study contrasted rehearsal of a single face for immediate recognition with memorization of a set of faces for later recognition (Ranganath, Johnson, & D'Esposito, 2003). The results suggested that the same brain areas may be involved in both short- and long-term memory.

A study by Clark and Wagner (2003) used fMRI to compare brain activation during a phonological decision task involving written presentation of words, highly wordlike pseudowords and foreign words. A surprise old/new recognition task was given to the participants 20 minutes after the scanning session. The amount of activation during task performance in the left inferior prefrontal cortex, bilateral superior parietal cortex (BA 7) and left inferior parietal cortex (dorsal BA 40) was positively correlated with later recognition performance for words and highly wordlike stimuli. There was no difference between activation elicited by real foreign (Finnish) words and highly wordlike pseudowords.

An event-related fMRI study (Davachi, Maril, & Wagner, 2001) explored the brain areas active during rote rehearsal of word triplets and subsequent memory for them. Rote rehearsal was found to boost behavioural memory performance. The study also found that greater activations in four brain areas associated with articulatory rehearsal – left prefrontal (BA 44/6), bilateral parietal (BA 40/7), supplementary motor and left cerebellar regions – predicted later recognition memory for the words.

Two MEG studies investigating the learning of new words in a picture naming task found increased activation in a left inferior parietal area for trained names. In one study (Cornelissen, Laine, Renvall, Saarinen, Martin, & Salmelin, 2004), four out of five participants showed the effect, one of them in the right hemisphere. The fifth participant had increased activation in inferior frontal cortex and one of the participants with a left parietal learning effect showed additional learning-related activation in a left paracentral lobule source. The second study (Cornelissen, Laine, Tarkiainen, Järvensivu, Martin, & Salmelin, 2003) explored the effects of re-learning of words by anomic patients in a picture naming training study. All three patients showed training effects in a left parietal area close to the lesioned area.

Finally, adolescents with SLI were studied during encoding and recognition in a working memory task involving listening to sentences and encoding their last words for later recognition (Ellis Weismer, Plante, Jones, & Tomblin, 2005). Dorsolateral prefrontal cortex, inferior frontal gyrus, superior temporal gyrus and parietal region, all in the left hemisphere, were selected as a priori regions of interest. The SLI group showed suppression of activation in the parietal region (compared to a tone monitoring task) and relatively lower activation in the precentral sulcus in the dorsolateral prefrontal cortex at the encoding stage. At the recognition stage, the SLI group had less activation in the insular portion of the inferior frontal gyrus.

In summary, parietal areas figure prominently in both STM and verbal learning studies. However, they behave as if they form the neural substrates of components of an attentional working memory network rather than separate stores of phonological material.

Conclusion

The reviewed neuroimaging studies are compatible with an interpretation that verbal STM and word learning both activate a network that incorporates frontal and parietal attentional components, as well as components customarily associated with articulatory rehearsal. At successful encoding, as well as recall, stronger activation is seen in the parietal components of this network. However, the neural substrate of the theoretically important phonological store component remains elusive.

The verbal STM patients in lesion studies often have extensive left-hemisphere damage. One possible explanation is that the type of phonological encoding assumed to be performed by the phonological store is supported by a distributed network in the left hemisphere. Patients' STM is not affected as a result of focal lesions but rather the joint effect of many small dysfunctioning units. These distributed lesions are not enough to cause speech perception to fail in a premorbidly well-developed system but affect tasks with high demands on simultaneous phonological representation, such as serial memory or pseudoword repetition tasks. The left ventral inferior parietal area, activated in immediate item recognition tasks (Paulesu et al., 1993, 1996; Ravizza et al., 2004), may be an indicator of the functionality of the network rather than the neural substrate of the store itself. Such a view would be in line with those lesion studies (Bartha & Benke, 2003; Luria, 1973) that associate verbal STM impairment in the absence of aphasia with temporal lobe lesions. It would also provide a working hypothesis for the neural causes of developmental disorders with specific impairments in phonological STM. This brings us back to our high and low repeaters. Is their MMN difference specific to phonological processing? We do not have an answer but we suggest that they do have a less efficient network for encoding phonological material, and perhaps also other stimuli requiring simultaneous representation.

References

Alho, K. (1995). Cerebral generators of mismatch negativity (MMN) and its magnetic counterpart (MMNm) elicited by sound changes. *Ear and Hear, 16*, 38–51.

Baddeley, A. D. (1986). *Working memory*. Oxford: Clarendon Press.

Baddeley, A. D. (2000). The episodic buffer: A new component of working memory? *Trends in Cognitive Sciences, 4*, 1364–1366.

Baddeley, A. D. (2003). Working memory: Looking back and looking forward. *Nature Reviews/Neuroscience, 4*, 629–639.

Baddeley, A. D., Gathercole, S., & Papagno, C. (1998). The phonological loop as a language learning device. *Psychological Review, 105*, 158–173.

Baddeley, A. D., & Hitch, G. (1974). Working memory. In G. Bower (Ed.), *The psychology of learning and motivation* (Vol. 8). New York: Academic Press.

Baddeley, A. D., Papagno, C., & Vallar, G. (1988). When long-term learning depends on short-term storage. *Journal of Memory and Language, 27*, 586–595.

Bartha, L., & Benke, T. (2003). Acute conduction aphasia: An analysis of 20 cases. *Brain and Language, 85*, 93–108.

Becker, J. T., MacAndrew, D. K., & Fiez, J. A. (1999). A comment on functional localization of the phonological storage subsystem in working memory. *Brain and Cognition, 41*, 27–38.

Bonte, M., Parviainen, T., Hytönen, K., & Salmelin, R. (2006). Time course of top-down and bottom-up influences on syllable processing in the auditory cortex. *Cerebral Cortex, 16*, 115–123.

Brock, J., & Jarrold, C. (2004). Language influences on verbal short-term memory performance in Down syndrome: Item and order recognition. *Journal of Speech, Language, and Hearing Research, 47*, 1334–1346.

Caplan, D. (1987). *Neurolinguistics and Linguistic Aphasiology: An Introduction*. Cambridge: Cambridge University Press.

Čeponienė, R., Service, E., Kurjenluoma, S., Cheour, M., & Näätänen, R. (1999). Children's performance in pseudoword repetition depends on auditory trace quality. *Developmental Psychology, 35*, 709–720.

Chein, J. M., Ravizza, S. M., & Fiez, J. A. (2003). Using neuroimaging to evaluate models of working memory and their implications for language processing. *Journal of Neurolinguistics, 16,* 315–339.

Cheour, M., Čeponienė, R., Lehtokoski, A., Luuk, A., Allik, J., Alho, K., et al. (1998). Development of language-specific phoneme representations in the infant brain. *Nature Neuroscience, 1,* 351–353.

Clark, D., & Wagner, A. D. (2003). Assembling and encoding word representations: fMRI subsequent memory effects implicate a role for phonological control. *Neuropsychologia, 41,* 304–317.

Connolly, J. F., & Phillips, N. A. (1994). Event-related potential components reflect phonological and semantic processing of the terminal word of spoken sentences. *Journal of Cognitive Neuroscience, 6,* 256–266.

Cornelissen, K., Laine, M., Renvall, K., Saarinen, T., Martin, N., & Salmelin, R. (2004). Learning new names for new objects: Cortical effects as measured by magnetoencephalography. *Brain and Language, 89,* 617–622.

Cornelissen, K., Laine, M., Tarkiainen, A., Järvensivu, T., Martin, N., & Salmelin, R. (2003). Adult brain plasticity elicited by anomia treatment. *Journal of Cognitive Neuroscience, 15,* 444–461.

Cowan, N. (1995). *Attention and memory: An integrated framework.* Oxford: Clarendon Press.

Cowan, N. (2005). *Working memory capacity.* New York: Taylor & Francis Group.

Cowan, N., Winkler, I., Teder, W., & Näätänen, R. (1993). Memory prerequisites of the mismatch negativity in the auditory event-related potential (ERP). *Journal of Experimental Psychology: Learning, Memory, and Cognition, 19,* 909–921.

D'Arcy, R. C. N., Connolly, J. F., Service, E., Hawco, C. S., & Houlihan, M. E. (2004). Separating phonological and semantic processing in auditory sentence processing: A high-resolution event-related brain potential study. *Human Brain Mapping, 22,* 40–51.

Davachi, L., Maril, A., & Wagner, A. D. (2001). When keeping in mind supports later bringing to mind: Neural markers of phonological rehearsal predict subsequent remembering. *Journal of Cognitive Neuroscience, 13,* 1059–1070.

Ellis Weismer, S., Plante, E., Jones, M., & Tomblin, B. J. (2005). A functional magnetic resonance imaging investigation of verbal working memory in adolescents with specific language impairment. *Journal of Speech, Language, and Hearing Research, 48,* 405–425.

Gathercole, S. E., & Baddeley, A. D. (1989). Evaluation of the role of phonological STM in the development of vocabulary in children: A longitudinal study. *Journal of Memory and Language, 28,* 200–213.

Gathercole, S. E., & Baddeley, A. D. (1990). Phonological memory deficits in language-disordered children: Is there a causal connection? *Journal of Memory and Language, 29,* 336–360.

Gathercole, S. E., & Hitch, G. J. (1993). Developmental changes in short-term memory: A revised working memory perspective. In A. Collins, S. E. Gathercole, M. A. Conway, & P. E. Morris (Eds.), *Theories of Memory.* Hove, UK: Lawrence Erlbaum Associates Ltd.

Helenius, P., Salmelin, R., Service, E., Connolly, J. F., Leinonen, S., & Lyytinen, H. (2002). Cortical activation during spoken word segmentation in nonreading-impaired and dyslexic adults. *Journal of Neuroscience, 22,* 2936–2944.

Hulme, C., Maughan, S., & Brown, G. D. (1991). Memory for familiar and unfamiliar words: Evidence for a long-term memory contribution to short-term memory span. *Journal of Memory and Language, 30,* 685–701.

Jacobsen, T., Schröger, E., Winkler, I., & Horváth, J. (2005). Familiarity affects the processing of task-irrelevant auditory deviance. *Journal of Cognitive Neuroscience, 17,* 1704–1713.

Kane, M. J., & Engle, R. W. (2002). The role of prefrontal cortex in working-memory capacity, executive attention, and general fluid intelligence: An individual differences perspective. *Psychonomic Bulletin & Review, 9,* 637–671.

Klimkovsky, M. (1966). *Disturbance of audio-verbal memory in lesions of the temporal lobe.* Unpublished Candidate dissertation (in Russian), Moscow University, Moscow.

Kujala, A., Alho, K., Service, E., Ilmoniemi, R. J., & Connolly, J. F. (2004). Activation in the anterior left auditory cortex associated with phonological analysis of speech input: Localization of the phonological mismatch negativity (PMN) response with MEG. *Cognitive Brain Research, 21,* 106–113.

Kujala, T., Myllyviita, K., Tervaniemi, M., Alho, K., Kallio, J., & Näätänen, R. (2000). Basic auditory dysfunction in dyslexia as demonstrated by brain activity measurements. *Psychophysiology, 37,* 262–266.

Laasonen, M., Virsu, V., Oinonen, S., Sandbacka, M., Vedenpää, A., & Service, E. (2006). Phonological and sensory short-term memory impairment in developmental dyslexia. Manuscript submitted for publication.

Laasonen, M., Service, E., & Virsu, V. (2001). Temporal order and processing acuity of visual, auditory, and tactile perception in developmentally dyslexic adults. *Cognitive, Affective, & Behavioral Neuroscience,* 394–410.

Laasonen, M., Service, E., & Virsu, V. (2002). Crossmodal temporal order and processing acuity in developmentally dyslexic young adults. *Brain and Language, 80,* 340–354.

Laasonen, M., Tomma-Halme, J., Lahti-Nuuttila, P., Service, E., & Virsu, V. (2000). Rate of information segregation in developmentally dyslexic children. *Brain and Language, 75,* 66–81.

Logie, R. H. (1995). *Visuo-spatial working memory.* Hove, UK: Lawrence Erlbaum Associates Ltd.

Luria, A. R. (1973). *The working brain: An introduction to neuropsychology* (B. Haigh, Trans.). Harmondsworth, UK: Penguin Books.

Marinkovic, K., Dhond, R. P., Dale, A. M., Glessner, M., Carr, V., & Halgren, E. (2003). Spatiotemporal dynamics of modality-specific and supramodal word processing. *Neuron, 38,* 487–497.

Merzenich, M. M., Jenkins, W. M., Johnston, P., Schreineer, C., Miller, S. L., & Tallal, P. (1996). Temporal processing deficits of language-learning impaired children ameliorated by training. *Science, 271,* 77–81.

Näätänen, R. (1992). *Attention and Brain Function.* Hillsdale, NJ: Lawrence Erlbaum Associates, Inc.

Näätänen, R., Gaillard, A. W. K., & Mäntysalo, S. (1978). Early selective attention effect on evoked potential reinterpreted. *Acta Psychologica, 42,* 313–329.

Näätänen, R., Lehtokoski, A., Lennes, M., Cheour, M., Huotilainen, M., Iivonen, A., et al. (1997). Language-specific phoneme representations revealed by electric and magnetic brain responses. *Nature, 385*(30 January), 432–434.

Näätänen, R., Tervaniemi, M., Sussman, E., Paavilainen, P., & Winkler, I. (2001).

Primitive intelligence in the auditory cortex. *Trends in Neurosciences, 24,* 283–288.

Papagno, C., & Vallar, G. (1992). Phonological short-term memory and the learning of novel words: The effect of phonological similarity and item length. *Quarterly Journal of Experimental Psychology, 44A,* 47–67.

Paulesu, E., Frith, C. D., & Frackowiak, R. S. (1993). The neural correlates of the verbal component of working memory. *Nature, 362,* 342–345.

Paulesu, E., Frith, U., Snowling, M., Gallagher, A., Morton, J., Frackowiak, R. S. J., et al. (1996). Is developmental dyslexia a disconnection syndrome? *Brain, 119,* 143–157.

Phillips, C., Pellathy, T., Marantz, A., Yellin, E., Wexler, K., Poeppel, D., et al. (2000). Auditory cortex accesses phonological categories: An MEG mismatch study. *Journal of Cognitive Neuroscience, 12,* 1038–1055.

Ranganath, C., Johnson, M. K., & D'Esposito, M. (2003). Prefrontal activity associated with working memory and episodic long-term memory. *Neuropsychologia, 41,* 378–389.

Ravizza, S. M., Delgado, M. R., Chein, J. M., Becker, J. T., & Fiez, J. A. (2004). Functional dissociations in the inferior parietal cortex in verbal working memory. *NeuroImage, 22,* 562–573.

Schweickert, R. (1993). A multinomial processing tree model for degradation and redintegration in immediate recall. *Memory & Cognition, 21,* 168–175.

Scott, S. K., Blank, C. C., Rosen, S., & Wise, R. J. S. (2000). Identification of a pathway for intelligible speech in the left temporal lobe. *Brain, 123,* 2400–2406.

Service, E. (1989). *Phonological coding in working memory and foreign-language learning* (Vol. B 9). Helsinki: University of Helsinki, General Psychology.

Service, E. (1992). Phonology, working memory and foreign-language learning. *Quarterly Journal of Experimental Psychology, 45A*(1), 21–50.

Service, E., & Craik, F. (1993). Differences between young and older adults in learning a foreign vocabulary. *Journal of Memory and Language, 32,* 608–623.

Service, E., & Kohonen, V. (1995). Is the relation between phonological memory and foreign-language learning accounted for by vocabulary acquisition? *Applied Psycholinguistics, 16,* 155–172.

Service, E., Maury, S., & Luotoniemi, E. (2007). Individual differences in phonological learning and verbal STM span. *Memory & Cognition, 35,* 1122–1135.

Service, E., & Tujulin, A.-M. (2002). Recall of morphologically complex forms is affected by memory task but not dyslexia. *Brain and Language, 81,* 42–54.

Smith, E. E., & Jonides, J. (1997). Working memory: A view from neuroimaging. *Cognitive Psychology, 33,* 5–42.

Steinhauer, K., & Connolly, J. F. (in press). Event-related potentials in the study of language. In B. Stemmer & H. A. Whitaker (Eds.), *Handbook of the neuroscience of language.* Amsterdam: Elsevier.

Tallal, P. (1980). Auditory temporal perception, phonics, and reading disabilities in children. *Brain and Language, 9,* 182–198.

Tallal, P., & Piercy, M. (1974). Developmental dysphasia: Rate of auditory processing and selective impairment in consonant perception. *Neuropsychologia, 12,* 83–93.

Thorn, A. S. C., Gathercole, S. E., & Frankish, C. R. (2005). Redintegration and the benefits of long-term knowledge in verbal short-term memory: An evaluation of Schweickert's (1993) multinomial processing tree model. *Cognitive Psychology*, *50*, 133–158.

Vallar, G., & Baddeley, A. D. (1984). Fractionation of working memory. Neuropsychological evidence for a phonological short-term store. *Journal of Verbal Learning and Verbal Behavior*, *23*, 151–162.

Vallar, G., & Shallice, T. (1990). The impairment of auditory-verbal short-term storage. In G. Vallar & T. Shallice (Eds.), *Neuropsychological impairments of short-term memory* (pp. 11–53). New York: Cambridge University Press.

Vuorivirta, A. (2006). *Development and validation of a Finnish-language verbal learning task*. Unpublished Master's thesis, University of Helsinki, Helsinki.

Winkler, I., Karmos, G., & Näätänen, R. (1996). Adaptive modeling of the unattended acoustic environment reflected in the mismatch negativity event-related potential. *Brain Research*, *742*, 239–252.

Winkler, I., Lehtokoski, A., Alku, P., Vainio, M., Czigler, I., Csépe, V., et al. (1999). Pre-attentive detection of vowel contrasts utilizes both phonetic and auditory memory representations. *Cognitive Brain Research*, *7*, 357–369.

Author index

Subject index

Page numbers in **bold** denote references to Figures/Tables.